URBAN AND ENVIRONMENTAL PLANNING IN THE UK

Yvonne Rydin

MACMILLAN

© Yvonne Rydin 1993, 1998

Published by
MACMILLAN PRESS LTD
Houndmills, Basingstoke, Hampshire RG21 6XS
and London
Companies and representatives
throughout the world

ISBN 0–333–73190–5 hardcover
ISBN 0–333–73191–3 paperback

A catalogue record for this book is available
from the British Library.

This book is printed on paper suitable for recycling and
made from fully managed and sustained forest sources.

10   9   8   7   6   5   4   3   2   1
07   06   05   04   03   02   01   00   99   98

Copy-edited and typeset by Povey–Edmondson
Tavistock and Rochdale, England

Printed in Great Britain by
Creative Print and Design Wales, Ebbw Vale Gwent

Contents

List of Tables, Figures, Maps, Exhibits and Summary Boxes

■ Tables

■ Figures

■ Maps

■ Exhibits

■ Summary Boxes

List of Abbreviations

AAI   Area of Archeological Importance
ACC   Association of County Councils
ADAS   Agricultural Development Advisory Service
ADC   Association of District Councils
ALARP   As Low As Reasonably Practicable
ALG   Association of London Government
AMA   Association of Metropolitan Authorities
AONB   Area of Outstanding Natural Beauty
BATNEEC Best Available Technology Not Entailing Excessive Cost
BEC   Building Employers' Confederation
BNF   British Nuclear Fuels
BPEO   Best Practicable Environmental Option
BPM   Best Practicable Means
CADW   Welsh Historic Monuments
CAP   Common Agricultural Policy (EU)
CBA   Cost Benefit Analysis
CBI   Confederation of British Industry
CC   Countryside Commission
CCT   Compulsory Competitive Tendering
CDP   Community Development Project
CEC   Commission of European Communities
CEGB   Central Electricity Generating Board
CIoTr   Chartered Institute of Transport
CLD   Certificate of Lawful Development
CLU   Certificate of Lawful Use
COPA   Control of Pollution Act
COSLA   Convention of Scottish Local Authorities
CSD   Commission on Sustainable Development
CVM   Contingent Valuation Method
DBRW   Development Board for Rural Wakes
DCF   Discounted Cash Flow
DCPN   Development Control Policy Note
DETR   Department of Environment, Transport and the Regions
DLG   Derelict Land Grant
DLO   Direct Labour Organisation
DoE   Department of the Environment
DoEm   Department of Employment

DoEn	Department of Energy
DoTr	Department of Transport
EA	Environmental Assessment
EC	European Community
EEA	European Environment Agency
EIP	Examination in Public
EPA	Environment Protection Agency
ESA	Environmentally Sensitive Area
EU	European Union
EZ	Enterprise Zone
GDO	General Development Order
GEAR	Glasgow Eastern Area Renewal Project
GIA	General Improvement Area
GLA	Greater London Authority
GLC	Greater London Council
HAT	Housing Action Trust
HBF	House Builders' Federation
HIP	Housing Investment Programme
HLW	High-Level Waste
HMIP	Her Majesty's Inspectorate of Pollution
HMIPI	Her Majesty's Industrial Pollution Inspectorate
IAP	Inner Area Programme
IDC	Industrial Development Certificate
ILW	Intermediate-Level Waste
IPC	Integrated Pollution Control
IPPC	Integration Pollution Prevention and Control
LA21	Local Agenda 21
LAW	Land Authority for Wales
LBA	London Boroughs Association
LDDC	London Docklands Development Corporation
LEA	Local Enterprise Agency
LEC	Local Enterprise Council
LEGUP	Local Enterprise Grant for Urban Projects
LENTA	London Enterprise and Training Agency
LGA	Local Government Association
LGC	Local Government Commission
LGPLA	Local Government Planning and Land Act
LLW	Low-Level Waste
LULU	Locally Unwanted Land Use
MAFF	Ministry of Agriculture, Fisheries and Food
MPG	Minerals Planning Guidelines
NCC	Nature Conservancy Council
NFU	National Farmers' Union

NGO	Non-Governmental Organisation
NIMBY	Not In My Back Yard
NNDR	National Non-Domestic Rate
NPG	National Planning Guideline
NPPG	National Planning Policy Guideline
NRA	National Rivers Authority
NSA	Nitrate Sensitive Area
ODP	Office Development Permit
PLI	Public Local Inquiry
PAN	Planning Advisory Note
PPG	Planning Policy Guidance Note
PPT	Procedural Planning Theory
PTA	Passenger Transport Authority
PTE	Passenger Transport Executive
PTP	Passenger Transport Plan
RCEP	Royal Commission on Environmental Pollution
RDA	Regional Development Agency
RDC	Rural Development Commission
RIBA	Royal Institute of British Architects
RICS	Royal Institution of Chartered Surveyors
RPG	Regional Planning Guidance
RSNC	Royal Society for Nature Conservation
RTPI	Royal Town Planning Institute
RWA	Regional Water Authority
SCA	Special Conservation Area
SDA	Scottish Development Agency
SDD	Scottish Development Department
SDP	Social Democratic Party
SE	Scottish Enterprise
SEA	Strategic Environmental Assessment
SEPA	Scottish Environmental Protection Agency
SERPLAN	South East Regional Planning Conference
SPA	Special Protection Area (for birds)
SPNR	Society for the Protection of Nature Reserves
SPZ	Simplified Planning Zone
SRB	Single Regeneration Budget
SSSI	Site of Special Scientific Interest
TEC	Training and Enterprise Council
TPO	Tree Preservation Order
TPP	Transport Policies and Programmes
UCO	Use Classes Order
UDC	Urban Development Corporation
UDG	Urban Development Grant

UDP	Unitary Development Plan
UKAEA	United Kingdom Atomic Energy Authority
UNCED	United Nations Commission on Environment and Development
UNEP	United Nations Environment Programme
WDA	Waste Disposal Authority
WDA	Welsh Development Agency
WO	Welsh Office
WRA	Waste Regulating Authority

Preface

This book is designed as a replacement for *The British Planning System*, published in 1993. Despite the gratifyingly positive feedback from reviewers and those who used the book as a text on a wide range of courses, I have opted for a thoroughgoing revision of both structure and content, both to take account of changed circumstances, including the end of the Thatcher era and the advent of New Labour, and to broaden its scope and make it more accessible and user-friendly. The major structural change has been the removal of Part 4 (Planning and the Market), which presented a range of alternative economic analyses relevant to urban and environmental planning; this has been replaced by a chapter of the same name which briefly considers such alternative economic analyses but places more emphasis on an account of land and property markets and development and valuation processes, including environmental valuation. This chapter is now placed alongside those on the politics of planning, previously in Part 3, to constitute Part 2 (The Politics and Economics of Planning). The detailed accounts of different aspects of the planning system now follow in Part 3 (Planning Today). It is hoped that this will enable the reader to understand these different aspects more fully, having encountered the political and economic analyses earlier in Part 2. Within Planning Today, there has been some rearrangement and reordering, which should be apparent from the chapter titles. The exhibits which present specific issues in box-format are now spread throughout Parts 2 and 3.

The other main thematic change has been the dropping of the framing device of contrasting New Right, New Left, Liberal Political Economy and the Institutional Approach. The shift from Thatcherism to New Labour and the maturity of the institutional approach, evidenced in Patsy Healey's *Collaborative Planning* (1997), have meant that a different kind of framing is now appropriate. At the start of each chapter in Part 2 there is a section which presents the different ways of analysing the institutions in question; this allows for more up to date coverage of key theoretical debates and developments. In addition there is a fuller account of institutional planning theory, as represented by collaborative planning, both in the last chapter in Part 1 (The Development of Planning Theory and Policy) and in the final chapter of the book. Elsewhere the changes have largely been of the updating kind. The extent of the changes are such that it seemed appropriate to give the book a new title. I have also taken the opportunity for it to be transferred into the 'Planning Environment Cities' series which I edit with Andy Thornley.

I would particularly like to thank Gerry Stoker, in whose 'Government beyond the Centre' series *The British Planning System* originally appeared, for suggesting the idea of writing a text of this kind. My thanks also to Steven Kennedy for his editorial care, and to all those who commented on drafts of the first and second editions – Erling Berge, Keith Hayton, Patsy Healey, George Myerson, Phil Pinch, Andy Thornley, Simon Zadek and the publishers' reviewers. I wish to acknowledge the extremely supportive environment provided by my colleagues at the London School of Economics, both within the Department of Geography and Environment and outside. Particular thanks to the Drawing Office and to those who provided research assistance for the two editions – Alison Greig, Shirley Maclean and Mark Pennington.

Needless to say I accept full responsibility for any errors and misinterpretations in the text.

YVONNE RYDIN

This book is dedicated to the four most important people in my life

George, Simon, Eleanor and Rita

to whom I owe the greatest thanks

Introduction

■ What is planning?

Planning, as discussed in this book, has three key characteristics. First, it is a future-oriented activity. Planning seeks to devise strategies which will lead to desired end states. Many dictionary definitions of the word planning begin with this idea of decision-making to achieve a given goal and it is at the heart of an influential theory of planning known as procedural planning theory (discussed in Chapter 2), which continues to influence much contemporary planning thought. Second, planning is primarily a public sector activity. It describes a process by which the public sector, at central, regional and local levels, seeks to influence the activities of firms and households through guidance, regulation and incentives. This is not to suggest that the decision-making that occurs within the private sector is not of interest. On the contrary, one of the arguments of this book is the need to understand these private sector processes in order to understand how the public sector conducts its planning activities (see Chapter 9). However, the starting point for a review of the planning system is an analysis of the policies, procedures and institutions of the public sector. Third, the particular type of planning covered by this book is focused on the physical environment, whereas in other contexts planning may refer to economic or social planning. This draws on another sense of the dictionary definition of planning, the association with drawings and layouts for buildings, sites and urban areas. The urban design aspects of planning have a history stretching back to Grecian and Roman times and many planning courses still emphasise drawing-board training for would-be planners. However much planning activity is now concerned with the physical environment without necessarily focusing on these design skills. Planning is about devising strategies for reshaping or protecting the built and natural environment. These strategies may take a variety of forms and their implementation need not necessarily be guided by a design blueprint. The aesthetic quality of the urban environment need not be the main goal. The goals may cover: the redistribution of resources to disadvantaged inner city groups; the longevity of the built stock; the conservation of wildlife; or the encouragement of urban development. A composite goal – such as sustainable development – may guide the planning process. The common strand is the focus on the use of the built and natural environment, and on strategies which can alter that use.

Such a definition is still, of course, very broad in scope. Planning activity describes a range of concerns, expressed through many specific policies. Accepting that planning is an umbrella term carries several implications. There is bound to be confusion over the boundaries of the planning system. Not all policies considered to lie within the boundaries will carry the label 'planning'. With an expanding range of state activities more and more policy concerns have come within the compass of planning textbooks: transport, housing, inner cities, pollution, to name but a few. Since these concerns are the subject of policy specialisms of their own, planning will overlap with several other policy areas and, indeed, can claim to include them. The scope of planning at any particular time will relate to the currently accepted limits to the public sector's role in devising strategies for the physical environment. It is important to recognise that as social and economic change occurs, the area shaded by the planning umbrella will alter. New (or old) problems will come (back) to the fore and new (or old) issues become politically salient (again). At times the emphasis will closely relate to the physical character of development, at other times to the social, economic or broader environmental implications of that development. The areas that a planning textbook should focus on will alter in line with current problems and political concerns.

So any useful definition of planning must be capable of coping with the changing scope of such activity. And a planning textbook should be relevant to the concerns and range of public sector policies currently constituting planning activity in the 1990s. For this reason, the policy areas covered by this book, and the relative depth in which they are covered, reflect my perception of the most significant areas within the planning system. Particular emphasis is given to two areas: land use planning which remains at the core of British planning, with the implementation of many other policy goals dependent on land use planning procedures (Chapter 10); and environmental planning which has become steadily more important within all public and private sector decision-making since the late 1980s (Chapter 11). Recognition is given to the place that countryside policy holds in the policy culture of Britain, despite (or perhaps because of) our high levels of urbanisation (Chapter 12) and, within urban policy, the current concerns with urban regeneration are reflected in the emphasis on promoting physical and economic development in and around our cities (Chapter 13). Housing and transport issues are dealt with only as they relate to these four main policy areas. The resulting survey should be appropriate to the needs of planning students and planners today.

■ The relevance of planning in the UK

Planning in the UK clearly has certain specific characteristics. It represents a response to the environmental problems of the first industrial nation, both in the twentieth century and then through the changes of the nineteenth century. It has been shaped by uniquely British versions of two of the major political ideologies of the postwar period. First, there is the commitment to the welfare state following the Second World War, seeking to redress inequalities of income but within a mixed-economy framework which fell short of the social democracy of, say, Sweden. Second, there is the impact of Thatcherism, a term widely given to the political project of the British government headed by Margaret Thatcher from 1979 to 1990, which sought to free the market from state control and interference. The detail of British policy, procedures and institutions reflects these specific British contexts.

However, there are cross-cultural dimensions to British planning. Many concepts have been borrowed from other countries' experience: Prussian land policy and urban design were influential on early conceptions of British land use planning; the environmental impact assessment is taken from the United States National Environmental Policy Act of 1969; national parks also have their North American precedents. In return the model of British planning has been transplanted to many other countries, both under colonial rule and by selective imitation. Thus knowledge of how the British system actually works in practice is of relevance to analysts from many countries trying to understand their own national systems and make proposals for policy innovations. The impact of Thatcherism may have been most pronounced in its home base, but similar political trends have been felt throughout many parts of the world. The detail of change in the planning system and the way in which it worked through to environmental change are relevant wherever Thatcherism was paralleled.

Across Europe the spread of new concepts and ideas in planning has been accelerated by the role of the EU. The British government has had to change procedures and institutions at the European Commission's behest and found itself subject to the rulings of the European Courts. Greater contact between policy-makers and professionals across the continent has also led to a diffusion of ideas at the same time that contact between economic actors is making the integrated market more of a reality. Knowledge of policy practice in the various nation states of our common European home is becoming more and more necessary for the student and practitioner alike. It is only lack of space that prevents a more directly comparative dimension in the book as it stands.

However, the relevance of knowledge of the British planning system does not lie only in the detail of procedures and institutions and their cross-national dimension. The British planning system is a long-running case study of public sector activity operating within a market or capitalist economy. As such, it can tell us much about the possibilities and constraints of such activity. There are many similarities in the environmental problems that countries based on a market economy face: in patterns of urbanisation and counter-urbanisation; in pollution generation; in inner city decay; and in demands on rural areas. The relationship between public and private sectors in market economies is a key element in explaining these problems and determining the nature of responses by the planning system. Analysis of the dynamic interrelation between public and private sector over the physical environment in Britain can raise questions and make suggestions for how that analysis could proceed in other national arenas, even if it will not directly provide knowledge of that relationship in other countries.

Finally, while many environmentalists may complain of the lack of progress in relation to an impending or even present environmental crisis, British planning has sought fairly systematically to engage with environmental or sustainability issues over the 1990s, if only at the level of rhetoric. There is a range of environmental policy documentation and legislation, and the British Local Agenda 21 process (see Chapters 6 and 11) has been a vigorous one. British planning, at least, provides a case study which can be assessed of how the sustainable development agenda may feed through into planning policy and practice.

■ Studying planning

How should we approach the study of planning to enable us to understand both the detail of the British planning system and, more generally how planning for the physical environment operates in practice? Two themes in relation to this question run throughout the book. First, to understand planning it is necessary to see planning in context, as a social, political and economic activity. An account which concentrates purely on the procedures of the planning system is, therefore, insufficient since it tries to divorce the planning system from those processes of which it is an integral part and which are essential to any understanding of planning in practice. This involves recognising the significance of economic dynamics for shaping both the impacts and the processes of planning. It also involves paying close attention to the interests and decision-making of key political actors involved in planning and considering how planning relates to the patchwork quilt of different groups that make up our society. These points are taken up in Part 2.

Second, there is considerable dispute over the analysis of these socioeconomic processes and, therefore, over the role of planning in relation to them. This dispute is not to be regretted, in my view. Vigorous debate is the indicator of a healthy and vital community in planning studies. It promotes new understanding of the role of planning, helps to prevent complacency among professionals and can engender new programmes for political action. It also prevents a too ready acceptance of planning policy statements in their own terms. Planning is a normative activity and planners represent themselves as a welfare profession. Its claims and pronounced intentions require careful examination and opposing theoretical positions can help in this task.

This book does not propose a single view of the relation of planning to socioeconomic processes and normative claims. It consciously takes on board a variety of disputing approaches and organises them to help the reader find their way around an otherwise confusing debate. The reader should not be put off by the variety of viewpoints presented. Such viewpoints develop in response to the conditions at the time of writing and, of course, each author adds their own personal gloss. In an interdisciplinary subject such as planning, the viewpoints are also influenced by the various disciplinary backgrounds of authors. Some order will hopefully be put on this variety. The author has a view also, of course, and this is set out most explicitly in Chapter 15, which concludes the book.

■ The structure of the book

□ *Providing a historical context*

Both the planning system and the debate about planning have changed over time and Part 1 of the book, 'The Development of Planning Policy and Theory', examines this development. Here the changing economic and social conditions are set alongside the emerging policies and institutions of planning. As new socioeconomic conditions are created, new problems are brought to the attention of policy-makers and some of these the planning system tries to address. At the same time, the development of the system has been associated with the growing professionalisation of planners and the increased sophistication of academic discussion about planning as planning organisations and their educational counterparts have matured in organisational terms. Thus the general socioeconomic context and the more specific institutional context for planning frame the detail of new and changing policies.

Key trends and discontinuities are emphasised, rather than attempting to provide a comprehensive and detailed historical narrative. A fairly rough and ready periodisation is used, suggesting links not only between specific forms of socioeconomic change and particular policy developments but also with the implicit or explicit theoretical positions adopted. The fit is not watertight but the coincidences are intriguing. It is possible, indeed common, to derive a history of planning policy in which change occurs naturally in response to the passage of time and the appearance of problems associated with environmental change. But at any time, there is a theoretical view implicit in the prevailing policy framework. As that framework changes, conflicts between theories can develop, with the theoretical debate becoming an element of policy change itself. Indeed the legitimating role of much planning theory can be clearly seen if theoretical developments are laid alongside the evolution of the planning professions and related academy. As Cooke argues, planning theory is stubbornly normative (1983, p. 25).

☐ *Analysing the politics and economics of planning*

In Part 2 attention is turned to the political and economic structures and dynamic processes which frame planning activity. The first four chapters explore the argument, so strongly put by urban sociologists in the 1970s, that planning is fundamentally a political process. There are three dimensions to this argument.

First, planning involves decisions about the allocation of resources. Land use planning will alter land values and the spatial pattern of those land values by development control decisions which grant or deny planning permission. For decades, countryside policy has had to deal with the demands from the farming industry for continued economic support, support which has had widely recognised adverse consequences on various groups. Pollution control can transfer costs from those affected by polluting emissions, whether in health or direct economic terms, to the polluter, making the polluter pay. And in urban areas planning has frequently focused on the struggle between different groups over the control of scarce land and the values it represents for direct use and exchange in the market-place. Through its influence on the allocation of resources, planning, therefore, has a distributive impact. This would be enough to earn the planning system the description 'political'. But such distributive consequences can also stimulate collective action to engage in political campaigning.

This second sense of the term 'political' refers to the quantity of activity generated by the planning system in which one group tries to influence the decisions and actions of another. In some cases this will involve non-governmental organisations (NGOs) or pressure groups trying to influence a government organisation, as when a local amenity society presses for a refusal of planning permission for a particular site. In other cases, the interaction will be between governmental organisations: a local authority negotiating with central government over grant allocations; conflicts between local authorities over green belt designations; disputes between various quangos, say between English Nature, English Heritage and the Environment Agency over the future of a riverside site of special scientific interest or SSSI owned by English Heritage. These examples also highlight the fact that the form of interaction between organisations will vary. A spectrum of such political action can be conceived with outright conflict at the one end, forms of campaigning and negotiation in the middle, and routine consultation and liaison at the other end. Organisations are more likely to engage in conflictual relations when two conditions are met: that the distributive consequences of the decision are certain, severe and adverse for one group; and that there is an ideological conflict underlying the specific circumstances of the issue at hand.

The third sense of political planning concerns this ideological dimension. There are left- and right-wing approaches to planning the physical environment. There are also views of planning incorporated in other political ideologies which may lay outside the Left–Right spectrum, as with green ideologies. The ideologies engage with each other in the debate over planning policy and its future direction. This debate concerns both means and ends in planning. The scope given to market forces in the urban regeneration, the extent to which local community groups should be involved in land use planning, and the extent of public expenditure on pollution control are all examples of differences over the detail of the planning system which may arise between adherents of different ideological positions. But there will also be differences in the criteria by which planning activity is judged to be successful. Generation of private wealth and profit may be a major goal for the Right, but not for the Left or Greens. Employment generation will be encouraged by the Right and the Left but not by Greens. Minimising the scale of public sector control over local decisions may be welcomed by the Right and Greens, but not necessarily by the Left. These issues of debate over principle and detail provide another political dimension to the planning system.

Planning is a political process but it is also essential for planners to understand the nature of economic processes. Indeed, it is because planning is engaged in resource allocation and has distributive consequences that knowledge of the market is so necessary. For British planning, like most examples across the world, operates in the context of capitalism based on market processes. As a public sector activity, planning constantly engages with these market processes, trying to regulate, stimulate and impose order and structure on them. In Britain's advanced capitalist economy, the state is so closely involved with the economy that it can be difficult to separate them in any analysis of a detailed planning situation. These are the issues tackled in the final chapter of Part 2 which looks at land and property markets and the development process.

In all chapters in Part 2, there is an emphasis on the range of different theoretical interpretations that can be offered of political and economic processes. There are also exhibits provided which highlight particular aspects of planning practice; similar exhibits are to be found in Part 3 as well.

☐ Detailing the planning system

A description of the details of the planning system is found in Part 3, 'Planning Today', which provides an account of the core elements of the planning system. Chapter 10 looks at 'Land Use Planning'. Land use planning remains at the heart of the planning system, providing the key tool of comprehensive development control and the flexibility of broad-brush and detailed development plans. The growing importance placed on environmental protection is reflected in the burgeoning area of 'Environmental Regulation' covered in Chapter 11. This looks at water management, pollution control, waste management and the integration of environmental concerns into land use planning, including the introduction of environmental impact assessment. In Chapter 12, 'Countryside Policy', the package of policies for rural Britain are examined, with their often contradictory attempts to provide for access to the countryside, protection of rural areas from development, nature conservation, rural economic development and resource exploitation. Finally, in Chapter 13, the twin themes of 'Regeneration and Conservation' are considered. Particular emphasis is placed on urban grant and subsidy systems, on measures to transfer land to private sector developers and the promotion of partnership. Conservation policy is closely linked to land use planning through the designation of conservation areas and the more rigorous application of development control to highly valued elements in the physical environment and thus returns the account to the concerns of Chapter 10.

While the aim is to introduce readers to the British planning system, the starting point is the operation of that system in England. Thus most of the references to legislation and other policy documents are restricted to those applicable within England. However, at the end of each section the significant variations that exist between the English situation and that prevailing in Wales or Scotland are identified. The imposition of direct rule in Northern Ireland renders the situation there even more distinct from that in England. It has not proved possible to provide parallel details for Northern Ireland in every policy area, but where points of particular interest arise, these have been noted.

☐ *Assessing planning*

Part 4 provides a overview, 'Assessing Planning'. This consists of two chapters. In Chapter 14 the assessment focuses on 'The Impact of Planning'. This chapter draws together statistical material and published research results to consider what the effects of the planning system have been. This is an ambitious task and it is in the nature of such a review that a comprehensive and conclusive judgement cannot be made: there are too many gaps in the research literature and space constrains review of what is available. But some clear trends are apparent; in many cases the research and data are fairly conclusive and a consequent critique of the planning system can be developed. Finally, Chapter 15 probes the necessity of a planning system, looking back at the general nature of the relationship between the planning system and economic change. It considers the potential planning offers for securing social change and the implications this has for political action surrounding planning issues. Finally, it reassesses the contribution of collaborative planning theory and suggests a rather different, more modest role for planners.'

■ *PART 1* ■

THE DEVELOPMENT OF PLANNING POLICY AND THEORY

Part 1 of the book reviews the development of planning policy over the past century alongside the changing nature of planning theory. Rather than being presented as a separate account of planning theory, the theoretical debates are seen as integrally connected to the changes in planning policy through the process of professionalising planning. All three aspects – planning policy, planning theory and the professionalisation of planning – are seen in the context of the changing nature of social and economic processes. Each historical period under discussion is thus considered in relation to: economic and social change; emerging planning problems and policies; and the planning profession and planning theory. The overall argument of the historical review in Part 1 is summarised overleaf.

	19th and early 20th centuries	1920s, 1930s and 1940s	1950s and 1960s	1970s	1980s	1990s
Economic and social change	Industrialisation Urbanisation War	Recession and restructuring War and reconstruction	Postwar boom Mixed economy Consensus politics	Turning point in economic growth Urban–rural shift Inner city decline	Recession (and recovery) New technology Collapse of mixed-economy consensus	Globalisation of: politics, economics and environmental change
Salient political issues	Public health Social unrest	Regional unemployment Suburban growth	Increasing living standards Rapid development	Racism and urban disorder Excesses of economic growth	Unemployment Track record of public sector	European integration Environmental crisis
Key planning activities	Housing Public sanitation	Regional planning	New towns Redevelopment	Inner city policy Rehabilitation and conservation Pollution control	Urban regeneration Countryside policy	Regeneration Sustainable development Flagship projects
Planning profession	Architects Engineers	Growth of separate identity	Corporate planners	Crisis of competence	Retrenchment Privatisation	Reassessment
Theoretical framework	Environmental determinism	Emergent planning theory	Procedural planning theory	Critiques: Organisation theory[1] Welfare economics[2] Radical political economy[2] Urban politics/sociology[3]	Political ideologies: New Right[1] New Left[2]	Collaborative Planning[1] Critiques (reprise): Environmental economics[2] Radical political ecology[2] Environmental justice[3]
Conceptualisation of planning	Urban design	Public sector direction of land use	Generic decision-making	1. Policy implementation 2. State intervention 3. Community empowerment	1. Economic development 2. Community empowerment	1. Place making 2. State intervention 3. Community empowerment

Figure 1.1 *The development of planning policy and theory*

■ *Chapter 1* ■

Establishing the Planning System

■ The nineteenth- and early twentieth-century origins of planning

□ *Economic and social change*

While some histories of planning trace its origins right back to the urban design practices of the Greeks and link its development to the town designs of the medieval and Renaissance periods, and the development controls of the Tudor, Stuart and Georgian periods, it is generally accepted that the impetus to modern planning activity came from the massive industrialisation of the nineteenth century. For this industrialisation brought with it large-scale population growth and, more important, population movement. Between 1801 and 1901 the population of England and Wales grew from 8.9 million to 32.5 million. The towns and cities grew at an unprecedented rate as people moved from rural to urban areas. Between 1821 and 1851 alone some 4 million people migrated to the towns and by 1851 some 50 per cent of the population was urban in residence. The resultant urban squalor is well-documented, most vividly in Engels's *Conditions of the English Working Class* (1845 German edn, 1892 English edn). Conditions for the average family were cramped, damp and insanitary. Along with an inadequate diet, this resulted in high mortality rates and a weak and unhealthy working-class population. Furthermore the conditions produced a general public health risk through the inadequate water and sewerage systems for the dense urban population. The resulting epidemics, particularly of cholera in the 1840s, spread the consequences of inadequate housing beyond the occupants themselves.

Urbanisation and industrialisation went along with rapid economic growth. This economic growth was underpinned by the creation of a labour force in the form of a proletariat, unfettered by links to land or craft and dependent on wage labour for meeting essential living costs. The factory system of production controlled the workforce with economic and organisational discipline. But such discipline could never be complete in its effectiveness. Resistance to the exploitation involved in such wage labour

13

and to the squalid urban conditions increasingly took the form of class-based politics as the labour movement slowly developed. In doing so, it had the examples of more revolutionary movements on the Continent to look to. The pressure from domestic and overseas labour movements created another impetus for reform to improve working-class living standards. The threat of revolution in Britain seems to have been most imminent just after the First World War with the mass demobilisation of soldiers into a collapsing economy. The postwar 'Homes Fit for Heroes' budget promised a programme of reform to stem the feared revolutionary tide (Swenarton, 1981) and helped lay the foundations for the future welfare state and rise of state planning.

☐ *Planning problems and policies*

The key concern arising from nineteenth-century industrialisation was with housing for the masses of the working population, and in particular with the public health aspects of that housing. In 1840 the Select Committee on the Health of Towns reported, followed by the Royal Commission on the State of Large Towns in 1845. The result was the Public Health Act of 1848 which created a Central Board of Health and local boards with responsibility for local sanitary conditions. The next three decades saw three Acts enabling the clearance of unfit housing: the Shaftesbury Act of 1851, the Torrens Act of 1868 and the Cross Act of 1875. The year of 1875 also saw the passage of a new consolidating Public Health Act which paved the way for sanitary district bye-laws specifying minimum new housing standards in terms of street width, dwelling design and construction. The appalling air pollution caused by emissions from factories was also recognised to be a public health hazard. Attention particularly focused on the alkali works, emitting corrosive hydrogen chloride gases, resulting in the introduction of the first of a series of Alkali Acts in 1863, the precursors of today's pollution control.

These series of measures had had little effect by the end of the nineteenth century, as was made clear in Chadwick's 1884 *Report on the Sanitary Conditions of the Labouring Poor*. The effects were beginning to concern a number of industrialists, both for philanthropic reasons and because of the assumed link between quality of environment and labour productivity. Certain notable individuals assumed responsibility for improving the living conditions of their workforce through the development of model towns, for example, Salt at Saltaire (1853), Lever at Port Sunlight (1887), and Cadbury at Bournville (1878). In each case considerable emphasis was given to providing housing which promoted clean, sanitary and healthy living. The idea of a pleasant, self-contained environment providing for work and leisure proved a powerful one.

By the end of the century, this idea had been given its fullest expression in the 1898 tract by Ebenezer Howard, *Tomorrow – A Peaceful Path to Social Reform*, whose title told of the perceived link between the threat of revolutionary change and planning activity; this was subsequently reissued in 1902 under the title *Garden Cities of To-morrow*. The tract propounded the idea of garden cities, which would combine the best elements of urban and rural life and provide a blueprint for urban growth. It was also a response to the suburbanisation that was beginning to occur with the building boom of the 1890s, linked to electrification of tramways and workers' concessionary rail fares. The garden cities concept was discussed further by the Committee on Unhealthy Areas, which reported in 1900, and given organisational support through the Garden City Association (later to become the Town and Country Planning Association) formed in 1899. In 1902 the Garden City Pioneer Company began trading, followed the next year by First Garden City Ltd which developed Letchworth. The development of Welwyn Garden City was begun after the conclusion of the First World War, in 1919.

The housing and public health concerns of the nineteenth century legislation and the comprehensive management of new urban areas implied by the garden city movement both influenced the first piece of legislation to bear the word 'planning'. Also influential was the example of German planning, used by both the National Housing Reform Council and the Association of Municipal Corporations to press for planning legislation (Hague, 1984, p. 55). The Housing, Town Planning, etc. Act of 1909 created permissive powers for local authorities or landowners to prepare schemes regulating suburban growth. The plan preparation procedures were, however, cumbersome, and of 172 authorised schemes, only 13 were submitted by 1919. The 1919 Housing and Town Planning Act sought to streamline the administrative procedures while extending the scope of planning control. Borough and urban districts with a population of over 20 000 were now required to prepare planning schemes for areas of new development and developers were advised to obtain interim development orders before undertaking development in scheme areas, otherwise they risked losing potentially valuable compensation. The Act also contained various provisions for building 'Homes Fit for Heroes' and, indeed, the land use planning provisions were curtailed in order to give the housing drive the fullest opportunities (Hague, 1984, p. 59).

It was soon recognised that the extension of state activity through planning would affect the pattern of land values, increasing them in certain locations and decreasing them in others. The 1909 Act had incorporated cumbersome compensation and taxation provisions to deal with the resulting changes in land values, but these were repealed along with the plan preparation process. This represented a broader shift in opinion on land taxation. The 1910 Finance Act had contained no fewer than four duties for land taxation, but none of these schemes proved successful, and the four duties were abandoned in 1920. The main success in this area was in clarifying the rules for compensation of land compulsorily purchased by the state: the 'Six Rules' of the Acquisition of Land (Assessment of Compensation) Act 1919 largely stand to this day.

By the late nineteenth century, it was also becoming increasingly apparent that urbanisation posed a threat to existing valued features of urban and rural areas. Therefore a conservationist and amenity-oriented strand of planning developed alongside the urban housing strand. This reflected general public concern with the countryside as evidenced in the number of societies formed around these issues: the Commons, Footpaths and Open Space Society in 1865, the Society for the Protection of Ancient Buildings in 1877, the Royal Society for the Protection of Birds in 1889 and the National Trust for Places of Historic Interest or Natural Beauty in 1895. Urban conservation concerns were given central government recognition in the 1882 and 1913 Ancient Monuments Acts and the creation in 1880 of the Royal Commission on Historic Monuments. The effect on amenity of increased roadbuilding and traffic, albeit modest by postwar standards, led to the 1925 Roads Improvement Act, which empowered local authorities to purchase land alongside highways for planting and amenity purposes; the Road Beautification Association, a voluntary body, was formed in 1928 to promote the use of these powers. A more specific area of planning activity, the 1907 Advertisements Regulations Act, also reflected an early concern with general urban amenity.

In rural areas, amenity concerns over inappropriate urban development were linked with evidence on the economic problems facing the agricultural sector. Financial support for the agricultural industry had been proposed by the Selborne Committee in 1917 and the 1920 Agriculture Act represented a first attempt at a support scheme, only to be repealed the following year because of the cost. The rural despoliation resulting from tree-felling during the First World War was addressed by the establishment of the Forestry Commission in 1919, though the primary concern of this body was always with timber production rather than rural amenity. Thus from the earliest days of planning, economic and amenity concerns went together in rural policy.

□ *Planning profession and planning theory*

Planning theory concerns an attempt to develop general ideas and principles, to go beyond the specific problem at issue. It draws on theory developed within the other social science disciplines such as economics, political science, geography and sociology but it brings a distinctive and integrated focus to bear on planning concerning the physical environment and the uses made of that environment. It also contains within it a normative slant, a concern with how planning *should be* carried out. Such theorisation is associated with the increasing maturity of the planning profession, the growth of institutionalised training and education for planners, and the establishment of planning as an academic discipline. In these early years, all such developments lay in the future. Planning was not professionalised and an explicit or even implicit 'planning' theory did not yet exist. In 1909 there were only four men practising in the United Kingdom as professional planners (Hague, 1984, p. 97). Planning activity during this period focused on physical aspects of urban design. This fitted with the sanitary engineering concerns that prompted the early planning legislation and with the consequent identification of planners with the engineering and architectural professions. Conferences held by the Royal Institute of British Architects in 1910 and the Institute of Municipal and County Engineers in 1911 discussed the development of planning and confirmed the urban design orientation. When the Town Planning Institute was founded in 1914, setting its first examinations in 1920, admission was on the basis of a professional qualification in architecture, engineering or surveying; the Town Planning Institute provided only post-professional training.

The analytic approach underlying such planning activity was not a fully fledged planning theory, but rather an assumption about the relationship between the physical environment and society: environmental or geographical determinism (see Summary Box 1.1). This proposed that through careful and expert design of the physical fabric of urban areas, an environment could be created which not only improved living standards but also improved the inhabitants themselves, physically, morally and socially (Pepper, 1984, pp. 110–13). The link with creating reformed urban residents and avoiding anti-social or, indeed, revolutionary behaviour was clear. Hague (1984, p. 54) also argues that planning activity at this time was linked with a concern over the physical well-being of the British race in the context of competition between imperialist nations, notably Britain and Germany, and in the face of evidence of the poor physical health of recruits to the 1899 Boer War, as revealed in the 1904 report of the Inter-Departmental Committee on Physical Deterioration and, again, during the call-up for the First World War. This is best expressed in the debate on the 1909 Housing, Town Planning, etc. Act itself, in which the Act's purpose was described as: to provide a domestic condition for the people in which their physical health, their morals, their character and their whole social condition can be improved (*Parliamentary Debates*, May 1908). These sentiments were echoed in the 1919 Housing and Town Planning Act, whose housing provisions followed on from a number of official reports drawing a link between poor housing and industrial unrest, such as the 1917 report of the Royal Commission on Industrial Unrest and the report of the Royal Commission on Housing of the Industrial Population of Scotland of the same year.

   This approach saw planning activity as essentially a technical process of design and drawing, separated in its operation from economic or political processes. The success of such activity depended on the technical ability of the planner, who could be considered an applied engineer. It was a strongly normative approach, based on a view of planning as a 'good thing' and setting out a detailed idea of what planning should achieve, an ideal model. Thus Ebenezer Howard, in the introduction to his volume, hoped 'to show how in "Town-country" equal, nay better, opportunities of social intercourse may be envisaged than are enjoyed in any crowded city, while yet the beauties of nature may encompass and enfold each dweller therein . . . how the bounds of freedom may be widened, and yet all the best results of concert and co-operation gathered in by a happy people' (1902, p. 49). But while the work of planners was limited to designing the new urban areas and was predicated on an environmental determinist rationale, the work of Howard himself went beyond this. It incorporated environmental determinism but the garden city project was essentially a social invention (F. J. Osborne in his preface to *Garden Cities of To-morrow*, 1902, p. 21). This involved considerable attention to the financial viability and management of the project and to the vision of a cooperative society, underpinned by the sharing of land rents. The project set a task for planners in designing dwellings, estates, towns and city regions, but it always went beyond the planner's professional remit. Or rather planners were charged with filling in the sketch diagrams of Howard's volume. Theirs was not yet the more comprehensive mission.

Summary Box 1.1   *Environmental determinism*

Definition of planning:	Urban design
View of planners:	Technical experts in built form and urban engineering
Process involved:	Design; map-making; technical drawing
Relation to economy:	Separate from viability concerns
Relation to politics:	Separate from community participation concerns
Outcomes:	Dependent on planner's skill
Research focus:	Areas of (re)development
Theoretical antecedents:	–

■ The 1920s to 1940s: towards the 1947 Town and Country Planning Act

□ *Economic and social change*

With the collapse of the inflated wartime economy upon demobilisation in 1918, Britain entered three decades of severe economic and social upheaval. A world recession in demand created mass unemployment, aggravated by the industrial restructuring that occurred. The resultant effects in the depressed regions are well-known: long-term unemployment, idle and abandoned plant, severe poverty, the urban dereliction of disinvestment. But this was also a period of rapid economic growth for the south-east and the Midlands. New industries located in greenfield sites on the urban periphery, using electric power from the National Grid rather than coal. In 1937–8 alone 372 factories opened in the London area. A speculative housebuilding industry and burgeoning building society movement translated this into large-scale residential developments for a new generation of owner-occupiers, with government encouragement in the form of tax relief on mortgage interest payments under the 1923 Housing Act. Some 2.7 million dwellings were built in England and Wales during 1930–40. At the outbreak of the Second World War one-third of all dwellings had been built since 1918. Operating at much lower densities than nineteenth century urban development, these residential, industrial and associated commercial areas spread over large parts of rural England, encouraged by the developments in energy supply and transport technology.

The housebuilding boom was just beginning to lift Britain out of recession when rearmament propelled the country once more into a wartime economy. This was a very different experience to that of the First World War, though. Whereas the war of 1914–18 had been supplied by entrepreneurs operating in a relatively free market, the war of 1939–45 was public sector-directed. The level of government involvement in the details of civil and military preparation for war was unprecedented. At the same time, mobilisation, evacuation of the cities and other population movements placed different social groups from different parts of the country in contact with each other, often for the first time. The effect was politically radicalising, preparing the way for a new form of public sector activity once peace was declared.

□ *Planning problems and policies*

The severe unemployment of the interwar years, concentrated as it was in particular regions in the north, created the impetus for regionally-based incentives to industrial activity. The earliest policies were property-based, providing new factory space in trading estates under the Board of Trade. Grants for industrial building and employment were also an early and enduring feature. At the other end of the country, in the more prosperous southern and midland regions, attempts were being made to cope with the rapid suburbanisation. From 1927 to 1939 there was an average annual loss of open land of 25 000 hectares. In 1925 the Town Planning Act, although largely a consolidating Act, for the first time separated planning from housing as an area of public concern. The 1932 Town and Country Planning Act introduced the power to prepare planning schemes for any land, including built-up areas and land unlikely to be developed in the near future. Once approved, development in the plan area was subject to local authority control and, prior to plan approval, the provisions for interim development control were extended. Ministerial approval was required for the plans and some scope for modification and amendment introduced; the minister responsible at the time was the Minister of Health. Policy-makers were also building on the model town and garden city concepts of the nineteenth and early twentieth centuries with the 1935 Parliamentary Committee on Garden Cities and Satellite Towns.

Alongside this planning activity for areas of growth went a concern with protecting rural areas from unplanned growth. The 1920s and 1930s saw a further increase in the number of societies based on such concern, the most notable example being the Council for the Preservation of Rural England (later the Council for the Protection of Rural England) set up in 1926, who soon pressed for a Rural Amenities Bill. Much of this concern focused around leisure use of the countryside, increasingly by urban residents. In 1929–31 Addison chaired a Committee on National Parks and in 1932, following the mass trespass on Kinder Scout, the Rights of Way Act provided some access rights for leisure users of the countryside. The Youth Hostels' Association was set up in 1921 and in 1935 the Ramblers' Association was formed. The latter pressed for further extension of access rights, lobbying hard for the 1939 Access to Mountains Act. However, the final legislation was much weaker than had been hoped for, reflecting the power of rural landowners and the other dominant thread of countryside policy – the support of the farming industry. The 1929 and 1931 Agricultural Marketing Acts re-established a system of financial support for the industry.

Much of this work on national parks, garden cities and regional development was sidelined when the international financial crisis brought down the Labour government in 1931 and led to a period of expenditure cuts. It was only after the declaration of the Second World War and the formation of a wartime coalition government that these issues were seriously examined again. A batch of major wartime reports under the auspices of the 1943 Cabinet Committee on Reconstruction, and the resulting legislation, provided the main basis for the postwar planning system. Also in 1943, the Ministry of Town and Country Planning Act established a separate and specific ministerial responsibility for planning, taking over from the short-lived Ministry of Works and Planning (1942–3). The same year saw interim development control extended to all land in England and Wales not already under an operative planning scheme; essentially permission was needed for all development if compensation rights were to be protected. This set the scene for the 1947 Act.

The crowning piece of comprehensive planning legislation was this 1947 Town and Country Planning Act, heralded by the 1944 White Paper *The Control of Land Use*. This imposed a compulsory planning duty on all local authorities for the first time. By 1 July 1951 all areas were to have development plans indicating the areas allocated to the main uses, the main transport routes, minerals areas, woodlands, green belts, reservoirs, and means of water supply and sewage disposal. Town maps supplemented such county maps and provided the detail for urban areas including any designated comprehensive development areas (CDAs) where major urban redevelopment was proposed. Some of these focused on war-damaged town centres, others on areas of slum clearance. These CDAs instituted a prolonged programme of clearance and redevelopment for reshaping and improving urban areas. Programme maps showed the stages by which development was to occur, given that development plans were to cover a twenty-year period. The preparatory work for the development plans included an extensive report of survey which focused on physical land use issues. All development, broadly defined in the 1947 Act but excluding agricultural development, was to be subject to development control, the need to obtain prior planning permission from the local planning authority. The 1947 Act thus introduced comprehensive and compulsory planning in the form of drawing up area-based plans and controlling development, case by case. This was a departure from the prewar planning system which was essentially a form of zoning in which the development plan itself created development rights.

These planning provisions were underpinned by two other policy changes. First, there was a degree of local government reorganisation of responsibilities. The 1947 Act identified county councils and county boroughs as the local planning authorities, rather than the county districts, thus reducing the total number of local planning authorities from 1441 to 145. The growing importance of the county councils had been anticipated since the 1929 Local Government Act which had given them highway responsibilities and the power to prepare planning schemes in default of the districts. Second, arising out of the 1942 Uthwatt Report of the Expert Committee on Compensation and Betterment, there was greater recognition of the role that public landownership and land taxation policies could play. The 1944 Town and Country Planning Act gave local authorities the power to compulsorily purchase land for planning purposes if it had been 'blitzed', that is, war-damaged, or 'blighted', that is, suffered from poor layout or obsolete development. The 1932 Town and Country Planning Act had already raised the betterment levy payable on increases in land values due to planning to 75 per cent but the 1947 Town and Country Planning Act went further. It compulsorily purchased all development rights, through the development control provisions. A global fund of £300 million, administered by the Central Land Board, was provided for once-and-for-all compensation and, on grant of any planning permission, a betterment levy, set at 100 per cent of the resultant increase in land values, was applied. As a result, all land was supposed to exchange hands at existing use value only, taking no account of the increase in value associated with the proposed development and planning permission.

Under this new planning framework, a number of policy ideas were consolidated. The garden city or model town idea was transformed into the new town concept. The 1946 Reith Report from the New Towns Committee and the 1946 New Towns Act effected the transformation. From this legislation, plans for 32 new towns would eventually be drawn up and implemented. In each case a master plan would design a town from scratch, with the public sector compulsorily purchasing the land and directing development to ensure the provision of facilities and limit the involvement of the private sector. This was a rather statist interpretation of the community sharing in development profits that Howard had envisaged. Meanwhile in existing urban areas, the burgeoning planning system took on the protection of urban heritage. During the interwar period, several more amenity societies had been founded: for example, the Ancient Monuments Society in 1924 and the Georgian Society in 1937. The 1932 Town and Country Planning Act had given local authorities powers to enforce the retention of significant trees in urban locations while the 1944 Act introduced the important power of listing buildings of architectural or historic interest.

In the field of regional policy, development areas were designated under the 1945 Distribution of Industry Act, with grants to encourage industrial relocation. This followed through the arguments of the 1940 Barlow Report of the Royal Commission on the Distribution of the Industrial Population (see below), and the commitment to maintaining full employment contained in the 1944 White Paper on employment policy. In addition, incentives in development areas were supplemented by restrictions on new industrial development in more prosperous areas. This took the form of the need to obtain an industrial development certificate

(IDC) prior to undertaking such development activity, under the provisions of the Town and Country Planning Act 1947.

In 1942 the Scott Report of the Committee on Land Utilisation in Rural Areas was published, enshrining the principle of protecting rural land and agricultural areas, to be followed by the Dower Report of 1945 and the Hobhouse Report of 1947. These reports proposed national parks in England and Wales overseen by a National Parks Commission. The purpose of national park designation included: landscape beauty, public access, wildlife conservation, and conservation of buildings or places of architectural or historic interest, as well as agricultural protection. The 1949 National Parks and Access to the Countryside Act established such national parks together with areas of outstanding natural beauty (AONBs) and nature reserves. However, the proposal for a powerful overseeing organisation, the National Parks Commission, was rejected. Instead local planning authorities took on these functions. The National Parks Commission was set up but with only an advisory role; a Countryside Commission was also formed. In Scotland the 1945 Ramsay Committee recommended five national parks but their proposals were not implemented. The 1949 Act did not apply to Scotland.

The Nature Conservancy Council was also established in 1949 by Royal Charter to provide scientific advice, establish and manage nature reserves and develop research. This followed the 1945 Special Committee on Wildlife Conservation and the 1947 Haseley Committee on Conservation of Nature in England and Wales. The latter Committee, while arguing for nature conservation measures, concluded that there was no fundamental conflict between access for amenity considerations and wildlife interests and the promotion of both aspects was encouraged. Provision was made under the 1949 Act for mapping rights of way. This followed on the report of the 1948 Subcommittee on Footpaths and Access to the Countryside, an offshoot of the Hobhouse Committee. While providing a framework for meeting leisure, amenity and wildlife concerns over rural areas, this entire countryside policy rested on the primary principle of conserving rural areas for agricultural activity. The 1947 Agriculture Act explicitly set out the commitment to the British farming industry and established a new system of financial support based on guaranteed prices for agricultural products. Failure to farm productively could lead to censure by the county council and, eventually, to notice to quit.

☐ *Planning profession and planning theory*

During the interwar period the planning profession gained confidence in its separate identity and specialist perspective, as more and more local authorities employed planners. The growing quantity of planning legislation was effectively creating a public sector profession. From 1931 the Town Planning Institute provided a town planning qualification rather than post-professional training and during the 1930s the first 'recognised' schools of planning were established. Planning-related groups also became more influential in promoting and developing planning policy. Early in the 1930s the Town Planning Institute and other professional and environmental bodies wrote to the Prime Minister regretting the apparent demise of active planning policy and pressing for new legislation. The Town and Country Planning Association is credited with being particularly important in shaping the 1947 Town and Country Planning Act through its general activities and the involvement of influential planners and members such as Frederick Osborne, also an active Labour Party member.

While the town planning educational syllabus still focused heavily on urban design, a more general vision of planning activity was gaining ascendancy. This can be described as a vision of comprehensive, integrated allocation of land uses. The public sector, through its planning functions, would provide and implement a general framework for resource allocation ensuring the best use of resources throughout the country. Both underutilisation (urban dereliction, regional decline) and over-exploitation (ribbon development, rapid urbanisation) would be avoided. A variety of tools would be available to ensure the implementation of this plan, emphasising the many dimensions to the problem of optimal land use. The key element of this vision was the need to provide a comprehensive strategy for tackling these many dimensions, which was also integrated in terms of recognising the interrelations between these dimensions. Thus the 1943 Ministry of Town and Country Planning Act could state the objective of the Ministry as securing consistency and continuity in the framing and execution of a national policy with regard to the use and development of land.

Of great significance in developing this view of planning was the Barlow Report of 1940. This argued that the problems of the depressed northern regions, with their high levels of industrial disinvestment, and the rapidly growing southern and midland regions, with their substantial suburban development, were two faces of the same coin. The problems were interrelated so that successful resolution of one problem depended on tackling the other. Also important was H. Warren and W.R. Davidge's book *Decentralisation of Population and Industry: A New Principle in Town Planning*, which argued for planning as part of national economic and social planning (Cullingworth, 1988, p. 5). Documents such as these provided the intellectual support for comprehensive, integrated planning, covering numerous dimensions of land use in relation to each other throughout the country. The logic of this approach could propose quite radical planning solutions. The 1942 Uthwatt Expert Committee argued that the key to securing the proper pattern of land use lay in solving the problems of compensation and betterment, that is, the recompense for downward and upward movements in land prices resulting from new patterns of land use. Following a comprehensive integrated planning approach, the committee recommended extending public sector activity to include land taxation and, logically, land nationalisation measures. Political considerations, however, meant that only the land taxation measures were considered realistic policy options.

The essence of this approach was the public sector direction of resource allocation, mainly through controlling land use. The role of economic processes through the land market in hindering 'proper planning' was recognised, through the pioneering work of the Uthwatt Expert Committee, but planning was seen as capable of externally directing those processes. While the whole programme of building up a planning system reflected the growing public acceptance of a socialist solution to interwar and wartime problems, the resulting planning activity was not seen as essentially political. Rather, planners were public sector urban managers in a technical, apolitical role. This was in line with the growing professionalisation of planning activity. The process of planning was seen as relatively problem-free; it involved devising appropriate policies and then implementing them. As Cullingworth (1988, p. 14) points out, what was new was the belief that the problems could be tackled in the same way as a military operation. Given the requisite powers this should be fairly straightforward, and little thought was given to potentially unsuccessful outcomes from this process. A naive view of socialist centralised planning dominated, closely related to the views propounded by the Labour government of the time. As Hague (1984, p. 64) says, the significance of the new legislation was that the idea of town planning could convey important symbols of a new social order. The political pressures of the postwar period were to curtail this vision of planning, limiting the directive role of the public sector and returning much control over resource allocation to the private sector. This division of responsibilities undercut the comprehensive, integrated nature of planning. Within the new mixed-economy consensus, a new model of planning activity would have to be devised.

This vision of planning was reflected in certain key writings of the time and sowed the seeds of what was to be the dominant form of planning theory for much of the postwar period (see Summary Box 1.2). A key figure in the development of this emergent planning theory was Patrick Geddes, a biologist who also turned his attention to issues of urban life and the development of an interdisciplinary approach that he termed 'civics'. His two key books in this area were published in 1905 and 1915, though he undertook influential work in India during 1914–24. His writings have allowed multiple interpretations of his legacy (Hebbert, 1982); one common view is that he was the father of the modern planning method through his espousal of a 'survey, analysis, plan' approach. This is wishful thinking but Geddes's writings do represent an important step on from the implicit environmental determinism of the early years. Geddes rejected the label of 'geographical determinist', arguing for the additional importance of visionary thinking and ideas in influencing urban life (Hasselgren, 1982, p. 33). He did argue for the need to understand the city in its historical context before undertaking any planning and proposed 'the survey method' but this fell short of contemporary social science meanings of the term. His surveys, though rarely carried out in practice, were intended to inform visual displays and pageants which would stimulate public discussion and even cooperative direct action. They were not primarily the basis for state planning action but rather for visionary 'civics'. He also proposed seeing cities in their regional context, 'the regional plan', and some see this as his more significant contribution (Hebbert, 1982).

His primary purpose and significance during the early formative period for British planning was to argue for planning: 'an ideal city is latent in every town' (Geddes, 1905, p. 159). He propounded the view that a better allocation of resources would lead to a better urban life and, in the context of interwar Fabianism and the emergent Labour philosophy, this was to underpin a new approach to urban planning, one in which state action would provide that better allocation. Geddes did not provide a theoretical basis for this view; rather his writings proved a resource for those who sought to develop this theoretical basis. In particular he elevated the discussion by suggesting that a general planning method could exist (even if he did not set it out) and that planning was a broad-based activity involving much more than issues of urban design.

Summary Box 1.2   *Emergent planning theory*

Definition of planning:	Public sector direction of land use
View of planners:	Public sector urban managers
Process involved:	Policy formulation and implementation
Relation to economy:	External direction of economy
Relation to politics:	Implementation of socialist programme
Outcomes:	Naive view of success
Research focus:	Particular policies
Theoretical antecedents:	–

■ Further reading

There are numerous histories of the origins of planning. Hague (1984) is particularly interesting. Other useful texts are Ashworth (1954), Cherry (1972 and 1996), and Sutcliffe (1981). Cherry (1974) covers the period 1914–74 but includes discussion of the RTPI. For detailed study there is the four-volume official history of the planning system by Cullingworth (1975a, 1975b, 1979, 1980 – see the end of Chapter 2 for more details). Volume 1 particularly focuses on the war years. Countryside policy is well served by Sheail's history of the interwar years (1981). To enable students to judge for themselves the contribution of two key 'founding fathers' of planning, Howard's and Geddes's original texts should be sought out, if only to convey the flavour of polemical writing of the time (Howard, 1902; Geddes, 1905 and 1915).

■ *Chapter 2* ■

Postwar Planning 1950s–1970s

■ The 1950s and 1960s: economic growth and the mixed-economy consensus

□ *Economic and social change*

Immediately after the war, the incoming Labour government faced serious economic problems, with a public sector deficit of £443 million in 1947 which severely limited their plans for a public sector-led economy. However, by the end of the 1950s, Britain was entering a long period of economic growth which brought with it an increase in and spread of living standards. National output rose, unemployment fell and the economy bumped up against the constraints of full resource use and productive capacity. With the replacement of the postwar 1945 Labour government, the state came firmly under the sway of the mixed-economy consensus. Whether Labour or Conservative governments were in power, their views on economic management were broadly similar. Butskellism (an amalgam of the economic policies of the Labour Chancellor Gaitskell and the Conservative Butler) ruled the day. Both were riding along on the economic wave of increasing national output based on the 'white heat of new technology' (as the early stages of the electronic industrial revolution were termed), together with increased concentration of capital and the culmination of Taylorism in production processes, whereby assembly lines organised a rigid division of labour.

Alongside economic growth went a variety of social changes. Population grew, largely from indigenous growth as family formation took off after the long interrupted war years. Near full employment also encouraged immigration from Britain's former Empire, now the Commonwealth. The increased living standards of the growing population stimulated many new forms of development: residential, industrial, office and shopping areas. The form of these areas was influenced by the greatly more mobile nature of the population as car ownership increased. This, together with the strains that growth placed on already dense urban areas, precipitated the decentralisation of first population and then employment that was to shape much of the postwar urban experience. The major focus of these decades was, therefore, on the scale of, and problems arising from, economic growth. Even the need to deal with the war damage of bombed town centres and residential and industrial areas was seen as much as a profitable development opportunity as a reconstruction task. But towards the end of the period it began to be acknowledged that the mixed-economy approach did not sweep away problems of inequality and deprivation. The 'rediscovery' of poverty at home and the example of the American 'race riots', as a response to ethnically concentrated deprivation, both raised questions about the future direction of public policy in Britain.

☐ *Planning problems and policies*

During this period a number of initiatives were undertaken in a variety of policy areas: new towns, regional policy, countryside protection, pollution control, urban poverty, housing, and transport. The land use planning system was also restructured. This variety indicates the growth that was occurring in the range of planning activity and also the implementation of many policy ideas merely discussed during the formative years of the planning system.

The implementation of the new towns programme showed how a simple idea could involve substantial resources. Thirteen new towns were designated from 1947 to 1950: eight round London – Basildon, Bracknell, Crawley, Harlow, Hatfield, Hemel Hempstead, Stevenage and Welwyn Garden City; two in the north east – Peterlee and Newton Aycliffe; two in Scotland   Glenrothes and East Kilbride; and one in Wales – Cwmbran. Within these new town areas, a development corporation directed the planning and building of the new settlement, working to a master plan. In an extension of the concept, the 1952 Town Development Act paved the way for expanded towns whereby population could be decanted from overcrowded urban areas in the major conurbations into newly developed areas adjoining existing small settlements. During the 1950s the policy focus shifted from new towns to expanded towns and only one further new town was designated in this decade, Cumbernauld in 1956. Then in 1959 another New Towns Act instituted the next generation of towns and set up a Commission for New Towns to oversee their operation. This second wave of new towns comprised: Skelmersdale, Livingstone, Telford, Redditch, Runcorn, Washington and Irvine. In addition Peterborough, Northampton and Warrington were designated for development under new town powers but on a partnership basis between the local development corporations and the local authorities.

Meanwhile regional planning took on new forms. The definition of areas, within which grants were available, changed several times. The 1960

Employment Act introduced development areas defined by exceeding a benchmark unemployment level of 4 per cent; the 1966 Industrial Development Act returned to fixed regionally-based areas; in 1967 special development areas were introduced where a higher level of incentive operated; and in 1969 intermediate areas were defined following the recommendations of the Hunt Commission. The Hunt Commission had noted a particular problem of dereliction in intermediate areas. Derelict land within these areas was made eligible for grants under the 1966 Local Government Act but the proposals from the Hunt Commission for a national programme and a derelict land reclamation agency were not implemented. Regional planning was also extended to offices as well as industry, in recognition of the growing importance of this sector and the pressure it was placing on the major cities, particularly London and Birmingham. The Location of Offices Bureau was established in 1963 to encourage the decentralisation of commercial activities and in 1965 the Control of Offices and Industrial Development Act introduced the need to obtain an office development permit (ODP) before undertaking any major commercial development in designated areas.

These incentives and controls of regional planning were further placed within a framework of indicative planning documents, intended to guide the private and public sectors. In 1965 regional economic planning councils and boards of local representatives and civil servants respectively were set up for the eight English planning regions, Northern Ireland, Wales and Scotland. These provided a mechanism for preparing regional plans. Briefly they were overseen by the Department of Economic Affairs, which issued its National Plan in 1965 before being promptly disbanded. Regional plans were supposed to provide a stage in the detailed implementation of this plan. The development plans of the land use planning system were to be the lowest tiers in this hierarchy of strategic planning.

Significant changes were made to the development plan regime towards the end of the 1960s. Concerned at the extent to which urban and rural development was running ahead of the rather inflexible development plans of the 1947 Act, the Planning Advisory Group was set up in 1964, to report a year later on *The Future of Development Plans*. Under the strong influence of the increasingly professionalised planning body, the Royal Town Planning Institute, the group recommended a two-tier system of development plans: broad-brush structure plans and more detailed local plans. This was put into effect through the 1968 Town and Country Planning Act. Structure plans consisted of a written statement and a key diagram, supported by an explanatory memorandum and a statement of public participation and other consultations. They were subject to continuous review rather than on a five-yearly cycle as with the old-style development plans. The ongoing survey which prompted review was broadly based, looking at social and economic forces and not just the physical land use matters of the 1947 plans. Local plans consisted of a written statement, maps and other descriptive matter as relevant. Three types of local plan were proposed: district plans covering all or part of a district; subject or topic plans looking at a particular issue; and action area plans effectively replacing plans for comprehensive development areas. At the same time, public concern at the rate of development and the changes it was bringing led to calls for more public involvement in planning. The 1969 report of the Skeffington Committee on public participation, entitled *People and Planning*, encouraged local authorities to involve communities in plan-making at every stage (Gyford, 1991, pp. 72–9).

Protecting the existing urban heritage remained a popular planning goal, with a wider range of architectural periods finding their supporters; in 1958 the Victorian Society was founded. In 1967 the Civic Trust scored a notable triumph when the Private Members Bill it had sponsored became the Civic Amenities Act. This introduced the concept of conservation areas within which special planning protection operated. The Act also set out the principle that all planning decisions should consider the preservation and enhancement of an area's character and appearance. Listed buildings gained greater protection with the provision of grants for maintenance and repair under the 1962 Local Authorities (Historic Buildings) Act. The first list of such historic buildings was completed in 1968.

The betterment levy provisions of the Town and Country Planning Act 1947 were abolished, along with the global fund for compensation, in the Town and Country Planning Acts of 1953 and 1954. This reestablished market value for most land market transactions but existing use value continued to determine compensation on compulsory purchase until 1959, when a further Town and Country Planning Act reestablished open market value as the basis for all transactions. This confirmed the shift from an assumption that the public sector would direct the allocation of land to a mixed-economy approach, where the state pursued its policies in the context of and within the constraints of market processes. Indeed provisions were introduced to compensate private landowners for some of the adverse effects of planning activity. The 1959 Act introduced the purchase notice, later termed a blight notice, whereby the local authority was forced to buy land which had been rendered incapable of reasonable beneficial use by a planning decision. For example, this covered the 'blighting' of houses on land allocated for roadbuilding at some time in the future.

The late 1960s saw an attempt by a Labour government to take development land out of the influence of market processes again through the Land Commission Act of 1967. This instituted a form of land nationalisation but insufficient financial backing rendered it largely ineffective. It was revoked in 1971 and landowners who had been holding their land off the market during the Commission's operation could now trade freely again. Capital Gains Tax, which was introduced in the Finance Act of 1967, proved more long-lasting. This taxed increases in the value of capital assets, including property and land, from a 1965 base date. Once inflation rates warranted it, the increased values were compared with the general level of inflation and only increases above the general level were taxed.

Countryside protection was extended in several ways. Countryside Acts for England and Wales (1968) and Scotland (1967) introduced a general duty to consider the desirability of conserving areas of natural beauty and amenity. The functions of the National Parks Advisory Committee were taken over by an enlarged Countryside Commission. In Scotland a separate Countryside Commission was established by the 1967 Countryside (Scotland) Act and in Northern Ireland, the Ulster Countryside Commission was established in 1965 with a largely advisory role. Coastal areas were given special attention. Two Ministerial circulars (56/63 and 7/66) provided advice on the preservation of such areas and requested local authorities to prepare special policy statements. Nine regional conferences on coastal planning were held during 1966 and 1967. This culminated in two 1970 Countryside Commission reports on *The Planning of the Coastline* and *The Coastal Heritage* and the concept of the heritage coastline was proposed for designation in development plans after consultation with the Countryside Commission.

But perhaps of greatest significance, the Ministry of Housing and Local Government issued a pamphlet in 1962 on designating green belts, which provided support and guidance on their widespread application. This followed the 1957 circular which had established the purposes and procedures of green belt policy. As a result many local planning authorities took up the invitation to designate such belts around towns and cities. While such designation does not provide for public access or landscape maintenance, the protection afforded from the main forms of urban development made green belts very popular with many suburban communities. As Elson (1986) has analysed, as a policy tool green belts had many attractions for planners, since they combined an element of simplicity and clarity with local discretion.

Leisure use of the countryside was a significant policy concern during this period. Under the Countryside Acts of 1967 and 1968, country parks were introduced, to be designated and maintained by local authorities. This picked up on the 1966 White Paper on *Leisure in the Countryside*. A special park was set up under separate legislation in 1967 in the Lee Valley managed by the Lee Valley Regional Park Authority. The leisure aspect was also highlighted in the reassessment of waterways that occurred in the late 1960s. Following a 1966 British Waterways Board report and a 1967 White Paper, the Transport Act of 1968 set out a Charter for Waterways which identified certain canals and rivers for cruising. It also established the Inland Waterways Amenity Council. Problems of access to the countryside led to the 1968 Countryside Act and Town and Country Planning Act. Following on the 1967 Gosling Committee on Footpaths, the legislation allowed for the maintenance of paths, sign-posting and finance for access. But the underlying rationale of countryside policy in supporting agriculture was not affected by these extensions of planning activity. In the 1950s, financial support took the form of minimum support prices for goods and deficiency payments for farmers. The 1957 Agriculture Act gave legislative basis to a system which, by its very operation, encouraged increases in agricultural productivity and capital investment. The contradiction between this and other goals of countryside policy were to become clear in the following decades.

Pollution control also came back on to the policy agenda. The famed 1952 London smog claimed 4 000 lives, leading to the appointment of the Beaver Committee to investigate air pollution. This committee estimated the economic cost of pollution at £350 million per annum due to corrosion, lost production in agriculture, industry and transport and inefficiencies in fuel-burning. Following the Beaver Report, emissions into the atmosphere were controlled by the 1956 and 1968 Clean Air Acts. These prohibited dark-smoke emissions, controlled grit and dust emissions, set standards for chimney heights and designated smoke control areas where smokeless fuels had to be used for domestic purposes. Discharges into rivers came under local authority control through the 1951 and 1961 River Acts, the latter following the Pippard Committee on Discharges into the Thames. In Scotland a Scottish Rivers Purification Advisory Committee and a network of river purification authorities were established to tackle water quality. A number of other government committees examined a whole range of environmental issues during these years. In 1961 the Key Committee considered household refuse disposal; in 1967 the Browne Committee looked at refuse storage and collection; and in 1970 the Jaeger Committee studied sewage disposal. Noise pollution was examined by the Wilson Committee in 1963, having already received consideration in the 1960 Noise Abatement Act. The 1968 Transport Act gave local authorities the power to prohibit vehicles in certain areas at certain times of day. The specific problem of aircraft noise was tackled in the 1965 Airports Authority Act and the 1968 Civil Aviation Act.

The rapid increase in car ownership and road freight traffic was recognised as posing environmental problems, though these were defined in essentially local terms. The problem was examined in the Buchanan

Report of 1963, *Traffic in Towns*. This highlighted the conflict between enhancing accessibility within, through and to urban areas and maintaining residential and historic amenities within those areas. As a result it was proposed that planning authorities should clearly distinguish environmentally sensitive and hence protected areas from areas where enhanced road provision was to be made. These ideas were never fully taken account of in road and land use planning and instead attention focused on organisational arrangements. Following the 1967 White Paper on *Public Transport and Traffic*, the 1968 Transport Act introduced passenger transport areas in the six major conurbations, within which passenger transport authorities planned and passenger transport executives operated public transport. Transport plans were formally considered part of the development plan under the 1968 Town and Country Planning Act (see above). The intention of the 1968 Act was to strengthen the transport role of local government and grants were provided to support this: capital grants for public transport infrastructure, a bus grant and fuel subsidies for rural areas. But in 1969 a Green Paper, *Roads for the Future*, set out plans for a new interurban network and this continued and expanded the substantial public funding of major trunk road construction programmes which has dominated transport planning throughout the postwar period.

Housing was one area where a strong continuity of concern was evident. The nineteenth century solution of slum clearance was carried through with major programmes of demolition and new build. Central government subsidies encouraged rapid high-rise building (Dunleavy, 1981). However by the end of this period, the problems of this approach were being recognised in terms of the high economic cost, the unsatisfactory nature of the resulting housing and the destruction of existing communities involved. The legislative framework for a housing policy based on improvement and rehabilitation already existed. Discretionary grants for housing improvement had been introduced in the 1949 Housing Act. Standard grants for installing amenities were covered by the 1959 Housing Purchase and Housing Act, and the 1964 Housing Act provided for the designation of general improvement areas, but without linking them to any specific grant provision. It was in 1966 that the Deeplish Study on *Improvement Possibilities in a District of Rochdale* demonstrated the practical potential of a shift from clearance and rebuild to rehabilitation in housing policy. Following this, the Dennington Committee produced a report into *Our Older Homes* in 1967; in the same year the Scottish Housing Advisory Committee produced a parallel report into *Scotland's Older Homes*. The 1968 White Paper *Old Houses into New Homes* heralded the 1969 Housing Act with its proposals for grant-aided general improvement areas (GIAs). The equivalent legislation for Scotland, the 1968 Housing (Scotland) Act, adopted a similar basic approach but, in its espousal of 'tolerable' housing standards as opposed to 'unfit' housing standards, it was ahead of English policy by eighteen years.

The consideration of housing problems merged into a more general concern with urban problems and laid the foundations for the inner city policy of the 1970s. The 1966 Local Government Act and the 1969 Local Government (Social Need) Act set up the Urban Programme, which consisted of grants to local authorities to finance expenditure arising from their location in an urban area of special social need. The Urban Programme was a flexible policy tool. Under its provisions, a variety of local authority projects could be funded by central government at rates of up to 75 per cent of costs. By the end of the decade, the Home Office became more concerned with inner city conditions, largely because of the law and order implications. This resulted in twelve community development projects (CDPs) being set up. Under this initiative, teams in deprived areas studied the root causes of deprivation and sought to remedy it through community participation. The radical analyses and recommendations of the various CDPs found little favour with the Home Office, and the programme was officially disbanded within a few years of its inception. The Home Office had assumed the root cause of the problem was a lack of local coordination; the CDPs tended to favour an analysis in terms of the uneven investment of capital in a market-based economy.

Finally, the process of reviewing the organisational structure of local government began in this period. Major reforms were to come early in the 1970s but in London these were already taking effect. London had always raised particular concerns generating a range of special reports in the interwar period, including that from the 1921–31 Royal Commission on the Local Government of Greater London. In 1963, following the Herbert Committee's report, London's local government was reorganised resulting in the creation of the Greater London Council (GLC), replacing the geographically smaller London County Council and coordinating the work of 32 London boroughs, plus the Corporation of the City of London. Change for the rest of local government was to follow shortly.

☐ *Planning profession and planning theory*

This growth of planning activity in response to the many problems thrown up by economic, population and urban growth was underpinned by the development of a sophisticated and precisely articulated planning theory. The planning profession was, by now, well-established as a separate profession. The Royal Town Planning Institute, having acquired a Royal Charter in 1959, had developed strong vertical links with its growing membership at central and local government levels. New city planning departments had been set up in many local authorities, Cardiff, Leicester,

Newcastle and Liverpool being among the first. Meanwhile central government was employing professional planners in relevant departments. The first full-time undergraduate planning schools were also established during the late 1940s and 1950s.

As the scope of the planning system had grown, with more and more issues seen as having a land use dimension, planning professionals were seen as much more than urban designers. In 1950s the Schuster Report of the Committee on the Qualifications of Planners was published. This recommended widening the entrants to the profession from mainly architectural, engineering and surveying backgrounds to include economists, geographers and sociologists. The syllabuses of planning courses were correspondingly broadened to include these social sciences. However this redefinition of the planning profession created some problems in specifying the specialist expertise of the planner. The result was a move beyond the physical, spatial conception of the planner towards a generalist planner with extended responsibilities. Planners claimed to have the capacity to deal with location decisions, population movements, urban growth, the use of land, slum clearance, city centre redevelopment, transport proposals, the design of new towns and rehabilitation. As public sector activity expanded, particularly at the local authority level, so planners seemed well-placed to advise on many of the new activities. Furthermore, within local government these activities were seen in the context of corporate planning, an approach whereby the interrelation between different local authority departments' work was considered important and in need of central coordination. Again planners saw themselves as well-placed to fulfil such a coordinating role through the medium of an appropriate development plan or other planning strategy. Land use was the map on which all public sector activities could be coordinated.

The theoretical rationalisation for this central role of professional planners was found by recasting planning as a general form of decision-making (see Faludi, 1973, and Faludi's edited volume, 1973, for a review). A distinction was made between theories for planning and theories of planning. The former covered theories explaining the phenomena that planning was seeking to control or respond to: demographic change, spatial location and so on. Computer modelling as an intrinsic element of such theories promised great advances in forecasting and developing planning strategies. However planning theory was properly construed as a theory of planning, concerned with the process of planning. It focused on procedural planning theory (PPT), which proposed optimal ways of taking decisions so as to devise solutions to predefined goals. The most idealistic of these decision-making prescriptions was the rational comprehensive model in which the planner collected all necessary information and data, and rationally devised a policy that would achieve the desired goal by selecting between alternative policies. The chosen policy was then implemented and feedback or monitoring ensured that decision-making could only improve over time.

Not surprisingly, this approach was criticised for its unrealistic assumptions concerning the planner's ability to collect the necessary data and foresee all the problems of implementation. More realistic modes of decision-making were recommended. Principal among these was disjointed incrementalism (Braybrooke and Lindblom, 1963) whereby the existing situation was taken as the starting point from which policy could promote change, rather than suggesting that planners had a clean sheet on which to impose their optimal plans. The constraints of available data and committable resources were recognised as limiting the extent of possible change so that planning policies edged forward, step by step, to desired goals rather than trying to achieve them in one leap.

In whatever form it took, procedural planning theory saw planners as generalist experts in decision-making, collating the necessary information and formulating policy solutions. As Faludi says, in a footnote on page 1 of his seminal 1973 book on *Planning Theory*:

> Definitions given to systems analysis . . . and operations research . . . are the same as that of planning given above. This underlies one of the points to be made about planning theory, i.e. the generality of the phenomenon planning, and hence its wide applicability.

The dynamics of economic processes which might hinder or enable the implementation of these solutions were hardly considered. Similarly the political system was seen as setting the goals for planning but, thereafter, planners operated in an essentially apolitical manner. The quality of information collection, plan formulation and monitoring processes, all aspects of the decision making process itself, determined whether planning achieved satisfactory outcomes. This theory proved quite unable to cope

---

Summary Box 2.1 *Procedural planning theory*

Definition of planning:	Generic decision-making
View of planners:	Rational decision-makers
Process involved:	Decision-making
Relation to economy:	Nil
Relation to politics:	Goals set by political process
Outcomes:	Dependent on information, monitoring and feedback
Research focus:	Professional planners
Theoretical antecedents:	Culmination of emergent planning theory

with the problems arising both from two decades of growth and its eventual collapse in the 1970s, factors which seemed essentially to be outside the control of planning as conceptualised through PPT (see Summary Box 2.1).

■ The 1970s: coping with growth and its collapse

□ *Economic and social change*

The decade of the 1970s saw the economic boom of the postwar period peak and collapse. The property boom of the early 1970s resulted in a tremendous increase in development values and activities, accompanied by substantial infrastructure investment, particularly in roads. The collapse of the boom in 1973–4, as oil prices and interest rates rose, proved no easier to deal with. Suddenly the pressure which had been driving a largely reactive planning system was taken away, and the extent to which economic growth had been relied on in devising public policy became clear. But even before this collapse the problems of substantial growth were becoming apparent, as was its inability to eradicate inequality. Existing public sector policies for managing growth were increasingly being criticised. Environmentalists were beginning to make their voice heard where issues of pollution and traffic generation were concerned. Providing adequate housing for the burgeoning population became a more politically vexed problem as the inadequacies of the previously adopted solution of public and private mass housing were highlighted. The procedures of the planning system were strained by the number and scale of the issues it was trying to tackle.

The problems of the decade were not just ones of the scale of growth. The end of the 1960s saw the beginning of the recognition that severe poverty was still a feature of many people's way of life. The social and economic policies of the postwar period had not successfully spread the increase in living standards to all sectors of the population. In particular the migrants from the Commonwealth and their British-born families were facing severe deprivation as a result of working-class poverty and racist discrimination. These features provided one facet of the 'inner city' problem increasingly recognised in the 1970s. The other facet was provided by the changing patterns of population and employment location. Over the years 1971–7 Merseyside lost 6 per cent of its population; London lost 0.5 million residents. Yet in 1976 the seven metropolitan areas accounted for 40 per cent of all registered unemployment. The suburbanisation of the 1960s had turned into a flight from the cities, as offices and industry moved premises and households who were able joined them. This trend was accelerated by the housing redevelopment policies of local authorities, the new towns programme, regional policies such as office development permits and the mobility afforded by roadbuilding programmes. By the end of the decade, the urban–rural shift in British society was well-established.

The problems of the inner city and persistent poverty were made worse by the downturn in the economy which followed the 1973–4 oil crisis and the resulting inflationary spiral. Unemployment rose, economic growth fell back and, under the conditions of a loan from the International Monetary Fund to cover Britain's balance of payments deficit after the oil price rise, the public sector was cut back. The conditions for the Thatcherism of the 1980s were set. The entry of the UK into the Common Market (now the European Union) also set in train the long, slow process of Europeanisation of British policy, which continues today.

□ *Planning problems and policies*

A few themes in planning policy were brought to a conclusion in this decade. The new towns programme was effectively wound up with the population targets for new towns being cut by 380 000 in 1977. This particularly affected the most recently designated new towns, such as Milton Keynes and Central Lancashire. In 1976 the New Towns Act made provision for the assets of the New Towns Commission to be transferred to local authorities as each town-building programme was completed. Regional planning was rapidly wound down with a greater emphasis placed on inner city problems within regions. But other themes continued and new ones were added.

Within land use planning, the procedures of the system were again under scrutiny. This time most attention was focused on development control rather than development planning. An important tool was made available to local authorities in their negotiations on planning applications in the form of Section 52 agreements contained in the 1971 Town and Country Planning Act. Three years later the Housing Act enabled positive covenants made under Section 126 to be enforced against subsequent purchasers of land, adding a further tool for controlling land use: generally only negative covenants, prohibiting an action, are enforceable. This opened the way for obtaining community benefits during development control, known as planning gain.

Considerable discussion centred on two analyses of development control procedures and practice. The first analysis was that carried out by the Dobry Committee. The Dobry Committee was appointed in 1973 and published its interim and final reports on *The Review of the Development*

Control System in 1974 and 1975, together with a separate report on the control of demolition. While highlighting many complaints of the system, its detailed recommendations for expediting development control were not taken up by central government at this time. These recommendations included separating two classes of planning application: A – minor and uncontroversial; and B – major and/or controversial. Time limits for consultation were to be set. For Type A applications, permission was deemed to be granted after 42 days. Extensive delegation of Type A applications to planners and/or small committees of councillors was proposed. For Type B applications, negotiation between planner and applicant was encouraged. A variety of other measures were also recommended: planning fees, use of design guides (such as the influential Essex County Council *Design Guide for Residential Areas* of 1973) and development briefs, strong control in special environmental areas, and setting up information and planning advice centres. Overall the reports argued that efficient and effective development control was linked to speedy development plan preparation, ensuring up-to-date strategic guidance. The second analysis came from the House of Commons Expenditure Committee's 1976–7 investigation of planning procedures. Gathering together a variety of opinions and data, the committee largely repeated concern with inefficiencies and delays in the development control process.

As far as development planning was concerned, local government was coming to terms with the new requirements of the 1968 Town and Country Planning Act. Structure plans in particular consumed large amounts of local authority planning resources with many district councils continuing to rely on the old-style development plans rather than preparing new local plans, although in Scotland the preparation of statutory local plans was obligatory. The particular circumstances created in Scotland by the exploitation of North Sea oil and gas resulted in an addition to the range of planning policy documents. In 1974 the Scottish Development Department (SDD) issued the first of a series of National Planning Guidelines, setting out national (Scottish) policy on *Oil or Gas-related Coastal Development*. The usefulness of this guideline led to the introduction of a number of others on key planning issues. The guidelines not only influenced subsidiary development planning but also required the local authority to notify the SDD if they planned to grant planning permission contrary to the advice contained in a guideline. Development planning in Scotland was also supplemented by the preparation during the 1970s of regional reports prepared by regional councils (see below) for the whole or part of their area. This reflected the fact that structure plans were generally being prepared for sub regional areas and a framework was needed to mesh the different plans together. Such reports were slim documents without formal procedures for preparation. They were quickly prepared to fulfil a need prior to the first round of structure plans being prepared. As such they were a one-off event.

Formal transport plans at the local level now supplemented development planning. The 1972 Local Government (England and Wales) Act required county councils, from 1975 onwards, to produce annual transport policies and programmes (TPPs), non-statutory comprehensive statements of objectives and policies together with expenditure programmes. These focused mainly on road provision, so in 1978 the Transport Act introduced annual rolling passenger transport plans (PTPs) prepared by the county council as passenger transport authority, which looked at public transport over five-year periods. The package of transport policy documents at the local level, therefore, consisted of the passenger transport plan, the transport policy and programme and the transport sections of the structure plan.

The context for land use planning was affected by a series of institutional reorganisations. The 1972 Local Government Act, following but acting against the advice of the Redcliffe-Maud Committee, instituted a two-tier system of local government in England and Wales. As from 1974 county and district councils across the country split planning functions. This reform cut across the changes made in the 1968 Town and Country Planning Act, which had assumed unitary local authorities preparing both structure and local plans under one roof. Now county councils prepared structure plans and district councils most local plans, opening up the opportunity for conflict and dispute. To coordinate the preparation of the various plans the 1972 Local Government Act required development plan schemes, setting out within each county who should do what and when. The 1972 Act also clarified those planning applications for which county councils as opposed to district councils were responsible, primarily minerals workings and applications in conflict with declared county council intentions. Following the reorganisation, national park functions also had to be redistributed. County council national park committees took on the main role although the Peak District and the Lake District had their own planning boards. District councils continued to undertake certain functions in conjunction with the planning committees or boards, or on an agency basis: tree preservation, derelict land reclamation and country park management in particular.

In 1975 local government in Scotland was reorganised along similar lines with regional councils operating as the tier above district councils, following the recommendations of the 1969 Wheatley Report and the 1973 Local Government (Scotland) Act. In Glasgow, however, the region, not the metropolitan authority, was the relevant transport planning body. Whereas in England and Wales, more and more local authority functions were being moved away to quangos, local authorities in Scotland continued to perform many of these functions. For example, in 1973 the Water Act created ten regional water authorities in England and Wales each charged with producing 20-year long-term programmes of development, 7-year medium-term programmes and 5-year rolling programmes of investment. In Scotland, however, water management remained a local government affair.

The 1970s saw the most recent and probably last attempt to tackle the issues of land value, compensation and betterment by nationalising development land. The 1974 White Paper *Land* was followed by the Community Land Act of 1975 and the Development Land Tax Act of 1976. The former provided for development land to pass through the ownership of local authorities or the Land Authority for Wales (LAW), thereby supposedly ensuring that the land was being used in the public interest. The latter taxed increments in land value arising from the grant of planning permission so that the land was sold on by the local authority (or LAW) at close to existing use value. Development Gains Tax had already been introduced in 1973 in an attempt to curb the substantial profits being made by landowners in the property boom of the early 1970s. Cumbersome procedures, substantial exemptions and exceptions and the hope of repeal once again undermined the effectiveness of the overall policy package, resulting in the legislation being used to channel land to developers rather than capture the development profit for the community and influence the nature of development in any meaningful way (Massey and Catalano, 1978). The failure of the Community Land Scheme was widely acknowledged and there have been no attempts at comprehensive land nationalisation since.

Countryside policy in this decade emphasised natural amenity. In 1971 the Sandford Committee was appointed to consider national parks policy. It reported in 1974, concluding that in cases of conflict natural beauty should prevail over public enjoyment of the countryside. A 1977 Countryside Commission report on *New Agricultural Landscapes* and a 1979 paper from the Countryside Review Committee discussed concerns over the effects of agriculture on lowland landscapes. A two-tier system of protection was proposed but not implemented. In 1978 the Countryside Commission for Scotland produced a report on *Scotland's Scenic Heritage* and also proposed identifying areas for special protection. To channel leisure pressures a 1974 Parks Strategy was developed in Scotland, which proposed a hierarchy of parks for public access: urban parks, country parks, regional parks and special parks. The particular needs of the Norfolk Broads, under pressure from agriculture and the leisure industry, led to a voluntary consortium of local authorities setting up the Broads Authority to protect the special landscape qualities and ecosystem of these

Norfolk waterways; the authority was grant-aided under the 1972 Local Government Act from Exchequer funds.

Following this trend, environmental planning was extended and significantly developed in this period, particularly with regard to pollution control. This was in response to the continuing growth of the environmental movement during this period and the evident problems of past growth. In 1970 a White Paper, *The Protection of the Environment: The Fight Against Pollution,* was published. The Royal Commission on Environmental Pollution was established and produced a series of reports from 1972 onwards. Its remit was to 'advise on matters, both national and international, concerning the pollution of the environment, on the adequacy of research in this field, and the future possibility of danger to the environment'. In 1974 the government issued a report on monitoring the environment and put forward the Control of Pollution Act covering waste disposal, water pollution, noise and atmospheric pollution. It also introduced the need for a disposal licence for tipping minerals. This was supplemented by the 1974 Health and Safety at Work Act which provided for scheduled industrial processes to be covered by the Industrial Air Pollution Inspectorate of the Health and Safety Executive. With regard to noise pollution, the Noise Advisory Council was set up in 1970 and the 1974 Control of Pollution Act allowed for the designation of noise abatement zones.

The shift towards more environmentally conscious public policy was becoming particularly evident at the European level. As Part 2 will detail, environmental policy has been one of the key areas where the EU has had a direct impact on the British planning system. The Treaty of Rome had contained no reference to environmental protection. However, 1970 was designated European Conservation Year and in 1972 the Commission drew up an environmental policy. The first Environment Action Programme was launched in the following year.

Despite these growing environmental concerns, roadbuilding continued with annual White Papers outlining national policy required by the 1978 Transport Act. There was, however, some marginal adjustment. In 1972 the Urban Motorways Committee reported on *New Roads in Towns.* This proposed that road planning should be integral to urban planning and include consideration of all the costs and benefits of construction. In 1977 the Leitch Report on *Trunk Road Assessment* was published which included discussion of the methods of valuing the environmental impact of road construction. The report also led to changes in the procedures whereby road schemes were assessed to accommodate the increasingly vociferous objections to major road proposals. The Sandford Committee (see above) further established that new road routes through national parks should be avoided.

The major policy initiative of the 1970s, though, centred around the inner city problem. While the key mover in the 1960s had been the Home Office, in the 1970s it was the newly created Department of the Environment (although the DoE did not officially take over the Urban Programme until 1977). Two early initiatives of the decade were the 1972 Shelter Neighbourhood Project and the 1974 Comprehensive Community Programme for areas of intense deprivation. The major policy action came in 1973 when the DOE commissioned the Six Towns Study which, during 1975–7, produced six major reports: three Inner Area Studies discussing the causes and dynamics of urban problems; and three Urban Guideline Programmes suggesting policy management strategies for remedying the problems. There was some conflict between the consultants and the DoE as the latter favoured an analysis in terms of improved intragovernmental coordination, a managerialist approach, while the consultants' studies tended to favour an emphasis on the lack of resources in the local economies. This echoed the dispute between the Home Office and the CDPs in the late 1960s.

The DoE line dominated and the resulting White Paper *Policy for the Inner City* was published in 1977, followed in 1978 by the Inner Urban Areas Act. This gave powers to local authorities to support the creation of employment opportunities and improve the environment of industrial areas by designating industrial improvement areas. Grant aid for derelict land reclamation was also provided; this supplemented the grant aid applicable in derelict land clearance areas within intermediate areas under the 1970 Local Employment Act and, more generally, under the 1972 Local Government Act. Seven partnership authorities were funded to make grants over a two-year period for subsidising industrial and commercial rents. These were: Birmingham, Liverpool, Manchester/Salford, Newcastle/Gateshead and three London boroughs, Hackney, Islington and Lambeth. Lesser funding went to 23 programme authorities and 16 other designated districts. The partnerships differed from the other arrangements in that a joint committee managed the programme, chaired by a DoE minister and with representatives of local authorities and central government departments and agencies. This committee produced an annual inner area programme (IAP) setting out the strategy for each partnership authority. Within these partnership areas, public authorities were to prepare schedules of void sites for reclamation and development. In Scotland, the Scottish Development Agency (SDA) was set up to promote local economic development, following the example of the Highlands and Islands Development Board set up in 1965. One of the SDA's main tasks was to act as the lead organisation for the GEAR project, seeking to renew Glasgow's East End.

Meanwhile the shift towards rehabilitation within housing policy continued. The Housing Act of 1971 increased the financial support for housing improvement in areas of stress unemployment. The 1974 Housing Act introduced housing action areas, areas of the worst housing conditions where grants and a public sector-led programme of improvement would operate. The aim was to prevent the ripple effect of deterioration spreading from one housing area to another. In 1977 a substantial and important Green Paper, *Housing Policy: A Consultative Document*, which undertook a comprehensive review of the adequacy of the housing stock and the effectiveness of housing policy, was published. The same year saw the introduction of housing investment programmes (HIPs), in which local authorities set out their strategies for capital investment in local housing. In Scotland, housing plans were introduced in 1978, paralleling HIPs. By the end of the decade there was increasing recognition of the problems of public sector housing with the Department of the Environment setting up its Priority Estates Project in 1979.

Urban conservation continued to be an important subsidiary theme within land use planning with conservation areas granted statutory status by the 1972 Town and Country Planning (Amendment) Act. Powers for enhancing such areas were included, along with measures on advertisement control and tree surgery, in the 1974 Town and Country Amenities Act. Demolition of most listed buildings in conservation areas now came under development control. The National Heritage Fund, administered by the Civic Trust, was set up in 1975 to give grants for maintaining and restoring historic buildings. At the end of the decade, in 1979, an Ancient Monuments Act was passed. This broadened the definition of an ancient monument and required that any works to any such ancient monument had to be approved by the Secretary of State. The Act also created the designation of areas of archaeological importance (AAIs) which provided for grants and restrictions on development to allow archaeological excavation. Grants for building preservation were also expanded.

☐ Planning profession and planning theory

The 1970s were a period of crisis for the planning profession. During the previous two decades, a variety of activities had been added to the repertoire of the planning system and planners had come to claim an expertise in all sorts of policy areas. But the period of economic growth saw the planning system showing signs of strain even before the economic collapse in 1974. Planning had not been able to fulfil its promise of balancing growth across the country and spreading its benefits widely within society. Excesses of development coexisted with areas of dereliction, severe deprivation with massive windfall development profits, and the environmental problems of growth were becoming increasingly apparent. The procedural changes in the planning system and institutional reorganisation were not leading to any apparent increase in efficiency and two successive attempts to increase the role of the public sector in directing development through land nationalisation had been spectacular failures. There was a pressing need for a reexamination by professional planners of their activities and for a renewed intellectual justification for planning. In particular the context for planning was reexamined to try and explain the failure to live up to expectations. The result was a critique on several fronts of the dominant procedural planning theory of the time, drawing on the new social science disciplines at the core of much planning education by now. The growth of planning activity had also meant that many other disciplines outside planning were examining planning, in particular urban planning, from their own perspective. A bewildering array of work on planning appeared. As Healey, McDougall and Thomas (1982, p. 5) point out: 'A distinctive characteristic of the urban and regional planning tradition has always been the readiness to adopt uncritically and often unwittingly the tenets of intellectual and ideological waves which sweep through the academic and para-academic world.' Much was highly critical and not all was conducive to a careful rebuilding of the case for planning. This placed planning in a weak position when faced with the onslaught of the ideological project of Thatcherism in the 1980s. However it also lay the foundation for post-Thatcher theorising on planning as will be seen in Chapter 4, and provided a fascinating and vigorous debate on planning in its own time.

One key distinction among the various critiques of PPT was between those who sought a managerial basis for improvement and those who looked to broader socioeconomic explanations of failures. Thus one strand focused inside government for its contextualising critique, and turned to organisation theory to explain the problems facing planning. Planning was seen from the point of view of policy formulation and implementation. The problems of implementation became the focus for attention (Child, 1977; Pollit *et al.*, 1979; Barrett and Fudge, 1981). Rather than concentrating on methods for devising the ideal plan, the key issue became the constraints on achieving policy goals. Identifying resource availability and enhancing monitoring mechanisms was one way of varying procedural planning theory but theoretical developments reconceptualised the formulation–implementation linkages. The policy process became viewed as continual renegotiation between policy actors. Networking and bargaining were seen as valuable skills for planners to aid the achievement of plan aims. It was also argued that the detail of policy goals became redefined in this process. This theoretical development reasserted the important role planners played, not only in drawing up plans and policies but in achieving the policy goals and, in the process, redefining these goals. Planners were seen as potentially political actors in that they engaged in negotiation over resource allocation but they were seen to do so in a relatively impartial manner, loyal to the overall goals of policy rather than any particular sectional interest group. On the other hand, while resource constraints were perceived as the key factor determining plan implementation and changing the nature of planners' activities, the relationship between planning and economic processes was left largely unexplored (see Summary Box 2.2).

The second strand of theoretical debate on planning in the 1970s focused externally to the planning organisation to consider the economic, political and social context for planning activity. Such theory ranged from friendly justifications of planning to wholesale rejection of its relevance. At the justificatory end, welfare economics represented both a set of tools, concepts and analyses which were a theory for planning, as well as a framework for understanding planning within a market context, a theory of planning. It centred on concepts of market failure applicable to urban and environmental problems (Evans, 1973; Harrison, 1977; Baumol and Oates, 1975). This suggested a number of justifications for planning in terms of dealing with externalities or providing and protecting public goods, and thereby achieving more efficient or equitable market outcomes (see Chapter 9 for a fuller discussion). Using a variety of economic techniques, exemplified by the cost–benefit analysis, planners could act as expert assessors of the impact of environmental change. Their ability to achieve an optimal balance in resource allocation depended on how these assessment methods were operationalised. A number of assumptions were involved in any such assessment, explicitly or implicitly, and the nature of such assumptions could greatly influence the recommendations and hence planning decisions. However, many of the most important assumptions,

---

Summary Box 2.2   *Organisation theory*

Definition of planning:	Policy implementation
View of planners:	Networkers
Process involved:	Negotiation
Relation to economy:	Nil
Relation to politics:	Planners bargain with interested parties
Outcomes:	Dependent on skill in handling resource constraints
Research focus:	Local authorities and quangos
Theoretical antecedents:	Critique of PPT

such as those concerning the weighting given to any distributional outcome, often remained implicit or were made in an apparently objective way by the planner. Thus planners were involved in taking political decisions in the guise of objective assessment. Within this theoretical approach, the relation of planners' activities to the broader political process remained unexplored, planners being presented as objective experts (see Summary Box 2.3).

A more critical account of contemporary planning practice was provided by political scientists and sociologists who studied local planning as an example of urban politics. Numerous empirical case studies documented the way in which planners interacted with local politicians, pressure groups and representatives of local business in generating various decisions concerning the local environment (Davies, 1972; Dennis, 1972; Dearlove, 1973; Elkin, 1974; Wates, 1976). The local economic structure provided the rationale for certain local actors to become involved in planning decisions, but planning was essentially seen as a political activity. The generation of inequitable outcomes was thus central to an understanding of the planning process. Planners were seen as having a degree of control over the generation of these outcomes through allocation of certain resources, that is, planners were seen as 'urban gatekeepers' (Pahl, 1975). As with radical political economy (see below), this provided a newly critical account of the planning system, with a much less sanguine view of the potential for improving the system's operation (see Summary Box 2.4).

The most comprehensive assessment, indeed dismissal, of planning came from radical political economy, which explicitly tackled the political nature of the planner's role alongside its economic nature. Using a Marxist model of society, radical political economy explored the ways in which the state influenced the flow of capital within the economy, its rate of turnover and accumulation (Harvey, 1973; Broadbent, 1977). While there is a large body of Marxist literature disputing the degree to which state actions are

---

Summary Box 2.3 *Welfare economics*	
Definition of planning:	Redressing market failure
View of planners:	Assessors of impact of environmental change
Process involved:	Economic assessment
Relation to economy:	Intervention based on quasi-market valuations
Relation to politics:	Nil
Outcomes:	Dependent on assumptions used in assessments
Research focus:	Social markets
Theoretical antecedents:	Contextualising development of PPT

Summary Box 2.4   *Urban politics/sociology*

Definition of planning:	Local politics
View of planners:	Urban gatekeepers
Process involved:	Allocation of scarce resources
Relation to economy:	Economics as source of conflicts
Relation to politics:	'Planning is political'
Outcomes:	Inequality in distribution
Research focus:	Political groupings
Theoretical antecedents:	Contextualising development of PPT

functional for capital accumulation, this approach inevitably involved a degree of functionality, particularly as it drew heavily on the work of French Marxists inspired by the functionalist philosophy of Althusser (Castells, 1977; Pickvance, 1976). It searched for the ways in which planning policy could serve the interests of capitalists, either in general or in specific fractions. Planners were not seen as apolitical professionals but as agents of an essentially capitalist state, continually responding to the drive for profit within a capitalist economy. Planning was, therefore, a political process and deeply implicated in the workings of a capitalist economy. In so far as planning was an example of state activity which was functional for capitalism, the outcomes of planning supported profit levels, maintained the class system and staved off economic crisis. Variants of radical political economy, which recognised the existence of dysfunctional state activity, usually explained this in terms of conflict between fractions of capital over the direction of state policy. In such situations there would be losers as well as winners amongst the capitalist class and there was, therefore, the potential for working-class victories over capitalist interests. It became a matter of empirical research to determine the exact outcomes in each case (see Summary Box 2.5).

Summary Box 2.5   *Radical political economy*

Definition of planning:	Supporting capital accumulation
View of planners:	Agents of a capitalist state
Process involved:	Influencing circuits of capital
Relation to economy:	Responding to profit drive
Relation to politics:	Example of functional role of state
Outcomes:	Dependent on conflict between capitals and classes
Research focus :	Production and collective consumption processes
Theoretical antecedents:	Contextualising development of PPT

■ Further reading

Readable accounts of postwar planning are provided in Cherry (1996) and Ward (1996), both of which carry the story through to the 1980s. Cullingworth's official history of the planning system covers the period 1939–69 in four volumes which look at: *Reconstruction and Land Use Planning* (1975a); *National Parks and Recreation in the Countryside* (1975b); *New Town Policies* (1979); and *Land Values, Compensation and Betterment* (1980). Other useful texts for this period are Hall *et al.*'s mammoth study of the land use planning system (1973), the MacEwans' history of national parks (1987), Johnson's environmentalist account of planning, including a study of the DoE (1973), and Ambrose and Colenutt (1975), Fraser (1984) or Marriott (1969) for a flavour of urban development cycles after the war. More detail on land nationalisation can be found in Cox (1984). Theoretical references can be found in Faludi's edited volume (1973) and Healey, McDougall and Thomas (1982).

■ *Chapter 3* ■

The Impact of Thatcherism

■ Economic and social change

The 1980s were the decade of Thatcherism, a political response to the economic and social conditions of the time which has had its own profound social and economic consequences. The decade began with the deepening and eventual bottoming-out of the economic recession that followed the 1973–4 oil crisis, accentuated by a tight monetarist budget in 1981. It was characterised by the worst unemployment and industrial disinvestment since the interwar period. Long-term unemployment among the young and those approaching retirement became a common occurrence. The effects of a cyclical recession were reinforced by the introduction of new technology based on computer microprocessors. As a result of recession and restructuring, industrial employment fell. However industrial output was also falling as the longer-term trend away from manufacturing towards service industries had an ever greater impact. By the end of the decade, the application of new technology and a spate of reinvestment, following the devaluation of capital in preceding years, was beginning to have an effect and economic growth went up again. This was a fragile recovery though and, by the end of the decade, the signs of a further downward trend for the start of the following decade were becoming clear.

Urban decentralisation continued to affect the location of economic activity. New technology often required new locations particularly as it went with a shift to new patterns of production, labelled post-Fordist or flexible specialisation, in which greater use was made of subcontracting together with part-time and often female labour. The search for appropriate labour pools and new industrial locations and the continuing push and pull pressures for residential decentralisation maintained the urban–rural shift. The inner city problem thus became ever worse as selective outmigration from the cities by the mobile and better-off was combined with the loss of working-class employment opportunities within urban areas. Large sections of the remaining population faced dependency on state benefits given the lack of available jobs. This was highlighted by the inner city riots of 1980–1 which the official inquiry under Lord Justice Scarman analysed as having their roots in economic deprivation, engendering alienation particularly among the young. By the end of the decade, however, evidence was coming forward that the process may have reached its peak at least as far as the residential sector was concerned, with selective reurbanisation.

These economic changes underpinned the growth of Thatcherism during the decade, as success for the Conservative Party under the leadership of Margaret Thatcher in the 1979 General Election was succeeded by success in 1983 and 1987. Thatcherism represented a significant ideological shift in British politics and, possibly, public opinion. The mixed-economy consensus was breaking up in response to the apparent inability of Keynesian economic management and welfare state social policies to deliver the promised results. The dominant theme within the shifting ideological framework was the emergence of a New Right philosophy emphasising the advantages of market processes, the role of the private sector in generating wealth, and the moral and economic dangers of both a large public sector and other forms of collective action such as trade–unionism. The stand of the government against the long and painful miners' strike of 1984–5 was emblematic of this anti-unionism.

However, other ideologies also emerged and would, from time to time, challenge Thatcherism. The third parties of the Liberals and Social Democratic Party (SDP), which became the Alliance and finally the Liberal Democrats, saw a rise in their attractiveness to voters. The Green Party (having been renamed from the Ecology Party) increased its support in recognition of the environmental damage caused by the postwar period of growth. And the Labour Party undertook a painful re–examination of its approach with different elements within the party promoting a quasi-Thatcherite line, the professional managerialism of the SDP or the radical socialist democracy of Ken Livingstone's rule at the Greater London Council (GLC) and the socialist–feminist wing. Slowly a New Left opposition began to emerge. This, together with the New Right legacy, was to shape the planning policies and politics of the 1990s, particularly under the New Labour government of 1997 onwards.

◼ Planning problems and policies

Certain aspects of the planning system, which had in any case been in decline during the 1970s, were finally killed off by the Thatcher administrations. Regional economic planning councils were disbanded in 1979, office development permits (ODPs) abolished soon after and regionally-based grants significantly cut back. The areas in which they applied were redefined, reducing their applicability. This had knock-on effects in that only development areas as defined by a national government were eligible for grants from the European Union (as it is now termed). Industrial development certificates followed ODPs in 1984 and the automatic entitlement to grants in development areas ended in 1988. Regional planning was effectively replaced by the application of inner city policy in depressed regions and an aspatial training policy administered through numerous special employment schemes. The apparatus of the new towns programme was finally dismantled with the accelerated winding-up of the New Towns Commission. The ailing Community Land Act was repealed in 1980 with the exception of the Land Authority for Wales (LAW), which remained on a self-financing basis as a means of directing land to private sector developers in pursuit of urban regeneration. The LAW's function was 'to make development land available as quickly as possible where the private sector finds it difficult to complete transactions'. Development Land Tax was abolished in 1985.

Within land use planning, the twin elements of development planning and development control were restructured in line with a more market-oriented approach. Government advice on development control made it clear that a more 'positive' approach to planning was to be adopted. This was particularly the case where small businesses were involved. The 1985 Department of Trade and Industry report *Business in the Community* led to a White Paper in the same year, *Lifting the Burden*, which set out the need to reduce planning constraints on business. A 1986 White Paper, *Building Business – Not Barriers*, again echoed this theme. Central government advice as issued in DoE Circular 14/85 established clearly that there was a presumption in favour of planning permission being granted unless planning objections could be sustained. And a series of circulars (DoE Circulars 2/86, 22/80 and 9/80) stressed the need to take account of market forces. Three DoE circulars focused on the needs of industrial development and business enterprises particularly: 16/84 on Industrial Development, 14/85 on Development and Employment and 2/86 on Development by Small Businesses. Several procedural changes were made to ensure that this advice was heeded. Joint housing studies undertaken by planners with housebuilders were introduced as a factor in deciding residential development planning applications by DoE Circular 9/80. Changes to the Use Classes Order in 1987 and the General Development Order in 1981 and 1988 removed some important and many minor developments from local authority control. Central government advice, such as Circular 31/85, emphasised that aesthetic control in particular should be removed from routine development control. Following the idea of zoning contained in enterprise zones (see below), special planning zones under the 1986 Housing and Planning Act created areas where development in compliance with an approved plan did not need specific permission.

The negotiation by planners of community benefits during development control, known as planning gain, was also regarded less favourably. Following a 1981 report on planning gain by the Property Advisory Group, a DoE Circular 22/83 was issued which restricted the use of planning gain by local authorities. In 1989 draft guidance and proposed legislative amendments were put forward for altering the nature of the planning agreements by which most planning gain was achieved. This was eventually covered by the 1991 Planning and Compensation Act. The use of planning conditions was also restricted by DoE Circular 1/85. Throughout all planning procedures, the emphasis was on speeding up the process and league tables were published of the speed of development control in different districts. There was a price to pay for such 'improvements' to development control – planning fees were introduced in the 1980 Local Government, Planning and Land Act. Similar fees for planning appeals were dropped from the Bill after opposition.

Development planning was also considerably affected, indeed diminished in importance. Early on in the decade the Secretary of State for the Environment made it clear that structure plans should be rapidly prepared and approved, and considerable departmental effort was put into processing the large number of structure plans still in the system awaiting final submission and approval. As part of the effort to speed up development planning, the DoE sought to restrict the scope of structure plans to land use matters. In modifications to development plans, the Secretary of State removed policies considered to stray outside such planning concerns. The requirements for survey work and public participation were also reduced. These procedural changes were summarised in DoE Circulars 23/81 and 22/84, the latter providing a memorandum on structure plans and local plans. The net result of these changes was that structure plans became shorter compared to the bulky documents of the 1970s. The relevant parts were even shorter as the 'reasoned justification' for policies became a non-statutory part of the plan after 1979 changes to regulations. These were readily identified as capitals were used for policies and lower-case print for all other parts of the plan. But it is not just that structure plans were shorter and more up to date; they were downgraded compared to local plans. The Inner Areas Act of 1978 had allowed local plans to be prepared and adopted in advance of structure plans in specified inner city areas. The 1980 Local Government Planning and Land Act extended this to all areas.

The government's attitude to local plans varied over this period. The changes in regulations meant that survey work for local plans was discouraged and, in the early 1980s, it was strongly suggested that local plans would not be needed for all areas. However, statutory local plans were clearly preferred compared to the non-statutory plans which had previously been commonly used by district councils. By the end of the decade, full local plan coverage was seen as a potential way of replacing structure plans altogether. The ideas for restructuring development planning were contained in the 1986 Green Paper *The Future of Development Plans* and a 1989 White Paper. The downgrading of the county council's role mirrored the removal of certain areas of development control from the county to the district council following the 1980 Local Government, Planning and Land Act. County matters now covered only minerals, waste disposal, cement workings and development across national park boundaries.

Taken together, structure and local plans were given less importance within the overall planning system during the 1980s. Two quotes from circulars illustrate this: from DoE Circular 14/85: 'the development plans are one, but only one, of the material considerations that must be taken into account in dealing with planning applications'; and from DoE Circular 16/84: 'where a developer applies for planning permission which is contrary to the policies of the approved development plans, this does not in itself justify reason for refusal'.

A further bout of local government reorganisation also had implications for development planning. In 1985 the Local Government Act abolished the metropolitan counties including the GLC, sweeping away six sites of increasingly troublesome opposition to Thatcherite policies. This also removed the structure plans that the metropolitan county councils used to prepare. Therefore, the Act and DoE Circular 30/85 provided for unitary development plans in metropolitan areas. These were to be prepared by the district council, comprising strategic and detailed policies and conforming to statutory central government policy guidelines. Passenger transport authorities were resurrected as separate organisations to replace the transport planning functions of metropolitan county councils. In London, London Regional Transport had already been established in 1984 to take public transport out of the GLC's hands.

Urban conservation remained a significant planning concern through the Thatcher years. The 1983 National Heritage Act established the Historic Buildings and Monuments Commission for England, known as English Heritage, which also took over the role of the GLC's historic buildings division, including its listed building control. In Wales the equivalent body was CADW or Welsh Historic Monuments, and in Scotland, the historic buildings and monuments directorate of the SDA, now known as Historic Scotland. The criteria for listing buildings of historic and architectural importance were extended in 1988. Previously only pre-1939 buildings could be listed in England and Wales, although in Scotland buildings over 30 years of age were eligible. Under the new rules buildings of only ten years' life have been listed. And following on from the 1979 Ancient Monuments Act, five areas of archaeological importance were designated in 1984: Canterbury, Chester, Exeter, Hereford and York. Within these areas an operations notice was now needed before development, even permitted development, could proceed. Thornley (1993, p. 161) describes the net effect of Thatcherism on land use planning as:

> to retain a strong planning system operating in certain areas where conservation and environmental factors are considered important. Elsewhere the system has been much modified and weakened and market criteria are expected to dominate with the removal of many previously adopted criteria.

Urban policy of the 1980s exemplified the market-led approach of Thatcherism. In housing policy there was a marked shift away from public sector provision; the sale of council houses to occupiers was one of the political flagships of the Conservative government. Local authority housebuilding fell from 130 000 completions in 1975 to proposed levels of only 6000 in England for 1991/2. Public spending on council housing fell by 80 per cent in real terms over 1979–89 (Spencer, 1989). There was a growing emphasis on private sector finance and complementing local authority grants with households' own resources. This was evident in the 1985 Green Paper on *Housing Improvement* and the improvement sections of the preceding 1980 Housing Act. DoE Circular 29/82 encouraged the use of enveloping schemes where the local authority undertook the basic external works on a group of dwellings, providing the physical and financial framework for other work largely financed from private sources. Meanwhile, DoE Circular 22/80 established the local authority improvement-for-sale scheme and homesteading, whereby local authority housing was sold for improvement by the purchaser. The 1985 Urban Housing Renewal Unit of the DoE and its Action Estate Programme was the logical next step; provision was made for whole local authority estates to be transferred to trusts, tenants' cooperatives or developers on the basis that this would facilitate their upgrading. Housing action trusts (HATs), introduced in the 1988 Housing Act, were an extension of this idea.

In Scotland, less change in housing policy occurred. The 1985 *Housing Improvement* Green Paper proposed three types of housing action area: for demolition, improvement and a combined strategy. This confirmed the greater role that the public sector continued to play, often in cooperation with local community groups. *Ad hoc* housing associations have often been the instrument for this cooperative policy under the Housing (Scotland) Act 1974.

In urban areas more generally, urban regeneration was based less on public sector development and direction and more on private sector development levered in by subsidy and land transfers. The activities of the Financial Institutions Group and Business in the Community were early examples of this. The Financial Institutions Group consisted of 25 private sector managers seconded for a year during 1981–2. This produced some 35 unpublished reports but one idea that really took root. This was the proposal for urban development grants (UDGs) along the line of American leverage grants (Jacobs, 1985). These flexible grants were introduced in 1982 in 80 local authorities in England and Wales: designated districts or those with enterprise zones (see below). Scotland had its own equivalent – local enterprise grants for urban projects (LEGUPs). They were intended to encourage marginal private development, with public sector funds levering in multiple quantities of private money. The legislative basis for the grants scheme was the 1969 Local Government (Social Need) Act. This was supplemented by urban regeneration grants for large-scale projects introduced in the 1986 Housing and Planning Act. The traditional Urban Programme was further revamped by a management initiative, which produced the City Action Teams of 1985.

However, the Enterprise Zones (EZs) and urban development corporations (UDCS) of the 1980 Local Government, Planning and Land Act were the mainstay of inner city policy during this decade. EZs were relatively small areas, proposed for Secretary of State designation primarily by local authorities. They lasted for ten years, during which financial assistance in the form of 100 per cent capital allowances against tax and exemption from business rates applied. A zoning scheme was prepared by the local authority which, when approved, overrode any local plan and structure plan in case of conflict. Development in accordance with the scheme did not require specific planning permission. The assumed problem that EZs were designed to tackle was a shortage of good quality commercial and industrial property and an excess of bureaucratic red tape. They were a unique planning experiment. Twenty-five zones were designated throughout the UK during 1981–5, covering some 3800 hectares in total.

UDCs covered areas, usually larger in scale than EZs, where a specially created body – the corporation – undertook a policy of levering in private sector development through cheap land and infrastructure investment. The inner city 'problem' was defined in terms of local government inefficiency, a lack of business confidence and problems in the supply side of the development process, principally the availability of land. The UDC had extensive planning powers within its area which effectively replaced the mainstream land use planning system creating, as Thornley (1993) argues, 'a dual planning system'. The first two UDCs announced were the London and Merseyside docklands, followed by five more in 1987: Cardiff, Trafford Park, Tyne and Wear, Teesside and the Black Country. A further three, in Leeds, Central Manchester and the Lower Don Valley in Sheffield, together with an extension of the Black Country Corporation area, were introduced by the end of the next year, with Bristol following, after local authority objections, in 1989.

In contrast to previous land nationalisation attempts, the Thatcher government sought to privatise much of the public estate. As already mentioned, the sale of individual council housing was a major plank in the Conservative Party's manifestos. Some one million council houses were sold at a considerable discount over 1979–89, contributing to the increase in owner-occupation among the population. As also mentioned earlier, under the 1988 Housing Act, whole council estates could be privatised as HATs. Nationalised industries such as British Rail were encouraged to sell any 'surplus' land and the 1980 Local Government Planning and Land Act set up Part X derelict land registers which collated data on and publicised the extent of surplus public sector land, available for voluntary or forced sale. These registers operated in designated areas: all districts in England and six areas in Wales, with no such provision in Scotland.

These policy changes went along with a stringent attempt to control the expenditure of local authorities. A series of local government finance changes set up repeated confrontations between central and local government. The basis of locally raised finance changed from the rates to the hugely unpopular poll tax and then, eventually in the 1990s, to the current council tax. Rate-capping and its later equivalents involved central government dictating the maximum level of locally raised funding. Locally set business rates were replaced by the National Non-Domestic Rate (NNDR), nationally set, locally collected on the basis of local property values and nationally redistributed on the basis of population. And local government became increasingly dependent on central government grants, both block grants allocated out by the Department of the Environment and specific grants, individually applied and competed for.

Heralding the reemergence of environmental concerns, countryside protection formed the basis of an unexpectedly popular piece of legislation, the 1981 Wildlife and Countryside Act, followed by the 1985 Wildlife and Countryside (Amendment) Act. This legislation covered a number of issues. Protection of specific species, such as bats and badgers, was enhanced and earlier Acts concerning birds (1954 and 1967), wild creatures and wild plants (1975) were replaced. A system of reciprocal notification, between the landowner and the Nature Conservancy Council, was set up with regard to sites of special scientific interest (SSSIs) and special protection given to moorlands. A system for monitoring applications for agricultural capital grants from an environmental point of view was also introduced. The 1985 Wildlife and Countryside (Amendment) Act extended this to the Forestry Commission also and conservation-oriented planting grants were introduced in the 1985 Broadleaved Woodland Grant Scheme. The legislation also covered the role of the Countryside Commission and access to the countryside. Under the 1981 Wildlife and Countryside Act a duty was placed on all county councils to inform the public about their access rights and, in 1985, a Countryside Access Charter was published. In Scotland the policy deliberations of the 1970s bore fruit in the 1981 Countryside (Scotland) Act which established regional parks and provision for management and access agreements between rural landowners and local planning authorities.

While reforms in the Common Agricultural Policy (CAP) were affecting farmers, countryside policy tried to ensure that the reduced production subsidy to agriculture did not lead to a shift of land out of predominantly rural use. The set-aside and environmentally sensitive areas (ESA) policies of the 1986 Agriculture Act exemplified this. In this Act it was established that the Minister of Agriculture had a statutory duty to balance agricultural interests with the economic and social interests of rural areas, conservation and the enhancement of the beauty and amenity of the countryside, together with any archaeological features, plus public enjoyment of the countryside. These pressures towards balancing the different interests in the countryside in the face of changing circumstances also led to the Farm and Countryside Initiative jointly sponsored by the Ministry of Agriculture, Fisheries and Food (MAFF), DoE, Manpower Services Commission, Development Commission, Countryside Commission, Nature Conservancy Council (now known as English Nature) and Agriculture Training Board. It investigated appropriate ways of changing the rural economy and training labour for a new economic structure. In 1987 MAFF further investigated alternative land uses, diversification and the environment in the countryside. This led to policies for encouraging farm woodlands, extending the ESA scheme and promoting diversification on farms with grants.

Concern for the rural environment guided several statements of minerals policy during this decade: 1981 saw a Town and Country Planning (Minerals) Act. The 1981 Act covered Scotland, England and Wales and created several possibilities for enhanced planning control of minerals workings. The case of coal, and in particular of opencast mining, was addressed by the Flowers Committee report on *Coal and the Environment* in 1981, a 1983 White Paper on *Coal* and subsequent 1984 guidelines. Opencast coal-mining had been considered merely a wartime emergency measure and had been controlled by the Minister of Power and, from 1958, the Secretary of State for Energy. Only in 1984 did such workings come within the general framework of development control. The separate need for Secretary of State authorisation was repealed in the 1986 Housing and Planning Act, so that such workings now required planning permission in the same way as any other minerals working.

As already indicated in relation to countryside policy, there was significant activity in the environmental policy area, heralding the changes that were to come in the 1990s. At the beginning of the decade the policy changes were marginal. In the case of noise pollution, the Noise Advisory Council was disbanded, but the 1980 Local Government Planning and Land Act allowed local authorities to designate their own noise abatement zones. Environmental concerns were introduced into derelict land policy. The 1982 Derelict Land Act, largely a consolidating measure, extended the power to declare derelict land clearance areas on environmental as well as economic grounds. But by the end of the decade more significant change was occurring. Moves were finally made towards implementing the integrated pollution control proposed by the Royal Commission on Environmental Pollution in the 1970s. In 1987 Her Majesty's Inspectorate of Pollution (HMIP) was created from existing pollution control agencies to control emissions to all environmental media: land, water and air. This was in pursuit of the 'best practicable environmental option' (BPEO) for controlling pollution. Particular attention had to be paid to water quality because, on the one hand, the European Community (now the European Union) was introducing new standards and, on the other, privatisation of the English and Welsh water industry in the 1989 Water Act created new structures of water management. Under EC law a new system of regulatory control was required. The 1989 Water Act, therefore, allowed the Secretary of State to set water quality objectives, which the new watchdog body for the water industry, the National Rivers Authority (NRA), should strive to achieve. By the late 1980s the DoE had also set up a Drinking Water Inspectorate and implemented part of the Control of Pollution Act 1974 on public registers of consented discharges and effluent samples.

A significant addition to environmental protection came in 1988 with the introduction of regulations requiring environmental assessments as a standard element of planning procedure. The Conservative government had opposed the 1985 European Commission directive on such assessments but eventually had to comply. A similar tale of British–European confrontation over environmental policy occurred over the highly salient issue of 'acid rain' or the impact of sulphur dioxide emissions. Britain's refusal to join the '30 per cent club' of nations committed to a reduction in such emissions was eventually overturned, largely due to pressure from other European countries. Britain had to agree to the 1985 protocol on sulphur dioxides and the EC's directive on large combustion plants (that is, the power plants that were largely responsible for these emissions) and require the installation of flue-gas desulphurisation equipment. Agreement to protocols on nitrous oxides and volatile organic compounds followed in 1988 and 1991. These cases represent the early signs of a key theme of the 1990s with European integration and the 'greening' of planning going hand in hand to reshape many of the changes of Thatcherism.

One area where environmental concerns continued to have only marginal impact was on transport. Transport policy continued to place emphasis on road provision and private sector transport. The 1980 statement on policies for roads in England set out that the first priority must be national economic recovery in which road provision would play a part. There was a general aim to introduce private sector funding, where possible, into transport provision and infrastructure investment. The 1987 Transport White Paper established the principle of developer involvement in financing road improvements. Similar emphasis was given to city, rail and tube systems where private sector funding could be demonstrated: for example, the Docklands Light Railway and the Jubilee Line Extension in London. Meanwhile British Rail restructured its services with an eye to breaking even and eventual privatisation and the Channel Tunnel struggled towards completion totally on the basis of private funding. In the case of public transport, conflict between local authorities and central government over the provision of a subsidised service eventually led to the 1987 Transport Act which reduced local government control over such financial matters. In the 1986 Transport Act, following the 1984 White Paper *Buses*, bus services outside London were deregulated to allow private sector operators to compete with the public sector on services over thirty miles. The underlying conflict between a transport policy based on supporting economic growth and increasingly financed by the private sector, on the one hand, and the environmental impacts of travel patterns on the other, was never acknowledged, let alone tackled, during this decade. It was to become one of the most significant themes for planning in the 1990s.

And finally, nuclear power and waste remained, perhaps, the most intractable of environmental problems. There were two highly publicised and politicised episodes in civilian nuclear planning during the 1980s. In 1980 the Central Electricity Generating Board announced that it proposed to build the first pressurised water reactor power station at Sizewell, Suffolk; this was a similar design to that involved in the Three Mile Island accident in the USA. A public inquiry into the proposal opened in July 1982 with the main public hearing beginning in January 1983. It eventually closed in March 1985, after 340 days of hearings. The inquiry was the focus of intense activity involving the CEGB, local authorities and environmental groups and discussed many issues of concern, effectively giving them a public airing. The Chairman of the inquiry, Sir Frank Layfield, submitted his report in December 1986 and, following debates in the Houses of Parliament, permission for development was given by the Secretary of State for Energy in March 1987. By contrast, a less publicised inquiry was held later in the decade. An application to build a nuclear reprocessing plant at Dounreay, Scotland, was submitted in May 1985. The inquiry opened in April 1986 but operated in a much more streamlined and less discursive manner than the Sizewell Inquiry; the major environmental groups had decided not to participate given the prohibitive costs.

The other episode related to the search for disposal sites for nuclear waste. During the 1980s a search was conducted initially for sites for high-level radioactive waste (HLW), and then for low- and intermediate-level waste (LLW and ILW). Exploratory drilling for HLW sites produced such opposition that disposal was abandoned in favour of a vitrification process to be undertaken at Sellafield, Cumbria. A number of sites for a LLW/ILW repository were identified where it was proposed to undertake preliminary investigations. Not surprisingly this gave rise to very vociferous local opposition and active campaigning by community groups, aided by national environmental groups. The strength of this opposition resulted in Sellafield again being chosen as the site for a repository for these wastes; an application by the nuclear waste body NIREX was eventually submitted in 1992.

■ Planning profession and planning theory

The planning profession came under severe attack during the Thatcher years. Planning departments were cut back in size and some even disbanded altogether. As with so many other areas of public sector activity, privatisation occurred. Planning consultancies grew apace, drawing professionals from the public sector, as private sector developers sought their expertise to challenge revised planning constraints in conditions of property boom and as local government made use of private sector planners to develop planning strategies. In this climate, the explosion of theorising on planning, often in a critical vein, which had occurred during the 1970s, came to a halt. The assault on planning under Thatcherism was backed by a New Right political analysis, which had expression as a practical political ideology and as a theoretical framework. Much academic effort went into understanding this analysis and categorising it. There then began an attempt to develop an alternative, a New Left position, which could similarly demonstrate practical relevance and intellectual coherence. Revising planning theory to arrive at a new normative stance had to await the clarification of these opposing political analyses. Early work on what was to become institutionalist planning theory began towards the end of the 1980s as an attempt to rejustify the role of planners. This is covered in Chapter 4. Here the focus is on the struggle during the 1980s of the New Left to challenge the hegemony of the New Right position.

The New Right position incorporates a stringent attack on the notion of the mixed economy and state planning (not just land use and environmental planning) with an economic programme based on the ideal of the free market and the application of monetarism at the macroeconomic level. Thornley (1993) describes the package as economic liberalism supported by an authoritarian and populist political style. The attack on the mixed-economy consensus was particularly destabilising to the postwar planning system. F.A. Hayek's 1944 text *The Road to Serfdom* was a key reference point taken up by contemporary political writers and advisers to the Thatcher Cabinet. In this Hayek argued 'that there was no half-way house between competition and planning, that the idea of social democracy was inconsistent, and that the "mixed economy" was nothing but the name for the transformation of the market order into socialism' (Gissurarson, 1984, p. 5). The 'road to serfdom' that this implied was a one-way road: 'it is impossible to stop deliberate control just where we would wish' (Hayek, 1944, p. 790). Therefore the granting of all discretionary power to the state was inherently dangerous.

Against the dangers of state planning were posited the benefits of allowing market processes free rein. The idea of markets as self-regulating derived from the eighteenth century political economist, Adam Smith (Heilbronner, 1983, pp. 33–57). He saw markets as places where self-interest drives the participants and competition controls them. The result of this competition between self-interested actors is social harmony. A key link in achieving this outcome is the 'invisible hand' of the price mechanism: the setting of prices and movements in prices. Of particular importance to urban and environmental planning is the application of this model to land, determining its allocation to uses and price. According to this view, the market for land operates to ration space between users so that each site is allocated to its 'highest and best use', that is, to the users who will pay the most for it. Since willingness to pay for the land represents the benefits arising from its use, allocating sites to the highest bidder maximises the total benefits to society from using this resource. In this way the allocation of land to urban and rural uses, to commercial and residential uses, and to high- and low-income households in free market conditions, can be said to be optimal (Newell, 1977, ch. 10) (see Figure 3.1).

The central argument of the New Right approach is that free market processes foster economic growth through their allocation of resources, thus satisfying a major, if not the major social goal. This role of markets in generating wealth and economic growth is an entirely positive one. Poverty and lack of purchasing power are seen as the root cause of urban and

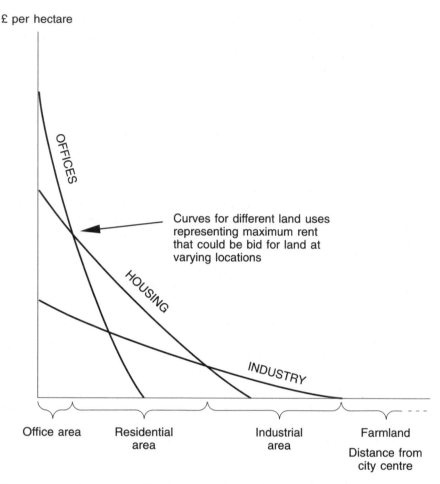

Figure 3.1   *Allocation of land uses in the ideal market model*

environmental problems, creating cycles of degradation whereby aspects of the environment are abused. Generating economic growth is, therefore, essential to combat these effects. This is the rationale behind promoting development in economically backward areas. Promoting private sector development, often including an emphasis on physical development or redevelopment of land or other application of capital investment, should be a priority for any urban or environmental planning. This is most readily achieved by giving market forces a free rein. For market actors will respond to urban and environmental problems, and do so in the most effective and efficient way, if they are allowed to do so. Markets respond to such problems because it is in their self-interest to do so. This point is made by John Elkington, Director of Sustainability Ltd and co-author of

The Green Capitalists: How Industry Can Make Money and Protect The Environment (1987, p. 21): 'Environmentally unsound activities are ultimately economically unsound.'

A prime use that was made of this kind of reasoning in the 1980s was to argue the case against restrictive planning where housing land was concerned. The availability of land for housebuilding was a heated political issue during the 1970s and 1980s. The House Builders' Federation and certain academics were effective in putting forward an economic argument concerning the role of the land use planning system in restricting the availability of land and, therefore, pushing up land and house prices. The analysis begins by considering the role of markets in transferring land from one use to another, and in particular from agriculture to residential development. In free market conditions, at the edge of the urban area housing land prices should approach agricultural land prices. If a substantial gap exists between agricultural and housing prices, then this suggests that market processes are being hindered. Currently such a gap exists. To quote a leading exponent of this view, Evans, in 1987 agricultural land in the south-east was selling for £4300 per annum while residential sites were fetching £984 000 (1987, p. 132). The planning system is blamed for creating this gap by restricting the supply of housing land. This bids up the price of such land above the free market equilibrium. As a result the supply of housing is also restricted and house prices are higher than they might otherwise have been (see Figure 3.2). The problem of high house prices, particularly in regions where restrictive planning policies operate, is explained in terms of the free market in land not being allowed to operate. To quote Evans again (1987, p. 6):

> Firstly . . . [l]and prices can push house prices in that restricting the supply of land can cause both land prices and house prices to be higher than they otherwise would be. Moreover, increasing the supply can cause both land prices and house prices to be lower than they otherwise would be. Secondly, land prices have risen faster than incomes, house prices, and the price of other goods which suggest that they are a legitimate cause for concern. And thirdly, the price of housing land is far, far higher than the price of agricultural land. Thus if the supply of land on which development were allowed were to be increased the value of development land would fall as agricultural land was developed.

The solution to such problems is clear. Planning restrictions must be eased so that the private housing market can expand to meet demand, driving prices down to more affordable levels. The pattern of suburbanisation and rural development that would result represents consumer preferences more accurately than the compact settlements desired by planners and politically active segments of the existing community. The NIMBY (Not In My Back Yard) attitude of people who already live in pleasant suburban and rural locations is the attempt by the few to exclude others; the market, by

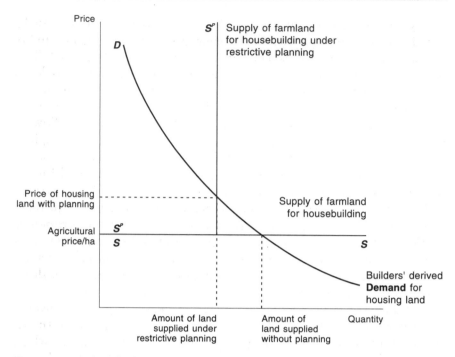

Figure 3.2 *The ideal market model: the effects of restrictive planning*

contrast, represents all potential residents and is a more democratic as well as efficient way of defining where housing should be built.

Similarly the inner city problem was seen as a result of state intervention. Planning policies actively promoting decentralisation, such as the new towns programme, the policies of inner city local authorities in raising local taxes (before the UBR) and diverting funds from business support, and the effect of restrictive development control decisions have all been cited as causes of the continued decline of employment in urban areas (Balchin and Bull, 1987, p. 104). From a New Right perspective, market process are fundamentally seen as a positive factor in the changing inner city. Planning has tended to inhibit the market in redressing urban decay and should be reoriented to a role in which it is subservient to the market and facilitates the private sector. In answering the question 'Why Wasteland?', Loveless identifies five causes: 'Four of these five major reasons. . . are the fault of government. The first is the fault of Central government; the next three are the fault of local government' (1987, p. 6).

The implications for planning again are clear. 'Planning is always inefficient; it can never co-ordinate individual activities as well as competition, even if imperfect; it can never marshall all the available information' (Gissurarson, 1984, p. 13). Normative procedural planning theory also fell under this analysis: 'Even when our knowledge can be stated in explicit theory, the synoptic view grossly exaggerates our ability to grasp the complex relationships of social life' (Gray, 1984, p. 30). This thorough assault on the very notion of planning proposed a much reduced role for planning. Planning, along with many other state activities, was characterised as potentially so much 'red tape' and an extravagant use of public funds. Planners were essentially state bureaucrats who, following the iron law of bureaucracies, sought to create and expand their empires. Their central concerns with 'equality', 'social justice' and 'the public interest' were mocked as meaningless. It was, therefore, essential for the economic well-being of society to cut back on such areas of state activity and minimise the effect on the public sector. Planning could be justified only to the extent that it reconstituted itself as facilitating economic development, a role which many planners actively took on. The extent to which it achieved this goal depended on its responsiveness to market signals and the ability to cut back on unnecessary bureaucratic procedures (see Summary Box 3.1).

Not all of the programme of the New Right was implemented (Thornley, 1993). Instead much policy change was in the form of experimentation with the principles of Thatcherism, experiments which contributed to a kind of social learning (Brindley *et al.*, 1996). It did, however, set an agenda for the Left to respond to. Left-wing movements began to develop, albeit incoherently, a vision of planning as community participation. Drawing on the experiences of the GLC Popular Planning Unit and the occasional success story, such as the Coin Street redevelopment in central London, a radically deprofessionalised planning was proposed (Brindley *et al.*, 1996; Wainwright, 1987; Montgomery and Thornley, 1990). In this model the planner would act as an advocate,

---

Summary Box 3.1   *New Right ideology*

Definition of planning:	State activity
View of planners:	State bureaucrats
Process involved:	Inhibiting or potentially facilitating development
Relation to economy:	Intervention in free markets
Relation to politics:	Potentially an example of the authoritarian state
Outcomes:	Dependent on relation between planning goals and market signals
Research focus:	Markets
Theoretical antecedents:	Critique of procedural planning theory and welfare economics

ensuring that local communities' wishes were fully expressed in local planning policy. Any other role for the planner would constitute the suppression of local wishes by professional interests or other vested interests operating through the medium of local planning. The rise of planning aid and the growth of community activism were related to this theoretical development. The allocation of resources was seen as a process of struggle between political groups formed around common economic interests. Community groups thus struggled for power in the context of constraining economic processes. Through struggle, an element of control over both private sector actors and central and local government could be exerted, resulting in environmental change for local needs. Struggle by community groups was a necessary process, forging political identities, mobilising local residents and building political resources.

The state, therefore, had a dual role to play. It should focus its energies on opening up the political arena to community involvement, decentralising state structures and actively empowering community groups (Livingstone, 1987). But the state's power resources could also be used by those on the New Left to challenge other interests in society (Stoker, 1991). Planners should actively assist local communities in this struggle. This view of local politics implies a debate about the concept of citizenship (Gyford, 1991). For some on the Left, effective political action can only come after economic and social change, otherwise all citizen action is token and empowerment is an empty shell; traditional class-based socialist politics, therefore, remained the route to change. However, many on the New Left foresaw an era of 'rainbow politics' in which coalitions of disadvantaged groups would come together to confront the power of capital and the Thatcherite state. Feminist politics was also centrally involved, with some arguing for a politics which went *Beyond the Fragments* (Rowbotham *et al.*, 1980) to find common interests and build a sufficient critical political mass to confront Thatcherism (see Summary Box 3.2).

As the language of the above makes clear, the links with class-based politics remained close. The character of this language and the imagery, emblems and metaphors of traditional left politics were considered highly relevant, as the New Left sought not only to identify policy proposals and political strategies, but also an ideological project to counter the highly successful Thatcherism: 'one thing we can learn from Thatcherism is that, in this day and age in our kind of society, politics is either conducted ideologically, or not at all' (Hall, 1988, p. 274). In political terms, this was an oppositional ideology still based in the socialist tradition; it derived its energy from opposing Thatcherism. While it sought to develop an alternative vision, the radical nature of the alternative largely served to create a wider gap between Right and Left politics. Given the established position of the Right under Thatcherism, this rendered the New Left position unachievable in the conditions of late twentieth-century politics. It was left to New Labour to create a realistic political programme by combining elements of New Right and New Left thought.

In academic circles, there was an attempt to marry the initiatives of New Left local authorities and other political actors on the ground with the criticisms of the radical political economy of the 1970s. In particular, the aim was to reconstruct a radical, left-wing analysis which was not driven by the inevitable dynamics of capital accumulation. This debate (within planning) originally centred around the work of Manuel Castells, one of the key figures in the development of an urban Marxism. The 1977 translation of his book *The Urban Question* was widely cited for its discussion of state planning, particularly urban planning, in relation to capital accumulation processes, and its Althusserian methodology, derived from the philosophy of Louis Althusser. This methodology proposed three structures which jointly determined social outcomes: economic, political and ideological; however, in accordance with the precepts of Marxism, the economic structure was considered to be 'determinant in the last instance', that is, in the end it was the economics of capital accumulation which drove the system. This resulted in a functionalist analysis (which Castells was later to reject in favour of an emphasis on urban social movements – see Chapter 7 below).

A profound disagreement grew up between those Marxist analysts who wished to maintain the primacy of the economic structure and those (of varying political persuasions) who wished both to elevate political and ideological factors to greater importance and to question the notion of structures driving social change. Some argued that a greater role should be accorded to human agency, to the actions of groups (classes, institutions, gender and ethnic groupings) and individuals within those groups in

---

Summary Box 3.2   *New Left ideology*

Definition of planning:	Community participation
View of planners:	Advocates
Process involved:	Struggle for local power
Relation to economy:	Economics as constraint on achieving community goals
Relation to politics:	Local pluralism as an ideal
Outcomes:	Dependent on ability to control public and private sectors
Research focus:	Communities
Theoretical antecedents:	Response to Urban Politics/Sociology and Radical Political Economy

generating outcomes, outcomes which could both reproduce the existing social system and achieve change (Dunleavy, 1980, p. 44). This debate was to inform the development of institutional planning theory in the 1990s.

■ Further reading

A historical overview of the 1980s can be found in: Brindley *et al.* (1996) which focuses on land use planning and urban policy; Lowe *et al.* (1986) which looks at countryside policy; and Weale *et al.* (1991) which provides an account of environmental planning in the 1980s. Healey and Nabarro (1990) gives a flavour of the concerns facing planners and planning academics in this period. For accounts of the key theoretical approaches, as they affect planning, the reader is referred to Thornley (1993) for an analysis of New Right ideas and Montgomery and Thornley (1990) for some suggestions of a New Left position. For a flavour of the New Right–New Left dichotomy, Livingstone's entertaining account of the New Left GLC (1987) can be contrasted with the Adam Smith Institute's publications (Jones, 1982; ASI, 1983; Loveless, 1987).

■ *Chapter 4* ■

Planning in the 1990s

■ Economic and social change

Margaret Thatcher was ousted from the leadership of the Conservative Party in 1990 and the formal period of Thatcherism thus appeared to be at an end. However, as the discussion of planning policies below will show, there was much continuity from the 1980s into the two terms of Conservative government under John Major as Prime Minister. There was a change of style and evolutionary change as circumstances altered but the significant juncture came in May 1997 when a Labour government was returned for the first time in eighteen years.

The context for this pattern of political events was shaped by three factors: the economy, the environment and Europe. In economic terms, the ups and downs of the 1980s culminated in a major world recession in the early 1990s which hit all regions and both manufacturing and service industries. Growth in real GDP (gross domestic product) had reached 5 per cent per annum in 1989–90 and fell to negative figures for 1990–2, with only slow recovery in the next few years. Unemployment during the 1990s remained at levels which would have been considered politically unacceptable in the postwar boom years. Of particular interest is the relatively poor position of the south-east (see Table 4.1). For much of the twentieth century, the south-east had been the focal point of economic growth but by the 1990s there had been a decisive shift towards the surrounding more rural regions. Yet urban areas, which had been in decline during the decades of the 1960s, the 1970s and the 1980s, were appearing to achieve a limited renaissance. Population loss in the main urban areas had been stemmed during the 1990s (see Figure 4.1) and growth in inner urban areas is now forecast into the twenty-first century.

However, given the continuance of anti-Keynesian policies by the Conservative government and the dominance of ideas of fiscal 'good housekeeping' as promoted by the Treasury, there was no possibility of public sector spending to induce a general economic recovery during the early 1990s. Rather there followed a period of persistent unemployment and economic restructuring associated with tight public spending restrictions, which appears to have brought a degree of economic recovery by the late 1990s but with little associated 'feel good' factor. This is

71

Table 4.1   *Unemployment* by region, 1995*

Northern Ireland	11.4%
Northern	10.6%
Yorks. & Humberside	8.8%
North West	8.8%
West Midlands	8.4%
Wales	8.3%
Scotland	8.2%
South East	7.9%
East Midlands	7.7%
South West	7.0%
East Anglia	6.4%

* As measured by benefit claimants as per cent of workforce.
Source: Annual Abstract of Statistics 1997.

because the restructuring has been a profound one, confirming the economic era of flexible specialisation or post-Fordism. In these economic circumstances, subcontracting replaced many in-house operations, flexible working replaced traditional labour practices, jobs became more short-term and work pressures more intense. Such an economy was also more open to global pressures. As such it was much more vulnerable to shifts in global economic activity, shifts of recession and recovery, shifts between locations and shifts in technology.

The sense of economic insecurity that many felt was compounded by an enhanced appreciation – some would argue an exaggerated appreciation – of environmental risks. The environment as an issue came to prominence in the 1990s in an unprecedented manner. The British planning system has always claimed that it is concerned with environmental quality and, as has been shown, there is a long history of environmental protection legislation aimed at pollution control. What was new about the 1990s was that the environment was conceived of as a global issue and seemed to achieve a new prominence in public opinion. The scientific evidence on and predictions of depletion of the ozone layer, enhancement of the greenhouse effect and loss of biodiversity meant that the environment became an issue of planetary survival rather than of local amenity. Global arenas became the key forums for developing environmental policy. An important early example of this was the Montreal Protocol, an international agreement signed in 1987 to control the production of CFCs and other ozone-depleting substances. But the prime mover has been the United Nations.

In 1972 the United Nations Conference on the Human Environment in Stockholm had been significant in raising awareness and produced a declaration comprising 26 statements which formed the basis for current

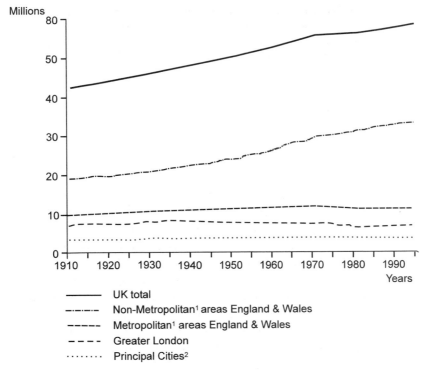

Millions

UK total
Non-Metropolitan[1] areas England & Wales
Metropolitan[1] areas England & Wales
Greater London
Principal Cities[2]

Notes:
[1] Excluding Greater London.
[2] Newcastle, Leeds, Sheffield, Birmingham, Manchester, Liverpool.
Source: *Annual Abstract of Statistics 1997*.

Figure 4.1 *Size and location of UK populations, 1910–95*

international environmental law. Following on from this conference, the UN created UNEP, the UN Environmental Programme which has been operating since 1974, largely playing a coordinating and catalysing role. Then in 1987 the UN World Commission on Environment and Development, chaired by Gro Harlem Brundtland, published its report *Our Common Future* (WCED, 1987). This argued forcefully for the existence of a global environmental threat and sought to popularise the concept of 'sustainable development' as a solution to that threat: that is, development which does not threaten the planet's ability to sustain life and which ensures that both our and future generations' needs are met. A leading environmentalist assesses the contribution of the Brundtland Commission as translating earlier policy ideas into a political process with its own momentum (Burke, 1995, p. 13). This momentum led to the setting up of a Centre for Our Common Future in Geneva and, most significantly, the 1992 Earth Summit held in Rio de Janeiro, Brazil. The Rio Summit saw an international gathering of world political leaders, other policy-makers and NGOs. This also provided a new political context within which the arguments of scientists would be heard, including the arguments emanating from the Intergovernmental Panel on Climate Change set up in 1988.

The practical outcomes of the Earth Summit were two conventions on global warming and biodiversity, and three statements with lesser legal standing: a statement on forestry principles; the Rio Declaration (the downgraded Earth Charter); and Agenda 21 (the agenda for implementing sustainable development). This last item may prove to be the most important outcome over time, as the UN has set up a number of institutions to follow up progress on Agenda 21: the Commission on Sustainable Development (CSD), which sets the major policy guidelines and priorities; the Inter-Agency Committee on Sustainable Development; the High-level Advisory Board on Sustainable Development; and the Department for Policy Coordination and Sustainable Development, which coordinates the different integrative, monitoring and reporting activities. There is also a Global Environmental Facility; this predates the Brundtland process but is now being used to fund development in less developed countries along sustainable paths. Further UN activity has continued, including the international conferences on population and development in Cairo in 1994 and Habitat 1996 in Istanbul. In 1997 an attempt was made to take the process further with an Earth Summit in New York and a Climate Change Convention in Kyoto. The latter forum was intended to agree a binding protocol on reductions in greenhouse gases; the resulting document is widely agreed to be disappointing, with the USA unlikely to ratify it and the developing countries exempt from its provisions.

As well as this considerable policy activity in international arenas, the new environmental agenda has had considerable impact at national and local levels within Britain. The CSD required national governments to prepare their own statements on how to achieve sustainable development and there were similar formal requirements to develop implementation strategies under the conventions. Particularly significant to local planning has been the emphasis on local action in Chapter 28 of Agenda 21 which has given rise to a Local Agenda 21 movement (see Chapter 5). Sixty per cent of UK local councils are committed to producing LA21 plans and worldwide between 1000 and 1200 local authorities are implementing LA21 strategies in 26 countries (Doran, 1996). Also of interest is the inclusion in the recommendations from the third session of the 1995 CSD meeting for an integrated approach to the planning and management of land resources. These top-down pressures for policy change have been reinforced by the changes in public opinion, the media coverage of environmental issues and the growth of environmental pressure group activity (see Chapter 7).

Yet for all this activity, progress on sustainable development is slow. One reason for this is the underlying tensions between action for environmental sustainability and current patterns of economic development. These tensions are also apparent in the growing influence of Europe, the third contextual issue of the 1990s. As will be seen in Chapter 6, the European Union has become a major influence on British environmental and planning policy, pushing for specific forms of regulation and taking the policy initiative in many areas, such as water pollution and recycling. However, the *raison d'être* of the European Union always was and continues to be economic. The 1990s saw steps being taken towards closer economic integration across Europe in order to promote internal trade as the provisions of the 1986 Single European Act were put into effect. The 300 or so measures identified by Commissioner Lord Cockfield for completing the internal market were largely in place by the end of 1992. Developments then focused on monetary and political union. The 1991 negotiations on the Maastricht Treaty on European Union revealed a lack of unanimous support for the federalist project among member states but it did at least set the fulfilment of the Union as a goal towards which members would progress, albeit at their own pace. Progress on monetary union was adversely affected by the crisis in the exchange rate mechanism in 1993 but the whole European project rolls on, most recently with the start of intergovernmental negotiations on revising the Treaty on European Union in 1996.

The trend toward greater European integration at all levels has implications for British planning in terms of detail of planning procedures and environmental regulation, the political processes involving the state and other actors, and the changing spatial pattern of economic activity. Together with the economy and the environment, Europe will continue to dominate the context for planning problems and policies in the 1990s.

■ Planning problems and policies

Most commentators (Thornley, 1993; Tewdwr-Jones, 1996; Brindley *et al.*, 1996) agree that the departure of Margaret Thatcher from the centre of the political stage did not signal a significant shift in policy content. Rather Thornley emphasises the change in style, back towards a traditional Conservative style of pragmatism and an emphasis on consensus. The content he sees as a continuation of the project of authoritarian decentralisation, whereby various decisions were devolved to lower-tier or quasi-governmental organisations but with strong central controls and reserve powers. This is exemplified in one of the few identifiably new policy initiatives of the Major incumbency – the Citizen's Charter launched in 1991 and implemented through the Local Government Act 1992. The Citizen's Charter notion sought to provide information for the consumers of public services so that they could 'shop around' or put pressure on local authorities and agencies to improve performance. The Audit Commission was to set out indicators of performance for services as measured by cost, economy, efficiency and effectiveness. Development control was, therefore, to be assessed in terms of speed of processing and costs.

Elsewhere there was an accommodation with the extremes of Thatcherite thought. The need to recognise the role of the market in achieving policy goals was now largely accepted but at the same time the limitations of New Right thought were becoming more apparent. In particular, the benefits of development planning were recognised. This was encapsulated in the amended Section 54A of the 1991 Planning and Compensation Act which marked an end to the anti-plan attitude of the 1980s. Whereas during the 1980s development control was urged to have regard to market factors often in preference to the development plan, the 1991 Act made it clear that development control decisions were to be based on the development plan unless there was a good reason to the contrary. As Gatenby and Williams (1996) argue, this represents a shift in balance when considering the various factors surrounding a development proposal; it does not represent a significant change in planning law. In the area of environmental regulation, the espousal of the BATNEEC (best available technology not entailing excessive cost) principle in pollution control could be seen to represent a similar accommodation between economic interests and environmental policy goals (see Chapter 11).

It is partly the rise of environmental concerns (see below) that has brought a more regulatory and proactive form of planning back into favour. But there had also been the disquiet with the effects of relatively unregulated development. In relation to granting permission for the development of new out-of-town retailing, for example, a more restrictive policy was introduced in 1993 (and again revised in 1996) in the form of Planning Policy Guidance Note 6 in order to deal with concerns over the transport and environmental implications of such development, as well as its rural land-take and the economic impact on town centres. Forecasts of housing need arising from demographic change raised the question of 'where will the 4.4. million dwellings go?', a question which it seemed the planning system and not the market alone should answer. (See Chapter 10 for more details on this issue.) In this context, the proposals to abolish structure plans were quietly dropped and central government sought to use the regulatory planning system – regional planning guidance and development plans – to begin discussions over the allocation of this development. Again environmental concerns had an influence. The UK

Round Table on Sustainable Development, which had been set up as part of the post-Rio process, urged the view that a proportion, 60 per cent or even up to 75 per cent, of this new development should be on brownfield sites to form more compact towns and cities (1997). Significant planning activity, using both 'carrots' and 'sticks', is clearly necessary if such a policy goal is to be realised.

On more specific one-off projects, whether for urban regeneration, local economic development or local environmental initiatives, there was now an almost universal emphasis on partnership. While this continued the central Thatcherite concern with facilitating private development, it also represented a move towards a more consensual style and a recognition that all parties can bring something to the policy process. The changes in urban policy exemplified this with a shift away from the traditional Urban Programme towards a system whereby local authorities were required to bid for inner city money in partnership with business and voluntary organisations, first through City Challenge and then for the Single Regeneration Budget, which combined various grant regimes. Bidding for money from the National Lottery, which in part supports built environment projects, has also taken this line. A similar approach was followed for much Local Agenda 21 work, which sought to implement sustainable development at the scale of the locality. Political theorists characterise this shift towards partnership as part of a broader change towards patterns of governance rather than government, which is explored further in Chapters 5 and 7.

However this emphasis on a partnership approach did not necessarily mean a decline in the significance of the private sector or economic interests. Rather it was a reorientation of the policy process to take account of the limitations of a market-led approach, when the buoyant economic conditions that underpinned property-led urban regeneration disappeared. The partnership approach provided a way of supporting as well as using private sector interests in the pursuit of goals which seem to marry the private and public interest. The widespread involvement of Training Enterprise Councils (TECs) in local economic development partnerships can be taken as an indicator that the market was still leading but from inside planning arrangements. The Private Finance Initiative can also been seen in this light. The PFI, introduced under the 1992 Finance Act, allowed for the use of public sector funds for key infrastructure projects, on which the private sector would earn a return partly through market prices and rents and partly through public sector payments for the services arising from the infrastructure. The public sector becomes the purchaser of services rather than the owner of an asset. While not taken up on as large a scale as the Conservative government hoped, there are a number of schemes existing and in the pipeline, subject to reassessment by the Labour government. A related scheme is the design–build–fund–operate formula for roadbuilding, whereby the private sector undertakes all four elements of the scheme, the 'operate' element comprising the collection of tolls or the payment by the government of a sum to represent the use of the road, that is, the traffic.

So mainstream land use planning and urban policy under the Major government essentially evolved during the 1990s towards a partnership approach without any significant new initiatives. As indicated above, environmental policy also followed this style, but this was a policy area of many new initiatives. Environmental planning achieved new importance in the policy climate of the 1990s. Significant environmental policy documents to date have included the 1990 White Paper on the environment, the first such White Paper ever produced. *This Common Inheritance* (which derived its name from the 1987 Brundtland Report, *Our Common Future*) was a glossy compilation of environmental statistics, a description of current policy and an outline of future policy commitments. On the one hand, it in no way addressed the global environmental concerns in a manner to satisfy environmentalists but, on the other hand, it did represent a new innovation in the DoE's policy thinking. A commitment was made to producing an annual update on the White Paper and further policy developments have followed. In response to the deadline proposed by the UN CSD, in 1994 the *UK Strategy for Sustainable Development* was published. The product of a standing committee of Cabinet ministers, this was regarded as a considerable improvement on the 1990 White Paper. Action Plans have also been developed to follow up the commitments of the two 1992 Earth Summit conventions, one on climate change and one on biodiversity. A 'green' minister in each government department was appointed to represent the environment's interests, a new environment service was set up inside the DoE (Northern Ireland), the Environment Agency has been created from HMIP and the NRA, and the DoE's own research has been skewed towards examining the implications of global environmental change on its traditional concerns such as land use planning. The recommendations of such research, if translated into policy, could significantly alter traditional practice. Another source of radical ideas on planning policy was the 1994 report from the Royal Commission on Environmental Pollution which looked at *Transport and the Environment* and proposed, among other things, that road users should pay the full social and environmental costs of their travel decisions (RCEP, 1995). Their proposals went well beyond the Conservative government's review and modest downsizing of the road construction programme.

The DoE also issued advice to other government departments on how to incorporate environmental assessment into their own policy appraisal (1991a). This drew heavily on the advice that the DoE received from environmental economists, such as Professor David Pearce who for a time was a special adviser to the Secretary of State for the Environment. Professor Pearce led a team on a DoE research project into the implications of the Brundtland Report's concept of sustainable development for the UK. In this research report (published as *Blueprint for a Green Economy* (Pearce *et al.*, 1989)) the use of environmental economics techniques to value the environment was advocated, and many of these techniques are mentioned in the DoE's policy appraisal advice.

This shift in Conservative government policy towards greater environmental protection was seen by some as evidence of the 'greening' of government. This is usually dated to 1988 when Margaret Thatcher made a speech to the Royal Society arguing for action to combat global warming and ozone depletion. However, this speech also emphasised that the health of the economy and of the environment mutually depended on each other. In this way it has been politically possible to advance a degree of environment policy innovation at the same time as meeting other political and economic commitments. Compact urban forms might reduce travel-based emissions but they also won the rural, middle-class NIMBY vote. Meeting the Rio Summit requirements to reduce CO_2 emissions to 1990 levels by the year 2000 could be largely met by, first, increasing road fuel duty and imposing VAT on domestic fuel (both of which helped with the government's economic goals concerning public sector borrowing) and, second, the results of the substitution of natural gas for coal in electricity generation (which was already in progress following electricity privatisation). In 1995 Gray could only conclude that 'There is a fragile momentum building up towards the development of a coherent environment policy' (1995, p. 10).

The European Commission similarly argued vigorously for high environmental standards as a corollary of economic growth, but it has used this view to push a more proactive agenda on the environment. It became clear in the early 1990s that the European Commission was leading Britain into whole new policy areas and new modes of policy practice. The Conservative government had tried to maintain its own particular environmental approach but the Commission increasingly criticised this approach, leading to conflict between Britain and Europe over the detail of policy (see Chapter 6). The EU continues to push its environmental policy agenda. The 1990s saw the publication of the fifth EU Environmental Action Programme, the Green Paper on the urban environment and another on 'sustainable mobility', together with numerous individual policy measures aimed at environmental protection and proactive moves towards sustainable development. Existing European policy was also affected by the new environmental concerns. One area where European and environmental policy are closely enmeshed is over countryside policy.

The debate within the EU over the Common Agricultural Policy continued with reforms put in place by Commissioner MacSharry which cut the subsidies to direct agricultural production from the EU's budget. In the context of heightened concern with the environment, the opportunity was taken to link these reforms with further measures for environmental protection. This continued a slow but significant trend of the late 1980s and contributed to a reshaping of rural policy. The EU also tried to bring transport and environment policy closer together but the conflict between economic demand for road transport and environmental policy goals is one which continues to bedevil planning at the European as well as the national level.

The remaining area of policy initiative under the Major government that deserves mention concerns local government structure and finance. In the early 1990s local authorities have had to cope with the imposition of yet another regime for local government finance, the council tax. Since this occurred in the context of recession and tight central government budget restrictions, there was considerable concern over the contribution that urban local authorities would be able to make to regenerating their areas, or even preventing further local economic and social decline. At the same time, a review of the structure of local government was announced. The purpose of this review has remained opaque to many; in England it has resulted in a Local Government Commission making individual recommendations on successive tranches of local authorities on whether to replace the existing two-tier arrangements; in Scotland and Wales a one-tier structure was imposed. The outcomes of these deliberations are discussed further in Chapter 5.

When the Labour Party won the General Election in May 1997, a new direction in policy seemed promised. While in opposition, the Labour Party had produced a substantial policy document *In Trust for Tomorrow* (1994), prepared by their Policy Commission on the environment. This was premised on four key themes which together comprised a quite different view on planning and the environment:

- the need to place the environment at the heart of all areas of policy;
- recognition that effective environmental protection requires use of the whole range of government action and cannot rely on the free market;
- a belief that high environmental standards drive economic efficiency;
- recognition that environmental progress and social equity go hand in hand. (1994, p. 5)

This is a view which draws heavily on the Brundtland view of sustainable development as modified by the doctrine of 'ecological modernisation' in which win–win opportunities for economic activity and environmental protection are sought (Weale, 1992).

There was much detail in the policy document from suggestions for greener industry to 'sustainable transport' and 'sustainable energy' policies. Demand management, environmental liability and an extension of the Trades Description Act all figured. Labour declared itself committed to preserving Britain's biodiversity and improving the rural and urban environment, as well as playing its part in the moves towards global sustainable development. In terms of institutions, it promised a strengthened Environment Agency, a parliamentary Environment Audit Committee, a special environmental division of the High Court and an Environmental Ombudsman with powers to investigate companies. Other interesting innovations were the proposals for an annual sustainable development plan and a bill of environmental rights. The annual plan was to be modelled on the Dutch National Environmental Policy Plan, setting out a vision, defining the environmental framework for social and economic activities including critical pollution loads and detailing targets, indicators and timetables for policy action. The bill of rights would cover rights to: clean air and drinking water; access to common land, open country, mountain and moorland; environmental information; consultation on environmental issues locally and in the workplace; and compensation for environmental damage.

Specifically on the town and country planning system, a number of reforms were suggested to strengthen it: extending coverage to forestry, agriculture, bulldozed tracks, power stations, overhead power lines and roads; including pollution, transport and other non-land use issues as material considerations in planning decision- and plan-making; extending the range of planning conditions to include energy efficiency or locally sourced building materials; requiring all major proposals to be accompanied by a full and public environmental assessment; and making relevant publications freely available to the public. In addition a right of appeal for objectors to a departure from a local plan and regularising planning gain procedures were also mooted. Regional planning was to be strengthened. Taken together this represented a package which many environmental and planning groups found a welcome new policy direction.

Not unexpectedly, such groups have been disappointed by the slow pace of implementation of this package. The 1997 manifesto highlighted education and economic policy issues, presumably not considering the details of environmental and planning policy to be vote-catchers. Transport and countryside policy were the only areas that were considered worthy of specific mention and the first Budgets were not notably 'green'. However there have been areas of action even within the first few months. The environmental and planning 'achievements' among the top 100 identified by the Labour Party in August 1997 include a 10-point plan for a better water industry involving action on water wastage, proposals for regional development agencies (see Chapter 13), the release of capital receipts from council house sales and the creation of a new Department of the Environment, Transport and the Regions (DETR) (see Chapter 5).

Signals on a stronger environmentalist line being adopted in the future were given in the 1997/8 Budgets and the Prime Minister's address to the United Nations Special Session on the Environment in New York in June 1997. This speech confirmed the Labour Government's target to cut CO_2 emissions by 20 per cent on 1990 levels by 2010 (as compared to the previous post-Rio commitment of reaching 1990 levels again by 2000). It also proposed 100 per cent involvement in Local Agenda 21 by local councils. The 1997 Budget itself did not include strong green taxes but the government claims it took the first steps towards environmental tax reform by increasing petrol and diesel duty, reducing vehicle excise duty for 'cleaner' vehicles and promising that road fuel duties would rise by at least 6 per cent per annum in real terms. This last commitment compares to Conservative government promises of November 1993 to increase road fuel duty by 5 per cent per annum in real terms (they had previously promised a 3 per cent annual real increase in March 1993). The Treasury promised that more radical measures would follow. Many of the interesting institutional changes have yet to be set in place but a new Cabinet Committee on the Environment has been established and a new environment committee within the House of Commons has been announced to monitor the environmental performance of all government departments. And in September 1997, a commitment was given to reducing pollution at sea by rescinding Britain's opt-out on the ban on dumping radioactive waste at sea and halting almost all harmful chemical discharges by 2020. After 100 days, New Labour claimed to be 'Britain's first truly green government' (1997) but these claims will have to be tested in full over the ensuing months and years. Particularly significant will be the content of the proposed integrated transport policy, due for publication in June 1998 which promises a radical new approach on traffic and transport.

In terms of the style of planning, there does not appear to be any evidence yet of a shift away from the partnership approach that resulted from the Major government's approach to the Thatcherite initiatives of the 1980s. The DETR has announced a modernising review of the land use planning system but consultation has only just begun on this (see chapter 10). Meanwhile, it appears to be 'business as usual'. As might be expected from the oppositional nature of New Left politics, little has found its way into the actual policies of New Labour, beyond a preference for referring to 'the people' rather than 'the market'. There does though appear to be a commitment towards greater openness and real partnership in government and encouraging decentralisation.

Perhaps the most significant changes to date have been in terms of constitutional politics, which sets the context for all planning activity. These include a form of devolution for Scotland, the Welsh Assembly and the new city-wide authority and elected mayor for London (see Chapters 5 and 6); there is also the possibility of new governmental arrangements in Northern Ireland. These will have considerable implications for urban, regional and environmental planning. With the prospect of regional government after the next general election, these might be the most lasting legacies of a Blair government.

■ Planning profession and planning theory

The 1990s have shown the resilience of planning as a state activity and as a profession. The numbers employed in planning departments have recovered from the low point of the 1980s (Cullingworth and Nadin, 1994) and the profession has been quick to pick up on the opportunities offered first by the growth of local economic development work under Thatcherism and then by the strength and spread of the environmental agenda. Planning theory has also proved resilient, determinedly redis-covering a positive rationale for planning activities after the theoretical critiques of the 1970s and the full-fronted attack of the New Right in the 1980s. This renaissance of planning theory centred around the work of Patsy Healey, initially under the heading of communicative planning theory and now as collaborative planning theory. This major approach is examined in more detail later in the chapter. First though, it is important to recognise that theoretical discussions of relevance to planning advanced on several other fronts. In particular, those analyses which sought to contextualise planning were given an added impetus by the emerging environmental agenda of the 1990s (see Summary Box 4.1).

Welfare economics found new outlets in its applications to environ-mental problems and policies and the development of a distinct area of environmental economics associated notably with David Pearce, R. Kerry Turner and their colleagues. This, in itself, provides an important new justification for state involvement in planning and environmental

Summary Box 4.1	*Theoretical debates and the environment*
1970s	*1990s*
Welfare economics	Environmental economics
Urban politics/sociology	Environmental justice
Radical political economy	Radical political ecology

regulation. In many ways it harks back to procedural planning theory for it suggests a view of the planner as a rational decision-maker, balancing all the costs and benefits of a policy or project. The planner can recoup a role as an objective, expert professional. This also emphasises the rationality of state organisations and the need for them to operate smoothly and efficiently. Welfare economics recognises that problems of urban administration can arise and that state planning activities are not costless, but the aim is to minimise these costs and then feed them into the analysis. The assumption often is that when such costs are taken account of, the benefits of planning activity will be valued well in excess of administration costs.

In this approach the public are seen, rather technically, as bearers of utility functions. This means that the public's preferences are considered important but that they are best accessed by professionals using a variety of valuation techniques. This goes beyond the idea of the public as consumers as it encapsulates the difference between marketed and non-marketed products, and emphasises the relevance of people's preferences even where a quasi-market cannot be created. Preferences are, however, a matter of markets or quasi-markets rather than democratic processes. Politics may set the policy agenda and prioritise goals, but the detail of policy formulation and implementation is the proper concern of planners.

The themes of distributive justice in the analyses within urban politics and sociology of urban planning in the 1970s were reprised in the environmental justice literature of the 1990s, which draws particularly on US experience. This literature again looked at the activism of groups who had been disadvantaged by planning actions in relation to the distribution of environmental costs and benefits. A particular catalyst was the citizens' protests arising from the Love Canal case in the USA in the late 1970s where low-income housing had been built on inadequately reclaimed land. During the 1980s localised protests mounted and evidence began to accumulate as to the widespread inequity of much environmental regulation and the ways that locally unwanted land uses, such as waste dumps, were predominantly situated near low-income groups and/or groups of colour. This led to a fully fledged First National People of Color Environmental Leadership Summit in Washington DC in 1991, and considerable networking and resource/information-sharing between the many local protests.

The academic attention to this grass-roots activism came during the 1990s with case studies of particular struggles and also assessments of the contribution that the movement could make to the broader goals of empowerment and/or environmental protection. The potential for a form of ecosocialism that embraced goals of distributive justice and environmental sustainability had been discussed by Dobson (1995) who had highlighted the potential contradictions between a socialist project closely allied with an industrial base and the more radical forms of ecological action (as opposed to mere environmental amelioration). The literature on environmental issues in the Third World, including but going beyond the Brundtland Report, had tended to emphasise the ways in which exploitation of communities in less developed countries goes along with exploitation of the environment (de la Court, 1990). Thus a route to sustainable development was seen to lie in the support of local and indigenous communities – the tree-huggers of the Chipko people in the Indian Himalayas have been cited repeatedly as exemplars of local activism protesting at exploitation of people and the environment.

However, just as the 1970s urban politics/sociology literature on urban protests was criticised by radical political economy for lacking a rigorous theoretical foundation for understanding these protests, so the environmental justice literature has been reassessed from a Marxist perspective. This literature seeks rather to consider environmental crises and struggles, as it did urban crises and struggles, in the light of an overarching Marxist analytic framework. This work both looks to Marx's original formulations for an account of capitalism and the environment, and seeks to amend the framework to account for contemporary understanding of ecological processes. One outcome of this work is the fairly bald statement that capitalism necessarily induces environmental degradation:

> A systematic answer to the question 'Is an ecologically sustainable capitalism possible?' is 'Not unless and until capital changes its face in ways that would make it unrecognizable to bankers, money managers, venture capitalists, and CEOs, looking at themselves in the mirror today (O'Connor, 1994, p 158)

In order to understand this, the notion of limits to economic activity as imposed by ecological systems is introduced. These limits are understood first, and sometimes only, in terms of natural resource depletion. Some work then incorporates insights, akin to those of Herman Daly, based on the second law of thermodynamics, the interrelation of matter and energy and the tendency towards entropy, whereby all transformation of matter inevitably involves a dissipation of energy into low-energy forms (Daly, 1992, Martinez-Allier, 1987). Some work also makes reference to the limited capacity of ecological systems to absorb the effects of economic activity without feedback effects which are harmful to the human species. This results in a rather pessimistic, even nihilistic, view (O'Connor, 1994).

Such approaches have been criticised by Harvey as essentially un-Marxist: 'Marx, of course, would have no truck with the eco-scarcity argument' (1996, p. 145); and he warns against 'the class content of the whole environmental–ecological argument' getting subordinated to 'an apocalyptic vision of a planetary ecological crisis' (p. 195). Harvey develops an alternative Marxist approach which sees ecological processes as also social processes, socio-ecological processes: 'all sociopolitical projects are ecological projects and vice versa' (p. 174). Therefore he sees all environments as socially created, not just socially constructed in terms of perceptions and understanding. 'Created ecosystems tend to both instanciate and reflect, therefore, the social systems that gave rise to them, though they do not do so in noncontradictory (i.e. stable) ways . . . natural environmental conditions [are really] historical geography of struggles over the social process (incorporating all of its moments) through which environments have been transformed' (p. 185).

The promise of this is that 'we can collectively hope to produce our own environmental history, but only under environmental conditions that have been handed down to us by way of a long historical geography of capital circulation, the extraction of surplus values, monetized exchange, and the circulation of commodities' (p. 196). And, therefore, he sees the environmental justice movement as a useful mobilisation tool though one riven with theoretical contradictions over attitudes to development and the environment. However, as befits a marxist, Harvey holds to the view that: 'This is fundamentally a class project . . . because it entails a direct challenge to the circulation and accumulation of capital which currently dictates what environmental transformations occur and why' (p. 401). This conclusion, and the rejection of ultimate environmental limits to social activity, would be questioned by many environmentalists, relying instead on an appreciation of the limits of global ecosystems in particular to continue to absorb impacts.

This range of work, together with the continuation of work on more urban themes from the welfare economics, urban politics/sociology and radical political economy schools, continues to provide challenging critical analyses of what planning and environmental regulation are doing. These critiques are particularly pertinent as they address the normative base of planning activity, the assumption that planning is operating in the public interest. They raise questions about how this public interest is to be defined – in terms of Pareto optimality or social justice? And they question the ability of practice to deliver on this goal.

A central function of normative planning theory, though, is to provide a model or at least an argument for how planning can achieve its goals. Collaborative planning theory is the contemporary manifestation of such a normative planning theory. This is a theory of planning to rival the hegemony of procedural planning theory (PPT) during the postwar period. It is work which seeks to reinforce the renewed confidence of the planning profession and to overcome the substantially separate professionalisation of academics and practitioners in planning fields noted by Breheny and Congdon (1989, p. 230). This theoretical development is closely associated with the work of Patsy Healey, who has termed it collaborative planning (earlier variants were termed communicative planning). This fits within a broader academic trend towards institutional theory, which considers in detail the nature of institutions (understood both as organisations and as social norms and habits) as well as the influence of broad economic, political and social structures.

In her recent full exposition of collaborative planning theory (1997), Healey identifies two key writers whose ideas have contributed to this theoretical development. The first is Giddens and his structuration theory. In an early account of the institutionalist approach to planning, Healey, with Barrett (1990), explains the use of Giddens's work as follows:

> The approach adopted in this paper draws in particular on the work of Anthony Giddens, who argues for a relational approach between structure and agency in which 'structure' is established by the way agents operate: deploying, acknowledging, challenging and potentially transforming resources, rules and ideas as they frame and pursue their own strategies. Structure, in terms of the framework within which individual agents make their choices, may be seen to inhere in the various resources to which agents may have access, the rules which they consider govern their behaviour, and the ideas which they draw upon in developing their strategies.

In *Collaborative Planning*, Healey expands on this (1997, p. 49):

> Giddens' theory of structuration thus emphasises that individuals are neither fully autonomous nor automatons. Powerful forces are all around us, shaping our lives, and presenting both opportunities and constraint. But structure is not something outside us. It is not an 'action space' within which we operate . . . How we act in structured situations not only 'makes a difference'; our actions constitute (instanciate) the structural forces. We make structural forces, as we are shaped by them. So we 'have power' and, if sufficiently aware of the structuring constraints bearing in on us, can work to make changes by changing the rules, changing the flow of resources, and, most significantly, by changing the way we think about things. Conscious reflexivity on our assumptions and modes of thinking, on our cultural referents, thus carries transformative power. The micro-practices of everyday life are thus key sites for the mobilisation of transformative forces.

Thus Healey sees local environmental planning as 'providing a locale within which people act in constrained situations' but where people are potentially able to transform those situations.

The other key thinker is Jürgen Habermas who 'provides a rich seam of ideas about how to reconstitute the public realm through open, public debate' (ibid.). The public realm is an arena where 'participants engage in open debate through which they explore each other's concerns and the context of these concerns' (p. 52) using a variety of different types of reasoning: instrumental–technical, moral and emotive–aesthetic reasoning. Through 'communicative action', participants 'exchange ideas, sort out what is valid, work out what is important, and assess proposed courses of action. In this conception, planning becomes a process of interactive collective reasoning, carried out in the medium of language, in discourse' (ibid.). This places collaborative planning firmly within the interpretive, communicative 'turn' within the social sciences more broadly which has emphasised the importance of how meanings are socially constructed and the influence that arises from the form of communication – the resort to rational analysis, storytelling, and various rhetorical strategies.

Healey draws on ideas from these two writers and places them together with the institutional economics (see also Chapter 9) of geographers Amin and Thrift (1995), which emphasises the web of social relations, the networks linking actors and organisations, and the institutional capacity of a place, that is, the quality of the collection of relational networks in a place. A view of planning builds up as 'part of processes which both reflect and have the potential to shape the building of relations and discourses, the social and intellectual capital, through which links are made between networks to address matters of shared concern at the level of neighbourhoods, towns and urban regions' (Healey, 1997, p. 61). Collaborative planning focuses on building links between networks, forging new relational capacity and doing so communicatively.

Putting detail on this theoretical framework, Healey looks to planners to manage a process of inclusionary argumentation (pp. 263–8). Here collaborative planning is defined in terms of power-sharing and five tasks are assigned to it: identifying and bringing together stakeholders; designing and using arenas for communication and collaboration; trying and using different routines and styles of communication; making the discourses of policy; and maintaining consensus. This last task of building and maintaining the consensus is central to collaborative planning: 'If the culture-building process of strategy-making has been rich enough and inclusive enough, the strategy should have become widely shared and owned by the participants and the stakeholders to which they are linked. It will express a robust consensus' (p. 279). Healey explicitly recognises the conflicts between interests and the multiplicity of different identities that coexist in contemporary society, but collaborative planning is premised on the hope that consensus can be forged between different interests and different groups; in this it represents a development of her earlier work on how planning mediated between different interests (Healey *et al.*, 1988). It is the work of planners to actively create this consensus across 'the fractures of the social relations of relevant stakeholders' (1997, p. 264).

Collaborative planning is, therefore, an explicitly normative planning theory that seeks to apply the institutionalist perspective. It searches for a role for planners, a role which is addressed to solving pressing economic, social and environmental problems and yet is people-sensitive (Healey and Gilroy, 1990). Planning has the capacity, it argues, to shape places, to bring

---

Summary Box 4.2   *Institutional approach: collaborative planning*

Definition of planning:	Shaping places
View of planners:	Enabling collaboration
Process involved:	Inclusive argumentation
Relation to the economy:	Economics as one source of structuration
Relation to politics:	Planning deals with conflict between stakeholders
Outcomes:	Dependent on contingent relation of factors
Research focus:	Locality case studies
Theoretical antecedents:	Integrating development of organisation theory, radical political economy and urban politics/sociology

---

together stakeholders and forge a consensus, an essential part of the planning process. Building on the consensus, negotiation and communication can broke deals, release resources and identify win–win scenarios. Planners can also identify strategies which could stimulate local economic development, such as institutional capacity-building or 'thickening' institutional capacity. Communication is a vital element of the planner's work: building a common vision, sharing knowledge, developing joint solutions, engaging in social learning. Such communication also achieves two less pragmatic and radical goals: enabling the empowerment of different voices through the planning system, including those previously 'voiceless'; and challenging the dominance of economic rationality within the planning system, whereby economic interests are rendered powerful, with the communicative rationality of the lifeworld, the ensemble of everyday experiences (see Summary Box 4.2).

This normative theory of planning has become widely influential within planning discourses and has, therefore, been set out at some length; the final chapter of the book returns to collaborative planning, to engage with it more critically and propose some alternative lines of development.

■ Further reading

A useful edited collection looking at planning policy and its context since Thatcher is Tewdwr-Jones (1996). Environmental policy is well served by Weale (1992) and Gray (1995) while rural concerns are covered by Goldsmith and Warren (1993) and urban concerns by Atkinson and Moon (1994). The main account of collaborative planning is Healey's (1997) book; for a critical article see Allmendinger and Tewdwr-Jones (1998) and for an overview of contemporary planning theory see Mandelbaum *et al.* (1996).

■ PART 2 ■
THE POLITICS AND ECONOMICS OF PLANNING

Part 1 has provided a historical overview of the development of planning policy and theory. In this part, the political and economic institutions of contemporary planning are examined. The political institutions encompass: central and local government, agencies, quangos and the European Union, and groups outside the state. The role of planners as professionals is examined, picking up on the theme of the importance of the professionalisation process introduced in Part 1. Finally, the economic institutions are discussed in terms of the market processes concerning the built and natural environment, including property markets, the key economic actors and the valuation processes. In each case, the chapters begin with an account of how the particular institution can be analysed, before moving on to the more substantive, descriptive material. This should provide the necessary background for the policy detail of Part 3. Throughout Parts 2 and 3, exhibits are introduced which highlight specific issues and debates, processes and procedures.

■ *Chapter 5* ■

Planning and the State

This chapter and the next look at the different organisations which together constitute the public sector where planning is concerned, outlining the main features of the various types of organisation. Four types are distinguished: those in central government, those in local government, quangos and the European Union. Much of the detail of how these different organisations are involved in different areas of planning practice will be covered in the separate chapters on particular policies in Part 3. It is not intended to anticipate those details here; rather, the emphasis will be on the characteristics of the organisations and the broad patterns of interrelation. To set these points in context, different ways of analysing the public sector are discussed first.

■ Analysing the state

The field of political analysis is a highly fractured one; a mix of theoretical approaches vie with each other. These approaches can be distinguished in terms of the assumed relationship of the state to economic and other interests involved in the political process. In liberal formulations, such as pluralism, the state is seen as essentially autonomous from economic interests, or interests based on other foundations such as shared values. The state is in a position to act as arbiter, mediator or referee to the pressures arising from these interests on the political system. In Marxism, in its most structuralist interpretations, the state is a capitalist state, captured by dominant economic interests and responding almost reflex-like to crises which threaten capital accumulation. Sometimes the state is given specific responsibility for ensuring the long-term survival of capitalism as a system, even if this entails acting against the short-term interests of any fraction of capital and/or giving concessions to the working class.

Other approaches take up a position along the spectrum from autonomy to capture. For example, less structuralist versions of Marxism allow a semi-autonomous status for the state so that it is not tied so closely to economic imperatives in each and every case, though a degree of linkage always exists. Marxist regulation theory provides a contemporary reworking of this theme with modes of regulation, principally but not exclusively based on regulation by the state, having a relationship to regimes of accumulation but not always neatly ensuring the continuance or smooth transformation of a regime (see also Chapter 9). Corporatism is another concept that has been applied by those at various points along the spectrum over the past twenty years (Lehmbruch and Schmitter, 1982). This describes a situation in which certain interests, particularly representatives of capital but at times representatives of other interests such as labour (through, for example, trade unions) develop a close working relationship with the state. Together they make policy, often behind closed doors and away from democratic scrutiny. Corporatism thus recognises the state as an independent actor with the potential for some autonomy but likely to have given up some of that autonomy to other actors. Marxists see the requirement to maintain the conditions for capital accumulation as the reason for corporatist politics. Liberal theorists such as Charles Lindblom (1977) invoke corporate discretion – the extent to which policy-makers rely on certain interests to fulfil policy commitments – as the reason. Corporatism is not, however, an explanation for a semi-autonomous state, rather it is a description of certain relations between the state and other actors at certain times and in the context of certain policy areas.

In line with developments in planning theory (see Chapter 4) and economic analysis (see Chapter 9), there has been in a shift in almost all variants of political theory towards a more explicit recognition of the significance of institutions. This 'new institutionalism' does not, as Hall and Taylor acknowledge (1996) constitute a unified body of thought but it can be dated back to certain key texts of the late 1980s, a period when institutional economics was also beginning to form a more coherent body of thought. Two central texts were Laumann and Knoke's *The Organisational State* (1987) and March and Olsen's *Rediscovering Institutions* (1989). Laumann and Knoke's work represents a detailed empirical analysis of energy and health policy in the USA during the late 1970s, seeking to explain events in terms of the history of institutional and organisational change. Important factors in the analysis included the identification of: actors inside and outside the state with interests and relevant mobilisable resources; networks linking the actors in terms of both communication and resource-exchange; and the structure of issue politics, including the boundaries of and linkages between issues. Information transmission, resource transactions and boundary penetration (across organisations) are the kind of interorganisational relationships that the researchers particularly focused on. There are strong parallels with the concerns of institutional economics and theoretical affinities with the structure–agency elaborations of Giddens which also underpins collaborative planning (1987, p. 19; see Chapters 4 and 9).

March and Olsen's work is a more general account of the role that institutions play in politics 'in creating and sustaining islands of imperfect and temporary organisations in potentially inchoate political worlds' (1989, p. 16). Institutions work by reducing comprehensiveness on the basis that the political system is better able to act on the basis of limited agendas, issues and problems. Institutions create barriers and reduce coordination because too much coordination can prevent action, and institutions help define identities through distinguishing collectivities. 'Thus, political institutions define the framework within which politics takes place, (1989, p. 18). Again, like institutional economists such as Hodgson (1988), they draw attention to the importance of rules, routine behaviour and socially constructed understandings of the world. The authors are happy for an institutionalist perspective to supplement other explanations of effects and, indeed, the ability of institutionalism to marry with other more specific frameworks may explain the many varieties of institutionalism that now coexist.

Hall and Taylor distinguish three main types of the new institutionalism (1996): historical institutionalists, who provide broad accounts of how norms, routines and procedures are embedded in the structure of the polity or political economy; sociological institutionalists, who focus on symbolic systems, cognitive scripts and moral templates in addition to norms and routines, and often judge these factors in terms of their impact on the legitimacy of organisations or participants; and rational choice institutionalism, which arises from the intersection of the line of analysis based on the assumption of rationality in political decision-making with the institutional economist's modification of that assumption in relation to economic decision-making in favour of an emphasis on property rights, rent-seeking and transactions costs. Indeed Hall and Taylor consider the relationship of rational choice and institutional economics to be so close that they more or less subsume the one into the other.

Rational choice institutionalism, or institutional public choice as Dunleavy terms it (1991), is becoming increasingly influential within political science. Much discussion of rational choice theory has drawn attention to its assumptions of rational and calculated decision-making, instrumental behaviour and given sets of preferences and/or tastes for actors. This is the defining characteristic of the rational choice approach in both economics and politics; it is similarly capable of adjustment in both contexts as proposed by institutional economists and political scientists such as Ostrom (1990), Dryzeck (1996) and Udehn (1996). However rational choice theory starts from the premise of this model of decision-making and asks how far it can explain contemporary patterns of decisions and outcomes in terms of strategic interactions by actors, using resources in an apparently rational manner. Its distinctive contribution is in two areas pertinent to planning. First, it sees politics as a series of collective action dilemmas – how to generate resources, support and legitimacy for policy actions which benefit the collectivity, though not necessarily all or even a majority of individuals. As shall be seen in Chapter 7, this collective action problem can also define the public reaction to and involvement in planning. Second, rational choice considers institutions in terms of the functions performed, arguing that the creation and persistence of a specific set of procedures or organisations depends on the balance of costs and benefits of its creation, continued existence, replacement or dissolution. Ostrom (1990) uses this approach to consider the role of institutions in managing common pool environmental resources. Dunleavy (1991) extends this into an analysis of the tendency of different bureaux within state organisations to expand, contract or remain stable in budgetary terms. In particular he replaces the traditional assumption of an iron law by which bureaucracies would expand with a more nuanced account that suggests only certain bureaux have an interest in expansion and core policy-making bureaux will rather favour a small elite composition.

There is, therefore, in this variety of new institutionalist work – but particularly within institutional rational choice – a development of the political science literature which brings it closer to the institutional economics literature and brings with it the prospect of bridging the great divide of these two dominating social science disciplines (outside the marxist tradition, that is, which has always refused to recognise this divide). As well as an interesting theoretical development, these accounts are particularly well-suited to analysing contemporary patterns of politics. This has been described as a pattern of governance, as opposed to government. Government implies: a hierarchical relationship between different state organisations with a significant element of top-down influence if not control; a firm boundary between the state and outside organisations; and the locus of authority and legitimacy remaining solely within state organisations. Governance implies a significant change has occurred over the past decade or so. More and more quasi-governmental organisations have been set up, such as the Environment Agency, urban development corporations (UDCs) or Training and Enterprise Councils (TECs). The Next Steps programme of creating executive agencies (see below) was an explicit process of this kind. The locus of responsibility for government policy is, therefore, somewhat indeterminate and the nature of the policy process, while it always involved negotiation between state and non-state actors, is now inherently an activity undertaken by state actors, quasi-state actors and non-state actors, with policy formulation and implementation based in *any* of these actors. This means that a considerable quantum of time, effort and resources goes into maintaining linkages between the different actors, and policy networks of all kinds (Dowding, 1995a) become an increasingly useful way of understanding these linkages.

Commentators have also argued that there is now a distinctive pattern of local governance which drives policy-making at the level of the locality (see below). Since the close relationships between state organisations, quasi-state organisations (quangos) and outside bodies is the defining feature of the new governance, this has implications for the study of outside bodies – pressure groups, non-governmental organisations, lobbies. Again at the level of the locality, the concepts of growth coalition and urban regime have been increasingly used to describe these relationships; this literature will be reviewed in Chapter 7 in the context of the business interests lobby. Here the emphasis will be on considering the institutions of the state, in the next chapter on the quasi-state and supra-state organisations.

■ Central government

The British government structure involves three main institutions at the national level according to the standard constitutional account: the Cabinet, headed by the Prime Minister and including Secretaries of State and senior ministers, which formulates government policy; Parliament comprising all elected MPs plus the Lords, which is the legislature and passes binding policy in the form of Acts; and the executive in the form of the civil service which provides non-partisan advice to ministers and organises the implementation of policy. In practice, the formal division of labour is overlaid with a complex pattern of interaction between the different roles. In the day-to-day running of the planning system, it is the executive that is most involved. The Cabinet may propose and the Houses of Parliament decide or legitimate new policy, but it is the civil service that administers. All three institutions will be the focus of lobbying for policy change since all three have a degree of influence on new and emerging policies. The influence of the executive in shaping new policy initiatives has been extensive in the past, although the 1980s has seen a shift towards greater ministerial control over policy formulation (Laffin and Young, 1990). The implementation of such new policy ideas remains the concern of the executive and it is the executive that has the ongoing responsibility for the operation of the system. The only exception to this is the system of parliamentary committees which provide for scrutiny and supervision of the activities of the executive. The House of Commons Select Committee on the Environment is particularly important as a watchdog over the planning system. A new Environmental Audit Committee has now been established with effect from November 1997 to monitor performance on environmental policy. Royal Commissions, established by Parliament and reporting to it but comprising a selection of the 'great and the good' outside Parliament, can also play such a role and the Royal Commission on Environmental Pollution (RCEP) has proved influential over the years.

The executive, or civil service, comprises some half million people, 48 per cent of whom are women and 45 per cent are non-specialists (Dowding, 1995b, p. 23). The institution is distinguished by a particular administrative culture. Civil servants are career administrators and generalists. They are not trained experts in the areas that they administer nor, in the past, was much use made of political appointees; the Blair government has shown a greater tendency to bring in its own people. Civil servants are sensitive to charges of political bias and hence tend to avoid controversial issues if at all possible (Chapman, 1984, p. 175). There is a strong sense of departmental loyalty and ethos, so that civil servants in one department tend to see themselves as much in relation to other departments as to outside groups, whether pressure groups, quangos or local government. These outside groups are often perceived as 'clients' of the department so that the world outside the executive is seen by civil servants to be divided up into the responsibilities of the various departments. Overall the civil service culture is a 'bounded culture' (Chapman, 1984, p. 178) which politicians, professions, policy advisers and the public can find difficult to penetrate.

Much of the actual implementation of environmental and planning policy for which the executive is responsible is delegated to regional or local institutions. These may be local offices of central government departments or ministries, or delegation may involve more autonomous institutions: local government or quasi-governmental organisations (quangos) discussed in Chapter 6. In recognition of the significance of these institutions operating at the subnational level, government offices for the regions have been established which bring together the interests of the Departments of the Environment, Transport, Trade and Industry and Employment at the regional scale and under a single budget. Local government now liaises extensively with these government offices. These have been called the 'ears and eyes' of central government (Stoker, 1991, p. 145). The Labour Party manifesto included a pledge to introduce regional chambers to shadow these offices and the proposed regional development agencies on issues such as economic development and European funding and to introduce an element of accountability.

Certain aspects of central government activities may also be hived off to quangos operating at the national level. At times it can be difficult to distinguish between the work of a central government department and that of a quango. For example, the system for appeals against development control decisions by local authorities is administered by the Planning Inspectorate. This used to be a branch of the DoE exercising central government control over local authority decisions. But during the 1980s the DoE emphasised a view of the Inspectorate as an independent body operating as a neutral, sometimes professionally informed, referee in planning disputes and the Planning Inspectorate is now a self-financing executive agency. Indeed it has been a feature of central government policy in the urban and environmental field, as elsewhere, to favour the creation of agencies at arm's length from the government and the executive. The Next Steps initiative, introduced in the late 1980s, sought to break-up the unified civil service, separating a policy-making core from a policy-implementing periphery, with the latter hived off into agencies where possible. The implications of this trend will be discussed further in the section on quangos in Chapter 6.

At central government level, the main institution responsible for the planning system in England has been the DoE. This 'superdepartment' was created in 1970 under the Heath administration, modelled on the Scottish Development Department (Selman, 1988). It combined the former Ministries of Housing and Local Government, Public Building and Works, and Transport and was charged with the responsibility for 'the whole range of functions which affect people's living environment'. It then lost the transport responsibility when the DoTr was set up in 1976 (but see below for recent changes to reverse this). The DoE lost further responsibilities due to the creation of a new Department of National Heritage in 1992. This covered historic buildings, royal parks and ancient monuments as well as sports, the performing arts and the media. It took over the listing of historic buildings but the DoE retained its development control function in respect of such buildings and the Secretary of State for the Environment remained superior to the Minister for National Heritage.

Under changes announced after the 1997 General Election, the Departments of Environment and Transport have been merged as of 16 June 1997 and the Department of National Heritage was renamed the Department of Culture, Media and Sport (see Summary Box 5.1). The new Department of the Environment, Transport and the Regions (DETR) is currently headed by the deputy prime minister but supported by two other Cabinet-level appointments, the Secretary of State for Heritage and for Transport. Below these three appointments are a number of ministers and junior ministers with responsibility for a range of issues from transport to film, regional affairs to housing, tourism to water, the countryside to the built heritage. This reinstates the superministry of the Heath administration but in a rather different policy context. Nevertheless the rationale for

---

Summary Box 5.1   *Department of Environment, Transport and the Regions*

Department of Environment (4768 staff, including 1323 in agencies)
- Legal Command
- Establishment and Finance
- Communication, Central Management and Analysis Unit
- Environmental Protection:
    Pollution control and waste
    Air, climate and toxic substances
    Energy efficiency office
    Global environment
    Environment Agency
    Water
- Local Government and Planning:
    Local government
    Local Government finance policy
    Town and country planning
- Cities and Countryside:
    Cities and countryside policy
    Cities and countryside and private finance
    Wildlife and countryside
- Housing and Construction:
    Housing policy and private sector
    Housing and urban monitoring and analysis
    Housing resources and management
    Construction sponsorship
    Land and property/building regulations.

---

doing so remains essentially the same: to bring together the different foci of planning – principally land use, environmental and transport – so that they should work together and not conflict with or undermine each other. In particular, it has been the recognition that transport issues are central to the achievement of environmental objectives that has driven the change, though the importance of transport infrastructure decisions to urban regeneration and local economic development should not be underestimated.

One of the key stated goals of the creation of the new DETR has been to create an integrated environment and transport policy. Achieving this may not prove easy. Partly this is because the DoE has not always held a strong environmental policy line. In practice the DoE has focused heavily on housing (particularly local authority housing), local government (especially local government taxation) and overseeing the procedures and operation of the land use planning system. As of February 1989 the staff within the DoE dealing with purely environmental issues (narrowly defined to exclude

---

Department of Environment (continued)
- Property:
    Property and buildings
    Principal Finance Officer and agency
    Sponsorship

Department of Transport (11071 staff, including 9100 in agencies)
- Legal
- Establishment and Finance
- Government Office for London
- Railways
- Roads, Local Transport and Transport Policy
- Aviation and Shipping
- Highways Executive Agency
- Information

Department of Culture, Media and Sport (1003 staff, including 666 in agencies)
- Historic Royal Palaces Agency
- Royal Parks Agency
- Heritage and Tourism
- Broadcasting and Media
- Arts, Sport and Lottery
- Libraries, Galleries and Museums
- Information
- Resources and Services

Source: *Civil Service Yearbook, Civil Service Statistics.*

---

land use planning and the built environment) amounted to only 10 per cent (McCormick, 1991, p. 17). And the DoE has also always acted as the 'sponsoring' department for the construction industry, a function performed by the DTI for most other industries.

However this appears a mixed set of policy goals, in which the environment at least figures, when compared to the DoTr. Historically the DoTr has interpreted its role largely in terms of road construction. Dowding explains the attitudes of the DoTr in terms of the high costs involved in overcoming inertia which encourages a culture of secrecy, and antipathy to public participation, and which will make change difficult to achieve (1995b). Herington has noted the conflicts that existed between these central government departments over the direction of planning policy. For example, the separation between the DoTr and DoE, and hence between land use and transport planning, means that the 'DoTr has been uninterested in the spatial impact of its programme' (1984, p. 75). This has been true in the past in relation to green belt protection and urban regeneration and is likely to remain an issue now with regard to constraining energy consumption and pollution.

One of the first tests of the ability of the new merged department to take a different policy line has been over the review of various roadbuilding projects in the pipeline. In July 1997 twelve contentious schemes were reassessed; only two were scrapped, five were left in the review process (including plans to widen the M25 to twelve lanes near Heathrow Airport) and five were given the go-ahead (including the first private toll road north of Birmingham). This outcome was reportedly only achieved after disagreement between the Secretary of State for the Environment and the Transport Minister, the former being on record as having supported the environmentalists' case, the latter apparently influenced by his civil servants. There was also pressure from eighteen pro-environment Labour MPs who tabled a Parliamentary motion which delayed the policy announcement by a week. In these circumstances it is not surprising that many regarded the final policy stance as at best a compromise, at worst a 'policy fudge'. A more stringent test for the new department will come with the promised delivery of an integrated transport White Paper in June 1998.

The range of the new Department of Environment, Transport and the Regions is indeed immense. Nevertheless certain key policy areas remain outside the its remit. Energy planning, which was located within the Department of Energy until 1992, is now within the Department of Trade and Industry. Industry policy, including selective grant-aiding of industry in particular regions and locations, is also the responsibility of the DTI although the proposal to set up regional development agencies may alter DETR/DTI relations in this policy area. The DTI is a substantial organisation with 9234 staff as of May 1996, including 3550 in agencies. The Ministry of Agriculture, Fisheries and Food (MAFF) is a similarly large department with 9993 staff, 3892 in agencies. It has the overall remit for agricultural land in the countryside and is currently organised into three substantive policy areas: food safety; agricultural commodities trade and food production; and countryside, marine environment and fisheries; with other sections covering the usual finance, establishment, legal and information responsibilities. There is also a Chief Scientist's Group within MAFF. Ironically both the nature conservation concerns of the Environment Department and any policy of planned urban growth potentially bring the department into conflict with MAFF.

Even within a single department, separate directorates or groups will sometimes clash. While the housing and construction sections may seek to promote speculative housebuilding, the planning directorate may be seeking to constrain it. While the cities directorate may promote concepts such as Enterprise Zones (EZs) where planning regulations are relaxed, the environmental protection group will be concerned over the possible consequences for local air and water quality. In 1984 Herington argued that 'the present division of responsibility within the DoE clearly makes it difficult for it to coordinate the twin policies of countryside protection and urban growth' (1984, p. 63); the establishment of a cities and countryside directorate is designed to deal with this problem but any structure creates divisions as well as unities. Furthermore separating central government functions off and handing them to quangos, such as the Countryside Commission which took over many rural concerns in 1982, or even private sector bodies such as the privatised water companies which replaced the regional water authorities in England and Wales in 1990, also makes for a potential problem of policy coordination. In these circumstances the institutional mechanisms for integration, networking and interorganisational communication become even more important, as does clear policy direction from the top on the overall priorities to be followed.

Over all the work of the different departments stands the financial control exercised by the Treasury. As Chapman (1984, p. 176) says: 'The Treasury has, in effect, a controlling role over all other departments through its financial responsibilities.' In addition Chapman notes that this functional control has been reinforced by the Treasury's elite status within the civil service and by the flow of staff in and out of the Treasury to elsewhere in the executive. It has been suggested that the desire to curb the growth in traffic owes as much to concerns over the costs of financing the necessary infrastructure as to the new environmental agenda (Button, 1995, p. 182). Similarly the financial work of the DoE, in regard to local government finance, has been a major influence on DoE's other policy work; the policy on the business rate may have had at least as much influence in determining the location of industry as urban policy or land use planning.

The problem of developing a unified policy stance within the DETR and within central government more generally is shown in the Environment White Paper (1990) *This Common Inheritance*. This was a document designed to respond to growing environmental concern, both at a local level and in relation to global issues. It aimed to be broad in focus. 'Environment' was loosely defined to include the built heritage, the countryside, nuclear waste, genetically modified organisms and energy use. The problem of interdepartmental coordination was met by a standing committee of Cabinet ministers who considered the draft document and advised on their particular ministry's concerns. Despite these arrangements, the White Paper was widely criticised for the extent to which it sacrificed demonstrable commitment to achieving environmental goals by way of institutional change and innovative policy tools to the gloss of presentation. Little in the way of substantial new initiatives was announced. Instead the emphasis was on listing the existing policies and practices of the various, largely divorced, government departments and quangos.

The standing committee of Cabinet ministers has been retained but, up to 1997, has met infrequently and always in secret. Ministers were nominated in each department responsible for the environmental implications of that department's policies and spending programmes but they have kept a low profile, focusing on housekeeping matters such as departmental purchasing policy (O'Riordan and Jordan, 1995). The criticisms concerning interdepartmental and intra-departmental conflicts over policies and objectives have not been met. O'Riordan and Jordan refer to low-level working groups of well-intentioned civil servants being the only attempt at interdepartmental coordination and points to the role of the Cabinet committee in resolving outstanding interdepartmental conflicts rather than working towards an integrated policy. Similarly, the environmentalists' concerns that the current institutional arrangements create a degree of inertia which prevents changed policies to enhance environmental protection also seem justified. The reluctance of the 1997 Budget to deliver on some of the promised green taxation measures – higher fuel prices, increased landfill charges – also demonstrates the traditional line that the Treasury continues to take in relation to environmental policy. It may prove difficult to alter this.

Outside England, the Welsh, Scottish and Northern Ireland Offices are the key central government departments (see Summary Box 5.2). Interestingly environmental and planning concerns are differently organised in each of these, and each again differs from the situation in Whitehall. The Welsh Office is the least powerful of the three. It has largely taken the lead from the DoE, setting out parallel policies for the Principality where necessary. Environment and planning issues are here organised alongside transport as social activities. Most planning policy is common for England and Wales, though an attempt is being made to develop a distinctive Welsh approach (see Chapter 10). However the smaller scale of the Principality means that it has a considerable hands-on role. It liaises directly with not only the local authorities, but also the TECs and various quangos such as Tai Cymru (Housing for Wales), the Welsh Development Agency, the Development Board for Rural Wales and the Land Authority. In many ways the Welsh Office acts as an unelected regional council; hence the proposals for a Welsh Assembly (see below) are regarded as democratising the quango state.

In contrast, the Scottish Office is a much more powerful institution based on the distinctive administrative and legal structure in Scotland. There are many policy areas, such as planning, where the Scottish Office has widespread autonomy, and other areas where the responsibility

Summary Box 5.2   *The civil service in Wales, Scotland and Northern Ireland*

Wales   Welsh Office (2139 staff, incl. 211 in agencies)

- Economic activities:
  - Economic development
  - Industry and training
  - Agriculture
- Health
- Social activities:
  - Local government
  - Health professionals
  - Nursing
  - Transport, planning and environment
  - Education
- Legal, establishment and finance

Scotland   Scottish Office (5045 staff, incl. 1238 in agencies)

- Agriculture, Environment and Fisheries Department
  - Agriculture
  - Fisheries
  - Environment: Pollution control
    - Water
    - Forestry
    - Rural affairs and natural heritage
    - Ecological Adviser
- Education and Industry Department
- Development Department:
  - Housing and urban regeneration
  - New towns
  - Local government and LG finance
  - Construction and building control
  - Chief Inquiry Reporter
  - Chief Planner
  - Economic infrastructure and public adminstration
  - Historic Scotland
- Home Department
- Department of Health
- Establishment, information and legal

Northern Ireland

- Northern Ireland Office
- Department of Agriculture for NI
- Department of Economic Development (NI)
- Department of Environment (NI)

Source: *Civil Service Yearbook, Civil Service Statistics.*

between Whitehall and the Scottish Office is at least ambiguous (Midwinter et al., 1991, p. 79). The Scottish Office has a range of relations with local authorities and other agencies which mirrors that of the DETR and other departments in England. This paves the way for the new Scottish Parliament (see below). Environment issues are dealt with alongside agriculture and fisheries, while many other planning issues are regarded as aspects of development policy.

The situation in Northern Ireland is quite distinct. The Northern Ireland Office is relatively small and is equivalent to the Home Office in Whitehall. Alongside it sit a number of other departments, including a Department of Environment (NI). The centralisation of most planning powers within the executive and the curtailed powers of local government since 1973 both creates departments with more direct responsibilities and also has absolved the DoE (NI) in the past of many supervisory and coordinating functions. As of 1 April 1996, however, the DoE (NI) was reorganised to redistribute many of its functions to eleven agencies covering planning, roads, water and works services, environmental protection and conservation, land registration, public records, the ordinance survey, rates and the testing and licensing of drivers and vehicles. The DoE (NI) retains only the core responsibilities of housing and transport policies, fire services, local government control, disposing of and managing DoE (NI) land and urban regeneration.

Following the 1997 General Election, the distinction between England, Wales and Scotland will no longer just be one of the organisation of the executive. The Labour manifesto promised a form of devolution for Wales and Scotland and the first steps towards this are already in place with referenda on the issue in September 1997. The 1997 White Paper *A Voice for Wales* set out proposals for how an elected Welsh Assembly or 'senedd' might work. The plan is for a 60-member Assembly elected in May 1999; 40 seats will be elected by constituencies and 20 seats chosen from a list with each voter having two votes. Existing Welsh MPs and MEPs would be able to stand for the Assembly. The Assembly will have a £7 million budget derived from the existing grants from Westminster which currently go to the Welsh Office and certain quangos; nine of the 45 main quangos are to be abolished although the Welsh Development Agency may have an expanded role. The key responsibilities of the Welsh Assembly will be for economic development, agriculture, forestry, fisheries and food, industry and training, education, local government, health and personal social services, housing, environment, planning, transport and roads, arts, culture and the Welsh language, and sport and recreation. Its legislative role will be limited to secondary legislation, filling in the details of primary legislation passed at Westminster, and Westminster would always be able to overrule the Assembly by passing new primary legislation. There will still be a Cabinet post of Welsh Secretary but most of the power will pass to the head of the Assembly.

In Scotland, however, there will be an elected Scottish Parliament with more extensive powers, including the power to vary national taxation rates, and a greater degree of autonomy from London-based government institutions. Elections are scheduled for 1999 with the Parliament operational from 2000. There will be 129 MPs elected by a form of proportional representation, with 73 elected from constituencies and 56 allocated to ensure that the distribution of seats reflects the shares of the overall vote; there will be a corresponding but not equivalent reduction in the number of Scottish MPs at Parliament, currently standing at 73. The head of the Scottish Parliament will be the First Minister for Scotland, and ministers will be able to deal direct with the European Union. The Parliament will also have wide legislative powers, be able to scrutinise European legislation and raise income tax by up to 3 pence in the pound, though the main funding will continue to come from a block grant from Westminster. Westminster will also retain responsibility for constitutional matters, foreign policy, defence and national security, economic policy, employment and social security and most regulation relating to health and safety such as that relating to transport and nuclear matters. The named areas of responsibility additional to the Welsh Assembly's remit are: education, law and home affairs, reflecting the historically different organisation of those areas in Scotland. The position of the Scottish Secretary will be retained but given the greater independence of the Scottish Parliament an additional mechanism will be set up to adjudicate in cases of disagreement between Scotland and Westminster, with the House of Lords acting as the final arbiter.

In addition, as of Easter 1998, there is the prospect of considerable and significant change in the governmental arrangements for Northern Ireland. All these constitutional changes are profound and are likely to impact on all areas of government policy, including urban, rural and environmental planning.

■ Local government

Local authorities in Britain employ two million people engaged in local planning and service delivery. Byrne (1986, p. 6) describes local government as a form of self-government providing for local initiative and freedom. As such it goes beyond both the decentralisation of central government functions to local offices and their delegation to non-elected but quasi-autonomous organisations. Local government and central government exist in an uneasy partnership, both claiming authority by virtue of their elected nature but with central government clearly in a position of greater power through various financial and administrative controls, power which increased considerably during the Thatcher years. Central government can also claim greater legitimacy through the higher turn-out at general than local elections (Stoker, 1991, p. 51); only about 40 per cent of the electorate turn out for local elections, about half the national figure. Local authorities are, after all, the creation of statutes enacted at the central level. They are bound quite tightly by the doctrine of *ultra vires* which means that local authorities can undertake only activities for which they have specific statutory authority; this contrasts with private sector bodies, who can undertake any activity unless prohibited by law. It is also distinct from the situation in many other European local government systems.

The nature of central–local relations between central government and local authorities is, therefore, of great importance in the British context. This can be analysed in terms of networks of linkages and resource exchange. Stoker, discussing central–local relations, defines a number of policy networks (1991, p. 148): territorial communities, based in regions such as Scotland or Wales; policy communities, based on specific policy areas such as housing renewal; the national community of local government (the national pressure groups representing local government), an example of an interorganisational network; producer networks based round a specific industry; and issues networks, the inner city problem being an example. Each policy network comprises a particular set of linkages between the centre and the locality, and between the state and outside groups at both levels. However, linkages between organisations tell only one part of the story. The strength of a linkage *vis-à-vis* others and the direction of power or dependency it represents is essential knowledge for understanding the interaction of organisations in practice. Rhodes (1981) has analysed this power–dependency relation between state organisations, particularly central and local government, as bound up with the resources available to the various organisations. Such resources may take five forms: financial, including the power to levy taxes or to give grants; constitutional and legal, set down in legislation, including the various reserve powers granted central government under planning acts; hierarchical, based on the supervisory role of one organisation over another and including the various forms of planning guidance that central government provides; political, founded on the electoral base of the organisation, either directly elected as with central and local government, or with political representation, say, on the board of a quango; and informational, using the expertise of professionals within an organisation, particularly important, say, in some pollution control quangos. These resources are used by actors in state institutions in a complex process of exchange, where resources are employed to achieve each organisation's goals according to the understood 'rules of the game'.

The existence of a variety of resources at both central and local government level at least ensures that local government does not degenerate into a mere agency of the centre. But as a result, 'difference and the possibility of conflict is structured in to the relationship' between central and local government (Ranson *et al.*, 1985, p. 24). The conflictual aspect has been particularly apparent during the 1980s, with the issue of local government finance being a flashpoint. Conflict is based in the fact that local government comprises political institutions capable of choice but it is exacerbated by organisational differences (see Summary Box 5.3), a lack of learning at both levels, a fragmented approach within central government (see above) and the random nature of the set of policy instruments used in the relationship between the tiers.

There are a number of specific control mechanisms included within the various policies of the planning system by which central government can limit the actions of local government. Many of these are indicated in Part 3. For example, development control decisions are subject to appeal to the Secretary of State. There are numerous reserve powers held by the Secretary of State. Central government can influence local areas by a variety of designations, even removing areas from full local government control by UDCs. There are also the supervisory aspects of the planning system and the mass of advice and information flowing between the tiers. Most important though, local authorities are dependent on central government for finance; 85 per cent of local authority income now comes direct from central government as grant. This level of grant, the revenue support grant, is based on centrally assessed notions of needs known as standard spending assessments in England and Wales and grant-aided expenditure in Scotland.

Summary Box 5.3 *Differences between central and local government*

Aspect	Central government	Local government
Focus	National, international	Local
Scale	Large scale	Smaller scale
Executive	Administrative culture	Professional culture
Political control	Ministerial control	Control by committee
Activities	Sets framework for action	Engaged in service delivery plus quasi-entrepreneurial activity

Source: Adapted from Ranson *et al.* (1985) pp. 27–8.

Central government also closely circumscribes the amount that local authorities can raise from local taxation and loans. Business rates are now levied according to their assessed property values and a nationally set, uniform rate poundage: rates paid are equal to the rateable values of the property multiplied by the rate poundage. The national receipts from the national non-domestic rate (NNDR) are then redistributed according to local authorities' share of population. Revenues from the council tax are determined by the value of domestic property (according to preset bands or ranges of value) multiplied by the local tax rate. The revenues are collected locally and remain available for the local council's budget. The amount that can be raised annually through loans and credit is limited so that councils cannot exceed an annual capital expenditure allocation. Within housing, controls are even tighter. There can be no transfer from or into the housing accounts, say from the general rate fund. A fixed percentage of housing capital receipts (largely from council house and land sales) must go to repaying debt with only the remainder available for new capital spending. The 1997 Budget though allowed for a phased release of a substantial proportion of these housing capital receipts to fund local housing, construction and employment schemes; £900m of additional loan approvals was granted to local authorities for the period to March 1999. The budget of a local authority may be 'capped' if central government considers it too high, and this may 'cap' local domestic taxation. The Labour government decided to retain these capping measures in the 1997 Budget pending a review.

Changes in local government finance and the use of central government powers have meant that the relationship of 'control' has increasingly replaced that of 'partnership' in recent years. A number of strategies have been used in engineering this shift: legislation, minimal consultation, targeted funding, bypassing local government procedures, and reorganisation and reform of local government (Stoker, 1991, pp. 153–7). The goal of this control under the Conservative government was fundamentally to alter the nature of local government. As Stewart and Stoker argue (1989, p. 2):

> From the mid–1980s the Government's concern about local government became wider in its focus and more far-reaching in its implications. The Government's programme has gone beyond the search for public expenditure restraint to a more broad-ranging attempt to restructure local government.

Stewart and Stoker identify a number of key themes in this restructuring process: the fragmentation of responsibilities, with service delivery, regulation and strategic planning shared with other institutions and agencies; a commitment to local authorities competing with private sector bodies and in the process separating service delivery from the responsibility for that service; a closer relationship between receiving the service and paying for it and a greater emphasis on consumer choice; all involving a challenge to current producer interests within local government and the development of a commitment to a more 'business-like' management.

Examples of this can be seen in: the opening up of building regulations inspections to approved private sector consultants; the payment of fees for planning applications; the competitive tendering for refuse collection and the creation of arm's-length bodies for waste disposal; the need for direct labour organisations (local authorities' internal construction, repair and maintenance organisations) to achieve a 5 per cent return, keep trading accounts and compete with private contractors; the requirement for bus undertakings to operate on a commercial basis. This list is potentially a very long one. The result has been a new style of management. Discussing land use planning, Maitland and Newman (1989) argue that there is a shift away from hierarchical and functional organisational structures towards new working practices which are customised to specific tasks. There is a new emphasis on 'customer care', on mimicking private sector planning organisations and developing new organisational cultures, often directly opposed to previously held values. Stoker argues (1989a, p. 159) that the 'aim is to create a local government compatible with the flexible economic structures, two-tier welfare system and enterprise culture which in the Thatcher vision constitute the key to a successful future'.

This has also involved a challenge to the existing political nature of local government, not just its role as service provider. Two more of Stewart and Stoker's 'key themes of restructuring' involved: initiating new forms of accountability to the centre and the local community; and challenging existing mechanisms of local representative democracy (1989, p. 3). The creation of local decision-making bodies which bypass directly elected local authorities (such as urban development corporations or TECs/LECs) has been complemented by tightening the constraints on local councillors. The Widdecombe Report of 1986, followed by a 1988 White Paper and the 1989 Local Government and Housing Act made substantial changes in the ways in which committees (the key decision-making arena) are convened in local authorities, the use of political advisers and cooptees on committees and the scope for local government officers to undertake political activity. The tasks of maintaining financial probity (avoiding unlawful expenditure), legal propriety (avoiding illegality or maladministration) and management coordination were also given a higher profile by the required appointment of three separate senior officers to these posts. The Audit Commission also maintains a watching brief on the probity with which local government handles its finances and powers.

These reforms were initiated largely to deal with urban local authorities who were seeking to implement and work out on the ground the ideas of the New Left (Gyford, 1985; Blunkett and Jackson, 1987; Livingstone, 1987; Boddy and Fudge, 1984). Drawing on spatially distinct social practices and cultures, these councils sought to mobilise local communities against the central state, in order to influence the local pattern of resource allocation, resulting from capital accumulation and (dis)investment and public sector policies. In doing so they often created innovative new political and organisational structures at the local level and sought to develop policy which both produced new benefits for the local community, particularly women, ethnic minorities, the disabled and other disadvantaged groups, and also politicised these groups. Empowering people, enabling them to govern themselves, was a watchword of such councils. Seen as a reaction to this activity within radical Left local authorities, the reforms of Thatcherism have, in their own terms, been largely successful, refocusing local authorities on service provision rather than broader political activity: 'What is clear is that the "tidal force" of the politicisation of local government will receive a severe and possibly terminal setback from the legislative proposals' (Leach, 1989, p. 121).

It remains to be seen how many of these trends will be reversed under the new Labour government. The requirement for compulsive competitive tendering (CCT) will be phased out but a replacement is being planned. The 'best value' initiative, announced in June 1997, is intended to replace the emphasis on economic criteria in CCT with a broader test of service delivery including effectiveness and quality; the aim is for local authorities to provide the quality of service that local people expect at a price they are willing to pay. It will encourage local initiative, rather than directly control, but it is still seeking to influence local public service delivery and may continue the involvement of the private sector. About thirty pilot schemes are to go ahead, monitored by the DETR and Local Government Association (the body representing local government), based on national and locally set performance targets and the identification of the local authority services most in need of improvement. Also under consideration by the government are new ways of involving the public in local government, both at election times and more continually. Changing the timing and location of local elections for councillors is a possibility as well as the method: proportional representation and electronic voting may be introduced. Other initiatives such as referenda, citizens' juries and innovative local participation measures are also being mooted (Kuper, 1997). This parallels some of the Local Agenda 21 work, discussed below. There is, therefore, more of an emphasis on changing the relationship between local government and local communities than between central and local government where an element of strong control will probably remain.

This is in recognition of the fact that the current pattern of local government elections and management does not always serve communities well. Elections are decided on national party swings in support, not local issues, and this can result in entrenched majorities for one party. The committee structure, whereby local government policy responsibilities are divided up and deliberated over by committees of councillors, drawn from all parties but controlled by the dominant party, can be difficult for the community to understand and influence. The key links are often between committee chairs and senior local government officers (that is, staff members), and between influential councillors and selected outside interests. Political parties can exert strong control over the management and decision-making of policy in some authorities, turning local government into an insider's game, which local people perceive as not interested in their needs. It is the deficiencies of this structure which the government's new initiative is intended to address. It should be noted that some local authorities have already adopted decentralised structures within their districts or boroughs to address these problems (Burns *et al.*, 1994). In some cases this is purely administrative, in others it involves mini town halls. This is discussed further in Chapter 8 in the context of the role of professionals.

It is unlikely that any new initiative will look again at the structural organisation of local government though (outside of the special case of London – see below). Local government structure has already been reformed more than enough. The reorganisation of 1972 in England and Wales and 1975 in Scotland created a two-tier system throughout most of the country, such a system having already been established in London. This was then amended by the 1985 Local Government Act which abolished the metropolitan county councils and the GLC. The result was a pattern of unitary authorities in the metropolitan areas – based on district councils and, in London, the boroughs plus the Corporation of the City of London – and two tiers everywhere else – counties and districts (some still called boroughs). This appears a clear and simple pattern by contrast with the outcomes of the latest reforms.

The latest round of local government reform was initiated in 1990 by the former Secretary of State, Michael Heseltine, along with the Welsh and Scottish Secretaries. The principle target of this reform was the two-tier system which existed in non-metropolitan areas. This was criticised for producing top-tier authorities which were too remote from the people being served, for inefficiency and for problems of poor coordination and excessive conflict. However, rather than proposing a universal solution along the line of the Redcliffe–Maud Commission or the 1972 Local Government Act, the government proposed in England to consider the applicability of the two-tier structure on a case-by-case basis. To this end a Local Government Commission (LGC) was appointed in England under the Local Government Act 1992 and this began reviewing the

---

Summary Box 5.4   *The structure of local government*

	Old system	New system	Representation
England	*Non-met. areas* 39 counties 296 districts	 34 counties 238 districts 46 unitaries	LGA[1]
	Met. areas 36 districts 32 London boroughs Corporation of City of London	 No change	LGA[1] ALG[2]
Scotland	9 regions 53 districts 3 unitaries	32 unitaries	COSLA[3]
Wales	8 counties 37 districts	22 unitaries	LGA[1]
N. Ireland	26 districts	No change	ALANI[4]

1. LGA = Local Government Association.
2. ALG = Association of London Government.
3. COSLA = Convention of Scottish Local Authorities.
4. ALANI = Association of Local Authorities of Northern Ireland.

---

organisational arrangements across the country in successive tranches. While central government indicated a preference for unitary authorities and for basing them on existing districts, the Commission was given a fairly free hand in the first instance. The aim was that the new authorities should be based on communities, as defined by people's preferences, geography, patterns of economic and social activity and any 'natural institutional focus'. However, cost-effectiveness was also a factor behind the reorganisation. The LGC published reports putting forward recommendations for each county, on which a final decision was then made by the government.

This is though an overly simple description of the resulting policy fiasco. A slow rate of progress and a tendency to recommend the retention of the two-tier structure in many cases resulted in the whole policy being reviewed in 1993, speeded up and the advice to the Commission changed to emphasise the unitary option above the others, if necessary subdividing counties and amalgamating districts. However, this advice was then subject to legal challenge by two counties and subsequently dropped. In 1995 the chair of the Local Government Commission resigned and a new LGC was formed to consider the case for unitary status of a limited number of 21 districts. This it duly did and was then disbanded (see Leach and Stoker (1997) for a brief history). The results of this process are summarised in Summary Box 5.4, the new authorities coming on stream from 1995 through to 1997. The final pattern produced only 46 English unitaries (largely due to public opposition to change, which was gauged through extensive survey and consultation work by the LGC (Game, 1997)) and a messy patchwork of local government has resulted. The broad consensus is that the work of the LGC was a failure:

> The LGC for England clearly failed to deliver what the government hoped for; there has been a minor restructuring only in most parts of England . . . it failed to ignite citizen interest in the issue, let alone support for major change, and was unable successfully to counter the intransigence of the local government lobbies with public desire for something new. (Johnston and Pattic, 1996, p. 110)

In Wales and Scotland there was no such review; rather a solution was imposed across each country. In Wales the Secretary of State issued a consultation paper in July 1991 setting out three options, each a different pattern of unitary authorities for the country. The resulting consultation has been criticised for its lack of openness, the token response to submissions, its undemocratic nature and the limited range of options offered. Nevertheless it has resulted in a new pattern of local government being established relatively quickly, with 22 unitary authorities operative from 1995 (Clotworthy and Harris, 1996). In Scotland a similar pattern of new unitary authorities – 27 in number – was announced by the Scottish Office in 1993 and again enacted through 1994 legislation. While Scotland already had unitary authorities in the islands and three rural regions, there has been great concern over the location of the boundaries of the new authorities and the replacement of a two-tier structure, which had been praised for its strategic planning potential, its lack of conflict between the tiers and its effectiveness.

The situation of London has been considered a distinct one, outside the concerns of general local government reform. London has for over a decade been the only major European city without a democratically elected representative body. Therefore the Labour government has proposed reintroducing a two-tier system in London, in a form that opens up the option of a political innovation, that of an elected mayor. The proposals for London, announced in a 1997 Green Paper and 1998 White Paper, involve an elected assembly – the Greater London Authority (GLA) – and a directly elected mayor. There was a referendum in May 1998 (with the local elections) among the five million Londoners on these proposals and, following a majority acceptance, legislation will proceed with the first elections taking place in May 2000.

The details of both the elections – some form of proportional representation – and the relative functions of the assembly and the mayor have yet to be worked out, but the present ideas involve the following: a relatively small elected assembly of 25 members with principally a scrutiny role akin to parliamentary select committees; a streamlined authority with a limited staff complement of about 250 (compared to 25000 for the GLC!), focusing only on metro-level issues such as transport, strategic planning, policing (including fire and civil defence), environmental protection (including waste and air quality management) and economic regeneration, together with any other relevant issue they wish to tackle such as tourism, homelessness or racism; and a mayor who will have the executive capacity, set the budget, and be the voice of London. The budget will comprise the precepts already included within borough council tax bills to cover the functions listed above, together with savings from abolishing some quangos; the boundary will be the old GLC area. The policy responsibilities will be administered by GLA-appointed boards, within the policy and budget parameters set by the Mayor but subject to scrutiny by the assembly. These proposals raise issues of the concentration of power in the mayoral office and the potential for corruption, the limited budget and hence power that the authority as a whole will command, and the scope for conflict between the assembly and the mayor, the mechanisms for resolving such conflict not yet being clear. If successful, however, the mayoral formula may well be repeated in other large cities.

Below this main structure of local government there is a patchy coverage of very localised organisations: over 900 active parish and town councils in England, about 800 community or town councils in Wales and over 1200 community councils in Scotland. These bodies have a largely consultative role *vis-à-vis* the rest of local government (Gyford, 1991, p. 89; Stoker, 1991, p. 57; Midwinter et al., 1991, p. 141) although they can undertake some local environmental management.

Although it would seem that a knowledge of this structure is essential for discovering which authority does what at the local level, it is not so simple. Responsibilities are generally allocated with strategic planning, transport, policy, fire services, education and social services (plus water in Scotland) going to the higher-tier authority. But there is considerable scope for sharing these responsibilities in a variety of ways: jointly providing a service; providing a service concurrently; dividing up the responsibility (as with development control); higher-tier authorities having reserve or default powers; lower-tier authorities claiming a responsibility back from a higher-tier authority (as with the maintenance of certain unclassified roads); or agency powers where one authority agrees to perform a function for another authority, usually for payment (Byrne, 1986, p. 59). Broadly speaking there are pressures for a higher-tier authority to perform a function where: there is a strategic dimension to the responsibility, involving some negotiation with central government and/or neighbouring authorities; the service is most economically or efficiently provided over a larger geographical area; or the function carries 'kudos' and the larger authority uses its political power to capture the function. The abolition of metropolitan county councils and the GLC has already necessitated alternative arrangements for many local government functions with a strategic dimension in these areas. The GLA boards will replace some of these in London. The complex local government restructuring in England will necessitate other new hybrid arrangements.

Local government functions, therefore, are not a simple hierarchy but are spread across the organisational structure of local government like a net, and the mesh of the net represents a complicated pattern of intraorganisational and inter-organisational communication. This communication is vital for resolving actual and potential conflicts between tiers of government or departments within local government. Such conflict not only arises from the existence of tiers with organisational boundaries but is also due to different professional and political judgements about policy and priorities (Midwinter *et al.*, 1991, p. 126). Godschalk (1991) distinguishes three types of conflict, each with its own resolution technique: issues resolved by informal negotiation or facilitation; disputes resolved by formal negotiation or mediation; and impasses resolved by arbitration, often to an external hearing or court. Situations can arise where there is insufficient liaison between departments, as with the conceptual and practical gaps between expenditure-based plans, such as HIPs and TPPs, and development plans which prevent local government taking an enabling role in relation to local development (Carter *et al.*, 1991).

But this account has so far only emphasised the governmental organisations at central and local level and their interrelations. It has been increasingly argued over the past decade that such an account misses important elements of the contemporary policy process. The concept of governance, introduced earlier, has been considered particularly applicable at the local level, giving rise to the term 'local governance' or 'new urban governance'. Stoker (1996) identifies five propositions concerning governance: it goes beyond the consideration of government; it identifies the blurring of boundaries and responsibility for tackling social and economic (and environmental) issues; it identifies the power dependence involved in relationships between institutions involved in collective action; it is about autonomous self-governing networks of actors; and – possibly most significant – it recognises the capacity to get things done which does not rest on the power of government to command or authorise, but rather sees government as using new tools to steer and guide. There is therefore an emphasis on the complexity of relationships between, at local government level, the local authority/ies, quangos (or qualgos at the local level – quasi-autonomous local government organisations), non-government organisations and citizens, and on how these complex relationships may achieve policy results in new ways. The balance of power in these new relationships remains largely uncharted; unsurprisingly those on the New Right see those arrangements which favour local economic interests as more efficient, while Marxists see the changes as part (albeit an unstable part) of a mode of regulation which has arisen in response to the crises of Fordism (Goodwin and Painter, 1997).

One policy area where networking and developing new patterns of relationships is an explicit theme is the Local Agenda 21 process (Young, 1997; Selman and Parker, 1997). As outlined in Chapter 4, the Rio Earth Summit spawned an Agenda 21 process oriented towards the implementation of policies for sustainable development, and the recognition that much of this change would have to occur at the local level in turn led to a Local Agenda 21 process. While the national process has focused on the development of policy documents, plans and strategies, LA21 has been distinguished by its self-characterisation as a process rather than a way of producing paper statements. The process of networking involved in LA21 and the ways in which more and more groups are involved are the purpose of LA21, not any document which may emerge. The aim of LA21 is empowerment, participation and changing attitudes. The reason for this is twofold: first, it is based on a definition of sustainable development which implies a radical democratic agenda; and second, it is argued that only by involving a broader cross-section of the community and changing their values and behaviour will the changes necessary for sustainable development occur. Thus the LA21 process can be a radical attempt to create new patterns of local environmental governance. Indicative of this is the fact that recent government advice on LA21 was jointly written by central and local government. Innovative techniques such as visioning, creating local events such as Green Fairs and forums which involve groups who have never previously participated in local policy (such as youth groups) are all examples of the more exciting potential of LA21. In many cases, though, it can degenerate into more traditional forms of participation activity and stall on the hard conflicts that are encapsulated within the concept of sustainable development between equity, economic and environmental agendas.

■ Further reading

An introduction to the theoretical issues is provided by Dunleavy and O'Leary (1987). Two good introductions to central and local government respectively are Dowding (1995) and Stewart and Stoker (1995b). Relevant journals to consult are: *Local Government Studies, Government and Policy, Urban Studies* and *Policy and Politics*. The official government websites contain a wealth of information: the main Government Information Service is at http://www.open.gov.uk and the Central Office of Information site is at http://www.coi.gov.uk/coi. Readers are also reminded that daily proceedings in Parliament are recorded and relayed on radio and television; this can be very revealing as well as entertaining. The formal printed version of parliamentary debates and hearings is obtained in Hansard, also available over the Internet. For individual local authorities, considerable information is held in local libraries and study centres, including council minutes; attendance at many meetings is open to the public and can convey the flavour of local politics much better than any text!

■ Chapter 6 ■

Agencies, Quangos and the European Union

The previous chapter looked at the formal organisation of the state at central and local levels. However the discussion emphasised the importance of processes of governance at both levels. This involves relations with a number of other organisations, both outside the state (as discussed in Chapter 7) and on the borders, the agencies and quangos. This chapter begins by considering such agencies and quangos and then goes on to discuss the rising influence of the EU on national and local policy.

■ Agencies and quangos

Agencies and quangos (quasi-autonomous non-governmental organisations) are non-elected bodies, appointed by central government to undertake specified functions often with a substantial degree of discretion. They stand between central and local government in the sense that either they have a regional geographical area to cover (for example, national park authorities) or they report directly to central government for a local spatial area or policy issue removed from local authority control (for example, urban development corporations (UDCs) or Training and Enterprise Councils (TECs)). But they also stand outside the central–local government relationship in the sense that they are not institutions with claims to representative democracy. Some are also spin-offs from local government and hence known as qualgos, quasi-autonomous local governmental organisations; grant-maintained schools are an example of a qualgo.

Such agencies may be charged merely with implementing or enforcing a tightly defined policy but they can also be given policy- or plan-making powers or even a general delegated responsibility. In Britain, delegation has been the norm (Rees, 1990, p. 367): 'Agencies not only have considerable flexibility to interpret what their responsibilities mean, but can develop their own strategies to meet them, set their own implementation timescales and decide their own enforcement practices.' In some cases delegation may even extend to discretion over whether to use their powers or not. In theory, these elements of delegation and discretion should enhance rational decision-making by allowing for spatial variation in needs and in the preferences of local communities. In practice, as will be explored below, they can insulate the organisation from popular pressure.

The importance and variety of these quangos has grown considerably in recent years as more and more functions have been allocated to them (Stoker, 1991, p. 61). Collective consumption functions, such as waste management and public transport, have been removed from local authorities to quangos. Resource development, as with forestry and water, has been placed in quangos prior to being proposed for privatisation or at least public–private partnership. Many regulatory environmental protection functions are located in quangos where, arguably, expertise and control powers can be strengthened by centralisation. Rees claims (1990, p. 373) 'there has been a tendency for all substantive aspects of environmental resource management to migrate away from local control'. In large part this arises from the ideology of the Conservative government of the 1980s, but also from the requirements of increased regulations under EU rules and from the heavy constraints that local government finds itself under (Shaw, 1990). The new Labour government has a commitment to make quangos more accountable but not to reduce their number. Shaw identifies a number of different organisations which can now be considered as quangos: central government arm's-length agencies such as UDCs; local government arm's-length agencies such as enterprise boards; corporatist development agencies such as English Partnerships, Scottish Enterprise or the Welsh Development Agency (WDA); joint boards such as police authorities; and hybrid agencies including TECs or Local Enterprise Councils (LECs). In his typology Stoker (1991, p. 65) replaces corporatist development agencies with public–private partnerships and adds user organisations (such as housing management cooperatives) and intergovernmental forums (such as the South East Regional Planning Conference, SERPLAN).

In many circumstances, the previous Conservative government has favoured the central government arm's-length agency, terming it the 'executive agency'. Seventy-four per cent of the civil service, some 387 000 people, are now in such agencies (see Summary Box 6.1). These agencies are directly modelled on a somewhat idealised private sector. For example, under the new agency model the Planning Inspectorate aims to cover all costs with fees and produces a corporate plan indicating targets such as speed, costs and efficiency savings, against which to measure their performance. Restrictions on the Inspectorate's activities are lifted allowing them to diversify, say into training and other profit making areas. There are varying figures for the total count of quangos depending on what is and is not included. Owen (1996) suggests that there are 1345

Summary Box 6.1 *Key non-departmental public bodies*

	Executive agencies (staff nos.)	Other
DoE	Audit Commission (1324) Countryside Commission (252) English Partnerships (407) Environment Agency (9450) 6 Housing Action Trusts (592) Housing Corporation (637) English Nature (753) Rural Development Commission (309) 10 Urban Development Corporations (586)	RCEP Property Advisory Group LG Commission Expert Panel on Air Quality Standards Advisory Panel on Standards for Planning Inspectorate Radioactive Waste Management Advisory Committee
	32 in total	*15 in total*
Department of Culture, Media and Sport	English Heritage (1567) Royal Commission on Historic Monuments of England (245)	
	37 in total	
Welsh Office	Countryside Commission for Wales (293) Development Board for Rural Wales (100) Land Authority for Wales (48) Housing for Wales (67) Royal Commission on Art and Historic Monuments in Wales (34) Welsh Development Agency (327)	
Scottish Office	Scottish Natural Heritage (625) Royal Commission on Historic Monuments of Scotland (68) Scottish Environmental Protection Agency (552) Scottish Enterprise (1443) Scottish Homes (1034)	
N. Ireland Depts.	Council for Nature Conservation and Countryside Historic Buildings Council	

Source: Civil Service Yearbook, Civil Service Statistics.

non-departmental public bodies and altogether 5000–6000 quangos, responsible for £50 billion per annum of public money and accounting for 60 000 board appointments. Of the appointments in public bodies, 69 per cent are male, rising for 76 per cent for executive agencies, and only 3.3 per cent are from the ethnic minorities.

The main complaint concerning the proliferation of such quangos, whatever their function, is their insulation from public pressure (Weale *et al.*, 1991). It is not just that they are unelected bodies and the chains of control from the public are weak. As Rees has outlined (1990, p. 373): 'Conflicts of interest are not, therefore, mediated by locating the different functions and decision-making modes of the state at different levels of government, but become buried by the mysticism which surrounds the technical expert.' This has implications for the role of professionals within quangos which is discussed further in Chapter 8. Given this divorce from democratic and popular control, Rees argues that 'Dissatisfaction with [quangos] has rarely resulted in their total abolition, rather new, higher-tier authorities are created as controls, or advisory and coordinating committees are provided to improve performance' (p. 381).

Isolated from democratic control these agencies can be subject to pressure from sectional interests through corporatist relations between the interest and the quango, in which policy practice is effectively jointly decided through extensive consultation. In particular they can develop close relationships with the very interests they may have been established to manage, regulate and control. The Industrial Air Pollution Inspectorate that preceded HMIP (now part of the Environment Agency) was criticised by the Royal Commission on Environmental Pollution as having too close a relation with the industry it was meant to control. Rees points out (p. 373) that once 'established central- and regional-level agencies are undoubtedly subject to corporatist pressures'. But she goes on to argue:

> But this should nor obscure the fact that the agencies develop an internal, professionally dominated, logic which critically affects the way they interpret their functions and by no means all professional groups support the expansion of private sector production and its profitability.

The nature of the professional and management culture will be decisive (see also Exhibit 8.1 in Chapter 8).

Whether this isolation from public pressure and tendency to corporatist pressures matters depends on the viewpoint adopted. For the New Right links with the commercial sector at the expense of local democracy are justified since the private sector is seen as dependent on and hence able to represent the public as consumers. The concern has rather been with the efficiency of the body and its value for money. To this end the National Audit Office maintains a scrutiny role in relation to central government-created quangos. However from other perspectives, the isolation may be a problem if it results in valuable information for decision-making being lost or the political goals of policy being misinterpreted. Quangos also thereby lose out on the opportunity to mediate between the full range of interests affected by the quango and the manner of a quango's decision-making can mask the inequalities arising from its actions. As Rees argues (1990, p. 346), many of these institutions become heavily influenced by the technocratic approach commonly adopted by the managers that run them. These 'tend not to see the political and allocative nature of their activities' and see their role rather in terms of technological fix, maintaining output or achieving economic efficiency.

Thus Rees concluded on the Industrial Air Pollution Inspectorate and its US counterpart (p. 397):

> the elitist and technocratic stance of the Inspectorates and their continued reluctance to involve the public in the bargaining process has produced much hostility and suspicion. The political nature of control decisions is ignored. Rather the whole process is viewed as a neutral technical matter. Calls for greater freedom of information have been dismissed as a 'waste of expert professional time', a 'distraction' from the 'highly technical job' which inspectors 'are employed to do' . . . However, no technical exercise can be neutral – all decisions on pollution control standards inevitably affect the distribution of real income and welfare between different groups within society.

This distributive issue is repeatedly ignored in the way many quangos tackle their tasks.

In some cases quangos may actively try to suppress concerns about this distributive impact. McCormick argues that agencies such as the NCC have in the past actively tried to moderate the demands of pressure groups with whom they are in contact in order to present a professional, apolitical face to central government (1991, p. 25). One of the advantages of maintaining a technocratic approach, which largely disregards outside political claims, is that central government will look on the agency with more favour and, after all, such agencies are dependent on central government for their very existence. For example, the NCC and the Countryside Commission were widely regarded as ineffective, powerless and secretive in the early 1980s (Lowe *et al.*, 1986, p. 133). They remained divorced from public concerns over the countryside and sought to remain aloof from the conflicts between farming and forestry interests on the one hand and rural conservation on the other. They were seen to be having a corporatist relation to these farming and forestry interests. But, as McCormick details (1991, pp. 17–18), by the late 1980s they were taking a more critical line with regard to government policy and the activities of key rural business interests. Many environmentalists saw a link between this shift in attitude and the proposals for merging the councils that central government announced in July 1989: 'There was a suspicion among environmental groups that the two agencies became too effective at slowing down the conversion of natural habitat to farmland.' This is a cautionary tale for quangos indeed.

Does this account of the critique of quangos and their operation suggest that quangos have no legitimate role? Certainly there has been widespread support for the new Environment Agency for England and Wales and its equivalent, the Scottish Environmental Protection Agency (SEPA) (Wilder and Plant, 1992). The Environment Agency is charged with a role in relation to contaminated land, air quality management, the national waste strategy and the producer responsibility for waste initiative, as well as taking over the functions of HMIP and the NRA and the local authorities' waste regulation duties; the SEPA has similar functions. In England the agency is organised into eight regions, largely based on the river catchment areas which defined the old water authorities, and 22 subregional areas (of about two counties each). There is a consultative framework in the form of Regional Environmental Protection Advisory Committees, with about twenty members each of whom five or six will be from the local authorities. Among the reasons put forward for supporting such quangos is their role in raising the profile of environmental protection, achieving a strategic overview and fostering integration between policy areas. They can also create career opportunities for specialists and thus foster education and training in these areas. It is also argued that the requirements of economies of scale in technical and research facilities and of integration in decision-making within pollution control support the need for such an agency.

However the above criticisms emphasise that safeguards are also needed to ensure the openness of the agencies' operation and the scope for democratic control of their activities in any particular locality. For this reason the Labour government issued a consultation paper in November 1997 entitled *Opening Up Quangos* to discuss ways in which quangos could be made more accountable. They are also ensuring that the proposed Regional Development Agencies are shadowed by a consultative body, which may in due course become an elected body.

■ The European dimension

There is no doubt that urban and environmental planning policy within Britain is increasingly having to conform with policy decisions made at the European and the international level. It is estimated that about 80 per cent of British environmental policy now emanates from the European Union. This section reviews the nature of that influence.

The European Community (EC) which became the European Union (EU) was based on six states sharing common borders and signatories to three treaties: the European Coal and Steel Community treaty, the Euratom treaty and the European Economic Community treaty (the 1957 Treaty of Rome). The emphasis was on establishing a free trade area. Since then the institutions and membership of the EU (as it is now known) have grown. The UK joined in 1973 with Ireland and Denmark; by 1986 there were twelve members; by 1995 there were fifteen, plus the old East Germany area. Six more former Eastern European countries are also due to enlarge the Union further. While the Union was set up to promote trade, it has from its earliest days pursued other policy objectives as well. In particular, there are two areas of policy activity where the EU has always had considerable significance. First, the strength of the farming lobby within original member states led to the Common Agriculture Policy (CAP) whereby an expensive system of financial support was provided for agricultural production. As Chapter 12 will explore, the CAP has had profound consequences for the British countryside. Eventually the high cost of the policy and the continued evidence of administrative failure in terms of butter mountains and wine lakes led to its reform, beginning with milk quotas introduced in 1984. Evidence of the adverse environmental impact of many agricultural practices promoted under the CAP further strengthened the case for reform. This reform has continued to reduce the amount of money directly pumped into encouraging agricultural production, although the total sum remains extremely high (Fennell, 1990). In 1996 the total CAP expenditure in the UK amounted to £2750 million.

Second, the EU has always sought to mitigate the effects of its competitive trade policy through programmes of grants to depressed areas, such as the Social Fund and Regional Development Fund. For a time these European monies merely reinforced British regional policy, for it had always been required that European funds can go only to areas and projects where some British government monies were already available; European support had been regarded as a supplement, not a replacement for national programmes. The EU and national subsidy programmes are now being delinked, in part as a response to the economic effects on regions of the integrated European market. The growth of European grant programmes is an important aspect of British planning now, as Chapter 12 and particularly Chapter 13 emphasise.

Economic issues continue to dominate the European agenda, as witnessed by the creation of a Single European Market under the 1986 Single European Act and the repeated attempts to move towards European monetary union. However alongside this overriding policy objective has gone a growing policy agenda concerned with social and other issues. The influence of socialists within the Parliament and Council of Ministers has fostered labour protection legislation for example. Of particular relevance to planning concerns has been the growing significance of EU environmental policy during the 1980s and 1990s. The original Treaty of Rome establishing the Community made no reference to the environment. However, following the 1972 United Nations Conference on the Human Environment, the first of five environmental action programmes at the EU level was announced. The first two contained largely remedial measures but more recent programmes have been increasingly proactive. Since these environmental programmes had no specific basis in the Treaty, policy measures were authorised under Article 110 concerning the removal of trade barriers or the 'catch all' Article 235. Specific responsibility for environmental protection was given to the EU by Article 25 of the 1986 Single European Act, provided that the objective of the policy could be better obtained at the Community rather than at nation state level. The 1986 Act also requires environmental protection to be written into all EU policy and states a commitment to the 'polluter pays principle', the latter underpinning moves towards full corporate liability for environmental damage. The 1986 Act and announcements at European Council meetings in 1988 and 1990 continued to argue that the single market and high standards of environmental protection were integrally related, the one supporting the other.

Under these various provisions, hundreds of measures of environmental protection have been passed at Community level since 1973. The Fifth Environmental Action Plan, covering the period 1993–2000 and supported by a Community environment fund, LIFE, has expanded EU involvement even further. Work is also under way within the Commission reviewing this plan, with a view to developing a more stringent and effective version for the next period. McCormick (1991, p. 20) concludes that:

> Against a background of variable government interest in environmental regulation, the role and influence of the EC in environment policy-making has grown. In fact, it is now arguably the single most important and effective influence on British environmental policy and politics.

It is therefore worthwhile briefly covering the way in which the EU works. The five principle institutions of Europe are the European Commission, the Council of Ministers, the European Council, the European Parliament and the European Court of Justice (see Summary Box 6.2). The Commission is the powerful executive of the union, employing 15 000 staff and headed up by 20 commissioners, appointed by national governments. The President is drawn from these commissioners. The Commission is divided into 24 Directorates-General. Those relevant to planning include: DGV Employment, Industrial Relations and Social

Summary Box 6.2   *The policy-making institutions of the European Union*

Institution	Function	Composition
European Commission	Policy formulation and implementation	Commissioners appointed, substantial executive
Council of Ministers	Decisions on Commission's proposals	Representatives of national governments
European Council	International summit	Heads of government
European Parliament	Debates, limited power	Directly elected Members of the European Parliament

Affairs, DGVI Agriculture, DGVII Transport, DGVIII Development, DGXI Environment, Nuclear Safety and Civil Protection, DG XVI Regional Policies, and DGXVII Energy. The roles of the Commission are to be the permanent secretariat, to act as a watchdog for the Union over individual states, to mediate between institutions or states and, most importantly, to take the initiative in developing policy proposals.

The Council of Ministers comprises departmental ministers from national governments meeting by portfolio (that is, finance ministers together, environment ministers together, and so on) and this has the final say on most issues unless there is strong Commission and/or parliamentary resistance. The business of the council is organised by the Committee of Ambassadors to the EU (COREPER) and various treaties determine whether majority or unanimous voting prevails on any particular issue; qualified majority voting is now increasingly the norm. The European Council brings together heads of state or government two or three times a year to set the overall agenda for the European project. The presidency is occupied by each member state for a six month period. The directly democratically elected institution of Europe is the European Parliament; it received a direct mandate from voters only in 1979 but its influence, power and legitimacy are growing. It is not a legislature; that role remains with the Council of Ministers. It can block, challenge and discuss and also, in extreme circumstances, dismiss the Commission. The European Court of Justice has become increasingly important also. It, together with the Court of First Instance, can interpret European treaties and legislation, hear individual cases, assert the dominance of European law over national law and impose fines. The UK government has been fined for not complying with European law.

In addition to these main institutions there are many other organisations and agencies: for example, the nascent European Central Bank, the European Monetary Institute and the European Environment Agency (see below). There are also some 380 committees which have been established to advise, consult and promote policy for specialised areas. One significant committee is the Committee of the Regions which seeks to represent the regional level more directly within the institutions of the Union, through the elected representatives of local government in the different regions.

In terms of direct influence on British or any other national policy, there are four tools available: regulations which apply equally in all member states and are directly binding; decisions which bind only the parties involved in the specific issue on which the Commission has been asked to adjudicate; directives which bind member states to the objectives of the policy but allow each state to find its own way of implementing these objectives; and recommendations and opinions which have no binding force but carry some weight given the other powers at the Commission's disposal. There has been a move away from the use of advisory policy documents and selective subsidies and grants to steer domestic policy towards a greater use of formal legislative tools. The significance of these tools is that the European Commission is the only international organisation in the world with the power to agree environmental policies which bind member states.

The EU has particularly relied on directives to prompt national-level legislation. The directive on wild birds required the government to enact new legislation leading to the Wildlife and Countryside Act 1981. Despite opposition from the government and major lobby groups such as the CBI, environmental assessments (EAs) were introduced using the 1985 directive. In 1988 the directive on large combustion plants required the introduction of new technology to reduce the emissions causing acid rain and in 1989 the EU took the British government to the European Court of Justice over failure to meet EU water quality standards set down in a directive. The directive has proved a very effective policy tool from the EU's viewpoint and new directives are in the pipeline. Golub (1996) argues that while there may be disagreements on individual cases, the use of directives allowed a degree of discretion to national governments. Under the Conservative Government this discretion was exploited to the full to maintain the traditional British stance on environmental policy and particularly pollution control. The traditional British approach embodies considerable discretionary power for enforcement agencies and an emphasis on indicators of ambient environmental quality. However, the negotiations between the British government and the European Commission on a series of directives have managed to modify the traditional approach. Britain has had to adopt a more technology-led approach and comply with many emissions-based standards (O'Brien and Penna, 1997). The requirement to adopt flue-gas desulphurisation equipment in power plants is an example of this. The discretion involved in the use of directives, therefore, provides a basis for negotiation between member states and the EU and does not directly determine the outcome of that negotiation.

It seems likely that the EU in the future will take a more directly involved role in environmental matters. This will take four forms. First, there is likely to be greater use of fiscal or market-based instruments, such as carbon taxes. These receive specific mention in the Fifth Environmental Action Programme. Negotiations on their introduction have stalled on the economic implications but they remain a policy option and may achieve more prominence now that targets for reducing greenhouse gas emissions have been agreed at the December 1997 Kyoto Summit. Second, there may be a shift from the directive towards the regulation as the main framework for environmental policy in many areas is established and the emphasis moves towards filling in the detail. Third, there is the operation of the European Environmental Agency (EEA) and the possibility of other European environment agencies. The EEA itself is charged with three main functions: to oversee the implementation of European environmental legislation; to encourage the diffusion of information and research; and to act as a reference centre or information clearing-house, with an EU-wide environment database. The agency is intended to support enforcement activity and policy-making rather than undertake enforcement itself.

Fourth, the EU is developing a sophisticated form of strategic policy advice to guide local policy-making. In 1990 it issued a Green Paper on the Urban Environment which sought to air some guidelines for urban planning practice and promote a vision for European towns and cities. In 1991 the first in a series of *Europe 2000+* documents was published setting out spatial trends within the Community. This established a form of regionalism as the likely key unit for EU indicative strategic planning. The UK falls into three interregional groupings: the North Sea Region; the North Western Metropolitan Area (approximately the south-east of England); and the Atlantic Arc. Work on a European Spatial Development Perspective (ESDP) has also advanced to the point where a full draft will be presented to ministers in June 1998. The full version should be complete by 1999. This will highlight the transnational, Europe-wide and cross-border implications of member states' regional planning policies. It will also consider the spatial implications of other EU policies and strengthen the interrelation between European urban and rural policies. Finally the ESDP seeks to act as a mechanism for synthesising the three EU goals of economic and social cohesion, sustainable development and the competitiveness of the Union.

Fifth, the EU continues to act as a focal point for networking across Europe on many issues, including sustainability. For example, the Commission has set up an Expert Group on the Urban Environment, which in 1993 launched the Sustainable Cities Project with the aim of contributing to thinking about urban sustainability, fostering the exchange of experience, disseminating best practice and formulating recommendations to influence policy-making at all levels. This has produced a number of reports including a good practice guide. And sixth, the significance of EU grant programmes continues to grow, not only funding new projects but also influencing the type of project that is put forward to funding (see Exhibit 6.1 and Chapter 13 for details of the proposed restructuring of EU grants schemes).

Certain EU actions also greatly strengthen the ability of third parties within Britain to challenge environmental policy practice. The 1990 EC directive on Freedom of Access to Information on the Environment No. 90/313 will open up public bodies to watchdog activity by pressure groups. And the proposed directive on Civil Liability for Damage caused by Waste suggests the prospects of new categories of environmental liability which can be enforced in British courts. This form of liability already operates in the USA and imposes considerable costs on polluters in accordance with the 'polluter pays principle'. As Faulks (1991, p. 20) says: 'It would not be unrealistic to suggest that the introduction of the concept of impairment of the environment as an actionable tort heralds a new era in the European Community environmental legislation programme.'

The Conservative government used negotiation over the 1992 Maastricht Treaty to try and 'repatriate' environmental policy to the national level, using the principle of subsidiarity – by which policies should be dealt with at the lowest possible level for effective implementation – as a negotiating tool. The debate about subsidiarity in relation to environmental policy has resulted in the Commission's power to enforce some directives being devolved to nation states, including water quality directives where the Commission was in conflict with Britain. The proposed legal action over failure to comply with the EA directive in the case of the M3 extension was also dropped in the wake of the subsidiarity debate. The emphasis of the government until 1997 has been to maintain as much discretion as possible for the traditional British approach to environmental policy – dilute and absorb – rather than accept the more preventative and technology-led European approach (Golub, 1996). In its negotiations in pursuit of this objective, the British government has been successful in blocking unwanted proposals and amending others. However Golub demonstrates how this has not slowed the pace of European environmental policy because of the impact of qualified majority voting and the results of individual bargains struck on specific issues. For these

---

Exhibit 6.1   *The European Union grant programmes*

The EU now exerts strong influence at the level of the region and locality through its grant programmes. The cornerstone of this is the structural fund package, comprising four key programmes: the European Regional Development Fund (ERDF), the European Social Fund (ESF),the European Agriculture Guidance and Guarantee Fund (EAGGF/FEOGA) and the Financial Instrument for Fisheries Guidance (FIFG). The expenditure of monies from these funds follows certain key principles: they are concentrated on areas of most need; grants are programme- rather than project-specific; they should involve a partnership between the Commission of European Communities (CEC), national, regional and local government; national, regional and local economic policies should be supported, not undermined, by the application of grants; and the principle of additionality applies, whereby grants supplement rather than replace other grant support.

The CEC has set out five objectives for these grant funds for the period 1994–9; these are currently under review for the period into the next century under the Agenda 2000 process (see Chapter 13):

Objective 1 – to promote development and structural adjustment in regions lagging behind;
Objective 2 – to convert areas affected by industrial decline;
Objective 3 – to combat long-term unemployment and integrate young people into the labour market;
Objective 4 – to facilitate adaptation by workers to industrial change;
Objective 5a – to speed up adjustment in agricultural and fisheries structures; and
Objective 5b – to facilitate development and adjustment of rural areas.

All parts of the UK currently qualify for funding under Objectives 3, 4, and 5a. 'Least favoured region' status under Objective 1 is accorded to Northern Ireland, Merseyside and the Scottish Highlands and Islands Enterprise Area. One hundred individual areas, mostly at the scale of a travel-to-work area, are listed as eligible for Objective 2 funding, and a more limited list of 26 areas, mostly at the scale of part of a county, are designated for Objective 5b funding. Designation under the structural funds provides a major opportunity for local authorities and others to apply for often substantial funds. The EU has effectively created a new map of regional and urban assistance which has

---

reasons, subsidiarity has not proved the brake on EU environment policy that was envisaged.

The real brake on EU environment policy remains the potential for conflicts with the economic agenda. For example the EU has developed a strategy for integrated trans-European networks (TENs); these should comprise an efficient, multi-modal transport system across Europe structured first and foremost by environmental considerations. This fits within the framework set out in the 1992 Green Paper on *The Impact of*

an impact on almost all areas of the UK; it would be difficult to find a region which does not contain at least one area eligible for funding under one or more objective. This means that it is worthwhile for local authorities to develop their linkages with the CEC, to upgrade information on European policies and priorities and to effectively lobby within the commission, and to a lesser extent within the Parliament.

In addition there is a package of thirteen initiatives which will take up 9 per cent of the structural funds during 1994–9:

ADAPT – focused on the labour market
European and Human Resources – comprising Now, aimed at women, Horizon, aimed at disadvantaged groups, and Youthstart, aimed at youth
Interreg II – focused on border areas
Konver – focused on defence sector areas
Leader II – focused on the rural economy
PESCA – focused on the fishing industry
Portuguese Textile and Clothing Industry
RECHAR II – focused on coal-mining areas
REGIS II – focused on island regions
RESIDER II – focused on steel industry areas
RETEX – focused on textiles and clothing areas
SMES – for small and medium enterprises
URBAN – focused on urban areas

Parts of the UK or specific industrial sectors are eligible for assistance under all these initiatives except Konver, REGIS and the Portuguese programme.

Other forms of assistance are also made available by the EU through business loans, business support and aid for technological innovation and development, education and training and cultural grant programmes. Finally the European Social Cohesion Fund is a major new programme for environmental and transport infrastructure projects announced in 1993; only Spain, Portugal, Greece and Ireland are eligible under this fund.

The net conclusion is that the EU is a significant source of funds, and in some localities can be more significant than national sources. This is not just a shift in policy detail but alters the pattern of relationship between organisations, encouraging many local authorities to bypass central government and engage directly in European governance networks.

Transport on the Environment which tackled the problematic issue of the relationship between transport and environmental policy, and suggested EU-led constraints on traffic growth in pursuit of the goal of 'sustainable mobility'. However, the demands of transporting people and goods arising from the Single Market remain a strong influence on policy and the concept of 'sustainable mobility' struggles to combine the different pressures on transport policy at the European level. Currently the European transport budget is split 60 per cent towards road and 30 per cent towards rail, while it is estimated that these proportions would have to be reversed to meet environmental targets (O'Brien and Penna, 1997). The EU has given £25 million to the UK for TENs schemes but it is notable that £15.6 million went to the Channel Tunnel Rail Link, a project not usually regarded in terms of its environmental benefits. Similarly the 1994 interim review of the Fifth Environmental Action Programme concluded that there was a general unwillingness to accept the goal of sustainable development within the Commission (as well as individual member states) and a tendency to see it as just the concern of those dealing with environmental policy. A larger quantum of European environmental regulation is one thing; achieving a higher priority for sustainability goals across European institutions is quite another.

■ Further reading

For work on agencies and quangos, the reader is referred to Rees (1990) and Dowding (1995b), and also to the annual reports produced by the individual agencies, many available on their websites. The National Audit Office produces reports on various agencies as well. The European Union is well-covered in McCormick (1991) for the general politics, Williams (1996) for spatial planning, and Holder (1997) for environmental law. Some recent case studies can be found in Baker *et al.* (1997) and Lowe and Ward (1998). Relevant journals include the *Journal of European Planning Studies*, *European Environment* and *European Environmental Law Review*. The Commission's website can also be consulted at: http://europa.eu.int.

■ *Chapter 7* ■

Lobbies and Interests

People and organisations outside the state interact with the planning system in a number of ways: as a 'client' applying for permission or authorisation or making representations on policy and decisions; by campaigning and through the lobbying tactics of pressure groups; and through the party political system. This chapter covers the last two forms of public pressure. It builds on the examination of the different state organisations in Chapters 5 and 6, which included an account of their variable openness to outside groups. The first form of public pressure, the client relationship, is discussed in the next chapter in the context of the professionalisation of planners. As before, the chapter begins with an account of how groups outside the state can be analysed.

■ Analysing groups

The terminology for analysing groups within political science is not undisputed. Indeed 'the tendency of different writers to espouse different terms is a source of confusion for many students approaching the subject for the first time' (Kimber and Richardson, 1974, p. 1). Some political analysts prefer to focus on interest groups where group formation is based on a shared location within economic processes. Pressure groups are then distinguished from interest groups by also having shared values, which may not relate directly to the participants' economic roles. Others see pressure and interest groups, so defined, as two sides of the same coin with little practical distinction possible. Again analysts differ in terms of how the interests, on which group formation is based, are defined. Some are willing to accept the group's own self-definition. Others argue that this is subjective and clouded by the operation of ideological processes within society. The analyst thus may more clearly be able to relate a group's interests to its role in economic and social processes.

These issues of interest versus pressure groups and subjective versus objective assessment of interests are hotly debated in the political science literature but it is not relevant to cover them in more depth here (see Saunders, 1979). Rather than adopting a strict definition of the type of

135

group to be examined, a broad range of groups will be discussed and issues of definition covered as they arise in particular cases. For working purposes, a pressure group may be defined as 'any group . . . which articulates a demand that the authorities in the political system or subsystems should make an authoritative allocation . . . such groups do not themselves seek to occupy positions of authority' (Kimber and Richardson, 1974, pp. 2–3).

However one defines a pressure group or interest group, the interesting questions really relate to how such a group is created and grows, and what kind of influence it has on government policy. Traditional liberal political science operates with a version of pluralism. In a pluralist perspective groups arise because of demand among their (potential) members. Where there is a concern, a group will form to express that concern and seek to influence policy accordingly. Such a concern may reflect the economic interests of members but may also be based on their values and beliefs. As demand changes so the pattern of groups will change, the supply of groups' services essentially responding to that demand. There may be inequalities in the resources that different groups of members can bring to groups but there is little consideration of there being fundamental barriers to the formation of such groups. Similarly pluralist perspectives find themselves at a point towards the autonomy end along the spectrum of state autonomy – state capture (see Chapter 6). The state is relatively unconstrained in choosing between groups in terms of the influence accorded during the policy process. And there is a presupposition that 'good' arguments and reasons put forward will enhance influence. Less extreme versions may acknowledge the existence of corporatist relationships and favouritism on the part of the state towards certain groups, which of itself enables those groups to present themselves as more successful and to attract more membership.

Marxist approaches have less interest in the range of groups that participate in the policy process. Their analysis is fundamentally based in the categorisation of interests in relation to the production process; hence as fractions of capital or labour. Work in the Gramscian tradition and exemplified by some of Castells's work has sought to supplement this class analysis with a recognition of the impact that campaigning by groups formed around consumption issues or identity politics can have. Such social movements might include environmental groups, gay and lesbian groups and women's groups, as well as residence-based resistances to development proposals. Castells has looked particularly at those groups which fulfil his definition of urban social movements, namely: organisation around issues of collective consumption, focusing on the use value of the city rather than its exchange value; the search for cultural identity, for the goal of community; and the demand for more power for local government, neighbourhood decentralisation and urban self-management, constituting a citizens' movement (1983). Where these three goals are pursued jointly in political action (in the group's praxis), then the group has the potential to become a social movement with the consequent scope for achieving change. For this potential to be fulfilled though the group must be self-conscious of itself as an urban social movement, connected to the key actors of the media, professions and political parties and yet organisationally and ideologically autonomous. When all these conditions are fulfilled, urban protest becomes something more significant. They have the potential to change the meaning of the city. However, the concern of Marxists is to identify the extent to which action by groups constitutes radical activity, which challenges the dominant capitalist mode of accumulation. Castells argues that an urban social movement cannot on its own transform society since they are not connected to mechanisms for transforming production processes and only operate at the level of the locality in an increasingly globalised world. Marxists, therefore, remain equivocal about the impact of such social movements and suspicious of some groups, such as environmental groups, which they regard as middle-class interest groups cloaked in an appropriate ideology. These points are taken up below in the discussion of the environmental movement.

Increasingly influential are more recent developments of public choice work on groups. This takes neither the rather complacent position of pluralists (and their variants) nor the single-minded view of Marxists, but rather asks for a reexamination of the internal dynamics of groups to explain their existence and actions. The classic text on which this work builds is Olson's *The Logic Of Collective Action* (1978; see also Dunleavy, 1991). This questioned the very basis of both the liberal and Marxist approaches in that it argued that even where a common interest or concern existed among a group of people, there could be good reasons why a formal group did not arise, or if it did arise why its growth might be constrained. Olson drew attention to the costs of group formation and to the imbalance that often exists between the costs and benefits to an individual of joining a group. Where a group's actions may benefit many, but there are costs to an individual of joining a group in terms of time, money and other resources, this may encourage people to free-ride on the group's actions, rather than be part of the limited number who bear the costs of the group's formation and continued maintenance. This is compounded where the chances of the group achieving its objectives are uncertain, while the costs of joining in are certain. Yet another contributory factor is the limited information many people have on a range of policy issues, there being no incentive to expend resources to obtain such information when the chances of influencing government policy through group action are low. Olson saw three solutions to the free-rider problem: keeping groups small; using surplus resources generated by a group formed for some other reason; and the use of selective material benefits to attract members. It is generally also acknowledged that there may be 'extra-rational' motives, such as altruism, which motivate people to join, though these are relegated to a marginal, not central, explanatory role.

Another mechanism identified for overcoming the collective action problems of group formation is the existence of a political entrepreneur, responding to some social disturbance – events, legislation, climate of opinion. A similar role is played in maintaining a group by patrons, who inject significant resources into a group to keep it going (Nownes and Neeley, 1997; Walker, 1991). This kind of questioning of the rationale and performance of groups, in terms of calculations between the costs and benefits of certain courses of action, provides a fresh perspective on groups which can challenge some commonly held assumptions about the desirability and effectiveness of pressure on government policy from such groups.

Groups relevant to planning policy can be divided into the following: business interests, particularly the development lobby and the farming lobby and, ranged largely in opposition to such groups, anti-development groups and the other elements in the environmental movement, including discussion of local amenity groups. Each category will be discussed in more detail below.

■ Business interest groups

Business interest groups are the classic case of an interest group where the members have a common role in the economic process. Although in competition with each other in everyday economic activities, such firms recognise the common benefits of grouping together to influence public policy. The aim is to restructure the policy framework to enhance conditions for profit-making. The business lobby thus comprises a number of interest groups from the overarching CBI to sector-specific groups such as the Building Materials Producers' Association or oligopolistic firms such as the electricity supply industry who lobby directly on their own behalf. In 1972 it was estimated that there were 2500 employers' associations, of which at least 1600 were active (Kimber and Richardson, 1974, p. 10). The potential membership of such groups is limited and fairly easy to identify but the coverage of that membership by a particular group will depend on the group demonstrating activity in lobbying policy-makers on behalf of its members. However there is always the possibility for a potential member to 'free-ride' on the successes of the group without actually joining.

Therefore, in some cases the tendency for members to abstain or exit from the group is reduced by the application of specific sanctions or selective incentives (Dunleavy and O'Leary, 1987).

The number of such groups is so great and they are so diverse in nature that is it is not possible to survey them here. Suffice it to say that in many areas of urban and environmental planning one or more business interest groups will be seeking to exert influence. This may take the form of the CBI's opposition to the introduction of environmental assessment (EAs). It may represent the demands of chambers of commerce for local economic development aid. Within the general business lobby there are bound to be conflicts and inequalities. Thus the electricity supply industry has different concerns from the energy efficiency industry. The former is represented by a small group of organised firms, until recently forming a nationalised industry. In their pursuit of a particular policy goal, the expansion of nuclear power, former Secretary of State for Energy, Tony Benn, has said: 'In my political life, I have never known such a well-organised, scientific, industrial and technical lobby as the nuclear power lobby' (Roberts *et al.*, 1991, p. 44). Yet, by contrast, the energy efficiency industry (that is, the business interests as opposed to the environmentalists) is represented by a fragmented group of over twenty trade associations. The strength of all business interest groups lies not in the size of their membership but in the control that members hold over economic resources and their use in production and investment processes. This 'corporate discretion' of business interests means that they are sought as consultees by government and do not have to push against a closed door in their political activities (Lindblom, 1977). Furthermore, those groups representing the more economically powerful firms will hold more sway than those comprising the smaller firms. This feature is particularly seen in the case of development interest groups which are considered further below, along with the farming lobby.

At the national level the operation of corporate discretion will mean that nationally powerful economic actors have easy access to ministers and, particularly, civil servants in the administration (Saunders, 1985). At the local level, the situation is not so clear-cut. In Conservative-controlled councils, a local business interest will have ready contacts with local politicians and may even be an elected councillor (Saunders, 1979). In Labour authorities, business interests may more readily make contact with local government professionals and administrators. It will also be easier for business interests to dominate the council where the councillors are not drawn from the commuter community, dependent on external income from outside the local area, but represent local business as employers or employees (Rees, 1990, p. 409). It is clear that during the 1980s business influence at the local government level increased. Since 1984, local authorities have had to consult non-domestic ratepayers, a consultative role usually taken by local chambers of commerce.

In response to these changes, a literature has developed which tries to conceptualise the current relationship of local authorities to such interests. Previously the assumption had been that local authorities were more open to interests based around consumption issues, while business interests largely looked to the central government level for access and effective lobbying; this argument was captured in Saunder's dual state thesis (1981). However the evidence of involvement of business interests in local economic development and local urban regeneration schemes suggested that local growth coalitions were forming to harness local planning to the promotion of a private sector economic agenda (Harding 1990). The term 'growth coalition' was borrowed from the US experience (Logan and Molotch, 1987), where the incentive of a local taxation system based on property values encouraged local councils to work closely with property development and other economic interests to undertake programmes of redevelopment, regeneration and urban expansion. The introduction of the NNDR and the historically different role of local government in Britain rendered this model less applicable than in the USA. More recently the concept of the urban regime has become more widely used (Harding, 1994, provides a review). Again a conceptual import from the USA, an urban regime describes 'an informal yet relatively stable group with access to institutional resources that enable it to have a sustained role in making governing decisions' (Stone, 1989, p. 4). It marries the formal characteristics of the local authority with informal relations among elites, and issues of the mobilisation of resources with those of the mobilisation of bias and leadership. As such it represents a consolidation and generalisation of corporatist decision-making at the local level since the purpose of urban regimes is to enlarge the local authority's 'capacity to act' (Stone's definition of power) by engaging in relations with other actors. The concept fits well with contemporary trends towards patterns of urban governance (see Chapter 5) but the particular local circumstances will determine the form that a specific urban regime takes. Stoker and Mossberger (1994) distinguish three regimes: organic, instrumental and symbolic.

While such a typology is helpful in generalising the concept, certain adjustments need to be made in transferring the concept to the European and British context. Newman (1994) identifies a number: acknowledging the greater importance of central government, central–local relations, access to central government resources and the specific structures of national institutions; the Europeanisation of policy and politics; the distinction between the scale of city governance and the scale of many coalitions on specific development projects; the continuing extent of public sector involvement in urban policy; the importance of non-material benefits in partnership arrangements; the greater role of professionals; and the continuing influence of party politics at the local level. However, despite this long list of adjustments, it has been argued that the urban regime concept is helpful in looking at how business interests work with local government, in a relatively stable rather than *ad hoc* way, to formulate and implement government policy at the local level. Reviewing the literature, Stoker and Wilson (1991, p. 30) conclude:

> The future world of local pressure group activity is likely to see increased influence for business and opportunities for it to take a leading role. But there are a number of limitations on the capacity of the business sector to offer leadership and on its ability to maintain a coherent and co-ordinated policy programme. It may not be as easy as some analysts imagine for business to usurp the local authorities' control and management of the local political agenda.

☐ *The development lobby*

Development interest groups are a business interest group defined by the common role of its members – housebuilders, property developers and construction companies – in creating and transforming the built environment (see Chapter 9 for an account of this process). They have a primary interest in the land use planning system given its central role in permitting development rights, but also in many of the other regulatory aspects of planning. Examples of such groups are the Building Employers' Confederation (BEC), the House Builders' Federation (HBF) within it, and the Federation of Master Builders. There are also the professions which work for or with development interests, notably the RICS, the RIBA and various property researchers' groups, such as the Society of Property Researchers and the Property Investment Group. As with other business interest groups, development interest groups use incentives and sanctions to maintain membership. For example, the BEC offers journals, advice services and indemnity schemes. Membership of a group, along with associated insurance or quality vetting, may be a substantial advantage in development activity. Dunleavy and O'Leary (1987) identify interest groups where selective incentives are used and there is a high-percentage membership as one example of a stable group with a relatively long-term presence in policy making. They are further characterised by strong leadership control and low participation by members in political activities. This provides a good description of most development interest groups.

There is, however, a limited number of smaller, more exclusive groups which do not seek a large membership base. These are closed groups of major economic actors who operate effectively as an advisory committee

within government decision-making. The small number of members is essential for the practicalities of government consultation and to enable the group to represent itself as the pinnacle of the development industry. Such groups, which include the Property Advisory Group, and in the past the Volume Builders' Study Group, are so incorporated into government policy-making that they look only inwards towards the public sector and have no function with respect to a wider membership (Rydin 1986).

The importance of such small development interest groups highlights the point that the influence of such groups is not necessarily related to their membership size, but to their control of economic resources. It is not the case that large numbers necessarily speak louder in policy circles. Hence the closed groups, representing only a few major firms, are incorporated into policy-making while other more open development interest groups, such as the Federation of Master Builders, have to engage in the routine campaigning and lobbying of other pressure groups. But while their position as economic agents responsible for undertaking development may give them advantages in such political campaigning, it does not always ensure that their viewpoint will prevail over other pressure groups' point of view. The above has largely focused on the importance of the development lobby in national policy-making, but the whole literature on urban regimes, growth coalitions and development coalitions has emphasised the important role that particular actors within the development industry may have in local politics and in local planning decisions.

Looking at individual property and development companies, Adams draws attention to ways in which companies commission professional expertise, both legal and planning expertise, in order to challenge local planning decisions and influence strategic planning (1994). While they do so in order to protect their development opportunities and the value of landholdings, they have the benefit of collective organisations. For example, for residential developers, the HBF will make representations on structure plans, unitary development plans (UDPs) and sometimes local plans on their members' behalf and will offer advice in relation to individual planning appeals, where documentation used to challenge development plans may also prove useful to the developer's case. The HBF is also involved in local housing land assessment exercises which can also be used to support individual applications and appeals (see Exhibit 10.1).

☐ The farming lobby

The farming industry is a key actor in planning policy, concerned over the transfer of land to urban uses under the planning system, the use of the countryside for recreational purposes and the pressure of nature conservation policy on their production activities. The farming lobby, comprising the National Farmers' Union (NFU) and the Country Landowners' Association (CLA), has been described as the classic case of an incorporated interest group with a relationship between the NFU and MAFF that was unrivalled in closeness (Self and Storing, 1962). McCormick (1991) recounts how this 'client' relation between the government department and the farmers' trade union arose from the 1947 Agriculture Act, which required government to consult representatives of producers in formulating government policy. By the late 1970s this was resulting in daily, even hourly, contact between the two organisations (see also Lowe *et al.*, 1986, pp. 87–95).

In addition to this legislative basis for consultation, the NFU, with its 115 000 members in England and Wales and parallel organisation in Scotland, can claim 80 per cent coverage of its potential membership of farmers, thus speaking with authority for the farming industry. Linkages to the legislature (Houses of Parliament) and government are also good due to the large number of Members of Parliament with farming interests, either directly or as a landlord. The NFU claims to have regular contact with some 100 MPs. McCormick argues that its relations with local government in rural areas were almost as good as those with central government, with a large number of farmers acting as councillors. But 1976 data suggest that only 7 per cent of non-metropolitan district councillors worked in farming, rising to 10 per cent in shire counties (Herington, 1984, p. 152). Such contact is probably heavily concentrated in specific local areas. As Herington points out (1984, p. 151) the local power of the farming lobby varies depending on the local structure of the agriculture industry, and the size and the productivity of local farms; political power reflects economic power.

However, McCormick also points to a decline in the influence of the NFU since the 1970s. He identifies five factors behind this decline. First, there is a growing concern among the public and government circles over the cost of agricultural support and its consequences in terms of food surpluses. Second, changes in the countryside receive considerable press and media coverage, usually hostile to the farming industry. Third, more people are questioning the morality of modern farming, linking the question of the treatment of animals with 'food scares' such as those over salmonella in eggs and BSE in cows. Fourth, there is growing criticism of MAFF and its role in relation to these problems. Fifth, the urban-to-rural shift in population is resulting in more and more people having a direct stake in how the countryside is used. As a result of these changes, the farming lobby no longer has as strong a foothold in central government and has to compete on slightly more even terms with other pressure groups. The importance of the farming lobby depends on the significance and extent of its economic power, on the importance that agriculture plays within the economy. As that importance is judged to decline, so will its influence. However, this decline in influence has to be judged against a position of unparalleled access to policy-making in the past.

■ The environmental movement

The term 'the environmental movement' covers a broad spectrum of groups from specific anti-development movements through local amenity groups to ecologists/environmentalists. There are clear and important differences between the individual groups within this movement, but they are united in their support of the protection afforded by planning and environmental regulations and the opportunities offered by participation in policy-making. Each group sees urban and environmental planning as providing a means for achieving their specific goals. Furthermore, many of these groups are convinced that their goals are or should be the goals of planning policy. Their involvement in the planning process is not therefore merely instrumental, a means to an end, but is also a question of legitimacy, of finding the right locus of power in decision making. While business groups owe their access to decision-making to their 'corporate discretion', environmental groups of all kinds owe their access to the need to legitimise planning decisions as in the public interest. This is not just a matter of the outcomes in the form of the decisions taken, but of the policy process itself. Therefore a key issue in considering environmental groups is the nature of the access that they have to decision-makers and their involvement in decision-making itself.

A classic way of looking at this issue is via Arnstein's 'ladder' metaphor (1969) which identifies successive rungs of participation from non-participation – manipulation and therapy – through degrees of tokenism – information, consultation and placation – to degrees of citizen power – partnership, delegated power and citizen control (see Thomas, 1996 for a discussion). This emphasises the way in which the planner or political decision-maker progressively cedes exclusive power over the decisions taken and, by implication, opens up the policy process to a greater degree of direct participatory democracy (rather than representative democracy in which the democratic act of voting cedes all power to the elected representative). Another way of looking at the same issue is to distinguish between the extremes of a top-down and a bottom-up strategy. Young uses this in his study of Local Agenda 21 participation strategies (1997). The top-down strategy keeps the policy-maker – here the local authority – firmly in control and sets up a one-way process in which information is passed down. The bottom-up strategy is described as 'a genuine dialogue between the council and local communities' (1997, p. 2), a two-way process which seeks to involve even traditionally passive groups. The local authority aims to empower rather than stay in control. A technique increasingly used in this kind of strategy is community visioning, which aims to get local groups to consider the range of possibilities of change for their area. In between, Young identifies two other strategies adopted by a local authority: the limited dialogue strategy which sets tight(ish) parameters for the dialogue with outside actors on its own agenda; and the 'Yes . . . but' strategy which is more open, at least to begin with, but which is prone to the local authority reasserting control when its prior commitments are challenged.

Political ideology has an influence on which kind of strategy, which rung of the ladder, is considered most appropriate. For those on the New Right there is always the probability that such pressure groups will be captured by highly sectional interests who will disadvantage the general consumer by restricting economic activity. Identification of the collective action problem by public choice theorists reinforces the argument of selectivity among environmental groups and the pursuit of sectional interests. But for others, pressure groups are a mechanism by which a variety of interests are represented within the policy process, and it is the role of the planning system to respond to these interests and mediate them. For those on the Left, the delegation of decision-making to such groups is a further desired step. And for the New Left, such groupings can form social movements, in which case they become the active motor of radical political change. Engaged in struggle with the state as well as groups outside it, they seek to achieve sufficient political power to challenge dominant economic interests and achieve a reallocation of resources. This process of conflict and struggle is a continuous one, which politicises groups and transforms them from mere pressure groups. As will be seen, such a transformation into social movements is rare in practice (Lowe, 1986).

☐ *Anti-development groups*

Anti-development groups are locally-based groups focused on opposition to a specific development proposal. They range from the anti-motorway campaigners of the 1970s to the NIMBYists (Not In My Back Yard) of the 1980s and the tenants' organisations seeking to prevent sale of their council estates in the 1990s. They differ from other types of environmental group in having a very limited purposed, a tightly defined geographical area of activity, being responsive to an outside stimulus (the development proposal) and, often, having only a limited lifespan. Sometimes an anti-development group may arise out of or turn into a broader-based amenity group (see below) but then it has lost the specific features of this type of group. Short (1984, p. 131) locates the growth of such groups in the 'failure of the formal political channels to either represent or articulate place-specific issues', itself a feature of the split between workplace and home. The finely grained nature of local community experience centred around the home has not been adequately reflected in the organisation of political parties, even at local government level, leading to an organisational vacuum. When development pressures threaten that local experience, community groups arise, focused on opposition to the development. The chief tactic of such groups involves intense local mobilisation to demonstrate the strength of opposition to development. This will then be demonstrated through existing formal channels, whether a public local inquiry (see Exhibit 11.2 in Chapter 11), the use of planning procedures or the vote required under housing action trust (HAT) procedures. More radical measures may also be adopted, including squatting, occupation of land and demonstrations. Short (1984, pp. 138–9) describes this as a spectrum of activities ranging from collaboration through campaigning to coercive and confrontational measures. One common feature, though, is that all such activities are focused on local rather than central government, unless some residents have a particular contact within the government. This contrasts with development interests which will commonly work through central government as well as using any specific local contact.

Much attention has been focused on middle-class, rural or NIMBY groups. Shucksmith (1990, p. 69) relates the rise of the NIMBY phenomenon to the migration of higher-status groups into rural locations with a vested interest in preventing further development and the resources, expertise and time to run local campaigns. He quotes the adage 'last one into the village runs the preservation society'. Given the overwhelming predominance of owner-occupiers among such migrants, the economic motive is clear. Short (1984, pp. 132–3) describes it as follows: 'Much resident group activity arises from owner-occupiers seeking to band together to protect and enhance their property values. The rise of owner-occupation has given a material basis for much community actions.' Thus in their study of residents' groups in Berkshire, Short *et al.* (1986, p. 227) identify the voice of the 'stoppers' (anti-development groups) as middle-class, middle-aged owner-occupiers. Again Rees (1990, p. 407) argues that:

> It is important to note that in the vast majority of disputes over the location of economic interests, *local* environmental interests have not questioned the need for the development; in other words, they have not challenged any dominant societal values or materialist goals. (Emphasis mine)

These groups are not concerned with conflicts between protection and development but with conflicts between groups of citizens. In this connection, Short cites the use of conservation area, AONB and other such designations in rural and gentrified inner city locations as an effective tool that middle-class anti-development groups seek to use to prevent further building and immigration. This is described by Rees (1990, p. 407) as: 'transforming legislation designed to preserve areas of special historic importance into a weapon for defending smart residential areas'. Shucksmith links this to Saunders's argument (1990, p. 70): 'that owner-occupiers must be seen as a distinct domestic property class because of their market interest in the accumulative potential of their homes, quite apart from their interest as consumers'. These issues are explored further in Exhibit 13.2 on gentrification and conservation in Chapter 13. However, others have emphasised that economic motive is not the only basis for NIMBYism. Such activity also represents a 'territorial defence of lifestyle' (Shucksmith, 1990, p. 69). Migrants to such rural locations are at least as much in search of particular social networks as a particular physical environment. Ironically as the migrants become established and come to dominate local social and political institutions, they replace the existing social order or, rather, replicate it in their own image.

The short-term, specific anti-development group may develop into (or arise out of) a local amenity group. Much research has covered amenity societies along with other environmental groups and they will therefore be covered in detail in the next section. But given their links to antidevelopment groups, they merit a short discussion here. Amenity groups share many of the characteristics of middle-class rural and urban anti-development groups, but they are usually longer-lived, and focus more generally on the local environment rather than the threat posed by specific developments. Some are locally based, others have a national level of organisation and many span national and local levels. However they differ from many environmentalist groups in that they concentrate on country-side issues, including access, recreation and wildlife, and on the quality of the built environment. They do not necessarily link these issues into a broader analysis of environmental systems. Amenity is primarily defined as a 'visual' feature from these groups' point of view. Another feature of these amenity groups which distinguishes them from all the groups discussed so far is that their activities are less directly linked to their members' material interests or, at least, relate to their consumption of the rural and built environment for leisure rather than to their ownership of parts of the environment as an investment. Many of these groups could be described as 'attitude' groups where people of like mind gather together irrespective of background (Johnston, 1989, p. 171). Membership is open with no obvious limits to the prospective constituency. This lack of direct material interest and the costs of joining in practice keep the membership well below potential numbers. In order to boost membership, amenity groups have to resort to a variety of incentives ranging from magazines, social activities, recreation information or discounts on entrance fees.

It is possible to overemphasise the extent to which commitment to an amenity group is an ideological as opposed to an economic issue. Some local amenity societies may function as long-term watchdogs against development interests. And the links between attitudes, social position and economic role are definite if not always clearly apparent. The difficulty of disentangling the economic and ideological can be seen in the attempt to understand the growth in local amenity societies. Over 1958–75 the number of such societies increased six fold to reach a membership of 300 000 by 1977 (McCormick, 1991, p. 33); the number of local societies registered with the Civic Trust grew from 200 to over 1000 from 1957 to 72 (Kimber and Richardson, 1974, p. 11). This increase did coincide with the surge of environmentalism focused on the consequences of economic growth, the threats of unlimited population expansion and the problems of exhausting certain natural resources. Yet the very fact of economic growth brought with it urban growth and pressures for migration to rural areas. A broader commitment to environmental protection could thus coexist with sectional material interests in preventing development.

Middle-class rural 'stoppers' are not the only form of relevant anti-development or amenity group. Many such groups have been in inner city locations and focused on tenant organisations rather than owner-occupiers. Short (1984, p. 133) describes these groups as forming out of 'dissatisfaction over housing provision in association with discontent over rising rents', but specific development proposals have also provided an impetus. Lack of opportunity to exit the local area by buying into owner-occupation or finding a transfer to another estate provides a captive membership which nevertheless can prove hard to mobilise. Lack of organisational skill, limited resources and resignation by residents all frustrate the formation of such anti-development groups. Often their formation is linked to broader programmes of social change. Short (1984, p. 134) highlights the role of the women's movement in many of these groups:

> There has been a reciprocal relationship. Much of the community action has involved women while some of the consciousness-raising of women has been because of and through community action. Much of the strength of community action has come from women while some of the new-found confidence within the women's movement has come through community action.

Short describes this kind of grass-roots movement as quite distinct from middle-class NIMBYism. This raises the prospect identified by the New Left that some anti-development groups may be seen as radical forces for social change rather than conservative protection of vested interests.

Castells (1983, p. 292) refers to: 'a new situation in which the management of the entire urban system by the state has politicised urban problems, and so translated the mobilisation of communities into a new and significant form of social challenge to established values'. Anti-development movements may, therefore, form such an urban social movement where the resistance to the development fundamentally challenges the premises of capitalist development and the role of the state. As indicated above, to qualify in this way, urban social movements must demonstrably pursue three goals: the organisation of the city as a collection of use values rather than exchange values; the search for autonomous local cultural identity; and the search for decentralised urban self-management (Castells, 1983, pp. 319–20). However, Castells warns that while such urban social movements may restructure the city, they will ultimately become institutionalised as they achieve elements of their programme and the change achieved will fall short of full social restructuring. But the appeal of such movements is great: 'when people find themselves unable to control the world, they simply shrink the world to the size of their community' (1983, p. 331).

☐ *Environmental groups*

Environmental groups cover a wide variety of interests and values (see Exhibit 7.1 for an example). As discussed above, some are locally based and are more long-lived, broader versions of anti-development movements. Others are nationally based, although perhaps with local branches. Some focus on amenity, on the visual aspects of the urban or rural environment, such as the Civic Trust or the Georgian Society. Some have developed an analysis of the interrelated nature of environmental systems which guides their work, such as Friends of the Earth and Greenpeace. Some focus on specific aspects of the environment, such as the Royal Society for the Protection of Birds. Others have more general concerns, such as the National Trust, the Council for the Preservation of Rural England and the Town and Country Planning Association. Groups vary in size and resources as well. Lowe and Goyder's survey in 1981–2 (1983) revealed a median size of 3000 members but a range from a few hundred to well over 100 000. The National Trust now has over one million members.

The lines of division are numerous yet the striking feature is that all such groups perceive themselves as part of one environmental movement (Lowe and Goyder, 1983, p. 80). This is partly because of common values and partly due to the perception of the movement as a unity by the media, public and policy-makers, but also due to extensive contacts between individual groups. Even at the local level of residents' groups, Short *et al.* (1986, p. 231) found a 'dense circuit of local connections to be used in

---

Exhibit 7.1   *The Wildlife Trusts*

The RSNC was established in 1912 as the Society for the Promotion of Nature Reserves (SPNR), with Lord Rothschild, the banker, as a key patron. Although it originally worked closely with the National Trust, its specific nature conservation interests and the recognition that active management of land was needed to conserve habitats meant that it soon branched out into ownership of nature reserves on its own account. It was active in the interwar period. Although membership was only 300 by 1939, it was instrumental in setting up the Natural Resources Investigation Committee during the Second World War, which led to the creation of the Nature Conservatory Council (NCC) in postwar legislation. Ever since it has maintained close links with the NCC.

After the war, however, the concentration on an elite membership meant that the society was largely moribund until it developed links in the 1960 with the growing number of country wildlife trusts. In 1969 the SPNR offered associated membership to all country trusts and in 1976 it received a new charter. In its modern form, the RSNC became the national representative and coordinator of these local-level nature conservation groups, and the partnership has benefited both. More recently, the RSNC has renamed itself The Wildlife Trusts and has also incorporated the urban wildlife movement, again representing local urban groups. It has also extended its national campaigning activities, both in terms of lobbying on legislation and in promoting the concept of Environment City.

The Wildlife Trusts now represents 47 wildlife trusts and 44 urban wildlife groups. These have membership of some 250 000 and manage over 1400 reserves amounting to 53 000 hectares. The number of full- and part-time staff employed is 716 and the total budget is £1.8 million. Members are in demand by local authorities and the NCC for their expertise and fieldwork, and The Wildlife Trusts both nationally and in local groups actively monitors, advises and educates on nature conservation issues. Yet, despite the huge

---

pursuit of common goals'. Such connections are certainly a feature at the national level, though they tend to be *ad hoc* and informal rather than under umbrella organisations (McCormick, 1991, p. 35). Spread of information is achieved by these means together with mutual cooperation on specific issues. McCormick (1991, p. 159) records an interview with Jonathon Porritt which suggested:

> that while the coordination of group activities may sometimes seem incoherent and unco-ordinated, most groups are working towards more or less pre-agreed sets of goals. The role of groups is often complementary. Porritt notes how Friends of the Earth, in working with other groups on changes to the Water Privatisation Bill, was often cast as the confrontational group. By taking this role, it attracted enough of the ire of ministers involved to allow other groups to portray themselves as less confrontational, and to succeed in having some of their proposals accepted.

membership, only 10 per cent of members were recorded in 1991 as actively contributing time to The Wildlife Trusts' activities. This suggests that a large number of people join the groups, not to become actively involved in nature conservation, but because of a general commitment to the cause. Members are not acting as direct consumers of The Wildlife Trusts' services. Neither do they gain social status and contacts from membership, resulting in new bases of social grouping and cohesion, for many members only rarely participate in the work of local groups.

It would appear that people join The Wildlife Trusts and its constituent groups because they reflect certain values and policy aspirations. These members value nature reserves regardless of their own 'use' of them. Such people hold an option value or existence value for nature conservation. 'Option value' refers to the desire to protect nature so that the person may benefit in the future or so that others - including but not only descendants - may benefit; 'existence value' refers to the desire for continued biodiversity regardless of its use to anyone (Pearce *et al.*, 1989). The argument that people are willing to put a substantial figure on both option and existence value provides a different perspective on the involvement of the public in environmental issues. It explains the pressures placed on planning policy quite beyond economic self-interest or the social dynamics of group formation. It also undercuts the arguments that all policy is driven by class-based conflict since the holding of such environmental values crosses class barriers. Nevertheless this emphasis on broad-based environmental values is only a supplement to the other dynamics of pressure group activity. It cannot replace other economic and social cleavages as a political explanation. Indeed the limited extent of nature protection measures suggests that, not only is it not the main factor in explaining pressure groups, it is fairly marginal in explaining policy outputs.

This does not mean that there is no room for greater coordination. In their study of electricity privatisation, Roberts *et al.* (1991, p. 27) note the disadvantages of there being no convenient coordinating forum for the energy efficiency lobby to challenge the electricity supply industry.

Whether considered individually or as a movement, environmental groups have seen substantial growth over the past two decades (see Table 7.1). In 1981–2, membership of environmental groups was estimated as 2.5–3 million or 4.5–5.3 per cent of the population. By 1990 the estimate was 4.5 million members, amounting to 8 per cent of the population. A 1990 directory of environmental organisations in the British Isles listed 1500 organisations including 65 non-government organisations operating at the national level, 62 local groups and 16 regional groups (McCormick, 1991, p. 34). This growth, which was particularly concentrated in the years 1987–9, builds on two previous phases of growth: the period of

Table 7.1   *Membership of selected environmental pressure groups, 1971–94*

| | Ten major environmental groups* | |
	Members	P.a. per cent growth
1971	747 000	–
1981	2 121 000[1]	10.0 %
1991	4 313 000	7.4%
1994	4 424 000	0.9%

* Civic Trust, CPRE, Friends of the Earth, National Trust, National Trust for Scotland, Ramblers Association, Wildlife Trusts, RSPB, Woodland Trust, WWF for Nature; not FoE (Scotland).
1. Assumed pro rata growth 1971–91 for Civic Trust.
Source: Digest of Environmental Statistics 1996, No. 18.

establishment in the late 1880s and 1890s and the first wave of environmentalism in the 1960s and early 1970s. The current expanded size of the environmental movement has significantly altered the way that environmental groups operate.

The growth in membership has increased the financial resources available to groups. Writing in the early 1980s, Lowe and Goyder were already commenting that (1983, p. 46): 'Perhaps the most important consequence of the growth in support for environmental groups has been their ability to take on or expand their professional staff. Increased staffing allows more contact with other groups, more expertise and skills to be brought into the group.' The increased membership itself brings greater skills. Groups do not just regard their members as sources of money, important though this is (see below). They can provide practical assistance at national and local levels and form a network of local watchdogs (Lowe and Goyder, 1983, p. 40). They also provide authority in relations with government departments though membership size alone will not suffice. The quality of the case is at least as important, and hence the ability to undertake research to support the group's case is central. In the case of the debate over nuclear power, although the groups involved were organisationally weak compared to the nuclear power lobby, the information they provided on the costs of nuclear power was critical, in this case in persuading financial investors that a privatised nuclear power industry was not viable (Roberts *et al.*, 1991, p. 118).

Growth has also brought other changes. The links with green consumerism have meant that environmental groups are faced with new demands from the membership and the public at large: demands which prompt new types of campaign. McCormick (1991, p. 117) argues that there has been a new emphasis on working with industry rather than in confrontation with it and on providing practical advice to the public. Within the movement generally a double approach has developed, using research to talk to government and industry while placing more emphasis on what the individual can do. Yet at the same time there appears to be public support for the more active groups and for more radical campaigning tactics. The ability to use professional media consultants and fund-raising advice has given the environmental movement a higher profile, perhaps a more aggressive corporate image. The growth of environmental legislation has also meant that government sometimes views environmental groups as a resource for implementing policy. Local wildlife trusts and offices of the RSPB can perform local environmental management and enforcement tasks concerning wildlife protection (Yearley and Milton, 1990).

The increasing importance of EU policy (as indicated in Chapter 6) has also changed the way in which environmental groups operate. There is a need for liaison with European environmental groups as well as with the European Commission and Parliament. The European Environmental Bureau was established in 1974 to liaise with the European Commission on environmental groups' behalf (Lowe and Goyder, 1983; McCormick, 1991). By 1982 it was representing 63 national groups. But internal problems regarding its direction and organisation for a time reduced its influence and some national groups bypassed the bureau and opened their own European offices. Since then it has reassumed a pivotal role. It now represents 160 environmental groups from 26 countries, which together account for 14 000 member organisations and 11 million members. It is funded by the EU DGXI, as well as member states and the non-governmental organisations (Butt Philip and Gray, 1996). In addition, the possibility of pressure groups themselves seeking judicial review before the European Court of Justice has given British groups a similar status to their counterparts in the USA under the National Environmental Policy Act. They can challenge policy practice directly, much enhancing their role as watchdogs. In all 'because the British Government has made few concessions on domestic environmental issues, British environmental groups have increasingly seen Brussels as a 'court of redress' and a means of out-maneuvering the government' (McCormick, 1991, p. 132).

This increased level of European representation has not only been in response to the groups' own perceptions of the need to influence European policy, but also because the Commission has actively sought out pressure groups. It has a habit of using such groups to help draft legislation, to provide information and data, to advise on the level of support for different measures, and to comment on draft proposals, partly due to its own limited resources and knowledge base (McCormick, 1991, pp. 128–47). This method of proceeding is in line with how British groups seek to influence British policy, but while they have to keep knocking on the British government's door, the European Commission's door has been open wide. More recently the Commission has had to make some changes to its mode of practice because of the volume of lobbying. Butt Philip and Gray (1996) note the 'massive influx' of lobby groups representing voluntary organisations into Brussels in the 1980s and also the number of industrial and commercial EU-wide pressure groups who have created environmental committees and working groups to reflect the importance of European environmental politics. The European Commission now prefers to deal with European-wide pressure groups which represent more than national interests. Twenty-seven such European-wide environmental groups have therefore been established or consolidated. The preeminent environmental group at the European level is WWF International, respected as responsible and informed by policy-makers and, with five million members/supporters, commanding more expertise, skills and resources than any other comparable group. By contrast, Greenpeace's European Unit is limited in the European arena by its unwillingness to compromise or to formally cooperate with other groups, preferring a principled if lonely position.

However, one must not paint too rosy a picture of the environmental lobby. While the membership and resources of groups have grown, they remain vulnerable to financial constraints. All such groups have no obvious constituency and membership is optional. There is therefore no guaranteed resource base (Johnston, 1989, p. 171). In their research, Lowe and Goyder (1983, p. 40) found that 72 per cent of groups surveyed considered membership as important first and foremost to provide income. Income from a stable membership allows the groups to plan its campaigning activities and membership services and gives it a degree of autonomy. Those groups reliant on grants, sponsors or donations find themselves dependent on donors in policy as well as financial terms and sometimes constrained by explicit or implicit conditions on the gift.

In the pursuit of effective influence on government policy, groups are not always successful. Government, particularly at central government level, plays an active role in determining consultation with environmental groups and can elevate some groups in importance while ignoring others (Lowe and Goyder, 1983, p. 24; but see Stoker and Wilson, 1991, on the situation in local government). Among the least receptive government departments to any environmental influence have been the DoEn, DTI and DoTr (as was). In some cases groups can be pushed from consultation with the centre of government out to marginal quangos or local government (McCormick, 1991; Lowe *et al.*, 1986, pp. 122–4). In any case, consultation implies acceptance of an unwritten code of moderate and responsible behaviour by the groups. Moving beyond this renders the groups and their demands illegitimate. Groups are dependent on government ceding access; they have no equivalent of business interests' corporate discretion, and attempts to mobilise the membership in overt political activity may be curtailed by the charitable status of many groups.

This suggests that constraints placed on environmental groups by their political role, as much as by their members' interests, may inevitably render them conservative supporters of the status quo. Lowe and Goyder, however (1983, p. 35), found both emphasis groups, whose demands did not conflict with the status quo, and promotional groups, seeking social or political reform, within the movement. The promotional groups were more likely to be democratic in political structure. They were described as having a representative leadership, a feature shared with certain recreational groups who drew their membership from a broad social background including substantial numbers of working-class members. This was in contrast to other groups, described as 'open oligarchies'. In these the elections were a formality and the leadership exercised strong control subject only to pursuing policies which did not openly split the membership. This covered both the older environmental groups, often formed before the First World War and hence dominated by upper-middle-class organisers, and also building preservation groups where there was a 'tyranny of taste' (Lowe and Goyder, 1983, pp. 51–3).

This issue of whether environmental groups can be a radical political force is a particular concern of the New Left. Castells (1978, pp. 152–66) reinforces the point that environmentalism embraces a number of fundamentally different elements. First, there are middle-class movements which adopt environmental issues on which concession can readily be exacted from dominant interests. Second, there are similar middle-class movements where there is a challenge to individual capitalists. Third, there are student movements (so active in the 1970s) which adopt a revolutionary programme and create the potential for linking environmental issues to a class-based challenge to capitalism. Fourth, there are the occasional cases of adoption of environmental concerns by black and other minority groups, primarily formed into urban social movements around other urban issues of collective consumption. Castells notes that this last important source of challenge to the capitalist state has, in fact, rarely taken up the banner of environmentalism. Castells concludes that environmental politics does have the potential to mount a challenge to capitalism through urban social movements (see above), but the linking ideology of environmentalism serves to mystify the true basis of the politics by reducing social conflicts into an overarching conflict between technology and nature. He questions the view often promoted by such groups that there is the possibility for all 'men of goodwill' to jointly and without internal conflict fight for environmental protection. As he says (1978, p. 159): 'The ideology of the environment, "apolitical", humanitarian, universalist and scientific, transforms social inequality into mere physical inconveniences and blends the social classes into an army of Boy Scouts.'

Therefore, while viewing environmental movements as conservative or, at least, diversionary, Castells accepts that the potential remains for environmentally-based urban social movements to transform the fight for the environment into 'a powerful level for change' (1978, p. 166). The problem is to activate this potential. This may be particularly difficult in Britain where pressure groups rarely seem to transform themselves into urban social movements (Lowe, 1986). The contrast with the North American environmental justice movement is striking. Contrary to Castells's expectations and despite Harvey's qualifications (reviewed in Chapter 4), this represents a set of locally based pressure groups which combine environmental demands with a concern over discrimination on the basis, particularly, of colour – the experience of racism rather class politics drives such North American activism. This has been effective in that it has prompted an official government report into the racial composition of the population living near waste facilities, though its findings were inconclusive. It has also gone beyond the bounds of NIMBYism to question the need for such polluting activities: 'In short, and by explicit extension, the grassroots movement for environmental justice represents a populist challenge to exclusive private control of the production process itself. Pollution prevention ultimately requires production control.' (Heiman, 1996, p. 113). In Britain this kind of linkage between environmental demands and working-class and/or ethnic minority struggles is less common than middle-class NIMBYism, though the anti-roads protests of the late 1990s have seen an unlikely alliance build up between local residents, including middle-class residents, and New Age anti-roads campaigners using non-violent direct action, including building underground tunnels on proposed road sites and incarcerating volunteers in them. This has resulted in prolonged legal and even physical battles to evict the protesters which has attracted considerable media coverage and increased the costs of roadbuilding through delays and the added security measures. Whether it constitutes a social movement is another matter.

■ Political parties

Pressure groups are not the only form of social organisation that seeks to influence public policy. In a representative democracy, political parties will, of course, play a major role. However, the growth in pressure groups outlined above can be explained in terms of the decline of party politics. As McCormick (1991, p. 41) says: 'it is arguable that interest groups are a more accurate (if not always more efficient) way of representing citizens' interests than political parties'. Nevertheless parties are a route to political power. Johnston (1989, p. 159) lists five ways in which policies may be brought to the forefront of the political agenda. Beyond influencing individual members of the legislature and changing the views of the population, the other three strategies all relate to political parties: influencing one political party, influencing all political parties, and creating a new political party.

First, one of the existing parties may be induced to adopt certain planning policies and implement them, if elected to government. The success in achieving this depends on the relationship of the new policy to existing ones and the impact those new policies will have on the voting intentions of current and potential voters. Second, planning policies (in general or specific aspects) may achieve the status of cross-party support adopted by every party in its manifesto. Green belt policy can be seen to be in this position (Rydin and Myerson, 1990). There is the danger that, if all parties adopt a specific or general pro-planning stance, then its relevance as a means of choosing between parties falls and in effect the policy slips back down the political agenda. As Johnston argues, in relation to environmental policies (1989, p. 159): 'if all parties agree on an issue, then it cannot be used to discriminate between them, unless evaluation of their performance on that issue will be salient when they next appear before the electorate for support'. The signal of this happening is interchangeable policy statements, say in manifestos. But a distinction should be drawn between a common commitment to an existing policy (as in green belts) when the common stance strengthens the policy, and a new policy area (as in reducing carbon dioxide emissions) when the common stance may deflect actual policy action, in the way Johnston suggests.

Certainly, all three major British parties have, until recently, paid little explicit attention to any planning policies (Kimber and Richardson, 1974). McCormick (1991, p. 44), focusing on environmental policies, has been able to say that 'British political parties have played only a marginal role in the environmental debate' and 'the environment tends to be a minor issue in election manifestos'. Between 1987 and 1992, a number of factors appeared to have created the potential for a changed situation. The change in policy stance of the Labour Party away from bolder forms of socialism and the departure of Margaret Thatcher as Conservative Party leader resulted in more flexible party lines. It was less easy to fit planning policy into an example of the overarching party line. At the same time environmental issues, broadly defined, came to have a much greater political saliency. Even before her departure, Mrs Thatcher made a series of speeches in 1988 and 1989 which demonstrated the significance of environmental concerns. Both inside and outside government and in the opposition parties, restructuring occurred to give all environmental issues a higher profile. The Conservative Party launched the Tory Green Initiative in 1988 to campaign on the basis of environmentally friendly free market policies and publicise current government policy in this light. The same year the Green Democrats replaced the former Liberal Green group and were charged with developing an environmental policy within the Liberal Democrats. Labour has had a separate environmental organisation, the Socialist Environment and Resources Association, since 1973 but this is probably too radical in its thinking for the current New Labour Party. In 1989 the party established a new campaign unit to promote an environmental policy. However, in line with Johnston's argument (see above), this cross-party stance effectively prevented debate on planning and environmental issues at the 1992 and again at the 1997 General Election. Once again other issues dominated the agenda. Reviewing British environmental politics in the 1990s, O'Riordan and Jordan conclude (1995, p. 237):

> Despite the Rio-imposed requirement of an environmental report to the nation, neither of the two major British political parties takes the environmental agenda seriously. Both John Major and Tony Blair have been conspicuous in their disinterest in matters environmental. Nor have the Conservative and Labour Parties been noted for their environmental output in the past. So, not much change there.

Beyond influence on existing parties, Johnston's third strategy for raising the political profile of environmental policy is the creation of a new party specifically focused on the environment. Britain has had a green party for over twenty years. The widespread success of the *Blueprint for Survival*, published first by *The Ecologist* magazine and then by Penguin, led to the formation of the People Party in 1973, to be called the Ecology Party as from 1975 and then the Green Party as from 1985. Electoral success has been much slower coming in Britain than in many other countries. Despite contesting a growing number of seats the Green Party has never polled more than 1.4 per cent of the vote in a general election. In 1997 they contested 95 seats and polled 1.3 per cent of the vote in those seats. They have fared somewhat better in other elections. In the 1987 local government elections, they received 5.9 per cent of the vote. Their peak performance came in 1989 when they polled a totally unexpected 15 per cent in the European elections. This doubled their membership from 1988 to 1990 to almost 20 000. Since then they have lost their high profile, losing members and voters and degenerating organisationally almost into anarchy. In the 1994 European elections they received 3.2 per cent of the

Table 7.2   *Green parties and the European Parliament elections*

| | Per cent share of the vote | | Number of seats |
	1989	1994	1994
UK*	14.9	3.2	0
Belgium	–	–	2
Denmark	–	8.5	1
France	10.6	5.0	0
Germany	8.4	10.1	12
Greece	–	–	0
Italy	6.2	3.2	4
Ireland	3.8	7.9	2
Luxembourg	–	10.9	1
Netherlands	7.0	6.1	1
Portugal	–	–	0
Spain	–	0.7	0

*Not including Northern Ireland which has one 3-member constituency.
Sources: R. Morgan (ed.) (1994) *The Times Guide to the European Parliament* (London: Times Books).

vote, much lower than in other Northern European countries (see Table 7.2).

There is no doubt that the electoral system in Britain works against the Greens. There is no Green MP, though one Plaid Cymrw MP also sits on a Green political programme. For all their relatively good support at local government level, by June 1989 they had only one county councillor, eleven district councillors and 90 parish councillors. When they received 15 per cent of the vote in the European elections they won no seats at all for their 2.29 million votes. On proportional representation, it is estimated that there would have been twelve British Greens in the European Parliament (McCormick, 1991). This contrasts with the West German situation where each voter has two votes, one for a constituency MP and one for a regional list candidate, a system which encourages voting for fringe parties. The preponderance of PR systems means that 28 of the 626 European Parliament seats were taken by Greens in 1997. However knowledge of the consequences of the British electoral system can influence voting in both directions. A vote for the Greens may be considered a wasted vote and thus depress electoral support. Yet when there is a move for a protest vote, as in 1989, Greens can be a ready recipient of votes, given that there is no chance of their actually being elected. The commitment to run the next European Parliament election on a proportional representation basis in Britain should have interesting results for the Green Party, depending on the precise system chosen and the reaction of the electorate.

Given this lack of effectiveness as a political party, it has been suggested that the Green Party is little more than another environmental pressure group. But Bennie and Maloney (1996) do see distinctive characteristics in Green Party members which distinguish them from members of a group such as Friends of the Earth. While finding considerable overlap in membership they found a more radical political consciousness among party members, in effect a party ideology. They therefore argue that the Green Party performs a separate and distinct role from that of the pressure group protest business. The problem has been how to resolve the pursuit of party political actions with this radical, deep green ideology. Dobson (1995) contrasts this ideology, which he labels 'ecologism', with light green 'environmentalism'. Dobson argues that ecologism stands outside and in competition to existing ideologies while environmentalism 'can be slotted with relative ease into more well-known ideological paradigms' and 'that the current vogue to green (small "g") politics shows this cooption at work' (p. 206). The battle between remaining true to deep green ideology and achieving status as a political actor within prevailing institutional structures is one which has bedevilled green politics at national level – as with the conflicts between 'Realos' and 'Fundis' in the German Greens – and continues to pose problems at the European level (Bomberg, 1996). It assures that it is environmentalism rather than its more radical counterpart, ecologism, that will continue to influence contemporary environmental and planning policy, though probably to a greater extent than in the past.

■ Further reading

A good basic introduction to the issues raised in this chapter is provided by McCormick (1991), and Johnston (1989) is also a useful review. For specific work on pressure groups, Lowe and Goyder (1983) is still the most authoritative reference on the environmental movement, with Richardson (1993) providing a theoretical and comparative dimension. A relatively recent publication on the role of political parties is Robinson (1992). Midwinter *et al.* (1991) contains detail on pressure groups, political parties and public attitudes in the Scottish context (see particularly pp. 41, 73–6, 210). For original documentation, the publications of the political parties (including their manifestos) and of pressure groups can be consulted.

■ *Chapter 8* ■

Planners as Professionals

The previous chapters have looked at the nature of various organisations involved in planning inside and outside the state, and on the borders, as with quangos. But within these organisations are the individuals who undertake the actual formulation and implementation of planning policy, the planners. For the moment, this term is used to denote all those who bring some claims to expertise to the planning process. These claims differentiate planners from bureaucrats who merely administer policy systems but with little or no discretion over the actual decisions taken. It is also a defining characteristic of those who call themselves professionals. Beyond this though, a number of different ways of conceptualising professions exist.

■ Analysing professionals

The traditional sociological approach has been to identify the 'traits' of professionals, starting with expertise: 'Whatever else they are, professionals are experts' (Freidson, 1984, p. 14). The professions represent the institutionalisation of knowledge so that it may fulfil social functions, and the specialisation between different professions represents functional differences in expertise. The price that professions may charge for their expertise, whether as fees or salary, is related to the process of acquiring that knowledge through education and accredited training. Higher salary levels are retrospectively justified in terms of the costs and the income and leisure foregone during this period of education. The education, usually conducted at undergraduate or postgraduate level, also justifies higher salaries in terms of the command over scarce specialist knowledge acquired and greater autonomy in work practices on the basis of the professional's superior knowledge. The scarcity of a profession's expertise effectively creates a monopoly situation in which only certain individuals and groups can charge for its supply.

Identifying the monopolisation of professional expertise has two other implications. First, it identifies the growth of professional expertise with the development of a market in that expertise, that is, with the rise and dominance of market processes. The ideology, or set of ideas, associated with increased marketisation is also a strong influence on how professions are seen; this ideology can be described as one of 'possessive individualism' (Larson, 1984, p. 32). Expertise is seen as something that belongs to individuals who invest to acquire it and, as such, can be bought and sold, commanding a high price due to scarcity. Professionalisation presumes a market in knowledge-based services. Second, where a scarce resource is owned by a select group, not only does it earn a high price but it becomes a base for exercising power in society. Thus professional accreditation is not just an advantage for individuals in the market-place but a source of social power for the professional group. This power is exercised *vis-à-vis* those who do not have the expertise: 'The presence of a lay public is what distinguishes modern professional expertise from other forms of scarce and esoteric knowledge' (Larson, 1984, p. 37). Hence professions are a form of social institution that certifies and credentialises knowledge and attributes it to certain groups at the expense of others, thereby granting professionals financial resources and social power.

In the traditional view, this analysis is modified by the attribution of other significant traits to professionals, traits such as altruism, social responsibility and a desire to pursue the common good. This makes the professional the guardian of the public interest, a view shared equally by those primarily in the public sector – such as town planners – and those primarily employed in the private sector – such as chartered surveyors. It is an additional justification for professionals being given safely considerable discretion in the exercise of their expertise, based on the assumption that they will not misuse it. However it is not always clear whether the exercise of monopolised power or the pursuit of the common good is going to dominate. Larson refers to the way that 'professional reformers logically defined expertise as that which they did or thought worth doing' (1984, p. 34), professional self-interest driving the processes of knowledge production, rather than objectively created knowledge being professionally used in the public interest.

This sense of professions acting in their self-interest is strongly promoted by the public choice approach. Public choice tends to be dismissive of the norms which might constrain professions. Rather they see professions as just another interest group, subject to the same collective action problems as other groups and requiring similar selective interests in order to maintain membership (Olson, 1978). A major incentive is the opening of employment opportunities only to those who choose to join the group. But other incentives are services provided by the professional body such as insurance, legal advice and defence, journals and information services. The balance of costs and benefits must be sufficient to maintain group membership. This done, the profession then also engages in the other activities of groups, protecting members' and the group's interests (though the two may not always be synonymous) by lobbying and other political action. For example, both the Royal Town Planning Institute (RTPI) and Royal Institute of British Architects (RIBA) were consultees on the annex to PPG1 on 'Aesthetic Control and Design Guidance', undoubtedly claiming professional expertise on a public policy matter but also staking a claim for their respective members in decisions on design matters. Similarly the RTPI lobbied to keep waste disposal a local authority function rather than transfer it to the new Environment Agency, since most of its members are within local authorities. In the public choice approach, there is little in the way of constraints on the self-interested action of professionals, unless self-seeking in itself undermines the group's effectiveness in the political sphere and its image in the market-place.

Between the two extremes of an altruistic profession and a self-seeking one lies the influential approach developed by Johnson of professions as a form of occupational control. Johnson (1972) argued that professionalism is a specific form of occupational control, of organising and restraining the working practices of specific groups of workers. It is a form of control which distinguishes these workers, termed 'members' of a profession, as being in middle-class, higher-status, service occupations. Entry is restricted and usually based on achieving formal educational qualifications, but as Collins (1990, p. 19) makes clear, technical knowledge by itself is not a sufficient guarantee of a professional occupational structure. It is the status that society confers on certain types of knowledge and the restrictions placed on access to it that is important.

The education process, involving selection at point of entry and at various examination points, is also part of a process of creating a uniform social grouping out of aspiring professionals. Collins argues (1990, p. 19) that: 'the academic organisational structure has a social rather than a technical impact: it affects the way in which an occupation is organised but not the amount of skilled performance'. Such educated, professional workers are distinguished by what they wear, how they conduct themselves, where they congregate for work and leisure, and the common language they speak. They can be described as: 'communities with a certain style of life, code of ethics and self-conscious identity and boundaries to outsiders' (Collins, 1990, p. 15). While not intending to imply there is no scope for individuality within a profession, nevertheless there are similarities between members of a profession which, in the majority of cases, are more marked than individual differences. This can make professions more resistant than other labour markets to widening entry, say to women or members of ethnic minorities when they have traditionally been white, male enclaves.

Exhibit 8.1   *Professionals in the English and Welsh water industry*

Professionals in the private sector sell their services to clients, who therefore exercise a degree of control over professionals, although a degree of autonomy based upon the professional's own expertise and status always remains. Where the employing firm is also owned by external investors, then consumer control is supplemented by owner control, and professionals may find themselves having to respond to quite distinct and potentially conflicting sets of pressures: concerning quality of service from clients; concerning expanding market share and cost-cutting from shareholders. Professionals in the public sector have a similar dual system of control. Here the 'client' is the user of the public sector service, traditionally a source of little pressure within the public sector, and the 'owner' must be the local electorate to whom the service is ultimately responsible. In the English and Welsh water industry, professional water managers have had to come to terms with a shift from the public to the private sector and this has highlighted the particular role they play within water management.

Prior to privatisation, water managers were located within quangos, the regional water authorities (RWAs). Here the 'control' exercised by the water authorities' customers, the users of water supplies, was fairly minimal since it was exercised indirectly. The scale of the RWA's organisation gave customers little effective access. Central government could influence RWAs on water customers' behalf and the boards of RWAs had a majority of local government delegates. In this way, democratic control was supposed to guide professionals in their work. Then, under the 1983 Water Act, the elected members were replaced by a small management board appointed by central government. Local authorities were represented via consumer consultative committees, where they held about a third of seats with RWAs themselves appointing the remainder. However, in practice this made little difference since water managers had come to operate with substantial autonomy, subject mainly to fiscal controls from their central government paymasters.

As a result, for much of the 1970s, water managers were promoting major public investment projects such as dams and reservoirs subject to relatively little external scrutiny (Rees, 1990). This has been severely criticised for being an inappropriate strategy, ignoring more mundane problems such as leaky pipes and inadequate sewage treatment. Even in relation to planning

---

While these features of uniform socialisation and controlled entry are hallmarks of the traditional profession, what Johnson calls the 'collegiate professions', he points out that professions can operate under two other forms of occupational control, and that the traditional collegiate form may coexist with either one of these. Some professions operate under corporate patronage in which one industry employs the majority of the members and, therefore, exercises a significant influence on their ways of working. For example, architects are predominantly employed by property developers and the values and norms of that industry affect their work. Alternatively, some professionals' work is defined by the actions of the state and they

infrastructure for new development, water managers remained distanced from the land use planning authorities, preparing their own strategies first and consulting afterwards rather than liaising during development planning. The RWAs in this period provide a good example of the New Right's bureaucracy running out of control. They were aloof from the community they served, hardly engaged in any negotiative activities inside or outside government and cannot be considered to have made rational planning decisions over water supply.

The transfer of the water supply industry from the public to the private sector has coincided with the greater influence of the European Commission. This meant that water managers have had to respond to a quite different pattern of pressures. The EC has required substantial upgrading of treatment facilities to improve water quality. Prior to privatisation this upgrading was blocked by financial restraints, but continued pressure from the EC and some private sector funding have helped loosen central government purse strings. As a result water managers are dealing with major new investment programmes again but are doing so under conditions of a requirement to produce profits for shareholders and the greatly enhanced consumer and environmental protection that followed privatisation.

First the NRA, and now the Environment Agency, monitors water managers closely and this is complemented by the work of the consumer watchdog, the Office of Water Services (Ofwat). Ofwat operates with a central and regional office structure, monitoring day-to-day management and guiding major policy decisions. It has responsibility for overseeing economic regulation, the standards of service, customer complaints and competition and discrimination. Thus the increases in water bills and the moves towards metering are not left to water professionals' discretion any more but are negotiated with a number of organisations; the same is true of water treatment investment. The direct control exercised by the community remains weak. Here quangos control each other, the public do not control the professionals directly. For water managers, this still represents a loss of autonomy but their authority as expert, objective professionals had already been eroded by the evidence of planning failures in the 1970s.

become subject to state mediation in establishing their professional identity. Many planning professions exist to operate a variety of regulations, from development control to pollution abatement to assessing suitability for council housing. The state, in setting the guidelines for this work and indeed creating the opportunity for its existence, is a preeminent influence on the profession. Exhibit 8.1 provides an example of the impact of privatisation on professional practice.

More recently, Johnson has used the work of Foucault to reconsider the process of professionalisation (1993). Foucault focuses on the role of the state in modern society and sees the state as an ensemble of institutions, procedures, tactics, calculations, knowledges and technologies. The institutionalisation of expertise in professions is one strand in 'governmentability'. Johnson sees the professions as socio-technical devices through which the means and ends of government are articulated. By identifying social problems and proposing means of solving them, they help render a realm of affairs governable. The institutions of the professions also provide staffed organisations to cope with politicised problems. The changes of the 1990s that he draws attention to are the ways in which established professional jurisdictions have been disrupted, networks of expertise reconstituted and the boundary between apparently 'neutral' expertise and politics shifted.

This more general analysis provides a backdrop for the following account of the planning professions. Aspects of self-interest, occupational control and a commitment to the public interest can all be seen in the current processes of professionalisation of planning. This will be explored by a focus on the core profession of 'town planning', as recognised by the Royal Town Planning Institute.

■ The planning profession

The majority of the professions that today deal with the built and natural environment were founded before the Second World War, particularly in the late nineteenth century and the 1930s (see Table 8.1).

The activities of these professions vary considerably from the more technically-minded public health engineers to the planners within the Royal Town Planning Institute (originally just the Town Planning Institute) who undertake more of a coordinating role. Some draw on knowledge from the natural sciences, others from the social sciences. Some of these professions are found almost entirely within the public sector, such as environmental health officers; others are oriented firmly towards the private sector, especially chartered surveyors and architects; some professions which were based within the public sector are facing privatisation. Some professions are high status, others lower status. Some professional organisations are large and powerful, others weak. The lines of division are many but nevertheless it is the nature of these activities as professions which is the common unifying thread.

State mediation has been a major factor in the creation of the planning professional, the chartered town planner. This professional remains the central figure in much planning policy for planners are charged with coordinating and synthesising the inputs from many other, more specialist professions. Data and policy inputs on roads from transport engineers, air quality from environmental scientists, housing need from housing

Table 8.1   *Dates of founding of the main planning professions (with selected current membership 1997)*

1834	Royal Institute of British Architects (22 500)
1868	Royal Institution of Chartered Surveyors (80 000)
1883	Institution of Environmental Health Officers* (9000)
1886	Royal Institution of Public Health (3000)
1895	Institution of Public Health Engineers
1896	Institution of Water Engineers and Scientists
1901	Institute of Water Pollution Control
1903	Institute of Hygiene
1914	Town Planning Institute (17 000)
1919	Chartered Institute of Transport (11 000)
1927	Institute of Energy (4000)
1930	Institution of Highways and Transportation
1931	Society of Housing Managers (now Chartered Institute of Housing) (14 000)
1937	Royal Institute of Public Health and Hygiene (4000)
1944	Institute of Road Transport Engineers (18 000)

* now chartered

managers, land drainage from water engineers all feed into the strategic planning and development control decisions of planners. The new informational requirements of environmental assessments (EAs) are also being handled by planners given the incorporation of most EAs into development control decision-making. This description of a planner's work reflects the image presented by the rational comprehensive model of planning theory, but a large amount of planning work is more bureaucratic in nature, particularly development control. Yet another area of planners' work is neither rational decision-making nor bureaucratic rubber-stamping. It involves negotiating with groups, whether from the commercial sector, pressure groups, or the general public, and liaising between the public and private sectors (Underwood, 1980; and see Exhibits 10.1 on joint housing studies and 10.2 on planning gain in Chapter 10). Here the discretion within planners' work is to the fore.

Planners, like other local government professionals, also have to operate within the context of responsibility to elected local politicians. This distinguishes them from professionals, say, in quangos. During the 1980s councillors have become more politicised along party lines (Stoker, 1991, p. 39 – but see Midwinter *et al.*, 1991, p. 137, for the Scottish situation), more aware of policy issues and more expert in managing and challenging their professionals. Laffin and Young (1990) point to a 'new breed' of councillor who is taking back much policy initiative from local government professionals, including planners. As a result local government professionals have had to redefine professionalism and reconceptualise both their competence and their claims to represent the public interest. A range of roles are available to the professional in this task: to act as a controller of a budget; to enable and facilitate council policy; to be a policy activist supporting radical councillors; and to be the professional advocate speaking out in the name of rational decision-making. Planners, too, have experimented with these roles.

But while the planning profession has been shaped by state mediation and the influence of the political context within which it operates, it also remains within a collegiate professional structure with all the consequences of monopolisation of expertise and exclusive socialisation outlined above. This raises the question of how the professionalisation process in planning deals with the major structural differences within society, those of class, gender and ethnicity. In many cases the filtering of entrants to the profession ensures a relatively homogeneous base on which professionalisation can work. But there is evidence that, at least in the case of gender, the barriers to entry are coming down. There are growing numbers of women entering all the professions associated with the environment, though this is operating from a low base (see Table 8.2).

In all the land use and construction professions, Greed estimates that less than 5 per cent are women. As she says (1991, p. 3):

> These factors may be irrelevant to urban policy-making, if women's needs are perceived as being no different from those of men; or if it is believed that the professional man is capable of sufficiently disinterested neutrality to plan equally well for all groups in society . . . But as research and human experience have shown, women suffer considerable disadvantages within a built environment that is developed by men, primarily for other men.

Greed argues that professions need to be restructured to allow more women access to senior posts in order to overcome this discrimination in the outcomes of planning activity, although she recognises (p. 181) that not all women in senior positions, particularly those that have achieved those positions on the basis of an agenda set by men, will automatically operate in a way that is conscious of this discrimination. The professional socialisation process may ensure that a female professional operates primarily as a professional (defined in terms of her male counterparts) rather than as a woman (defined in terms of exploitative relationships in society).

The planning profession has been particularly vulnerable to the changes of the 1980s and 1990s that Johnson (1993) identifies as it is not a strong organisation. It is relatively young and small among the broader range of professions concerned with the environment. It is a common focus of criticism and attack over the inadequacies of the environment and its

Table 8.2 *Women within the built environment professions*

Royal Institution of Chartered Surveyors	
60 000 members, excl. students	3 per cent women
	6 per cent including students
Royal Town Planning Institute	
11 750 members, excl. students	15 per cent women
	18 per cent including students
	7 per cent of FT working members
Royal Institute of British Architects	
28 000 members	8.5 per cent women
	4 per cent of working members
Institute of Housing (now Chartered)	
9 000 members	39 per cent including students
Chartered Institute of Building	
28 400 members	Less than 1 per cent
Institute of Civil Engineers	
70 100 members	2 per cent including students

Source: Greed (1991) pp. 202–4.

perceived failure to protect the environment from adverse change. When individuals and firms interact with planners, there is a high degree of dissatisfaction. Twenty-nine per cent of all cases referred to the Local Government Ombudsman concerned planners, amounting to some 6728 cases in 1989/90. From the New Right have also come criticisms of the restrictions that planners place upon development activity and the obvious failure of planners to manage environmental change in a rational manner. Planners suffered as part of the broader attack by Thatcherism on the professions generally, which included a report by the Monopolies and Mergers Commission in 1986 on the provision of professional services (Laffin and Young, 1990). Faced with this attack the professions found little support from the Left, who had long criticised planners and others for their treatment of disadvantaged groups and the inequitable use of their expertise, powers of negotiation and control over the allocation of resources.

As a result of the political assault on the planning profession, the RTPI faced a difficult time during the 1980s. Planning departments in many local authorities were cut in staff numbers, with departments merged or even abolished. Unit costs per planning application actually fell during 1985–9. In the case of the Milton Keynes Development Corporation, the planning functions were privatised to be taken over by Chestertons, a firm of chartered surveyors; a similar situation resulted in Berkshire County Council. There was increasing privatisation of planning work through the use of consultants, with many private sector planners members of alternative professional bodies, such as the RICS, or holding less allegiance to the RTPI which is predominantly public sector-focused. At the same time the role of the RTPI in controlling access to the profession came under challenge from the National Council for Vocational Qualifications and from the implications of European integration in allowing foreign professionals to practise in Britain and claim membership of British professions (Morphet, 1992a and 1992b). However, by the 1990s the planning profession had recovered somewhat. Recruitment had increased and only in London were planning departments understaffed, according to the Audit Commission (1992), although many departments still find themselves under daily pressure. The New Right also tempered its views somewhat with an emphasis on customer care, quality and efficiency rather than deprofessionalising planning.

Indeed the professional values have been held up as an antidote to the disturbing tendency for planning within local government to become the focus of accusations of misconduct and inappropriate behaviour. Too close relations between planners and other officials, councillors and property developers were an occasional feature of the postwar building boom – as with the well-publicised cases of T. Dan Smith's era in Newcastle or the Poulson corruption scandal in Birmingham. But the 1980s saw councils as diverse as Labour Lambeth and Conservative Westminster charged with the inappropriate exercise of their powers and resources and, as recently as August 1997, an investigation into corruption surrounding planning issues in Doncaster was announced, including the grant of planning permissions to develop housing on 'protected' land. The Committee on Standards in Public Life, chaired by Lord Nolan, considered a number of different institutions including the roles of councillors and professionals in local government (1997). By and large, it considered the cases of improper behaviour to be the exception in the context of 20 000 councillors and 2 million local government employees. The Audit Commission, who monitor local authorities in England and Wales for fraud and corruption, found 1475 proven cases of fraud in 1995/6 and 21 cases of corruption (although 99 per cent of the cases of fraud were committed by outsider persons against local authorities).

However the committee did note a persistent concern and related lack of clarity over appropriate standards. A particular problem that the

---

Summary Box 8.1   *The Nolan Committee's Seven Principles of Public Life*

Selflessness – Holders of public office should take decisions solely in terms of the public interest. They should not do so in order to gain financial or other material benefits for themselves, their family or their friends.

Integrity – Holders of public office should not place themselves under any financial or other obligation to outside individuals or organisations that might influence them in the performance of their official duties.

Objectivity – In carrying out public business, including making public appointments, awarding contracts, or recommending individuals for rewards and benefits, holders of public office should make choices on merit.

Accountability – Holders of public office are accountable for their decisions and actions to the public and must submit themselves to whatever scrutiny is appropriate to their office.

Openness – Holders of public office should be as open as possible about all the decisions and actions that they take. They should give reasons for their decisions and restrict information only when the wider public interest clearly demands.

Honesty – Holders of public office have a duty to declare any private interests relating to their public duties and to take steps to resolve any conflicts arising in a way that protects the public interest.

Leadership – Holders of public office should promote and support these principles by leadership and example.

---

committee identified was the lack of ownership of the standards by the local authorities, as other bodies had increasingly taken on the role of standard-setting. Therefore they sought to develop ways in which all those involved in government, the administration of government or quasi-governmental agencies would adopt and work by their 'Seven Principles of Public Life' as set out in Summary Box 8.1. Substantial recommendations were made in relation to codes of conduct for councillors but the committee also drew attention to the changes involved in the officer–councillor relationship (1997, p. 5):

> One particular area that gave us cause for concern was the potential for improper behaviour if the normal relationship between member and officer became unsatisfactory by being either too comfortable or too combative. A number of councils already adopt a formal protocol setting out the relationship between officers and members; we believe that principle should now be extended throughout local government.

Land use planning was a particular focus of concern. 'Planning is probably the most contentious matter with which local government deals and is the one on which we have received by far the most submissions from members of the public' (1997, p. 6). This is partly because of the win–lose nature of many planning decisions. But there is also the tendency for formal contact between officers and/or councillors and those seeking planning permission to develop into something improper, for too much discussion to take place away from public scrutiny or go unrecorded, and for the granting of planning permission to become the sale of planning permission through the mechanism of planning gain. The grant of planning permission by local authorities on their own land and property was also a matter for concern.

Central to all these matters is the relationship between professional planners and the councillors who formally take decisions. Planning officers advise planning committees of councillors. Professional planning bodies proposed to Lord Nolan that the balance should be altered by excluding councillors from various stages of planning decision-making, such as the site visit, and constraining their influence. The Nolan Committee rejected this and instead chose 'to approach planning by accepting and under-standing the duty of elected members to listen to their constituents' (1997, p. 74) and favoured giving planning committee members more training in planning law and procedures. In a sense this is an attempt to professionalise councillors, in the belief that this will reduce improper behaviour by imbuing elected members with the norms of their professional officers, though Nolan also recognised the importance of independent scrutiny of the activities of councillors and officers by the Audit Commission, the Local Government Ombudsman and central government.

Paralleling these political criticisms of planners, there has been a critique developed in academic circles of the intellectual standing of planning as a profession. Broadbent (1977) has argued that planners had a less established body of knowledge and code of practice than many other related professions. As a result they were oversensitive to other professions poaching their areas of work and tended to be swayed by fashion. They readily adopted new theoretical approaches and sought to capture new planning procedures before other occupational groups. It has proved, therefore, very difficult to identify a coherent ideology for the profession (Foley, 1960). In a stringent attack on planners, Reade (1987) argues that planning lacks any credible theoretical basis, that it is a profession which was prematurely legitimised before its function could be fully clarified and that, consequently, it tries to disguise this fact by jargonising and confusing the issues it deals with: Reade terms this 'legitimation by obfuscation'. Again he emphasises the willingness of planners to take on board new ideas and concerns, without due consideration or a thorough grounding in the knowledge of these new areas.

Evidence of the changing flavour of planners' self-perception can be seen in the rapid shift that has occurred from a concern with economic development during the Thatcher years to the current attempts to take on board the growth of environmental policy. In 1983–5 an analysis of papers in the professional journal *The Planner* found that 45 per cent dealt with economic development, 13 per cent with the environment, and 11 per cent each with the development industry and public administration (Leyland, 1986, p. 34). Now planners are arguing for a key role in local environmental auditing, in EAs and in plan preparation with a 'green' slant. In support of this, they can cite a debate within the RTPI that took place in 1971 which adopted environmental planning as the broad description of the Institute's concerns. But this option was chosen out of no less than five very different definitions of planning, an indication of the lack of a certain professional identity.

Given the recent adoption of environmental concerns within planning, how easily does this fit with current patterns of practice? O'Riordan and Turner (1983, p. 136) find three reasons why planning should be more oriented towards environmental concerns. First, there is the impact of environmental scientific knowledge on the general consciousness of planners and planning policy-makers at central and local levels. Second, there is the interconnection between local economic prosperity and environmental degradation, affecting tourist and farming industries within certain areas. Even with a primary commitment to economic development, this encourages planners to take environmental concerns into account. Third, there are the procedural changes surrounding the introduction of EAs. However, O'Riordan and Turner question the ability of planners to deal effectively with the new problems they are facing. Most environmental data draws on knowledge of the natural sciences and thus planners are placed in the position of consulting external experts and assessing their material, often couched in highly technical terms. Second, there is a divergence between the time-scale on which environmental research is conducted and that for planning decision-making. The latter is relatively short-term, geared to local authority or other organisational decision-making cycles; the former can require a period of over five years to be conclusive. Third, the environmental scientists providing the raw information have a value system which emphasises their objectivity and neutrality *vis-à-vis* sectoral interests and is opposed to the political nature of much planning activity. This suggests that the ability of British planners to deal with the integration of environmental issues into planning may be limited: they lack the theoretical base or a consistent value scheme to do so.

These criticisms by O'Riordan and Turner, however, accept the traditional view of a professional as an expert rather than recognising the power base that monopolised and credentialised expertise can create. Rejecting the ability of planners to protect the environment and deliver sustainability on these bases may just hand the discretion and the power over decision-making to other professional groups, other environmental managers. If the implications of the professionalisation project for all these other types of environmental expertise are also accepted, then a more radical programme for involving lay publics or local communities in environmental decision-making may be needed. This is implied by the idea of the empowering professional (see below) and much Local Agenda 21 work (see Chapter 5). An essential element of this is a more modest conceptualisation of the contribution of the professional (including the professional planner), recognising the limits to expertise and questioning any automatic claims to serving the public interest. Planners' tendency to fall back on the rational comprehensive model, together with their view of themselves as welfare professionals to justify their activities, has supported their claims to be leading the sustainable development policy process; but the literature reviewed here both questions these justifications and suggests that planners may be pursuing 'green' topics because they are an organisationally and intellectually weak profession (Evans and Rydin, 1997).

Of course, such criticism from planning academics makes the profession even more vulnerable. Breheny and Congdon (1989) locate the reason for this in the division that exists between planning academics and professionals, so that the academics tend to develop knowledge, theories and research about planners rather than for them. This contrasts with many other professions, such as surveying and environmental engineering, where the academics and practitioners share common values and approaches, and academic work seeks to support everyday practice. It is, however, evident in other areas of work such as housing management, where radical critiques of the role of state professionals have also been developed.

■ The empowering professional

The legacy of these decades of criticism has resulted in a search for a different role for the planning profession, as an empowering profession. The new role for professionals looks back to ideas current in the 1960s to develop the concept of the 'empowering professional'. This goes beyond the New Right's concept of the 'enabling' professional who lets people 'help themselves' in the context of market processes; in this context, the

1985 Local Government (Access to Information) Act and 1987 Access to Personal Files Act are as much ways of constraining and checking on professionals as putting information in the hands of citizens. The concept of empowerment involves people using information to take political control in order to reallocate economic resources in the recognition that market processes systematically disadvantage certain groups. This often involves restructuring planning organisations, alongside changes in the attitudes and working practices of planners.

Organisations can be opened up to allow community groups to become directly involved in the decision-making that occurs within them, as the GLC showed. Organisations can also be decentralised to encourage participation. Local area offices and professional teams, even local mini town halls can give government a new, more approachable and challengeable face (Burns, 1988; Gyford, 1991; Hambleton and Hoggett, 1984). As Hambleton and Hoggett have shown, there is a wide range of motives informing the moves towards decentralisation. It is not automatically linked to radical notions of empowerment but it can be used as part of an attack on a professionalised welfare state. It can seek not only to improve public services and the accountability of those providing services, but also to alter the distribution of resources towards the disadvantaged and, most important, to raise political awareness among the local electorate.

There is now also a concerted effort among planning academics to develop work supportive of practitioners. This has shaped the nature of the institutional approach and Healey's collaborative planning theory (see Chapter 4). For example, the work of Forester (1989) has had a great influence. This recognises the constraints under which planners work but argues that they can play a positive role in achieving benefits for the environment and disadvantaged groups by means of 'communicative action' and 'mediated negotiation'. Drawing on ideas in American institutionalist politics, the analysis argues that 'political democracy depends not only on economic and social conditions but also on the design of political institutions' (March and Olsen, 1989, p. 17) and further (p. 27) that:

> Regardless of the way in which institutions are structured, attention is a scarce good in politics; and control over the allocation of attention is important to a political actor. By inhibiting the discovery of and entry into some potential conflicts, a structure of rules organized into relatively discrete responsibilities channels political energies into certain kinds of conflict and away from others.

Central to this process is the role of language, 'the ways in which participants come to be able to talk about one situation as similar or different from another' (p. 25).

The professional is important within this process of communication. It is not enough for the planner to stand aloof as the expert. For though Healey argues that 'techno-rational processes have at times been important safeguards for interests not otherwise actively represented in the social relations of policy formulation and implementation' (1990, p. 100), they have also suppressed interests. Hence the new mediating professional must be much more aware of the social and economic position of interests involved, of how the communication involved in planning is structured and of the relation between a mediating planning process and policy outcomes (Healey, 1992b):

> A full understanding of the impact of what planners do must address their contribution to the interrelated activities of knowing, acting and valuing . . . in interactive situations. This means analysing communicative acts.

Above all the planner must be reflexive about his or her own actions (Healey and Gilroy, 1990).

This will prove difficult (Myerson and Rydin, 1991). For the discourses of professions are themselves a source of power. As Murphy notes (1988, pp. 178–9), 'those who can develop and monopolise the language and concepts to be used in an area of social life do indeed have power rooted in knowledge'. The professional discourse is a way of cementing relations between professionals and distancing them from others, the lay public and clients: 'This discourse provides a basis of mutual understanding among professionals which is not shared by others' (Torstendahl, 1990, p. 2). This means that much professional communication is not about using knowledge systems to serve a 'problem solving capacity' but rather has a symbolic value unrelated to that capacity (p. 3). The political consequences of such discourses can be deeply undemocratic. Larson has argued that 'containing an issue within a discursive field controlled by professions is a depoliticising strategy' (1990, p. 39) and again that the 'inevitable recourse to scientific and technical expertise is one more factor that reduces legitimate citizen participation in decision-making' (1984, p. 39).

For these reasons, the hope that professionals may open up their discourses in the service of empowerment may be a pious one. They prefer to modify their discretion in decision-making by reference to the concept of 'client' (Kitchen, 1997), another market metaphor for a knowledge services market. Larson describes professional discourses as exercising their influence 'silently and invisibly'. Therefore changing such discourses and the associated professionalisation of planners is a considerable task. As Newman says, reasserting the rights of the citizen (rather than the client) within planning implies a reassessment of professional practices and values and requires 'a radical shift in attitudes and complete reform of the ways in which local and central government officers are trained. The prize for such a change would be strategic planning decisions arrived at through debate rather than conflict' (1991, p. 30). The broad model behind this vision is of a radical reworking of the enabling state concept as proposed, for example by Stewart (1995), in which the community is enabled to take a full part in, even control over, decision-making.

■ Further reading

Rees (1990) provides a good account of the role of professionals within environmental quangos, while Laffin and Young (1990) is a review of the situation in local authorities. Evans and Rydin (1997) provides a recent critique of the town planning profession in the context of the sustainability agenda. The issue of women in such professions is dealt with in Greed (1994) and Little (1994). Forester (1989) is a good introduction to the idea of the 'empowering' professional. These could be usefully set alongside the policy documentation of the RTPI and reports of its viewpoint in *Planning*, the weekly journal.

■ Chapter 9 ■

Planning and the Market

The previous chapters have considered the political processes of planning. However, it is now accepted that planning policy has an economic dimension. Economic processes underlie the problems that urban and environmental planning seeks to tackle; planning policies have their own economic impacts; and the interaction of planning and economy generates many of the political pressures on the planning system. Knowledge of economic processes is, therefore, as important as understanding the political process of the planning system. This chapter will review these economic processes, looking at the markets in land, property and environmental assets, the role of the construction and development industries and of financial institutions, and considering the valuation of land and the environment.

■ Analysing economic processes

The dominant model used to understand economic processes is the neo-classical account which is based on the market model and its development through welfare economics. The idealisation of the market model of the New Right has already been set out in Chapter 3, when the theoretical basis of Thatcherism was discussed. Few economists would accept this as an adequate account of contemporary economic processes. Rather the neo-classical formulation of economics, which is the dominant one within the academic social sciences and the economics 'profession', seeks to build on the market model, critiquing and adjusting it from inside. Welfare economics, the main such development, was introduced in Chapter 2, where its role in supporting procedural planning theory (PPT) with a theoretical justification and techniques such as cost–benefit analysis (CBA) was set out it. In Chapter 4 it was suggested that the approach had been reinvigorated through environmental economics and the application of valuation techniques to environmental services and assets, as a tool for achieving sustainable development policy goals. Some of these applications are covered later in this chapter.

The central concepts within the neo-classical model are equilibrium, efficiency and market failure. Market failure describes those situations in which market processes do not result in an efficient equilibrium, itself defined strictly in terms of a balance of the marginal costs and marginal benefits in the market ('marginal' here refers to the calculation of the additional costs or benefits arising from increasing an economic activity by a small amount at the margin). Market failure occurs because real-life markets fail to live up to the assumptions of the perfect model. These include: perfectly competitive markets with standardised commodities, numerous buyers and sellers and a ready exchange of market information. Examining the ways in which reality diverges from this ideal model identifies four distinct types of market failure (Harrison, 1977).

First, market processes may be 'distorted' by the existence of monopolies or other forms of imperfect competition. Second, it is not necessarily the case that the marginal revenue and cost schedules facing suppliers and consumers in the market represent the full costs and benefits of production and consumption. Externalities occur wherever the actions of a consumer or producer affect other consumers or producers other than through market prices. In these cases the private cost to the supplier diverges from social costs to all affected actors, and/or the private benefit to the consumer diverges from social benefits. In either case the operation of market processes will result in an equilibrium which is not efficient and at which there is a loss of social welfare. A third form of market failure is provided by the existence of 'public goods'. A public good is strictly defined by welfare economics in terms of non-excludability and non-rivalness. Essentially once a public good is supplied at all, it can be supplied to any who want it and may even be supplied to some who do not want it: street lighting is a good example. Furthermore consumption by another individual will not reduce the level or quality of existing consumption. In the case of such goods, the market has little incentive to supply them, for costs cannot be covered by revenue. Consumption have no incentive to pay for the good as they have the opportunity to free-ride on the provision of the good to other consumers. Many of the concerns of British planning have public-good characteristics. Enjoyment of a landscape is a public good as is a high level of local amenities: street furniture, planting, maintenance of the built environment, parks and playgrounds. Public rights of way and other access rights are by definition public goods as are also the fundamental functions of the environment in providing clean air and water. And fourth, market failure can result from other missing markets, in particular those in future goods, risk and information.

These various forms of market failure suggest the need for government intervention to rectify such failure or, at least, create a *prima facie* case for such intervention. However, it is not necessarily appropriate to intervene to remove the particular market failure that has been identified. First, this is because introducing a government policy, such as a tax, in one market may generate distortions in other related markets. Second, the economic theory of the 'second best' argues that the best way to deal with distortions in one market may be actively to create distortion in other markets. Third, the costs and benefits of the policy intervention itself must be assessed to ensure that greater inefficiency is not created by intervening than by leaving the market failure alone.

The main opposition to the neo-classical orthodoxy has traditionally come from the Marxist school. Marxists criticise the dominant neo-classical position on the grounds that the focus on supply and demand within a market framework uncritically accepts the appearance of equal exchange between buyers and sellers. Neo-classical economics, according to Marxism, focuses on epiphenomena rather than the underlying causal processes. The key to unravelling these causal processes is a recognition of the central importance of 'class'. Relations in society are essentially class relations and the actions of individuals and groups can be understood only in terms of their class position. The starting point of any Marxist analysis is the production process through which capital accumulation occurs (Ambrose, 1986). The exploitation of labour through the sale of labour power in the market-place and the appropriation of 'surplus value' – created by labour – by the owner of capital, the capitalist, is the source of wealth creation under capitalism. The system is driven by the capitalist seeking to use the exploitation of labour to accumulate capital over time, to generate a larger and larger quantity of surplus value and accelerate the rate at which accumulation occurs.

Unlike some equilibrium theories of neo-classical economists, the Marxist analysis of capitalism does not assume a steady state. On the contrary it presupposes that the tendency of the system is towards contradiction and crisis. Capitalism continually has to respond to these contradictory tendencies and seek to avoid crisis. The generation of urban and environmental problems is seen in this light (Harvey, 1985; Burkitt, 1984). Crises within capitalism can take a number of forms. The most famous, perhaps, is the tendency of the rate of profit to fall. But there is also the way that the drive to accumulate capital results in the overproduction of goods relative to the capacity of the economy to absorb them. Third, crises can result from the anarchy inherent in a fragmented market system (Desai, 1979, Part III). A particular form of this problem, which may be termed a fourth crisis tendency, is posed by the existence of a separate sector focused on landownership and investment in landed property assets (Massey and Catalano, 1978). And we could now add the environmental crisis to this list (O'Connor, 1994). Redclift (1987, p. 48) argues:

Marxists see the commitment to commodity production under capitalism as making ecological externalities inevitable. Indeed it is part of the contradictory nature of capitalism that the environmental crisis presents a massive threat to the earning powers of entrepreneurs, as underwritten by the capitalist state.

The outcomes of such a crisis-ridden process of capital accumulation take a number of forms: cyclical activity in all sectors of the economy, aggravated by speculation; the unemployment of certain resources, coexisting with the overexploitation of others; and periodic collapses of capitalist enterprises. Each of these outcomes has urban and environmental consequences.

More recently the regulationist school has focused attention on the means by which crisis has to be continually avoided and the expanded social reproduction of capitalism continually secured. This school looks to the analysis of social norms, mechanisms and institutions as a way of understanding this process of seeking to achieve continuity and adjust to change. As Jessop, among others, points out, regulationists cover a broad spectrum from the more functionalist Marxists through to institutionalists. The Marxist variant is interested in how institutions are implicated in the survival of capitalism 'even though the capital relation itself inevitably generated antagonisms and crises which make continuing accumulation improbable' (Jessop, 1990, p. 308). To continue the Jessop quote:

> The answer was found in regulatory mechanisms, i.e., institutional forms, societal norms and patterns of strategic conduct which successfully expressed and regulated these conflicts until the inevitable build-up of tensions and disparities among the various regulatory forms reached crisis point. When this occurred there would be an experimental period from which a new accumulation regime and a corresponding mode of regulation might – or might not emerge.

The intention is certainly to provide accounts which are not economically reductionist and are more sensitive to non-economic bases of explanation. But while the existence of a single objective development logic of capital may be denied (Jessop, 1990, p. 10), Marxist regulationists still search for logics of capital, logics determined by the law of value at some level (ibid., p. 311; Leyshon and Thrift, 1997, p. 270).

These two economic paradigms are increasingly being challenged by an institutional economic analysis. In economics, institutionalism describes both a distinct mode of analysis and a variety of work (see Eggertson,1990; Veblen, 1976 Myrdal, 1957; Galbraith, 1981; Granovetter and Swedberg, 1992; and particularly Hodgson, 1988). What is common to all these applications is, of course, a concern with institutions. Institutions can be defined as organisations such as the firm, the networks for organising contact between actors or the bodies which shape the labour market. But these approaches also define institutions in the sociological sense as sets of rules and norms which shape behaviour and decision-making. This twin focus can be seen in all work under the institutional label. Furthermore there is a normative dimension to the work. The current social structure is seen as centrally relevant, particularly the issue of social status and the pursuit of goods and economic roles to reflect higher status. The existing inequalities of property ownership are the starting point for much analysis and many trends in economic activity are seen to reinforce, not eliminate, those inequalities. The state is also integrated within the analysis and not a *deus ex machina* which intervenes from outside the economic system. Institutionalists, therefore, have a normative analysis of the state which promotes a role for public policy in redressing economic and social inequalities.

Four key themes can be identified in institutional economics work. First, there is a concern with markets as institutions which require state or societal action to create and maintain them, particularly with regard to regulating and enforcing transactions. Second, there is the nature of economic actors as organisations, including the organisation of the firm and the management of the processes of consumption and retailing. Third, economic decision-making is not taken for granted but requires detailed examination; a range of motives for economic action such as satisficing are relevant. And fourth, regimes of property rights are seen as centrally important. Many institutional economists see economic action as socially situated so that economic action is embedded in ongoing networks of personal relations rather than being carried out by atomised economic agents. This emphasis on networks is reminiscent of the concern with mediation, negotiation and networking of collaborative planners (see Chapter 4).

■ Land, property and development markets

The focus of the planning policies covered here is on the built and natural environment. Of course the economic processes involved in all production, consumption and distribution activities have an environmental and spatial impact and there are policies, such as those aimed at 'greening business', which try to ameliorate some of these impacts. But the planning policies detailed here are essentially seeking to influence and control more directly the use made of the environment. Therefore the economic processes that such planning interfaces with are those involving rights to the natural and built environment, that is, land and property markets. To reemphasise a point made by institutional economists, such markets are not markets in the physical environment itself (or parcels of it); rather the object of exchange processes in the markets is rights: rights to build on land, to obtain a rent from occupiers, to draw on or emit into watercourses, to extract minerals or to deposit waste. Such rights are defined by law and enforced by the state. While for well-established markets, such as those in houses, it is easy to forget that it is not the physical object that is being traded and the role of the state in creating and sustaining the market can be overlooked, for newer markets such as those in pollution permits, the complexities of defining the object of exchange, setting up institutions for exchange and enforcing those exchanges are all too apparent.

The key distinction between different markets in rights to the environment is between use, investment and transformation. Use markets are concerned with the built and natural environment as a site for occupation, a location where other activities can occur. Large sections of the residential, commercial and industrial markets fall into this category as households and firms seek sites for their domestic and profit-seeking activities. The ownership of the countryside and undeveloped parts of urban areas for nature reserves and leisure access by organisations such as the National Trust can also be considered part of the use market. Investment markets comprise those seeking ownership of rights for the stream of income and/or capital appreciation that they represent. Much of this market – and all of it in the 'prime' category of best quality property – consists of freeholds which are bought in order to create leaseholds and tenancies and thereby generate a flow of rental income. More specialist submarkets comprise leaseholds which are then sublet so that a positive income is generated by the differential between the rent from the occupier and the rent to the freeholder; more complex arrangements are also possible. The third market involves those who seek to use the built and natural environment as a raw material, and have an interest in transforming that material. This includes the rural primary industries of agriculture and mining, both of which rely on the land and its ecological and geological characteristics as the source of profit. It also includes the development industry whose primary interest is in using a piece of the environment as a location for construction, and in transforming the use and character of that local environment (see Exhibit 9.1). Many polluting and waste disposal activities are also of this nature, using the absorptive capacity of the environment, whether a landfill site, a water course or the atmosphere. Here the interest in the environment is in its ability to support other production and consumption activities. Many of these environmental services are provided free but increasingly a charge is being made: the landfill tax adjusts the market price for waste disposal facilities; charges for emission to water create a new cost for the polluter (see Chapter 11). Neither of these examples are tradeable and therefore do not constitute marketable rights, but proposals for emission permits, as already exercised

---

Exhibit 9.1   *The development process*

As the following flow diagram shows, the overall development process is a complex ensemble of different actors undertaking many different tasks. As well as the entrepreneurial organisor – the developer – the other actors involved will be professionals (lawyers, valuers, architects, surveyors), construction companies, raw materials suppliers, financiers and landowners. The commercial entity that is the developer may fulfill almost all these functions in-house or may be involved with a range of other organisations. One developer may already own the land, raise at least part of the finance internally, have their own architects and other professionals, and do the building work themselves. Another may be dealing with a separate landowner and financier and sub-contract all the commercial and professional work to other firms. And of course overseeing all development activities are the public sector regulators – planning, building regulations, health and safety, environmental standards.

The development process

Assessment of potential: firming up on plans to develop

⬇

Development appraisal: requirements for construction to proceed
    Landownership – acquire property rights to site
    Public procedures – acquire planning permissions and
    building consents
    Financing – acquire financing on profitable terms
    Site preparation – clear, service and prepare site
    Demand assessment – assess market price and client/buyer/occupier
    requirements

⬇

Construction: physical production process + organisation of that process
    Letting tenders and contracts
    Management of labour and materials
    Using professional advice

⬇

Disposal: marketing, agreeing prices, legal exchange of property rights

Note: While the diagram depicts the development process as sequential, the different stages may not take place in this order.

in USA, would create such a market in environmental rights (Pearce and Turner, 1990)

The length of time that rights in any of the three markets may be exercised varies from short tenancies and permits to 'outright ownership', the holding of a freehold that defines owner-occupation. Another characteristic that distinguishes exchanges in a market is the functionality of the physical parcel of the environment for the purpose of the owner. This is partly a matter of the physical characteristics of the environment – the layout of the house, the road access for a shop, the quality of the fixtures and fittings, the quality of the soil, the beauty of a view. But the spatial configuration of the environment and the way the different aspects relate to each other are also important. For valuers of property rights, this distils down to the importance of location and the distinction they draw between prime and secondary locations, the former commanding higher rents and prices. Thus in retail property markets, the prime pitch identifies that part of the shopping area with the greatest footfall, the largest number of shoppers passing by; this is partly the result of the physical layout of the shopping centre and the access points to transport and parking facilities, but it is also a result of the prior location of certain retailers who will almost always attract large numbers of customers – such as Marks and Spencer. In industrial and commercial markets, factors such as ease of access, the existence of new purpose-built properties that meet the exact up-to-date requirements of contemporary users and, again, a conglomeration of such uses all help define the prime as opposed to secondary areas. In residential markets, the different value areas are distinguished by a variety of local amenities: visual character, access to transport facilities, the local schools, and so on. The residential market example also makes it clear that the more desirable locations will go to those with the greatest purchasing power, the greatest income. Hence the prime and secondary property categories have strong class connotations.

While these three markets are conceptually distinct, it is possible for one piece of the environment to be viewed in terms of use, investment and/or transformation, either at different times or by different owners. The landlord of a property will primarily be interested in its performance as an investment while the occupier will be interested in its usefulness for occupation. A residential owner-occupier will combine both these interests. Even the owner of pollution permits may have an eye to their capital appreciation if they are tradeable. And development interests, though seeking profit through construction, may also hold the ownership of the subsequent development and become longer-term investors; developers can also hold land prior to construction, aiming to make profits from capital appreciation of the site and not just the construction activities.

Table 9.1   *Land prices as at 1 April 1997 (£ per hectare)*

	England and Wales		Scotland	Northern Ireland
Agricultural land:[1] Vacant				
possession	3190–8550		403–5856	3285–11 547
Tenanted	1208–3227		151–2779	–
	England and Wales (excl. London)	London	Scotland	Northern Ireland
Residential development land:				
Bulk land	663 000	1.9m	513 000	258 500
Small sites	726 000	1.8–3.0 m	626 000	290 000
Industrial development land:	351 000	1.0–1.2 m	183 000	–

[1]Lower figures for hill farming; higher figures for arable or dairy farming.
Source: Valuation Office, *Property Market Report, Spring 1997.*

The interaction of these different reasons for holding rights in land, building or parcels of the natural environment can be further examined by looking at the different submarkets as defined by activity (see Table 9.1). The agricultural land market comprises both those seeking owner-occupied farms and those seeking tenanted farms as an investment, together with those who might purchase a small farm primarily as a rural dwelling and those developers interested in the potential for conversion of at least part of the land or buildings. There will also be a demand for options from developers interested in the future development potential of the land; an option gives the developer the opportunity to purchase the land on specified terms. Because of this range of types of demand, the factors influencing the market also vary: the profitability of farming affects the occupying farmer and investment market; the residential amenities and access to transport affects the housing market; and the profitability of development and chances of getting planning permission affect the development market. These factors obviously vary from time to time, region to region and property to property.

While the agricultural land market thus overlaps with the development land market, there is also an explicit market in land with development potential. This is strongly influenced by the profitability of development –

Table 9.2   *Rental values as at 1 April 1997 ($£/m^2$)*

Region	Shops GIA basis[1]	Offices Modern, $1000 + m^2$	Industry Modern, $500\,m^2$
Northern	70–110	55–105	20–38
Yorks. & Humb.	60–97	70–180	22–53
North West	85–115	65–195	34–43
W. Midlands	85–140	72–215	28–48
E. Midlands	65–115	50–124	28–50
E. Anglia	85–130	85–145	33–53
South West	75–100	60–135	28–50
South East	65–145	60–180	38–75
Outer London	80–320	95–190	45–75
Inner London	–	150–400	50–58
Wales	70–140	45–115	25–45
Scotland	62–195	90–180	30–60
N. Ireland	115	110	35

Note: Data may be based on a small sample of transactions in the relevant period.
[1]GIA = gross internal area; rents for shops can also be worked out on the basis of a zoning pattern where the front of the shop is assumed to be worth more than the back.
Source: Valuation Office, *Property Market Report, Spring 1997.*

for example, by house prices, mortgage rates and changes in disposable income. Changes in local economic development can shift the spatial location of the most profitable development sites. The higher incomes of the London labour market plus the limited supply of sites available pushes up residential development land prices to over £1 million per hectare compared to half that in Wales. Similarly industrial development sites achieve over £1 million per hectare compared to less than £200 000 in Scotland.

The property market data for shops, industrial premises and offices show great variation between regions and between types of property. Table 9.2 gives some rental value data for the different sectors from the Valuation Office reports for 1 April 1997 and this shows ranges for each region even within specific categories for offices and factories. This variation is indicative of the importance of the individual characteristics of the buildings and sites – age, condition, suitability for function – and also the location of the properties – near transport, prime pitch, surrounding uses, level of local economic development.

Table 9.3   *Property yields as at 1 April 1997*

	England and Wales	Scotland	Britain
Agricultural land[1]	5.25–6.50	6.00–8.50	–
Shops[2]			
Average	–	7.9	8.3
Prime	6.25	–	–
Offices[2]			
Average	–	9.5	9.6
Prime	9.25	–	–
Factories and warehouses[2]			
Average	–	10.3	11.5
Prime	11.75	–	–

[1]Simple percentage yield.
[2] All risks initial yield.
Source: *Valuation Office, Property Market Report, Spring 1997.*

The investment market is measured by rates of return, the yield. Table 9.3 gives some figures for the different sectors: agricultural yields are calculated on a simple percentage basis of rents divided by vacant possession value; for the shops, offices and industrial sectors, initial all-risks yields are given which is the rate used to capitalise initial rents (that is, calculate the capital value from initial rents) and also the yield for prime property in each sector. Industrial property yields a higher return (10-11 per cent) but this is because shops and offices (to a lesser extent) are considered to be a safer long-term investment. The yield for shopping centres is now taken as an indicator of town centre viability, following planning advice in Planning Policy Guidance Note 6 (see Chapter 10). Therefore the Valuation Office provides detailed prime retail yield evidence for 550 shopping centres in England, plus 44 in Wales and 41 in Scotland. This shows that yields can fall as low as 4 per cent for a prime new shopping centre such as Meadowhall outside Sheffield, or rise as high as 12 per cent for a sleepy seaside location such as Shoreham-by-Sea in Sussex. Even small spatial distances can separate very different local property markets: rental yields are down to 6 per cent in Camden Town, London, but rise to 12 per cent in Cricklewood only a couple of miles away.

Attention now turns to two sets of key actors in property markets: the construction industry and the property investment sector.

■ The construction industry

The construction industry is a major economic actor. It comprises over 194 000 firms, employs over 1.3 million people and in the third quarter of 1995 undertook work amounting to over £10 million. Housing production alone amounted to almost 4 per cent of gross domestic product in 1995 (it was 5.4 per cent at its peak in 1988). These aggregate figures cover a wide variation within the industry. There is, for example, a wide variation in the size of firms: some 99 000 (51 per cent of the total) are one-person firms; 95 per cent employ seven people or less. Yet the few large firms account for the vast bulk of the work done in the industry (see Table 9.4). The largest 189 firms, less than 0.1 per cent of the total, account for 28 per cent of all work done by value and 37 per cent of all new work. Many of the small firms are either engaged in the repair and maintenance sector or are subcontractors to larger firms, in an industry where extensive subcontracting and the use of self-employed labour has always been the norm: 45 per cent of all those employed in construction are self-employed. Repair and maintenance has been a growing sector within the industry, as might be expected in a country with a significant proportion of older stock, particularly in housing where demolitions and closure are only running at a few hundred a year. But even within the new work category, there is tremendous variety from road and infrastructure building to large shopping or commercial complexes to smaller estates and one-off buildings. In total housing comprises 28 per cent of all new orders, infrastructure 19 per cent and other work 53 per cent. As can be seen from Figure 9.1, housing and commercial work dominate the orders.

Figure 9.1 also shows that the public sector is a significant customer of the construction industry, accounting for 30 per cent of all new orders: road orders and work for the education and health sectors stand out as

Table 9.4 *Structure of the construction industry (GB), 1995*

No. employees	No. firms	% total no.	% all work done[1]	% new work[1]
1–7	184 224	95	31	19
8–59	8 755	5	23	22
60–299	1 909	< 1	18	22
300–1199	156	–	15	19
1200 +	33	–	13	18

[1]Relates to work done in 3rd quarter 1995.
Source: Housing and Construction Statistics 1997.

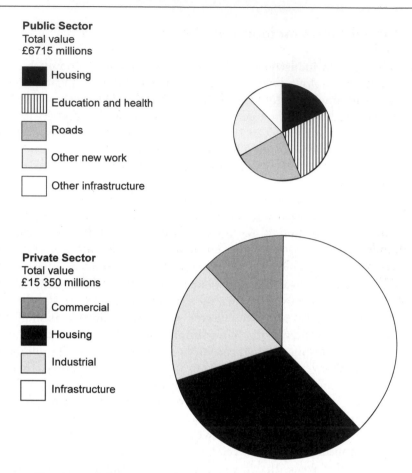

Source: *Housing and Construction Statistics 1985–1995.*

Figure 9.1   *Public and private sector construction orders*

significant categories. The role of the public sector as a major builder and provider of housing is now in the past. Of the 199 000 dwellings completed in the UK in 1995, only 21 per cent were public sector and these were overwhelmingly housing association schemes (20 per cent of the total) – less than 3000 dwellings were built by local authorities. These figures cement the predominance of owner-occupation in the housing sector: 67 per cent of the stock of 24 million houses is owner-occupied; 4 per cent housing association owned; 10 per cent privately rented; and 19 per cent in the hands of local authorities and new town corporations. Neither do local authorities undertake much construction themselves any more. In the past many local authorities had direct labour organisations (DLOs) to undertake construction work. In the 1980s such DLOs were required to compete with private sector firms and demonstrate a rate of return, that is, effectively operate at a profit. This was despite the claims that such DLOs worked to a higher standard of output and offered better and safer working conditions to their employees. As a result the significance of DLOs has fallen considerably. In October 1995 423 local authorities had DLOs, employing 77000 operatives (less than 6 per cent of total employment). They were responsible for £810 million of work done in the third quarter of 1995, about 8 per cent of all work done. Ninety-five per cent of this was repair and maintenance, 55 per cent was housing repair and maintenance.

The other significant feature of the construction industry is the highly cyclical nature of its activities. There are cycles in all business activity but those affecting construction are particularly pronounced. Figure 9.2 shows the trends in construction output and housing completions in Britain for the past two decades. The impact of the onset of economic recession after the 1973/4 crisis can be seen in the series for all output while the impact of spiralling house prices can be seen in increasing housing completions in the same period. Thereafter a construction boom can be seen in the late 1980s as the Conservative government policy of property-led regeneration reinforced economic recovery in that period. Meanwhile the fall in house

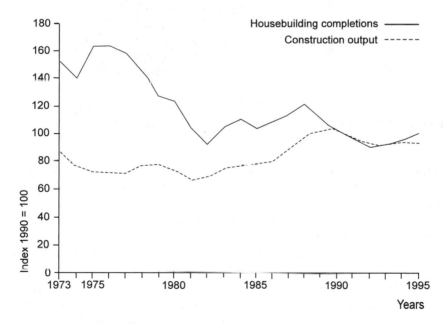

Source: Housing and Construction Statistics 1985–1995.

Figure 9.2   *Housebuilding completions and construction outputs*

prices from 1991 onwards led to a corresponding fall in housebuilding. This cyclical pattern in turn leads to a high rate of entry and exit to and from the industry: in 1995 there were 2783 bankruptcies and 1844 liquidations, 13 per cent of the total; construction forms the single largest category.

While these strong cyclical patterns are undoubtedly problematic for individual firms, there are other implications. Ball has argued that there is little prospect of industry investment in improving the skills of construction workers or the quality of the output while such instability remains endemic (1988). British construction remains a relatively low-skill, low-quality industry with low levels of innovation. This is currently retarding the potential for more environmentally-friendly buildings. This is not just a matter of conservatism within the industry or due to the industry being a passive victim of economic cycles. Rather there are sectors within the industry who actually benefit from and therefore actively contribute to this instability.

It has been mentioned above that certain interests in the construction industry also hold land for investment purposes. This is particularly true of the housebuilding sector at certain periods of time. The rationale for this is shown in Figure 9.3 which sets out a price index for new dwellings and housing land. The huge variation over just fifteen years is readily apparent. It is also notable that housing land prices fluctuated more than dwelling prices. There is a powerful rationale in these figures for buying land when it is cheap and holding it, if this is financially feasible, during a rising part of the cycle to build it out when house prices are high. If resources allow, this means housebuilders should seek to acquire land banks either outright or via options to purchase land at preferable terms in the future. Of course, this is a risky strategy as a fall in the housing market may leave a builder with expensive land banks that can no longer be built out at a profit. Such speculation in housing land has had and continues to have a significant impact on the housing market, fuelling instability and diverting resources from product improvement to land accumulation. It can also result in pressure on the land use planning system to skew planning permissions towards housebuilder-owned land. And the competition over land can seriously disadvantage social housing providers by bidding up prices; a recession when private builder interest is low may prove the time when housing associations can most readily acquire sites for social housing. Finally these cyclical patterns follow quite different timescales in different parts of the country in response to local conditions and policy initiatives, but also as changes in property prices in one part – usually the south-east – slowly create a ripple effect across space. This will also affect the pressures that a local planning system will face from development pressure at any particular time.

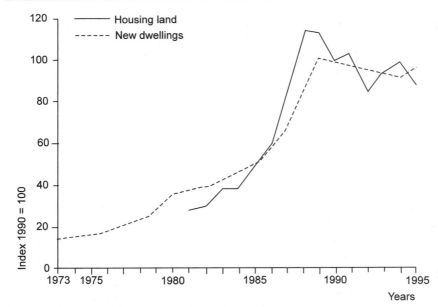

Source: Housing and Construction Statistics 1985–1995.

Figure 9.3   *Housing land and new dwelling prices*

Some developers do seek to insulate themselves from the cyclical patterns. This can be done by finding a stable niche in the market. For a time demographic change meant that accommodation for older households provided such a niche. Luxury or specialist property may also constitute such a niche but any such submarket is unlikely to persist for any length of time. Another strategy is to concentrate on grant-related urban regeneration schemes (Rydin, 1998a). As in the mass housebuilding schemes of the 1960s (see Dunleavy, 1981), use of public sector monies can provide a profitable alternative to a reliance on market activities provided a close enough, in effect corporatist, relationship is built up with the state body holding the funds.

■ The investment sector

As emphasised above, many different property owners can have investment interests, seeking capital appreciation of their asset, whatever that may be. In this section, the influence of the major property investors is explored.

The distinguishing feature of such investors is that they seek to hold property for at least the medium and often long term. Beyond this they vary in terms of the kind of risk they are willing to take on; risk here means volatility in returns, either through changes in rental income or the capital value of property. Pension funds are generally the most risk-averse of investors since they have a fairly certain commitment to meet in the future that is, paying out pensions – and they need to be sure that the income and value of their investment portfolio matches those commitments. Insurance companies' commitments are less certain and less long-term, though actuarial methods reduce uncertainty and the growth of life insurance business makes them more akin to pension funds. Together these institutions comprise the commonly used category, financial institutions. They show a preference for prime property, which is the least risky as defined above. However risk, in a capitalist economy, is also the source of profit and less risky investments tend to show lower returns. The standard relationship is given in the following formula where: capital value = rental income/rate of return or yield.

	Prime property	*Secondary property*
Capital value	£3m	£3m
Rental income	£240 000	£450 000
Yield	8%	15%

A prime property with good prospects of capital value growth and a secure rental income will have a low rate of return so that rental income will be relatively low for the same capital value compared to more secondary property, though of course the rent or value per m2 will be higher for prime property.

Property has been a good investment for this sector because of its long-term durability, the ability to obtain a low-risk investment by buying or developing only prime property and its good returns in certain past periods compared with other paper assets such as equities (stocks and shares) and bonds, particularly government bonds (known as gilts). By mixing investment in all these assets, the institutions can build up a portfolio which gives a good return for low risk. As a result financial institutions have bought into the best quality agricultural land, new office developments, major retail schemes and prime industrial property including science parks. But when property markets are not performing well, as has been the case during the recession of the early 1990s, then institutions will shift out of property into other assets, notably equities. The weight of property in institutional investment portfolios fell by 50 per cent from 1990 to 1996, resulting in an average holding in property of only 5 per cent (see Table 9.5). At the same time the development activity of institutions, which was very evident during the 1980s as institutions sought to create the prime property that was in short supply in the market, has declined. This means less pressure on local planning authorities for

Table 9.5   *Direct investment in UK property by financial institutions[1](£m)*

	Pension funds		Long-term insurance companies	
	£m	% total	£m	% total
1989	27 359	8	38 854	16
1990	26 943	9	34 828	15
1991	24 527	7	32 185	12
1992	19 914	5	30 074	9
1993	21 932	5	33 939	8
1994	24 353	5	35 914	9
1995	24 259	5	36 369	7

[1]Financial institutions also invest in overseas property (over £2000m in 1995) and indirectly via property unit trusts.
Source: Annual Abstract of Statistics 1997.

planning permissions for development schemes but also less possibility of manipulating that development pressure to meet regeneration objectives and fewer possibilities for planning gain on such schemes. Despite this overall decline in the importance of property and property development to institutions, total investment by this sector in land and property is still considerable: over £60 000 million in 1995. The management of existing portfolios can have a significant impact on the built environment. The Investment Property Databank (1997), the premier source of information on institutional investment, notes the following re-engineering of property portfolios over the past sixteen years: a shift from offices to the retail sector; disinvestment from central London; and a preference for shopping centres and retail warehouses. In certain localities these shifts will form a significant context for local planning activity.

Not all development is undertaken by financial institutions though. In between the institution and the construction company are the development or property companies. These companies are speculators. Working in the commercial and industrial sectors, they will build developments and look to let and sell them on to others as an investment, or if market conditions are not right for this, they will hold the development as an investment. The key indicator of activity in the property company sector is the amount of bank lending to such companies. As at the end of December 1995, £30 732 million was lent to property companies by UK banks, just under 6 per cent of all bank loans outstanding (see Table 9.6). One of the concerns of financial regulators has been that the activities of such developers – spurred on in the pursuit of fairly short-term profit, without a commitment to the long term stability of the property sector and with the fuel of often

Table 9.6   *Bank lending to property companies*

	£m	% of total amount outstanding
Third Wednesday of November		
1986	9 349	5
1987	13 360	6
End November		
1988	21 348	7
1989	31 963	8
1990	38 996	9
1991	39 670	8
1992	37 944	8
End December		
1993	34 249	7
1994	32 181	7
1995	30 732	6

Source: Annual Abstract of Statistics 1997.

generous bank lending – can generate speculative bubbles in property development which can cause oversupply of new buildings and excessive vacancy rates. One of the tasks of strategic planning has been to try and regulate this process through the supply of planning permissions. However, given the strength of the financial pressures, the relative weakness of development control and the time lags that exist in the development process, this can be a very ineffective form of regulation.

In addition to the activities of pension funds, long-term insurance companies and property companies investing in a portfolio of individual parcels of land and buildings, there have been repeated attempts to create a larger and more liquid investment market based in land and property, where transactions can occur more readily and speedily. This would comprise paper units, more akin to equities. Just as equities represent a share in the profits generated by commercial companies, so property units would represent a share of the rental income and capital growth of a property, which might take a variety of forms of the built and natural environment. Property unit trusts – equivalent to equity-based unit trusts but based on property ownership – have been available for some time but only to pension funds, essentially to allow smaller funds to benefit from this type of investment. Pension funds invested £2443 million in this way in 1995. Proposals for unitisation or securitisation aim to create a market in paper assets based on a share in an individual property's or a portfolio of properties' returns. The redevelopment of the old Billingsgate Fish Market in the City of London as office space was financed on this basis but plans for a fully securitised property market are still just plans (Howells and Rydin, 1990).

■ Pricing, valuation and appraisal processes

In the neo-classical model, pricing is a result of the operation of the invisible hand, the interaction of supply and demand through the pursuit by individual producers and consumers of their own self-interest. In reality, as institutional economics has stressed, there are powerful societal influences on the pricing process, including the professionalisation of valuation and the exercise of norms and behavioural routines. In this section, some of these conventional aspects of pricing, valuation and appraisal in the market-place are examined.

There are five conventional methods of valuing land and buildings. These arise because there are insufficient exchanges of homogeneous (that is, similar and equivalent) goods in the property market. Characteristics of the buildings, the site, the local environment and the precise property rights, together with the spatial location, all distinguish any particular item to be exchanged in the property market from almost all others. Therefore there is no 'invisible hand'. Professional valuers have to determine the price at which rights should be offered. The methods they use are: the comparative method, trying to find recent similar transactions; the contractor's test which uses an adjustment of the cost of building a replacement; the profits method which deduces a value for land and buildings based on the profitability of the occupying activities – used for hotels, public houses and mining locations; the residual method, used for determining the value of development land; and a discounted cash-flow approach, which assesses property as an investment. The last two methods are well-used in the development and investment sectors and therefore deserve further explanation. They also raise issues concerning the environmental impact of property development.

The residual method is used both to determine the value of a development site, working backwards from the value of the proposed development, and to calculate the viability of a development project taking into account the asking price for the site. The broad outline of the calculation is as follows:

	Gross development value
less	Total construction costs
less	Development profit
equals	Residual site value

Exhibit 9.2   *Environmental valuation and CVM*

The variant of welfare economics known as environmental economics has been increasingly influential in policy circles. The overriding recommendation of the environmental economics approach is to find a way of valuing the environment which approximates to market prices. In this way a more efficient allocation of resources is achieved, social welfare is increased and environmental degradation can be reduced to optimal levels. The goal is not the absolute elimination of pollution and other degradation. Rather it is a matter of balancing the costs of that environmental damage against its benefits, i.e. the welfare generated by the economic activities causing that damage. Hence the need is to find a unit of measurement for environmental damage (or obversely the value of environmental goods and services) which can be taken into account alongside the profits and prices which measure the benefits of production and consumption. A number of techniques are available within environmental economics: hedonic pricing in which econometric techniques are used to establish the relationship between aspects of the local environment, such as a view, and local property prices so that a price for changing the local environment can be calculated; the travel-cost method which uses the costs of travelling to a particular environmental asset such as a country park, including the time taken, to assess the value of that asset; the risk premium method is where the additional wage for undertaking a job in environmentally risky conditions is used as an indicator of the cost of that risk; and the contingent valuation method, where a complex set of iterative questionnaires is used to identify how much people would be willing to pay for an environmental good or asset, or alternatively willing to accept as compensation for the loss of that good or asset.

CVM is now increasingly advocated as a valuation technique; the results of such surveys can then be fed back into neo-classical analysis and corresponding policy prescriptions. However, as Jacobs points out, there are considerable problems with this method (1994, p. 74). He identifies problems of: refusal to participate in the surveys; different results arising from

---

The detailed calculation involves allowances for all elements of the development process, including contingencies for unexpected events and the costs of development finance. The stage in the development process when each cost occurs is estimated and a discount rate – equivalent to the cost of finance – is used to reduce all figures to a present-day value (see below for further discussion of discounting in the context of environmental valuation). The development profit is worked out at a conventional proportion of gross development value. The calculation expresses the fiction that land values are a residual which passively accrues to landowners. In practice, the sum of the development profit and the residual land value represents a surplus over the commitments to the construction contractors, the financiers and all professionals involved in

asking people about their willingness to pay for goods and services and their willingness to accept compensation for the loss of those same goods and services; and aggregation when the results of different surveys in different aspects of the environment are collated. There is also doubt over the meanings of the results since it seems unlikely that respondents' interpretations of the questions and their answers is on a par with the economist analysing them. In the case of the environment, Jacobs argues that 'there are no individually expressed preferences' and that what is at stake 'is the design of the institutions through which social choices are made and enforced' (1994, p. 77). Thus Jacobs also favours an institutional economic paradigm.

There are also issues of how CVM treats issues of equity. In the neo-classical model, distribution is seen as a distinct issue from allocative efficiency within the model. If the outcome of market processes is seen to be unjust, then this is a matter for a separate policy effort. Others would argue that it is necessary to be more aware of the distributive consequences of policy recommendations. While the environmental valuation techniques and cost-benefit analysis are presented as neutral and objective, they incorporate normative assumptions about the values of different income groups. Higher income groups will bid more for assets and services, because they can afford to and they exhibit a lower marginal utility of money. Therefore they 'count' more in any valuation technique than low income groups. Negative impacts on high income groups will result in a greater loss of social welfare than the same impact on a lower income group. At the extreme, the loss of life of a high earner is worth more than that of a low earner. Many find these implications of the neo-classical approach highly distasteful. Proponents defend them in the name of maximising total social welfare and the most efficient use of scarce resources. But a concern with equity remains a key impetus in the search for alternative theoretical frameworks, techniques and methods.

the development and this surplus is bargained over by the landowner and the developer. From a planning perspective, the significance of the residual calculation is that the surplus is also available for the planning authority to try and extract planning gain. The larger the gross development value, the lower the costs of development and the greater the availability of development sites (which weakens the landowner's power in negotiations), and the greater the opportunity for extracting sizeable planning gain from the developer (subject to legislative restrictions, of course – see Chapter 10).

Discounted cash-flow (DCF) techniques are now gaining ascendancy not only in the investment sector but also as a way of appraising development projects and obtaining valuations of a growing range of projects and properties. Simple computer software is readily available now for undertaking such DCF calculations. The essence of the approach is that all the costs and benefits of a project are set out in a matrix which has time periods (years, quarters, months) as one axis. The sum of costs and benefits – the net cash-flow – is then discounted using an appropriate discount rate. The rationale for such discounting is that, in a capitalist economy, there is a cost involved in waiting for income to accrue equivalent to the lost interest that would have been earned if the monies had been invested; similarly there is an advantage if costs are delayed. When all the cash-flow has been discounted to present-day values, then the sum of present values can be assessed to see if any profit remains, if there is a positive net present value. This is essentially the same technique as cost-benefit analysis (CBA), although a CBA will typically involve items for which there is no market price and a proxy needs to be estimated (see below). As might be expected, the final outcome of the calculation is dependent on which elements are included, at which price and the choice of discount rate. Sensitivity analysis can be undertaken to see how robust the outcome is to changes in any of the elements of the calculation.

For market-based calculations, most of the elements should be fairly accurately assessed with sufficient knowledge of market conditions. Where non-market elements are included this can be more difficult. This is where the literature on market-based appraisal meets that on environmental valuation. There has been a recent attempt to try and incorporate more environmental costs of development and other projects into the calculation of the viability of the scheme. Environmental economists argue that as the goods and services the environment provides are largely unpriced, they are effectively ignored in the assessment of whether a scheme should proceed or not; they have to be protected by regulation, but regulation of a scheme which has already been assessed as viable. Therefore a range of techniques are proposed for valuing the environment so that it can be included on a par with market goods and services (see Exhibit 9.2). Some environmentalists remain sceptical and even hostile to the attempt to value the environment, claiming this misrepresents people's relationship to the environment and merely allows environmental concerns to be bought off rather than contributing to environmental protection. Environmental economists retort that valuation provides better protection than leaving such assets and services unpriced, and further that a trade-off between economic benefits as measured by the market and environmental values is a route to a more optimal allocation of resources.

A similar dispute exists over the role of discounting. Environmentalists argue that the discounting in DCF and CBA techniques inherently disadvantages future generations by diminishing the value of the costs they will bear and the benefits that they will receive, and therefore is in conflict with the goal of sustainable development. There is, therefore, a proposal for reducing discount rates to zero, that is, not discounting or at least reducing the discount rate below market levels. Others argue that this is unrealistic in a capitalist economy, that there is no guiding principle for reducing the rate and that a lower rate will lead to environmental degradation and resource use by encouraging more development, since a lower discount rate will render more projects viable (unless there is an overwhelming tendency for benefits to be front-loaded and costs delayed into the future).

While environmental economists have developed these techniques of environmental valuation to a high degree of sophistication, there is little evidence of their widespread adoption in project appraisal. The DoE produced two key documents advocating such techniques (1991a, 1993a) but they have not been more widely used than the already current applications in road scheme appraisals. Their effectiveness in current scheme appraisals must be questioned given the number of such schemes in environmentally sensitive areas that pass through the appraisal process and are only stopped by pressure from environmentalists at a later stage. Hence environmental protection may have to rely on the politics of planning to achieve changes in priorities rather than adjusting its economics, in an apparently technical manner.

■ Further reading

The main texts to consult concerning property and land markets are Fraser (1984) or Ratcliffe and Stubbs (1996), with Adams (1994) and Gore and Nicholson (1991) specifically covering the development process, while Ball (1984 and 1988) looks at the construction industry and housebuilding. For references on environmental valuation, a good starting point is Pearce and Turner (1990).

■ *PART 3* ■

PLANNING TODAY

Part 3 surveys the current planning system with a view to providing a description of its main elements. The emphasis is on clarifying the procedures of planning. The planning system is taken to comprise: land use planning (development planning, development control); environmental regulation (land use planning and sustainability, water management pollution control, waste management); countryside policy (countryside protection and access, nature conservation, rural economies, minerals); and regeneration and conservation (physical improvement grants, transfers of land, regeneration through partnership, conservation). Each area of the planning system is covered in terms of: the organisations involved; the focus of this specific planning activity; the aim of that activity; the timing and geographical scope involved; and the main methods used to achieve the desired end result. The emphasis is on the situation in England. The situation in Wales is usually broadly similar. Reference to the main differences in Scotland is made at the end of each section. Generally, the situation in Northern Ireland is not covered, although particularly interesting points of comparison are made where appropriate. As in Part 2, exhibits highlight examples of the application and practice of specific policy regimes.

For any practical application, the reader will have to make reference to up-to-date policy documents, indicators of current practice and data. This text does not attempt to replace such reference material. To guide the reader to more detailed material, references are given to sources of data and policy statements at the end of each chapter. Much contemporary policy documentation and legislation is available in full-text or summary form on the Internet; the Government Information Service is the main access point (see Chapter 5). A List of Abbreviations is provided on pp. xi–xiv.

■ *Chapter 10* ■

Land Use Planning

This chapter sets out the procedures and policies of the comprehensive system of land use planning which is at the core of the planning system. Many aspects of environmental, countryside and regeneration policy are dependent on the powers contained within the land use planning system. Land use planning has remained remarkably resilient, enduring in largely the same form since the founding 1947 legislation. Change has occurred but in an incremental form. Even the attempt to create a more market-led planning system under the Thatcher government did not remove the preexisting planning system but rather modified it and created additional experimental regimes. Just before it left office, the Conservative government had issued a consultation paper on 'tidying up' the land use planning system, proposing some streamlining; the incoming Labour government has promised a more thorough-going review of planning looking at current efficiency levels and the case for more decentralisation. Four issues are flagged up for consideration: the speed of preparing development plans; the treatment of national projects; regional planning; and planning at the local level. In addition, an expenditure review of the DETR is to be conducted. However a really radical overhaul is unlikely. The two central elements of land use planning are, and are likely to remain, the provision of indicative guidance through development plans and the control of development proposals on a case-by-case basis through development control.

■ Development planning

Development planning (see Summary Box 10.1) is one of the two key elements of the comprehensive land use planning system in the UK: the other is development control (see below). Under development planning, plans are prepared by local authorities to guide development and environmental change for all parts of the country. These plans operate at two levels: a strategic level and a detailed local level. Above these levels, there is the control afforded central government by certain statutory provisions and the guidance offered by certain policy statements. The exact form of this tiered structure varies across the country depending on

```
┌─────────────────────────────────────────────────────────────────┐
│              Summary Box 10.1   Development planning              │
│                                                                   │
│   Organisation:    All local planning authorities                │
│   Focus:           Scale of development, patterns of land use     │
│   Aim:             Comprehensive planning                         │
│   Timing:          As change in strategy necessary                │
│   Scope:           Local authority areas or sub-areas             │
│   Planning tool:   Indicative guidance                            │
└─────────────────────────────────────────────────────────────────┘
```

the structure of local government in the area. In areas where there is a two-tier structure of county and district councils, then strategic planning is provided by structure plans prepared by county councils. These are documents which set out general policies, in respect of the development and use of land, and which must include specific policies relating to the conservation of natural beauty and amenity, and proposals for improving the physical environment and traffic management schemes. They have a time-scale of 10–15 years and, under the 1991 Planning and Compensation Act, it is the intention that full coverage of a local authority area will be provided by one structure plan.

Under government advice (set out in Planning Policy Guidance Note 12 – see below), structure plans should be made concise by concentrating on key land use issues and excluding detail more properly left to local plans (see below). Key structure plan topics are listed as: new housing; green belts and conservation; the rural economy; major employment-generating development; strategic transport and highway facilities; minerals; waste disposal, land reclamation and reuse; and tourism, leisure and recreation. Economic issues must be considered and social issues may be considered only in so far as they relate to land use and development. Structure plan policies should also make reference to any regional or strategic planning guidance, current national policies, the availability of resources and other matters that the Secretary of State identifies. The structure plan document comprises a written statement of policies, supported by a key diagram (including inserts as necessary), which is explicitly not a map. Individual properties and the precise boundaries of areas where policies apply are not identifiable. The structure plan is accompanied by an explanatory memorandum which sets out the reasoning for the policies or any alterations to previous policies. This is not strictly part of the structure plan and carries less force than the policies themselves, because it is non-statutory in nature.

The policies may be further supported by descriptive material such as a report of survey, in which statistics and other data are used to analyse the situation in the county. Local authorities have to keep under review the

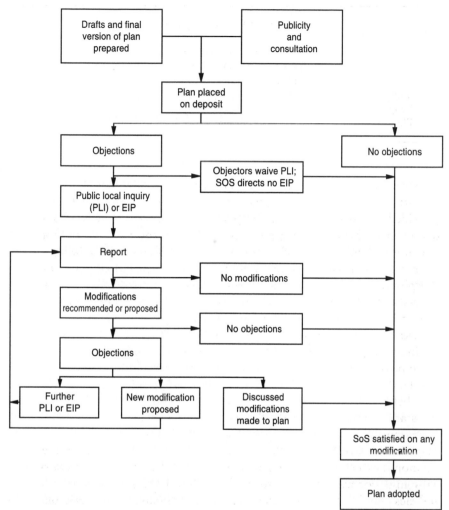

Source: Adapted from PPG12, Section 4.

Figure 10.1 *The development plan process*

need for a fresh survey examining the local area, particularly with regard to physical factors, economic structure, population trends and communication networks. Where the review of strategy in the light of this survey work indicates that a change of structure plan policies is needed, then fresh policies can be devised resulting in an alteration to or complete replacement of the plan. A structure plan may be revised or replaced without any fresh survey work at all but, in all cases, an explanatory memorandum is needed. Government advice is that plans should be revised every five years. While local authorities have discretion in reviewing structure plans, they can be directed so to do by the Secretary of State.

Until the 1991 Planning and Compensation Act, the structure plan was submitted to the Secretary of State who approved or rejected it, following any appropriate modifications. However, county councils are now able to approve their own structure plans, subject to certain reserve powers held by the Secretary of State. This change is intended to speed up the overall plan process. Plans are subject to specified consultation and publicity before the final version is placed 'on deposit' for public inspection. Prior to the council's final approval and adoption of the plan, an examination in public will usually be held. Here a chairman, appointed by the Secretary of State, invites selected participants to debate selected policy issues. There is no right of appearance at an examination in public, and not every policy will necessarily be examined in detail. The details of procedures are set out in the Town and Country Planning (Development Plan) Regulations 1991.

With the strategic framework set by these structure plans, the detailed land use policies are set out in local plans (see Figure 10.1). These are written documents accompanied by one or more annotated maps, specifying the location of new development and areas of protected land. There are two kinds of local plans. District or general plans cover the whole or part of districts. They are also known simply as local plans and provide the main basis for development control. Subject or topic plans cover a specific policy issue. There used to be a category of action area plan, but such action areas, selected for comprehensive treatment by development, redevelopment or improvement, can now be designated in district plans. In general local plans are prepared by districts with certain topics of county-wide interest being dealt with by county council subject plans, for example, derelict land or recreation. County councils and national park authorities must prepare separate subject plans for minerals and (in England only) waste management covering the whole of their areas (see Chapters 11 and 12). National park authorities also have to prepare a general local plan for their area. Under recent legislation and policy advice it is the clear intention that every local authority should prepare one local plan for their area. Full coverage in England was expected by 1996 but latest estimates are that by the end of 1997 development plan coverage of the country would only be 70 per cent; at the end of 1996, 43 per cent of authorities had reached adoption stage with area-wide development plans.

Local plans fill in the details left unspecified by the strategic policies of structure plans, and generally should conform to them. The county council, in response to being sent a copy of a local plan in compliance with publicity requirements, sends the district a statement of conformity or non-conformity. A similar statement is issued if the structure plan is revised or modified. If there is conflict between a structure plan and local plan prepared by the same local authority, the local plan will prevail. But a statement of non-conformity acts as an objection to a newly prepared local plan and, where it arises from a modified structure plan, may suggest the need for alterations to the local plan. It is intended that, after allowing for the time-scale of the plan-making process, local and structure plans should agree with each other. However, conflict between local authorities over development planning can occur and has done so in the past. An exhibit of conflict over green belt designation in development plans is provided in Exhibit 12.1 in Chapter 12.

Local authorities are entitled to prepare alterations to or replacements for their local plans at any time. In doing so, they are encouraged to rely on the survey supporting the structure plan rather than preparing their own. Once a local plan or proposals for alteration to or replacement of a plan are prepared by the local planning authority, they undergo public consultation and are placed on deposit for a time to allow for objections to come forward. If there are any objections, then a public local inquiry is held before an Inspector. Those who do not object to the plan have no right of attendance, a fact which may disadvantage some if they would object to alternative policies which arise during the public inquiry process. Any modification arising from the local inquiry process must be advertised but the final local plan is adopted by the council without reference to a higher-tier authority. Nevertheless the Secretary of State does retain the reserve power of calling in a local plan or proposals for alteration to and replacement of such a plan for final decision and approval. The Secretary of State can also make a direction modifying a local plan.

In the metropolitan areas of England and Wales, structure and local plans have been replaced with a unitary development plan (UDP) prepared by the district councils. Such a plan has two parts. Part 1 consists of general policies (along similar lines to a structure plan) and Part 2 sets out detailed proposals. The detailed (Part 2) policies have to be in general conformity with the strategic (Part 1) policies. Adoption of UDPs closely follows the procedure for local plans including the provisions for a public local inquiry. A Secretary of State may call in any part of a UDP, including individual policies or one of the two parts. Public participation already undertaken for an existing local plan may be taken into account when preparing a UDP. The situation is less clear in those non-metropolitan areas of the country where local government reorganisation has removed the two-tier system of county and district councils, that is, in over half of all county areas. Now a mixture of unitary, county and district councils can coexist within any one county. Circular 4/96, which provides advice on the implications of local government change for the planning system, indicates that any of three options are possible, depending on the Secretary of State's view of the preferred outcome in any locality: the unitary authority may prepare a UDP; it may retain the structure and local plan system; or the authority may be required to agree on joint working arrangements with other local authorities to prepare the structure plan for the county.

Similarly, the creation of the Greater London Authority, operative from the year 2000, creates the need for reconsidering development planning in the capital. The experience of the Greater London Development Plan in the 1960s and 1970s has resulted in an emphasis on a development plan process which is streamlined, focused only on strategic issues and which does not involve substantial resources in terms of GLA staff or anyone else's time. Proposals are still being worked through but it is likely that a development plan will be prepared by the GLA using the resources of the London Planning Advisory Committee, which was established as a statutory body to advise boroughs on strategic issues following the demise of the Greater London Council and which will be absorbed by the GLA. It is intended that this London land use development strategy will also reflect the London transport and waste strategies (two other functions that the GLA will take over) and there may even be an integrated land use and transport plan. The boroughs UDPs will need to take account of the GLA land use development strategy but there is currently no intention that the boroughs would need to certify their own plans with the GLA.

In any area where a structure plan, local plan or UDP has not been prepared and a development plan under the 1947 Town and Country Planning Act exists, then the 'old-style' development plan has statutory force as 'the development plan'. Some local authorities also prepare supplementary planning guidance and other 'bottom drawer' plans. Central government advice (in the form of Planning Policy Guidance Note 12 – see below) makes it clear that informal plans which have not been subject to public consultation and formal procedure are discouraged. Supplementary planning guidance, which has been through such processes, may form a material consideration in development control decisions (see below) but will not be accorded equal weight with the statutory development plan. There is therefore an impetus towards preparing statutory development plans, but there is also a concern with the length of time taken by plan preparation. This is likely to be a key focus of the Labour government's review of the planning system.

An important aspect of strategic planning is the relationship between land use planning and transport policy. While central government has overall responsibility for motorway and trunk roads, local authorities cover other roads. Similarly, while the DETR (and equivalents) oversees rail services and sets the framework for registration of bus services, county councils and metropolitan local authorities have a duty to coordinate an efficient system of public transport. In most metropolitan areas, passenger transport executives (PTEs) have been created to administer the largely privatised public transport services on behalf of passenger transport authorities (PTAs), themselves a joint board of district representatives from the relevant metropolitan district councils; special arrangements operate in London where public transport remains within central government's remit until the election of the new Greater London Authority.

At the local level, the relevant policy documents comprise development plans, transport policies and programmes (TPPs) and passenger transport plans (PTPs). Structure and local plans are required to include traffic management proposals, defined as the coordination of public transport services, the movement of freight, the control of parking and the improvement of cyclist and pedestrian safety. The ability to implement these policies has been enhanced by the 1991 Road Traffic Act. This provides for the designation of a network of red routes, routes on which all stopping and parking is restricted. The Act also introduces a new system of decriminalised on-street parking control operated by local authorities. Local authorities can also prepare parking policies, subject to DoTr guidance, which match the needs and character of their areas. Residential areas may be designated as 20 m.p.h. zones as part of local traffic-calming measures. These measures have proved popular with many urban local authorities and are going some way to altering local traffic management and driving patterns. Emphasis continues to be given though to proposals for improvements to the road network and safeguarding land for new routes which will be developed within ten years. However, a counter-emphasis will result from the Road Traffic Reduction Act, as this will require national, and presumably local, targets for reducing road traffic and local measures to achieve these targets.

Transport policies and programmes were originally intended to be broad ranging documents integrating transport and structure plan policies, but they have been narrowed in scope to the point where they comprise an annual single purpose bid to central government for highways capital funding. These funds are provided in the form of a Transport Supplementary Grant, a form of block grant. Local authority attempts to use the general rate fund to supplement this grant were curtailed by the House of Lords ruling over the GLC's 'Fares Fair' policy. Passenger transport plans focus on public transport but bus deregulation has limited their relevance.

While simplified planning zones (SPZs) were originally presented as a way of removing areas from planning control, in practice they have become areas where a distinctive form of development planning operates. Although the policy itself is of largely historic importance, the provision for SPZs remains. Under the Housing and Planning Act 1986, the plan for the SPZ itself conveys permission to develop. In effect, in an SPZ a system of zoning operates rather than the plan being a precursor and guide to case-by-case development control. The plan for an SPZ is known as a scheme and new schemes or proposals for alterations to existing schemes are prepared under procedures akin to those for any development plan: the 1991 Planning and Compensation Act has effectively created one streamlined set of plan-making procedures (see Figure 10.1). SPZ schemes can take two forms: a specific scheme which itemises the desired development in detail, leaving all other development proposals to fall within normal development control; and a general scheme which gives a very broadly-defined planning permission and lists specific exceptions to that permission. The scheme may grant planning permission for almost any development or specify permitted development very closely. It can specify whether the planning permission granted under the scheme is unconditional or subject to certain conditions. All development which is not specifically permitted requires permission under normal development control procedures (see below). This contrasts with zoning schemes in certain other countries where a change to the zoning scheme itself would be required in such circumstances. SPZs last for ten years and on their demise only permitted development which has already begun continues to carry planning permission.

SPZs cannot be set up in national parks, conservation areas, the Broads, AONBs, green belts or SSSIs (see Chapter 11). Certain types of development are also not considered suitable for SPZs: minerals workings; waste disposal facilities; special industrial areas as listed in Use Classes B3-B7 (see section on Use Classes Order below); and some other developments such as slaughterhouses and fun-fairs. SPZs were considered particularly appropriate for large sites which are either proposed for new development (such as an industrial park or residential estate) or consist largely of derelict land (an old industrial estate or railway siding, for example). They can be used to implement a development brief prepared by a local authority, but the legislation does permit the initiative for an SPZ to come from outside the local authority, say a private developer. Anyone can request a local authority to make or alter an SPZ scheme and the Secretary of State has default powers to direct the preparation or alteration of a scheme and to call the scheme in for approval. Relatively few SPZs have been designated.

While much of this development planning activity occurs at the local level, central government retains control through the various reserve powers identified. In addition to these control mechanisms, central government also issues guidance. In England and Wales, the DETR and its predecessors have prepared a series of planning policy guidance notes, setting out its interpretation of policy on a number of issues to guide local

Summary Box 10.2   *Planning policy guidance notes (as at February 1997)*

PPG1	General Policy and Principles	February 1997
PPG2	Green Belts	January 1995
PPG3	Housing	March 1992
PPG4	Industrial and Commercial Development and Small Firms	November 1992
PPG5	Simplified Planning Zones	November 1992
PPG6	Town Centres and Retail Development	June 1996
PPG7	Countryside: environmental quality and economic and social development	February 1997
PPG8	Telecommunications	December 1992
PPG9	Nature Conservation	October 1994
PPG10 } PPG11 }	replaced by Regional Planning Guidance Notes	
PPG12	Development Plans and Regional Planning Guidance	February 1992
PPG13	Transport	March 1994
PPG14	Development on Unstable Land	1990
	Annexe on landslides and planning	March 1996
PPG15	Planning and the Historic Environment	September 1994
PPG16	Archaeology and Planning	November 1990
PPG17	Sport and Recreation	September 1991
PPG18	Enforcing Planning Control	December 1991
PPG19	Outdoor Advertisement Control	March 1992
PPG20	Coastal Planning	October 1992
PPG21	Tourism	November 1992
PPG22	Renewable Energy	February 1993
PPG23	Planning and Pollution Control	July 1994
PPG24	Planning and Noise	September 1994

authorities in their local planning activity (see Summary Box 10.2). These can be influential in changing the direction of local planning. For example, planning policy guidance has not only clarified the national policy on out-of-town retailing by replacing ad hoc decisions on appeals or called-in planning applications (see below) with a consistent statement, it has also strengthened and refined that policy. PPG6 has introduced the concept of the 'sequential test' whereby a clear priority is established for retail development locations: town centre, followed in order by edge-of-centre, district and local centres and only then out-of-town locations. Local authorities are expected to follow this set of preferences in their development planning and developers will be required to argue their case in relation to its ordering in seeking to obtain planning permission. PPG6 also sets out that the location of retail development should be influenced by the amount of pollution it would generate, including carbon dioxide emissions. This is a innovation in planning for retailing, one which is also likely to influence planning for leisure developments. It parallels the changed advice on transport and planning contained in PPG13. In the past, this PPG concentrated on issues such as sight splays at road junctions and site access points. The new PPG13, however, examines the whole question of how development decisions permitted and promoted through the land use planning system have environmental consequences, particularly through the amount of travel, the fossil fuel consumed and the associated greenhouse gas emissions. PPG13 recommends that development planning should promote urban forms which minimise the need to travel, which may include more compact and dense settlements as well as development linked more closely to the provision of new public transport infrastructure (see also Chapter 11).

In England there is also regional planning guidance which advises local authorities of central government's view on the broad distribution of development across the country as well as how to deal with any special features of a particular region that are of national importance, such as a major airport. The purpose of regional guidance (see Summary Box 10.3) is to provide a broad development framework for the next twenty years or more (fifteen years in the case of housing). While the guidance is issued from the DETR, it is devised by the Government Offices for the Regions and takes account of advice given to the Secretary of State by regional conferences of local authorities. There is, therefore, a degree of negotiation between the centre and the locality in coming to the final figures, though in practice they are heavily driven by the forecasts generated by the Office for Population and Census Studies (OPCS). The Labour government do not propose to give regional planning powers to the Regional Development Agencies (see Chapter 13). However they are considering the possibility of the regional conferences of local authorities themselves preparing draft regional guidance.

The distribution of development needs arising from forecast population change is a particularly important and contentious aspect of regional planning guidance. For example, the most recent forecasts of population change issued by the OPCS suggest that the number of households in England will grow by 4.4 million between 1991 and 2016; most of this growth is accounted for by single-person households, at both ends of the age distribution. This is clearly a substantial number and will require local authorities to make allowances for increased development in their plans, as is clearly set out in the White Paper *Household Growth: Where shall we live?* (Cm 3471) published in November 1996. How much development in which regions will be advised in the RPGs. A central issue will be the assumptions made concerning the proportion of the development that will occur on brownfield sites, that is, urban land, as opposed to greenfield land. Following the current heightened concerns with sustainable development, central government advice is that 60 per cent of new build should be on brownfield sites; this appears to be a compromise between original estimates that about half could be accommodated within urban areas and the suggestion from the UK Sustainable Development Round Table that the figure could be as high as 75 per cent (1997). Most recent revisions of the forecasts suggest that the additional number of households may be as many as 5.5million The introduction of a sequential test for residential development, akin to that for retail development is likely; following the 1998 Budget, greenfield land tax is a more distant prospect.

These guidance notes, both planning policy guidance and regional policy guidance, are advisory, not statutory, documents. They gain their authority from: the ability of central government to use its reserve powers over development plans and individual development control decisions to influence local planning; the widespread consultation undertaken before final versions are issued, particularly among local government itself; and the general relationship of local to central government in which greater authority is claimed by the latter (see Chapter 5). Other forms of central government guidance include White Papers, minerals planning guidance notes, development control policy notes (DCPNs) and Department circulars, although DCPNs are being progressively withdrawn and the use of circulars restricted.

Summary Box 10.3 *Regional planning guidance (as at November 1997)*

RPG1	Tyne & Wear	1989
RPG2	West Yorkshire	1996
RPG3	London*	1996
RPG4	Greater Manchester	1989
RPG5	South Yorkshire	1989
RPG6	East Anglia	1991
RPG7	Northern Region	1993
RPG8	East Midlands Region	1994
RPG9	South East	1994
RPG9A	Thames Gateway Planning Framework	1995
RPG10	South West	1994
RPG11	West Midlands Region	1995
RPG12	Yorks. and Humberside	1995
RPG13	North West	1996

* Advice to the London Planning Advisory Committee.

On transport issues central government guidance to the local plan-making process used to be provided by separate and ad hoc policy statements for the different transport sectors issued by the DoTr. Only in the case of motorways and trunk roads is there a statutory requirement to issue an annual policy statement, in the form of a White Paper listing the programme of construction by region. As of summer 1998, the DETR will issue an integrated transport strategy covering all transport sectors. This is intended to provide substantial environmental and economic benefits by reducing congestion and promoting the use of public transport. It should address the potential for joint planning of different infrastructure networks and the use of various financial instruments to achieve policy goals.

A Thatcherite addition to the statutory development plan is the joint housing study. This is prepared jointly by local authorities and house-builders and compares the housing land requirement for each district over the next five years, as derived from structure and local plans, with an assessment of the land which is agreed to be available for housebuilding. Each study usually covers the area of a county and identifies all potential housing sites of 0.4 hectares or more, with an allowance being made for the contribution of smaller sites, known as intensification. Joint housing studies are normally reviewed every two years. Joint housing studies do not apply in London where, instead, there is a requirement to identify the capacity of urban housing sites. There is some debate over the methodology to be used for determining housing land requirements over the joint housing study period. Where the five- or two-year period coincides with the development plan period, including any of its phasing programmes, there is little difficulty. Assessments for identified land can be compared with structure plan proposals. Where the periods do not coincide, then central government advice, contained in PPG3, is that the 'residual method' should normally be used. This subtracts dwelling completions to date from plan targets and transforms the resulting figure into an annual requirement. This is then grossed up to cover the five-year period. The main exceptions are when local housebuilding rates in the recent past have diverged substantially from the level provided for in the development plan. Further discussion on joint housing studies is provided in Exhibit 10.1.

There is evidence that joint housing studies are not being pursued enthusiastically across all counties; housebuilders have less interest in becoming involved where and when the pressure for residential development is low. Furthermore, the market-led methodology for identifying a five year supply of readily developable land sits uneasily with the new methodologies that will be needed to bring forward urban sites sufficient to account for 60 per cent of forecast household requirements. Llewelyn Davies have proposed such a methodology (1997) which combines a site search with exploring detailed alternative design options for the sites – including those that relax local plan policies particularly on density and parking standards– and identifying the 'gap funding' needed to facilitate development of those sites.

☐ *Scotland*

While the broad structure of development planning is the same in Scotland, there are some important differences. The consolidation of planning legislation contained in the 1990 Town and Country Planning Act for England took until 1997 for Scotland with the Town and Country Planning (Scotland) Act, together with the Planning (Listed Buildings and Conservation Areas) (Scotland) Act, the Planning (Hazardous Substances) (Scotland) Act and the Planning (Consequential Provisions) (Scotland) Act.

Until local government reorganisation, structure plans were prepared by the regional councils with local plans falling to the district councils. The three island councils were already unitary authorities and the regional councils of Dumfries and Galloway, Borders and the Highlands were unitary authorities for the purpose of planning, combining regional and district functions. Since reorganisation all of Scotland is covered by unitary authorities. These cannot, however, prepare UDPs as there is no statutory provision within Scottish law for UDPs. They will, therefore, have to make arrangements to prepare structure and local plans. The old regional planning authorities had the authority to prepare regional reports, quite separate from structure plans, and these will continue to inform development planning for some time.

The Scottish Office is the central government department with overall responsibility for planning in Scotland and it issues guidance in the form of national planning policy guidelines (NPPGs). These are the equivalent of the PPGs and RPGs in England and Wales. They replaced National Planning Guidelines and the Land Use Summary sheets which supported them. The Scottish Office also issues planning advice notes (PANs), which set out good practice in relation to local planning and cover some of the material set out in PPGs in England and Wales. For example, PAN37 recently advised local authorities to make full use of structure plans, PAN51 looked at planning and the environment, while PAN52 set out advice on planning for Scottish small towns.

Other differences are that Schedule 4 of the 1991 Act for streamlining the development plan system does not apply to Scotland and the requirement to prepare joint housing studies is not operative in Scotland. There have been some concerns over the time taken to deliver development

---

Exhibit 10.1   *Joint housing studies*

The concept of professionalism implies a degree of autonomy in everyday work and some specialist or monopolised expertise that underpins the higher social status of the professional. In more technocratic areas of planning, such as pollution control or nature conservation, the basis of expertise may be clear-cut. But in some areas it is more difficult to conceive of planners as experts in the rational decision-making mould. Joint housing studies provide a good example of the nature of 'expertise' that planning can involve.

Joint housing studies have the appearance of a technical document. They consist of a commentary on a series of tables with figures purporting to identify the availability of housing land. Planning policy guidance indicates the methodology for such studies and refers to the 'residual method' using formulae and numeric examples:

The residual method

The general formula used is:

$$TLA = 5 \times (SPT - C)/Y$$

where

TLA is the target land availability figure
SPT is the structure plan target for dwelling completions
C is the number of dwelling completions to date
Y is the number of years remaining for meeting SPT

This formula has to be adjusted where the structure plan has less than five years to run or there are exceptionally high or low completion figures.

The whole concept of the study fits within a model of planning and development drawn from neo-classical economics: demand for housing land arises from the housing market and is represented by housebuilders seeking planning permission on new development land; supply is controlled by the planning system issuing such permissions and making land allocations in development plans. Planners could thus collect data on the housing market,

---

plans in Scotland. In 1996 of the 211 adopted plans, 42 per cent were more than 5 years old and the mean local plan preparation time was 5.5 years compared to 4.25 years for England and Wales; the maximum was a staggering 14.25 years (compared to 8.6 years for England and Wales).

☐ *Wales*

Most circulars and PPGs used to be issued jointly by DoE and the Welsh Office (though sometimes with different numbers). There were very

demographic and otherwise, and on the outputs of the planning system concerning residential development, and make decisions on future policy.

However, joint housing studies were introduced in the early 1980s precisely because a New Right government would not accept this view of planners (Rydin, 1986 and 1988). It argued that planners did not have the expertise to assess housing and development markets. This expertise resided in the housebuilding industry. Therefore joint housing studies involved planners discussing their land allocations with housebuilders, involving the private sector in planning policy. To the Left this was further evidence of the Thatcher administration's redirection of the state from the needs of local communities to the demands of private capital. The issue of expertise was an irrelevance since the main issue was the use of planners and the planning system to allocate development rights in line with housebuilders' wishes. In particular, the redefinition of housing land allocations in terms of market-based criteria meant that planners were not allocating land resources in line with the needs of low-income, poorly housed or homeless groups.

In fact, the use of joint housing studies cannot be simply represented in terms of local working-class needs versus private capital. For, in many of the areas where conflict and debate between planners and housebuilders over the studies was fiercest, the local community, and in particular the most politically active parts of the local community, was middle-class. Joint housing studies were caught in the struggle between housebuilders wishing to build and NIMBYist local populations resisting development. In this situation joint housing studies became a mechanism through which the conflict was negotiated with planners playing a mediating role. The pseudo-technical nature of the joint housing study became a resource in this mediating role. Many of the arguments over the relevance of the residual method and the precise formula used represent the form that the mediation between conflicting interests took. So that, when central government states that the residual method is not appropriate in areas of unusually low or high housebuilding rates, this represents an influence on the outcome of mediation, favouring one party at the expense of the other. Technical dispute is a rationalisation for decisions with distributional consequences.

limited exceptions where the Welsh Office chose to issue its own advice, notably on the Welsh language (No. 53/88) and on conservation policy (Nos. 60/96 and 61/96). The Welsh Office has also issued some advice in the form of technical advice notes: these currently cover joint housing studies, affordable housing, SPZs, retailing and town centres, nature conservation, development involving agricultural land, outdoor advertisements control and renewable energy. It has now been decided that there will be a distinct line of Welsh planning policy advice set out in a separate collection of PPGs issued by the Welsh Office; DETR PPGs will not apply in the Principality. The new Welsh PPGs are appearing only slowly and the old DoE advice is, in some cases, persisting in Wales after it has been revised in England. Two Welsh PPGs were issued in 1996: Planning Guidance (Wales) on Planning Policy and on UDPs.

Development control

Development control (see Summary Box 10.4) is the cutting edge of the land use planning system. It is the mechanism by which planning affects most people and, arguably, could be said to have its most direct effects. The essence of development control is that prior permission is required for most categories of development (Figure 10.2). This is a comprehensive requirement covering all locations, and it means that a vast number of development proposals are discussed and decided on within local planning authorities, that is, the district or unitary council for most purposes. In 1996 English local authorities dealt with 473 000 planning applications; 88 per cent of these were granted.

The definition of development for which planning permission must be sought is given in Section 55 of the 1990 Town and Country Planning Act. Broadly speaking this covers all building, engineering, mining or other operations and any material change of use of land and buildings. Exceptions include operations which affect only the interior of a building and which do not materially affect its external appearance (but do not include underground excavation). Partial demolition has always required planning permission but under the 1991 Planning and Compensation Act all demolition has been formally brought within the definition of development. In most cases it will be considered permitted development under the General Development Order (see below). The intention is that most residential demolition should be controlled. Two other important exceptions from the definition of operations subject to development control are works for road improvements or maintenance within the

---

Summary Box 10.4   *Development control*

Organisation:	Usually district or unitary councils, the Planning Inspectorate
Focus:	Individual development proposals
Aim:	Implementing development plan, other material considerations including environmental impact
Timing:	*Ad hoc*, responsive
Scope:	Development site and surroundings
Planning tool:	Regulation and bargaining

boundaries of a road and work on sewers, mains, pipes, cables, and so on by local authorities or statutory undertakers.

There are also three exceptions from the definition of material changes of use: use incidental to the enjoyment of a dwelling-house; use for agriculture or forestry; and change of use within the same use class (see the Use Classes Order below). Changes of use that are specifically included within development control are the use of a dwelling as two or more units and the deposit of refuse and waste material. Case law has clarified that in certain cases intensification of a use may also constitute a material change of use. This is where there is a change in the character of the use such that the use before and after the change can be identified by separate names. Resuming a temporarily discontinued use is not development but resuming a permanently discontinued use does require a further planning application. Where there is doubt as to whether planning permission is required, the developer can apply to the local authority for a certificate of lawful use or development. Such a notice can be applied for before or after any development is carried out, that is, to decide whether a planning application is necessary or as a defence against enforcement action (see below). Appeal against such a notice can be made to the Secretary of State. The issue of such a certificate effectively grants planning permission so that, thereafter, uses may lapse and be legally resumed.

While the use of a site for agricultural or forestry does not require specific planning permission, a system of prior notification now exists for all farm and forestry building proposals (see Chapter 12). Where development is proposed, notification must be given to the local authority to allow intervention on matters of siting, design and external appearances, nature conservation and heritage. New buildings, significant extensions and alterations, farm and forestry roads and certain excavations and engineering operations are covered. Fish farming has been brought fully into the development control system under an amendment to the definition of development by the 1991 Planning and Compensation Act. In addition certain intensive farming activities now require environment assessment (see Chapter 11).

Exemptions and exceptions from development control are further provided by two central government policy instruments: the Use Classes Order (UCO) and the General Development Order (GDO). The Use Classes Order defines sixteen classes of use to which a building may be put; change of use within a class does not constitute development and does not, therefore, require planning permission. It does not necessarily mean that a change of use from one class to another is always development. It will still be necessary to decide if a material change of use has occurred. The order divides uses into classes under the headings shown in Summary Box 10.5. Recent proposals to include a rural business class have been shelved.

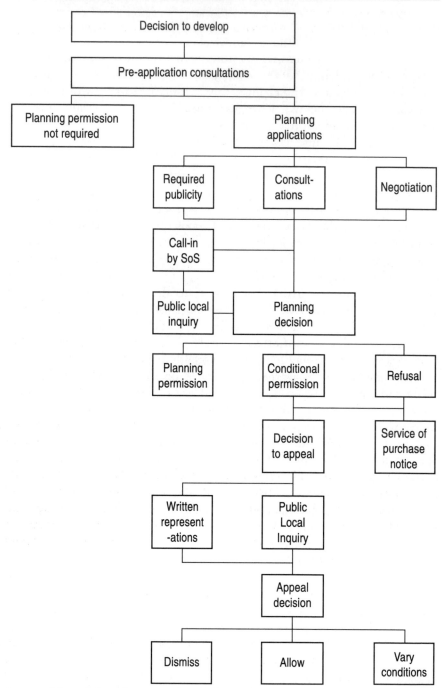

Source: Adapted from Burton and Nicholson (1987) Figure 7.1.

Figure 10.2 *The development control process*

Summary Box 10.5		*The Town and Country Planning (Use Classes) Order 1987 (England and Wales)*
Part A	A1	Shops
	A2	Financial and Professional Services
	A3	Food and Drink
Part B	B1	Business
	B2	General Industrial
	B3–7	Special Industrial Groups A to E
	B8	Storage and Distribution
Part C	C1	Hotels (hostels were removed from this class with effect from April 1994)
	C2	Residential Institutions
	C3	Dwelling-houses
Part D	D1	Non-residential Institutions
	D2	Assembly and Leisure

The General Development Order, which requires parliamentary approval, defines minor forms of development, such as extensions, which may be undertaken without explicit planning permission. Legally such actions still constitute development. The list of such permitted development is categorised under the parts shown in Summary Box 10.6. Many of the provisions have size restrictions which limit the general applicability of the GDO. The order also provides that certain changes of use between different classes as identified in the UCO shall not require planning permission. This covers certain changes between Part A uses (shops, financial and professional services, and food and drink) and between B1, B2 and B8 uses (business, general industrial, and storage and distribution). The GDO may not apply in all instances. The Secretary of State or a local authority may issue an Article 4 direction removing GDO rights in respect of an area, such as a conservation area (see Chapter 13). Planning conditions may also remove GDO rights in respect of a site or building. The 1995 version of the GDO removed permitted development rights for any development requiring environmental assessment (see Chapter 11).

Strictly speaking applications for planning permission are not required in the case of development on Crown land or development by government departments or the local authority themselves. In these cases, deemed planning permission is currently granted for which there is a simplified non-statutory procedure. Some types of development by local authorities and statutory undertakers is covered by the provision in the GDO and

---

Summary Box 10.6   *The Town and Country Planning (General Permitted Development) Order 1995 (England and Wales)*

1	Development within the curtilage of a dwelling-house
2	Minor operations
3	Changes of use
4	Temporary buildings and uses
5	Caravan sites
6	Agricultural buildings and operations
7	Forestry buildings and operations
8	Industrial and warehouse development
9	Repairs to unadopted streets and private ways
10	Repairs to services
11	Development under local or private acts or orders
12–17	Development by local authorities, local highway authorities, drainage bodies, the Environment Agency, sewerage undertakers and statutory undertakers
18	Aviation development
19–23	Mining-related development
24–25	Telecommunications development
26	Development by Historic Buildings and Monuments Commission for England (English Heritage)
27	Use by members of certain recreational organisations
28	Development at amusement parks.
29	Driver information systems
30	Toll-road facilities
31	Demolition of buildings
32	Schools, colleges, universities and hospitals
33	Closed-circuit television cameras

---

local authorities have deemed permission for development which has been authorised by a government department. Section 299(2) of the 1990 Town and Country Planning Act however enables the Crown to apply for planning permission so that it can sell land with the benefit of that permission.

For developments and changes of use which require permission, a planning application is made to the relevant district or unitary council on specified forms, providing all the necessary detailed information and, in 82 per cent of cases, paying a fee (Audit Commission, 1992, p. 5). Pre-application negotiations with the planning authority are encouraged; under a House of Lords ruling, local authorities may not charge for this. Planning applications may be made for outline planning permission, where certain 'reserved matters' are held over for further approval by the local authority at a later date (usually within three years), or full planning permission. Reserved matters may include siting, design, external appearance, means of access and landscaping. Submission of a planning application involves a certain amount of publicity, which is the responsibility of the local authority, not the applicant. Construction of oil refineries and private hospitals require additional authorisation to accompany the planning applications. Once submitted, the application is investigated by a planning officer who consults with affected parties, for example the Health and Safety Executive in the case of hazardous development or development within a hazard consultation zone (see below), or MAFF for development on more than 20 hectares of Grade 1, 2 or 3a agricultural land. In most non-minor cases, the highways authority and water authority are important consultees and parish and community councils have specific rights of notification. The details of the procedures to adopt within development control, including who should be consulted, are set out in the Town and Country Planning (General Development Procedures) Order 1995. This also includes proformas for various notices and certificates.

In the case of hazardous installations the role of planning has been extended by the 1990 Planning (Hazardous Substances) Act, itself a response to a strengthened EC directive. Already, in 1990, local authorities consulted with the Health and Safety Executive on 5046 applications, with 620 applications considered by its major hazards assessment unit. The 1990 Act now requires local authority consent for the storage of prescribed quantities of defined dangerous materials, as set down in regulations (see Chapter 11). The removal of the distinction between processing and storage of hazardous substances increases the number of sites covered by the regulations from 300 to 450. Environmental policy and development control have also been brought closer together by the introduction of environmental assessments, again in response to an EC directive (see Chapter 11). The 1991 Planning and Compensation Act now includes the requirement for environmental assessment of certain development proposals in key planning legislation.

The decision on the application is formally taken by a planning committee of the council, to whom the planning officer presents advice, although the decision may be delegated to sub-committees or the chief planning officer. In some exceptional cases, the application may be 'called in' for decision by the Secretary of State, following a public inquiry held before an inspector, in a manner similar to an appeal (see below). This power is used in only about 140 cases each year in England and Wales. Over the last decade central government has placed great importance on the efficiency of the development control and tried to minimise delays. The goal set for local authorities is that they should decide 80 per cent of applications within eight weeks. It appears that the new Labour government will continue this emphasis.

The councillors on the committee or the planning officer (or the Secretary of State) cannot take any view they wish on the proposal. The planning legislation requires the decision to be made as follows: 'Where, in making any determination under the planning officer, regard is to be had to the development plan, the determination shall be made in accordance with the plan unless material considerations indicate otherwise.' This change, introduced by Section 26 of the 1991 Planning and Compensation Act, creates a presumption in favour of the development plan. Included within material considerations is central government advice on development control as provided in DETR circulars and planning policy guidance notes. In general material considerations must relate closely to the purpose of planning legislation and must also fairly and reasonably relate to the application itself. In addition acceptable decisions may be based on: the fear of creating a precedent, the availability of alternative sites, the risk of piecemeal development, preservation of existing uses and, exceptionally, the personal circumstances of the applicant. Planning permission can be refused on the grounds of prematurity, that is, because the relevant development plan is in process of being revised. However, in such a case, it must be clearly shown how the development will prejudice the outcome of the development plan process. Refusal on the basis of prematurity is allowed, for example where the development contravenes a phasing programme in a development plan setting out how much development should occur each year or over a specified number of years. Local authorities may also refuse to determine repetitive applications where an appeal has been dismissed by the Secretary of State within the past two years.

The planning decision taken by the local authority need not be a simple reject or accept. Conditions may be attached to the planning permission provided that they: fulfil a planning purpose; are necessary, precise and enforceable; are related to the permitted development; and are not unreasonable. This can include limitations on changes otherwise permitted under the UCO. Advice on planning conditions is contained in DoE Circular 1/85. If there is a choice, planning conditions are preferred over the pursuit of planning obligations. Under Section 106 of the 1990 Town and Country Planning Act or Section 52 of the 1971 Town and Country Planning Act, a planning agreement may be made between the applicant and the local authority to obtain planning gain or, as it is now termed, enter into planning obligations. Such an agreement is an enforceable local land change which can restrict the use or development of land, require specified operations or activities to be carried out, require land to be used in a particular way, or require money to be paid to the local authority. Whereas previously, such matters had to be mutually agreed between the local authority and the landowner, a planning obligation can now be offered unilaterally by the landowner under Section 12 of the 1991 Planning and Compensation Act, in which case it may be become a material consideration particularly in an appeal situation. After a specified period of time, there are provisions for discharging or modifying a planning obligation on application to the local authority or, on appeal, to the Secretary of State.

Further advice on planning obligations is given in DoE Circular 1/97 which sets out five tests for their acceptable use. Planning obligations can only be sought if they are: necessary; relevant to planning; directly related to the proposed development; fairly and reasonably related in scale and kind to the proposed development; and reasonable in all other respects. Obligations which fail these tests are seeking 'extraneous benefits' and cannot be used by local authorities. Local authorities can set out in their development plans the basis on which they will seek planning obligations, and this is now encouraged to avoid uncertainty. Such development plan policies are likely to encourage the practice of seeking planning obligations (Ennis, 1996). Legislation is currently being proposed to require local authorities to place planning gain agreements on the planning register; this is already practised in some authorities. Given the current concern over undue secrecy in the conduct of negotiations over planning obligations, the advice is that this should be conducted as openly, fairly and reasonably as possible. Exhibit 10.2 is on the role of planners in negotiating planning obligations.

From time to time, local authorities have sought to use the planning system to ensure that housing is provided for low income groups. Some governments have discouraged this practice. The DoE circular 13/96 on 'Planning and Affordable Housing', which eventually appeared after several draft versions, currently sets out the policy guidance for promoting low cost market housing and subsidised housing. This states that local plans can include policies on such affordable housing and also that the 'community's need for affordable housing' can be a material planning consideration, i.e. influence decisions on planning applications subject to a minimum size threshold for residential development sites. Furthermore, it is acceptable that a commuted payment be made by the developer so that affordable housing provision can be made elsewhere in the local authority area, off the development site under consideration. Further draft revisions to this circular have been put forward in 1997. There are, however, no major changes in policy other than replacing the term 'affordable' with 'social' housing and lowering the size thresholds for sites where the provision of such housing can be a legitimate issue. Chapter 12 also considers the special provisions for providing affordable housing for local people in rural areas.

If a planning permission is refused or unacceptable conditions attached

---

Exhibit 10.2   *Negotiating planning gain*

Few areas of planning practice have been as controversial as planning gain. To the New Right it epitomises the attempt by the local state to exert undue influence over private sector activity, siphoning off profits and deterring wealth generation. Many uses of planning gain are considered outside the legitimate scope of a planning authority's role. According to this view, the planner would be seen as a bureaucrat, tying up development proposals in unnecessary red tape. But others would argue that planning gain presents, at least potentially, a much more positive role for planners. The welfare economist places most emphasis on the outcomes, on the ways in which planning gain can deliver a compromise which reflects all the costs and benefits of a proposal. The planner is here cast in the role of an expert assessor of these costs and benefits, using the resources of the governmental organisation to pool internal and external information. The outcome is then judged in terms of the extent to which a balance is achieved and social welfare increased. By contrast, the institutional approach looks to the process by which the gain was arrived at, and stresses the negotiation involved. The planner is seen as an active mediator between vested interests both within local government and outside. Recognition may be given to the possibility that the planners have vested interests of their own, but it is usually assumed that these do not dominate the mediation process. The skill of the planner lies in balancing the demands of these various interests and devising an outcome which, if not a compromise, is seen as legitimate. In such circumstances, central government plays an important role in providing advice and determinations on what constitutes a legitimate use of obligations, although scope for conflict always remains.

The 1980s saw considerable conflict between local authorities on the one hand, and developers and central government on the other, over the definition of legitimate planning gain. Recent policy pronouncements by central government represent a temporary halt in that conflict. The current situation

to a planning permission, then the applicant has the right to appeal to the Secretary of State for the case to be reconsidered. In 1994/5 12 236 appeals were decided in England and Wales. In completing the appeal forms, the appellant must choose the procedure by which the appeal will be considered: written representations, that is, by correspondence; or public local inquiry, that is, in a fairly formal local tribunal. Eighty per cent of cases are dealt with by written representations. For certain minor categories of development, local informal hearings can be used which attempt to overcome some of the off-putting procedural aspects of local inquiries. The procedures for appeal cases are set out in detail in regulations, which include a timetable for the exchange of statements of case by the parties and for the holding of the inquiry and the decision itself.

reflects both a slight softening in the rather hostile attitude of central government to planning gain and the revised expectations of local authorities in achieving social benefits through planning gain. DoE research has shown that planning agreements are now being used fairly cautiously to control and regulate developments and not to achieve wider planning objectives or community benefits (Grimley J. R. Eve *et al.*, 1992).

To the Left, however, the existing situation is disappointing. They see considerable potential in planning gain for redressing the inequalities that inevitably result from a weak planning system trying to control powerful capital flows. Planners could use planning gain to channel resources to groups disadvantaged by current patterns of resource allocation. Ethnic minorities, the working class, and women could have their special needs met by diverting some of the developer's profit into community facilities. But planners are heavily constrained gatekeepers and the combination of central government control and the underlying dynamics of capital accumulation ensure that community benefits are limited. In addition, planners cannot be assumed automatically to reflect the wishes of community groups. Their own interests, in terms of status and career advancement, may result in identification with the promotion of the development process rather than the problems of disadvantaged groups. Community groups, therefore, have constantly to fight to maintain their needs at the forefront of planners' agendas.

The local plans of the 1991 Planning and Compensation Act could provide a new possibility for doing so. Under recent government advice, a planning agreement may legitimately seek to implement local plan policy and research suggests that local plans are recognising that planning agreements are an important policy tool. So the more open debate that occurs about development plan policy may open up the opportunities afforded by planning gain to a wider range of community groups, if planners recognise the opportunities (Healey *et al.*, 1995).

Once both sides have put their cases in public or in writing, then the inspector allocated to the case will write a report. In 95 per cent of cases, the inspector will also make the binding decision, but the Secretary of State has the right to recover a case for final decision. For major developments the inspector's report will be passed on to the Secretary of State for this decision. The appeal decision can be challenged in the courts only on fairly restricted legal ground, referred to as proceedings for statutory review. Costs may be awarded against either party to an appeal under the Local Government Act 1972 and Town and Country Planning Act 1990. The principles on which costs are awarded are set out in DoE Circular 2/87: unreasonable, vexatious or frivolous action which has resulted in unnecessary and unreasonable expense, including unreasonable cancellation of a public local inquiry. Under the 1991 Planning and Compensation

Act, the Secretary of State has the right, with due notice, to dismiss an appeal if there has been an undue delay on the part of the appellant.

There is provision for the Secretary of State to constitute a Planning Inquiry Commission to deal with applications that have been called in, appeals or other public sector projects. This provides for a broader-ranging debate over the development than may occur at a public local inquiry. Although this provision has been on the statute book for over twenty years, a planning inquiry commission has never been convened.

Central government can, in occasional cases, take over the role of the local authority in development control and grant planning permission through a special development order. As such the development order is debated in the Houses of Parliament and signed by the Secretary of State. They are generally used for particular areas, such as new towns, urban development corporations (see Chapter 13), national parks or AONBs (see Chapter 12) or particular developments which raise issues of national significance such as Stansted Airport or the Windscale nuclear reprocessing plant. Planning consent can also be granted by private bill procedure, again debated within the Houses of Parliament rather than at a public local inquiry. Under the 1992 Transport and Works Act many of the types of development involved with orders and private bills will be dealt with in future by making a ministerial order and using a public local inquiry. This is of particular relevance to transport schemes (see below).

If a development occurs without the benefit of planning permission then the district council has certain enforcement powers (see PPG18 and DoE Circular 21/91). These include the power to issue a variety of notices. A recent innovation under the 1991 Planning and Compensation Act is the planning contravention notice which a local authority issues to give warning of a breach of planning control without instituting full enforcement proceedings. Such a notice can be used to ascertain information about the development, owners of interests in the site and the extent of compliance with planning consent and, further, to encourage contact with the local authority with a view to rectifying the apparent breach of planning control. There is an equivalent breach of conditions notice. An enforcement notice requires the developer to comply with a particular planning permission, including its conditions, or to discontinue an existing use. An enforcement notice must be issued within four years of any building, engineering, mining or other operations occurring to be effective. In the case of unauthorised uses, enforcement action must be taken within ten years. There is a right of appeal against the issue of an enforcement notice to the Secretary of State and it is possible to apply for a certificate of lawful use or development retrospectively to obtain planning permission for the unauthorised activity. Under the 1991 Planning and Compensation Act the local authority can serve a breach of condition notice requiring that any conditions attached to a planning permission are complied with within a prescribed period. There is no appeal against this notice. Non-compliance with any of these notices is an offence. The maximum fine is currently £20 000. The use of these notices is further strengthened by the right of the local authority to enter a site with a warrant to ascertain if a breach of planning control is occurring. Local authorities have the power to enter the site, take steps to ensure compliance with any planning consent and recover the costs if an enforcement notice has not been taken notice of. They can also apply for an injunction to prevent breaches occurring. Where the breach involves demolition, then a replacement building may be required.

A stop notice is issued after an enforcement notice and requires the developer to stop all activities on site in breach of planning legislation. If the developer successfully appeals against a stop notice, then the local authority may be liable to compensation for the financial loss incurred. The scale of such financial loss, particularly to a commercial developer, can be many times the scale of fines for non-compliance with an enforcement notice. Registers of both enforcement and stop notices are held by local authorities for public inspection. Finally, a completion notice seeks to encourage completion by stating that the planning permission will lapse after a certain period of time, of one or more years, unless development is begun. Otherwise planning permission lapses if development has not begun within specified time limits, usually five years or two years from the approval of reserved matters.

In addition to these enforcement powers, local planning authorities have certain powers for altering planning permissions. A revocation or modification order is issued prior to development beginning and negates or changes an approved planning permission. Such an order requires ministerial confirmation. A discontinuance order requires the developer to halt development even if permission has been granted. A strong case must be made before the necessary ministerial confirmation is given. Central government advice states that enforcement or discontinuance powers are not normally to be used in the case of small businesses unless alternative premises can be found. Issuing a revocation or modification order will render the local authority liable for compensation for expenses incurred by the developer since the grant of planning permission and any loss of development value. The developer is also entitled to compensation for the costs of complying with a discontinuance order. There is therefore a disincentive to using such orders.

Finally, the allocation of land for certain uses by public authorities or its designation as a new town, urban development area, clearance or renewal area, general improvement area or for roadbuilding may 'blight' that land in the interim period before the development or designation takes effect. In these cases the landowner may find the value of the land has fallen substantially and a blight notice may be served on the local authority requiring the authority to purchase the land. Ministerial confirmation is necessary.

Local authority development control powers are extended in the case of specific categories of development, notably advertisements, caravans and minerals (the latter are dealt with in Chapter 12). Advertisement control is covered by Sections 220–4 of the Town and Country Planning Act 1990, the Town and Country Planning (Control of Advertisements) Regulation 1992, PPG19 and DoE Circulars 5/92 and 15/94. The display of advertisements also constitutes development under Section 55(5) of the 1990 Act so that local authorities may use either development control or advertising regulation powers to control unauthorised advertisements. With limited exceptions advertisements require consent, although some, such as bus stops, have deemed consent. The Secretary of State can make directions removing the benefit of deemed consent from specific classes of adverts in defined areas: this power is rarely used. Rural businesses are entitled to advertise their whereabouts. Consent for advertisements is given on the basis of two criteria only: amenity and public safety. A discontinuance notice can be issued which requires the display of an advert with consent to cease: there is a right of appeal. The local authority can designate areas of special control in which stricter advertisement controls apply, including prohibitions on certain types of advert. Such areas have to be reviewed every five years and local consultation is expected before designation. Currently, 50 per cent of the land area of England and Wales is so designated. The Conservative government was considering proposals to remove the areas of special control designation; this has now been abandoned by the Labour government.

Caravans are covered by the 1960 Caravan Sites and Control of Development Act and the 1968 Caravan Sites Act. Sites require prior permission in the form of a licence from the local authority as well as the usual planning permission. For travellers in particular, local authorities now have a duty to provide sites within their area, but compliance has been very patchy. Guidance is provided in DoE Circulars 28/77, 57/78 and 23/83.

Specific proposals for major transport schemes, usually roadbuilding, are subject to DoTr procedures. Under these procedures public inquiries are held for all major schemes where there are objections and local authorities usually follow similar procedures for other road proposals. The Inspector is now chosen by the Lord Chancellor, rather than by the Minister of Transport as has been the case in the past. Information on the reasons for the road proposal must be published in advance along with practicable alternative routes. Consultants' reports must be made available to protestors and library facilities provided. All trunk roads are subject to an environmental assessment following the 1992 DoTr manual *Assessing the Environmental Impact of Road Schemes* proposed by the Standing Advisory Committee on Trunk Road Assessment. There has, however, been a tendency to use private bills for new railways and tramways. This includes both major development associated with the Channel Tunnel and various innovative urban light rail schemes. Under the private bill procedure, the proposal is heard and considered within the Houses of Parliament. There is no public local inquiry and the method of making representations is both archaic and expensive. Under the 1992 Transport and Works Act, the private bill procedure has been reformed, so that proposals for new railways, tramways, and so on, are covered by an order-making procedure which is subject to ministerial rather than parliamentary approval. This provides for public consultation, environmental assessment and a public local inquiry if there are objections.

☐ *Scotland*

While, again, the broad principles of development control are similar in Scotland to the rest of Britain, there are procedural differences. Of course, where reference is made to the DETR, in Scotland the relevant reference is the Environment Department of the Scottish Office. Again, whereas PPGs are material considerations in England and Wales, NPPGs and PANs are relevant in Scotland. Other differences are more specific.

First, the reference point for the definition of development for which planning permission is required is provided by the 1997 Town and Country Planning (Scotland) Act, not the 1990 Town and Country Planning Act, which did not apply to Scotland. Second, there are separate policy instruments setting out the provisions of the UCO and GDO for Scotland. These are: the Town and Country Planning (Use Classes) (Scotland) Order 1989; and the Town and Country Planning (General Permitted Development) (Scotland) Order 1992. The terminology to describe the classifications in these instruments varies slightly from the English and Welsh equivalent. Third, the 1991 Planning and Compensation Act does apply to Scotland but the section which establishes the presumption in favour of the development plan in development control decisions is Section 58. Fourth, the provisions on Section 12 of the 1991 Planning and Compensation Act relating to planning obligations do not apply to Scotland. Fifth, the power to call in planning applications for decision used to rest with the regions but will now, presumably, pass to the Scottish Office. Sixth, planning appeals are dealt with by a recorder, not an inspector.

☐ Wales

The Welsh Office is building up a separate set of planning advice so that development control in Wales is influenced either by recent and specific Welsh Office PPGs and circulars, or the old circulars and PPGs jointly issued by the DoE and the Welsh Office. Given that the pace of producing Welsh advice is slower than that of revising the English advice, the old circulars and PPGs can still apply in Wales even when they have been superseded by newer versions in England. For example, Circular 1/97 on planning obligations does not apply in Wales; rather the DoE Circulars 16/91 and 28/92 continue to apply until replaced by Welsh advice. Similar the new PPG13 on transport, which radically altered the role of transport considerations in land use planning, does not at the time of writing have an equivalent in Wales.

☐ Northern Ireland

In Northern Ireland planning appeals are dealt with by a Planning Appeals Commission. A separate line of planning advice is also provided through Planning Schemes rather than the PPGs which apply in England.

■ Further reading

In this area there is little substitute for consulting the actual policy documents themselves: legislation, circulars, PPGs and so on. They are often more accessible than the student fears! Documents for England and Wales are gathered together in the *Encyclopedia of Planning Law*; the Internet site is http://www.smlaw.pub.co.uk. A parallel text for Scotland is the *Scottish Planning Sourcebook*. Useful journals are *Planning*, the weekly magazine for the profession, and the monthly *Journal of Planning and Environmental Law*. The annual reports of relevant organisations – such as the Planning Inspectorate – can also be consulted. Other texts on land use planning include Cullingworth and Nadin (1994), Greed (1996) and, specifically on development control, Thomas (1997).

■ *Chapter 11* ■

Environmental Regulation

Environmental policy is a rapidly growing area of planning activity. Public concern, the results of scientific research, and the role of the EU are all increasing the scope and stringency of environmental policy tools. In this chapter four aspects of environmental regulation are covered: the recent 'greening' of the land use planning system, already anticipated in Chapter 10; the management of water resources; pollution control including integrated pollution control and air quality management; and waste management. Issues relating to derelict and contaminated land are considered as part of regeneration policy in Chapter 13.

■ Land use planning and sustainable development

The previous chapter has outlined the main procedures of the British planning system, which have persisted with remarkable resilience through periods of reform rather than root-and-branch restructuring for over half a century. As Part 1 outlined, though, there have been shifts in the goals of the planning system with varying emphasis on economic development or social issues running alongside the more enduring concern with amenity. Most recently, there has been a significant realignment associated with a broadening of the environmental focus of planning in the wake of the Brundtland process. Chapter 4 introduced the new policy goal of sustainable development but here the main alterations to planning practice are outlined. Some of these, such as environmental assessment, are procedural changes which have affected all local authorities. Others are more in the nature of innovations which are being taken up and developed with more enthusiasm by some planning authorities than others.

The most significant change to procedures has been the introduction of environmental assessment. The concept of environmental assessment of projects is now well established in land use planning (see Summary Box 11.2 and Figure 11.1). The origins lie in the 1985 European Directive No. 85/337, Assessment of Effects of Certain Public and Private Projects on the Environment. Exhibit 11.1 discusses the role of the EU in promoting environmental assessment. The directive was implemented in Britain in

```
┌─────────────────────────────────────────────────────────────────────┐
│              Summary Box 11.1   Environmental Assessment              │
│                                                                       │
│   Organisation:           Local planning authorities                  │
│   Focus:                  Environmental impacts                       │
│   Aim:                    Sustainable development                     │
│   Timing:                 Continuous                                   │
│   Scope:                  Projects, extending to plans, programmes     │
│                           and policies                                │
│   Planning tool:          Research, indicative guidance, regulation,  │
│                           negotiation                                 │
└─────────────────────────────────────────────────────────────────────┘
```

1988 through amendments to a variety of regulations which deal with different types of development: for example, ports, harbours, roads. The main form of implementation in England and Wales was through the Town and Country Planning (Assessment of Environmental Effects) Regulations 1988. This effectively required environmental considerations to be specially considered during the development control process for certain projects. The 1991 Planning and Compensation Act gave this process statutory recognition. More recently the EU has issued a revised directive, No. 97/11. This has extended the categories of projects subject to assessment as well as strengthening the process in other ways (see below). The revised directive has to be implemented by 14 March 1999.

Under the British procedures, all developments which fall within the remit of the schedules attached to the 1988 Regulations require an environmental statement to be submitted with the planning application; these schedules replicate those in the EC directive. The 'environmental statement' presents 'environmental information' which allows an 'environmental assessment' to be made. An environmental assessment is defined in DoE Circular 15/88 as:

> a technique for the systematic compilation of expert quantitative analysis and qualitative assessment of a project's environmental effects, and the presentation of results in a way which enables the importance of the predicted results, and the scope for modifying or mitigating them, to be properly evaluated by the relevant decision-making body before a planning application decision is rendered.

Under the amended EU directive, local authorities will have to give advice to developers on the scope of information to be included in the environmental statement, that is, on the 'scoping' stage of environmental assessment. They will also have to ensure that there is a system of development consent for all projects requiring environmental assessment; this particularly affects forestry projects, which are not current subject to development control.

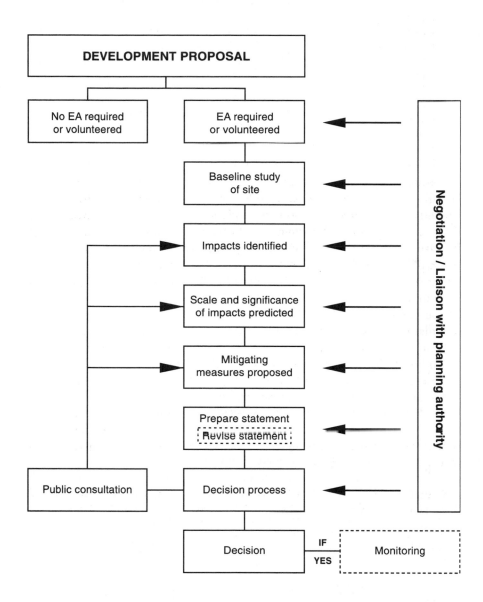

Figure 11.1 *Environmental assessment*

Schedule 1 lists all those developments for which an assessment is compulsory, usually subject to specified size limits (see Summary Box 11.2). Schedule 2 lists all those developments for which an assessment may be necessary if it is of a type, scale or form to have significant environmental consequences by virtue of factors such as the nature, size or location of the process or land use (see Summary Box 11.3). DoE Circular 15/88 gives guidance as to when an environmental assessment should be undertaken with regard to Schedule 2 uses and activities, including various 'indicative thresholds'. The general rule is that an environmental assessment will be needed for projects which are of more than local importance, or where they are in particularly sensitive or vulnerable locations or for unusually complex projects with potentially adverse environmental effects. Under the revised directive, the scope of Schedule 2 has been considerably extended; the British government is, therefore, proposing to make more extensive use of thresholds and specified size limits to exclude certain smaller projects automatically from environmental assessment. The new directive also requires that modifications to all listed projects should undergo environmental assessment, whereas previously only amendments to those in Schedule 1 did.

A developer may choose to submit an environmental assessment with the planning application without waiting to discover if the local authority requires it. Alternatively a developer may make an application to the local planning authority for a determination on the need for an assessment. Otherwise the local authority, or the Secretary of State in the case of called-in applications, will decide whether an assessment is necessary. Any appeals against any determination or decision are made to the Secretary of State.

In principle, the environmental statement is prepared by the developer with the local planning authority undertaking the assessment but, in practice, the process of preparation and assessment involves considerable consultation with various bodies, public participation and communication between developer and planner. The new EU directive requires the developer to provide an outline account of the main alternatives considered in deciding on the proposed project and the environmental implications of that decision. The purpose of the environmental statement is to inform the planning decision and, in particular, to propose mitigation measures which will lessen the environmental impact of the project. Under the revised directive, local authorities will also have to give the main reasons for their decisions in relation to the environmental assessment and set out the main mitigation measures they require. The local authority decision and rationale must now also be communicated to the public. The environmental statement may become a focus of debate in appeal or call-in situations and resulting public local inquiries.

Summary Box 11.2 *Environmental assessment: Schedule 1 projects*

- oil refinery or liquefaction/gasification plant
- power station (other than nuclear power station) and combustion plants
- nuclear power stations and reactors, including dismantling or decommissioning[1]
- production, reprocessing or storage of nuclear fuel or waste[1]
- cast-iron and steel melting; production of non-ferrous crude metals[1]
- asbestos processing
- integrated chemical installation[1]
- certain roads; long-distance railway lines; airports[1]
- trading port; inland waterway; inland port; piers outside ports[1]
- waste disposal, including treatment of special waste[1]
- ground water abstraction or artificial recharge schemes[2]
- transfer of water resources between river basins[2]
- waste water treatment plants[2]
- extraction of petroleum and natural gas[2]
- dams and similar installations[2]
- pipelines for transport of oil, gas or chemicals[2]
- installations for intensive rearing of poultry and pigs[2]
- pulp, paper and board factories[2]
- quarries, open-cast mining and peat extraction[2]
- overhead power lines[2]
- storage of petroleum, petrochemicals and chemicals[2]

Notes: There are additional size thresholds in several instances.
[1]Indicates modification to class of projects.
[2]Indicates new projects included in EU directive 97/11.

Summary Box 11.3 *Environmental assessment: Schedule 2 projects*

- agriculture, silviculture and aquaculture
- extractive industry
- energy industry
- production and processing of metals
- mineral industry[1]
- chemical industry
- food industry
- textile, leather, wood and paper industries
- rubber industry
- infrastructure projects
- other projects
- tourism and leisure[1]
- modification of Schedule 1 and 2 developments[1]
- short-term development and testing for Schedule 1 activities

[1]Main modifications.

Exhibit 11.1   *The EU and environmental assessment*

The relationship between the EU and Britain over environmental assessment (EA) has not been a happy one. Britain held out against the imposition of the 1985 EC directive, contributing to the lengthy delay between first draft and final version. When the adoption of the directive required that Britain introduce EA within two years, the DoE sought to simply graft EA on to land use planning by means of amended regulations. The view that Britain was complying with the words rather than the spirit of the directive was reinforced by the apparent reluctance to apply EA to infrastructure proposals approved by private bills and to projects which were in the pipeline at the time the EC directive came into force on 3 July 1988.

The latter led to an acrid exchange of letters between Britain and the Commissioner for the Environment, including a request from the Commission not to proceed with four major transport projects: the Hackney Wick–M11 link; the East London River Crossing; the Compton Down M3 extension; and the Channel Tunnel rail link. Only in the 1990s has EA been integrated into the private bill procedure and new orders under the Transport and Works Act, and given statutory recognition in the 1991 Planning and Compensation Act. Even so the EU remains unhappy that British regulations require only that the environment statement, and not the assessment of information it contains, is recorded in writing. The statement is provided by the developer while it is the public body who undertakes the actual assessment.

The British government's point of view has been that the Commission was imposing unnecessary regulations, that the British land use planning system took environmental factors into account in development control anyway, and that the EA directive was an example of exactly the creeping bureaucratisation that the Thatcher government had been trying to dismantle since 1979. Further it represented not only more red tape within Britain but also the empire-

---

The EU is also currently in the process of adopting a directive which will extend this process of environmental assessment beyond specific projects to plans, programmes and policies as well; this is termed strategic environmental assessment. In Britain, central government has been advocating the environmental appraisal of development plans for several years. The 1991 Planning and Compensation Act required that development plans should include policy for the conservation of natural beauty and amenity and for the improvement of the physical environment, while the Town and Country (Development Plan) Regulations 1991 expressly required local planning authorities to take environmental considerations into account when preparing development plans. Most significantly, PPG12 contains a substantial section on development plans and the environment and requires local planning authorities to conduct an environmental appraisal of plans, policies and proposals as they are being drawn up. The DoE Good Practice Guide defines such an environmental appraisal as (1993b, p. 2):

building tendencies of the Commission. In this context the bureaucratic nature of the Commission, as opposed to the relatively less powerful but elected European Parliament, is significant.

Against this view are ranged those who see the EU as acting in the interests of the environment. They see the EU as acting to impose a decision in the public interest; the environment is seen as a public good on a European, if not a global, scale. The EU is acting in the best interests of all members by insisting on a common and rigorous standard of environmental protection. Certainly EA has added another layer of procedures to the planning system (Clark and Herington, 1988). Documents have to be produced, information obtained, and organisations consulted. The relevance of EA to the role of local government in taking planning decisions depends on the use made of such documents. If the information and judgements therein do not influence planning decisions, then there has been unnecessary procedural red tape, but the lack of effective constraint on the development process means that the term 'nanny state' is hardly justified. Rather, it would seem as if the state is engaged in a legitimation exercise, appearing to promote environmental protection when in practice the development process has continued as before.

However, if it appears that EA is influencing planning decisions – and the early experience supports at least some marginal impact – then the role of government must be construed differently. Enhanced environmental protection will restrict development, preventing projects from going ahead or requiring extra expenditure along the way. Whether this restriction is seen as unnecessary interference or a rational policy tool depends on the value placed on the environment compared to the economic activity of the development process and also on the assumed interrelation between environment and economy, the central assumption of the sustainable development concept.

- an explicit, systematic and iterative review of development plan policies and proposals to evaluate their individual and combined impacts on the environment;
- an integral part of the plan making and review process, which allows for the evaluation of alternatives;
- based on a quantifiable baseline of environmental quality.

This environmental appraisal will often be supported by a State of the Environment report for the locality, which collates relevant statistical and other material. The proposed EU directive on strategic environmental assessment will require all appraisals of development plans to be submitted to the local authority as well as programmes in sectors such as transport, energy, waste management and water resource management. The procedures mirror those for project-based environmental assessment.

Underpinning this work on development plans and State of the Environment reports has been considerable effort going into devising appropriate ways to categorise and quantify environmental assets and functions. One move has been directed towards developing environmental indicators. At a national level, such indicators can challenge the dominance of conventional economic indicators such as gross domestic product; at the local level, indicators can perform a number of functions, summarised by Brugman (1997) as educational, assessing current conditions, guiding planning decisions and evaluating actions. The task of devising local environmental indicators can be used as a means of involving local communities and revising policy practice in line with their priorities and expectations; such indicators can be relatively non-technical. However, there has also been an emphasis on defining environmental assets and services more rigorously, as a technical tool for use in guiding and evaluating planning policy. For example, environmental capital has become widely used to denote the natural counterpart to man-made capital. Environmental capital can further be disaggregated into: critical capital, which must be maintained, and other environmental capital, where substitution is possible – either environmental asset for environmental asset or man-made asset for environmental asset (Owens, 1994). This then allows a redefinition of sustainable development in terms of maintaining capital stock, either aggregate capital stock, total environmental capital stock or critical environmental capital stock (Pearce *et al.*, 1989). As outlined in Chapter 9, valuation of environmental assets and services is promoted as a way of arriving at assessments of these capital stocks (DoE, 1993a).

Environmental capacity is another term which has been imported into planning. Drawing on analyses from the biological sciences, which determine the maximum animal population that a specific area can sustain, the idea is to analyse the amount of development that a locality can accommodate without severe negative environmental impacts (Jacobs, 1997; Selman, 1996). Identifying environmental capacity in this way has clear implications for development planning and development control. However, central government have not looked favourably so far on development plans using the concept as a rationale for restrictive planning policies. Much more attractive has been the idea that land use planning can play a role in shaping the urban form in a way that minimises the need to travel by road and, therefore, reduce the greenhouse gas emissions associated with road travel. This is in reaction to the 1996 forecasts of increased traffic growth of between 53 and 83 per cent by 2025.

Over the past few years a rapid consensus has built up that planning for more compact and high density urban areas will reduce the length of individual journeys and encourage the use of walking, cycling and public transport (Owens and Cope, 1992; Owens, 1994; RCEP, 1995). More recently though, there have been doubts expressed as to whether land use planning can effectively influence travel behaviour in this way given: the slow rate of change of urban form; the over-riding importance of the relative cost of different modes in determining travel decisions; the problems of capacity in public transport that might result; and the other adverse effects of increasing urban density (Breheny *et al.*, 1997; Breheny, 1995). A more effective planning strategy may be to bring together the planning of new development and the planning of public transport infrastructure so that public transport becomes the more obvious choice for travel. A significant move towards endorsing this approach came with the issue of PPG13 on transport and planning which advocated both the urban compaction approach and the pursuit of joint transport–development strategies. A good practice guide has been published, based on research into the application of PPG13 (DoE, 1995a). With the merging of the Departments of Transport and the Environment and the publication of an integrated transport policy in summer 1998, this is a theme that is likely to influence land use planning for some time.

It should not be forgotten that global warming does not only suggest a new proactive role for land use planning in promoting development patterns which reduce the emission of greenhouse gases. It also requires a adaptive role for planning, promoting development patterns which anticipate the effects of global warming. Coastal planning advice covers the need to restrict development in areas prone to flooding and at risk of such flooding in the foreseeable future. In a situation of global warming and sea-level rise, this could be a significant new consideration for local planning in many areas. Managed retreat for low-level coastal areas may be the most realistic approach to adopt in undeveloped stretches.

□ *Scotland*

In Scotland environmental assessment was introduced through a separate range of regulations: the main one being the Environmental Assessment (Scotland) Regulations 1988.

■ Water supply management

Water management used to be a wholly public sector activity undertaken in England and Wales by river water authorities, until water privatisation split responsibility between the private water companies and a new regulatory body, the National Rivers Authority, now part of the Environment Agency (see Summary Box 11.4). Investment in water supply infrastructure, whether reservoirs or pipe networks, is planned and implemented by the water companies using a mixture of public and private finance. For example, under the 1989 Water Act the companies may levy

---

Summary Box 11.4   *Water management*

Organisation: Water utility companies, Environment Agency, Ofwat, Scottish local authorities
Focus: Supply of water
Aim: Matching and managing demand
Timing: Continuous
Scope: Lithosphere
Planning tool: Investment, regulation and charging

---

an infrastructure charge on developers of new residential estates. Since many of the water companies are based on the old regional water authorities and, therefore, cover river basins and their catchment area, in theory this enables integrated management of the basic water unit to continue. In practice, a mixture of commercial considerations and regulatory constraints drive investment decisions. Whereas in the past most investment went into new reservoir capacity, attention is increasingly being focused on the loss of supplied water through leaky pipes. Demand management is also receiving more attention, with the use of pricing and metering to restrict the demand for water. The water consumers' watchdog, the Office of Water Services or Ofwat, is playing an important role here in monitoring the water companies' use of the price structure as a tool of water management in a commercial, profit-making context.

Privatisation has made a considerable difference to water management in England and Wales, effectively removing a major area from the remit of the planning system. However, in many ways the explicit regulatory framework has been improved. Decision-making discretion within the public sector has been replaced by external scrutiny of the private sector. Ofwat has the power, under the 1995 Environment Act, to set water efficiency standards for the water companies; it can also use the power of publication of information about the companies to influence their behaviour. The current government has particularly emphasised the need to monitor the water companies and ensure a high standard of performance in customer and environmental terms; its attitude concerning the possibly excessive level of water companies' profits is reflected in its 1997 decision to levy a 'windfall tax' on the former public utilities, including the water companies. The implications of these changes for the role of professionals in the water industry was explored in Chapter 8. Meanwhile regulatory pressures, particularly from Europe, are pushing more investment into meeting pollution control conditions. Hassan concludes: 'Universally, the directives are forcing Member States to increase greatly water investment' (1995, p. 48). The changes to the pollution control regime for water due to EU directives is explored below. But the broader framework for the management of water resources is likely to be influenced by the Water Framework Directive which the EU is developing. This will establish a common framework for water management across Europe.

Within Britain the Environment Agency, which absorbed the National Rivers Authority as from April 1996, is responsible for overall water resource management alongside functions with respect to water pollution (see below), flood defence and land drainage, fisheries, navigation and harbours. Under the 1991 Water Resources Act, these functions are carried out having regard to the conservation and enhancement of natural beauty and amenity, conservation of flora and fauna and recreational use. A number of regional and local advisory committees help the Environment Agency to perform its functions having regard to these goals. The water management function charges the Environment Agency with conserving, redistributing and augmenting water resources in England and Wales and securing the overall proper use of such resources. This is achieved by agreeing water resources management schemes with water companies, determining minimum acceptable flows and minimum acceptable levels or volumes for inland waters and issuing certain licences. Such licences are required for abstracting water and for impounding water by means of some obstruction. Conservancy notices may also restrict the use of wells or boreholes which otherwise might not need a licence. Applications for licences may be called in by the Secretary of State and provision is made for appeals against refusal or failure to issue a decision. Existing licences may be modified or revoked, although compensation may then be payable. The Environment Agency is required to keep details of licences available in a public register.

In situations when a serious deficiency of water exists or is threatened, then the Secretary of State may make drought orders, either ordinary or emergency orders. These allow extra restrictions on the taking of water from any source, the discharge of water, its supply and any treatment. The use of water by consumers may also be regulated under such an order. This is the source of the numerous hosepipe bans in south-east England and elsewhere. The Environment Agency also liaises with local planning authorities on development planning and development control to ensure that water resources are protected from inappropriate development, for example in a vital catchment area or in a flood plain.

☐ Scotland

The Water Act 1989 did not apply in Scotland so that water management and supply remains within the public sector and is largely administered by the local authorities, who directly manage the use of water resources, sometimes cooperating in joint boards. They are subject to regulation by the Scottish Environmental Protection Agency with regard to abstractions and treatment. There are proposals for altering this long-standing system of public sector planning of water.

■ Pollution control

Pollution control covers a great variety of incidents from smoky bonfires to major accidents at hazardous installations and can affect all media: land, air and water. The range of pollution control measures reflect this variety (see Summary Box 11.5).

Smoke control and local nuisances are dealt with by local environmental health authorities, that is, district and unitary councils. In general this is *ex post* control, coming into effect after the nuisance is created. Pollution from domestic chimneys is controlled under the successive Clean Air Acts by local authorities creating smoke control zones. Within these zones only smokeless fuels may be used and, in newly declared areas, grants for installing new boilers and fires are available. In 1990 there were 6342 smoke control orders covering 962 000 hectares and over 9500 premises in the UK. Local authorities also have powers to control a variety of other specific sources of air pollution, such as bonfires, under the 1974 Control of Pollution and various Public Health Acts. The Environmental Protection Act 1990 extends the powers of local authorities to deal with the air pollution aspects of a number of industrial processes as well. These are referred to as local authority air pollution control processes, or Part B processes. The control of these process dovetails into integrated pollution control (see below) by ensuring prior authorisation for some 11 000 manufacturing processes and 10–15 000 waste oil-burning plants. Both new

---

Summary Box 11.5   *Pollution control*

Organisation:	Environment Agency, Scottish Environmental Protection Agency, local authorities
Focus:	Discharges, hazardous substances
Aim:	Integrated pollution control, best practicable environmental option, best available technology not entailing excessive cost, polluter pays principle
Timing:	Prior authorisation, nuisance control
Scope:	Sources of pollution
Planning tool:	Regulation and inspection

and existing processes require such authorisation. The system for such processes is run by local government through air pollution officers or chief environmental health officers within district, metropolitan borough or unitary councils.

More complex industrial operations, or Part A processes, are covered by integrated pollution control (IPC) under the 1990 Environmental Protection Act. IPC considers emissions to all media – air, water and lands – and recognises their interrelation; the aim is to achieve the best practicable environmental option (BPEO). In 1976 the fifth report of the Royal Commission on Environmental Pollution suggested that each industrial process should be looked at as a whole so that the best overall pattern of discharges from the environmental point of view might be authorised. This means that a higher level of air emissions, say, may be acceptable if it can be traded off against a lower level of water discharges, providing a net environmental benefit. In practice achieving BPEO can be time-consuming and expensive. The first move towards integrated pollution control was made with the creation of Her Majesty's Inspectorate of Pollution (HMIP) for England and Wales in 1987 from three other organisations: the Industrial Air Pollution Inspectorate; the Radiochemical Inspectorate; and the Hazardous Waste Inspectorate. HMIP used to liaise with the NRA on authorisations concerning emissions to water (see below). Then HMIP was amalgamated with the NRA and the waste regulation functions of local authorities to create the Environmental Agency, operative from April 1996.

The Environment Agency has a statutory responsibility to control emissions from scheduled industrial processes to all environmental media in a system of prior authorisation. Controlled processes for IPC are classified into some 35 process areas with a distinction drawn in most cases between Part A processes (which are subject to IPC) and Part B processes (which can be left to local authorities to consider air pollution alone). IPC covers some 5500 complex industrial processes. In issuing a licence for these processes the Inspectorate traditionally required the operator to use the 'best practicable means' to prevent pollution and render any residue harmless and inoffensive. This has been amplified by the concept of BATNEEC (best available technology not entailing excessive cost), under Section 7 of the 1990 Environmental Protection Act. Licences require operators to use BATNEEC to: prevent or minimise the most polluting emissions; render harmless all substances released; and control releases to achieve the best practicable environmental option. The onus of proof with regard to BATNEEC lies with the operator of the process.

Guidance papers covering some 200 processes detail the operation of IPC and all prescribed processes, whether existing or proposed, should have applied for authorisation within six months of the issue of the final guidance note. The timetable was that all new and substantially altered processes should have been brought under control between1 April 1991 and the end of 1996. Fees are charged for the issue of the licences, the aim being that 75 per cent of the Inspectorate's costs would be recouped. Three types of fee apply: for the application; for inspection, monitoring and enforcements; and for variation of a licence. The fee depends on the complexity and size of the process involved. Applications are made to the regional office of the Environment Agency, and a response is required within four months. The authorisations and any conditions attached are legally binding so that breach carries financial penalties. In addition to granting the initial authorisation, the Environment Agency has the power to issue notices; vary the conditions attached to a licence; revoke an authorisation; enforce compliance with a licence; or prohibit the continuation of an authorised process. Appeals in each case may be made to the Secretary of State. In cases of a breach the courts may order the harm to be remedied or the Environment Agency has the power to undertake remedial actions itself, subject to the Secretary of State's approval and that of any other land users affected (other than the prescribed operator). The public have an opportunity to comment before any authorisation is granted and information on authorised processes, including breaches of authorisation, is held on a public register. The registers are held nationally and locally by the Environment Agency and by local authorities. Commercially confidential material and information affecting national security is excluded. The aim, however, is that the public will have greater opportunity than before to assess the effectiveness of IPC.

The operation of IPC in Britain will be substantially affected by the EU Integrated Pollution Prevention and Control Directive No. 96/61 which will come into effect in October 1999. The directive applies to five sectors: energy, metals production and processing, minerals, chemicals, waste management, plus a catch-all 'other' category. It sets out a number of principles to guide pollution control prioritising: the prevention of pollution and of accidents; the avoidance of waste production and the need to recover or safely dispose of waste; achieving energy efficiency; protecting and cleaning up sites; and ensuring that no significant pollution is caused. IPPC therefore differs from IPC in having a more preventative focus and integrating waste management and resource use more closely with pollution control. However both systems fall short of full life-cycle analysis for production processes. The standard to be adopted under IPPC is at least best available technology, where 'available' is interpreted to mean economically and technically viable. IPPC does not espouse BPEO as currently IPC does. However, IPPC goes beyond IPC in other respects. It applies to intensive agriculture, covers noise and vibrations and operates with a broader list of pollutants for which it specifies mandatory emissions limits. It links together environmental assessment with pollution prevention and control regimes, at the same time as integrating pollution concerns with waste management. The information requirements set under IPPC exceed those currently operating under IPC and IPPC also requires the reporting of incidents. The introduction of IPPC will therefore have a considerable impact on pollution control regimes in Britain.

In addition to this control over emissions, there is a separate set of controls over particularly hazardous materials. For the manufacture of dangerous chemicals an Advisory Committee on Major Hazards has been appointed by the Health and Safety Executive. This has produced reports which have increased the safeguards for such installations including the production of a written safety report, on-site and off-site emergency plans and the provision of public information on the hazard. EU directives also control hazardous chemical production. The 1990 Planning (Hazardous Substances) Act establishes a new system for authorisation of the storage of hazardous materials. Hazardous substances consent must be obtained from the relevant authority for holding more than certain controlled quantities of specified substances. These are obtained from district, borough or unitary councils, except in the case of statutory undertakers' land when the appropriate minister issues the consent. The Secretary of State can also call in applications. Prior to the issue of consent, the Health and Safety Executive must be consulted and there is provision for appeals against refusal or the imposition of conditions. Holders of consents can also apply for consents to be varied or revoked, and hazardous substances authorities can revoke or modify given consents, subject to confirmation by the Secretary of State. In the latter case, compensation may be payable. Although the consent runs with the land, application must be made for continuation of the consent if ownership of that land changes. Compensation is payable if continuation is not granted under such circumstances. Enforcement is dealt with by issuing hazardous substances contravention notices and details of all consents are held in a public register.

Discharges to water are the prime responsibility of the Environment Agency. This body incorporated the National Rivers Authority which was specifically created to act as a regulating body in England and Wales following privatisation of the water industry and the creation of private water companies. It has the responsibility imposed on it by the 1989 Water Act, now consolidated in the 1991 Water Resources Act to monitor water quality and achieve water quality objectives. The Environment Agency also has a general responsibility for controlling pollution in inland, coastal and estuarial waters. To this end a licence for discharges to water is required from the Environment Agency, either under the 1991 Water Resources Act or under some other specified legislation such as the 1974

Control of Pollution Act. Where discharges of 'special wastes' or 'Red List' substances are involved, both the water and pollution control sections of the Environment Agency are involved, under the 1990 Environmental Protection Act. Disposal into sewers is under the control of the water companies who own the sewerage network but discharge from the sewers requires consent from the Environment Agency.

Compliance with authorisations is monitored by the Environment Agency and public registers on the consents and effluent samples are kept. The Environment Agency has powers to prosecute offenders in Magistrates' Courts or Crown Courts with penalties of fines up to £20 000 or up to two years in jail. It can also undertake remedial works and reclaim the costs if a site operator knowingly caused or permitted water pollution. The Environment Agency has been given powers to charge for processing consents and monitoring them. These charges seek to recover the costs of administration; they are not primarily targeted at generating incentives for pollution abatement. However, the banding for determining annual monitoring charges does relate to the quantity and type of discharge and some crude estimate of the carrying capacity of the affected watercourse.

Where the Environment Agency considers that a particular area requires special protection from pollution then a water protection zone may be designated by the Secretary of State. This extends the potential scope of regulation. Nitrate-sensitive areas (NSAs), which affect agricultural activities, are a particular form of such protection zones. Pollution from agricultural sources is a particular problem for water resources. Run-off and seepage from slurry, silage, yard water and herbicide or pesticide application all pollute rivers or aquifers. An 1989 joint survey by MAFF and the NRA highlighted this issue and the EC Nitrates Directive No. 91/676 sets standards for nitrate pollution which largely arises from this source. The Farm and Conservation Grants Scheme provides 50 per cent grants for capital works to prevent such pollution and MAFF and ADAS provide free advice including codes of good agricultural practice. The designation of NSAs is, however, a more effective way of tackling the problem as it allows for management agreements to control farming activities with payments to encourage farmers to enter into such agreements. Ten pilot NSAs were originally designated in England; there are now over 40 designated areas. Due to the continuing evidence of pollution of groundwater sources, the Environment Agency proposes to establish source protection zones or vulnerability zones (so called to avoid confusion with the SPZ acronym). Within these, certain developments would be restricted to protect water supplies. This is likely to affect waste facilities, chemical stores, mineral excavations, intensive livestock units and chemical spraying. Three types of zone are suggested: inner source protection, outer source protection and source catchment areas. This would be an extension of the water protection zone concept.

The effectiveness of pollution control is judged in relation to quality standards set for water and air. The 1989 Water Act provided for statutory water quality objectives and these are being established by the Environment Agency. Under the scheme all water (inland, coastal and groundwater) is covered by a three-part classification. This considers the application of EU directives, sets standards for key chemical parameters and biological measurements, and considers appropriate uses for the water. The objectives are formally set by the Secretary of State serving notices on the Environment Agency in relation to specific stretches of water. The objectives will help determine decisions on discharge consents. Overall compliance with the objections is monitored by five-yearly river quality surveys. The National Air Quality Strategy, the final version of which was published in April 1997, also sets standards for air quality in relation to eight emissions: nitrous dioxide, particulates, ozone, sulphur dioxide, carbon monoxide, lead, benzene and 1,3 butadiene. The strategy sets objectives to be achieved by 2005 and establishes a system of local air quality management to help achieve these objectives. Under this system, all local authorities have a duty set out in the Environmental Protection Act 1995 to assess their areas with a view to determining where monitoring is necessary. There is already a national monitoring network but most monitoring stations are set up and run by local authorities. Where local monitoring reveals levels in excess of the national standards, then local authorities have the power to declare air quality management areas. Within these areas, local authorities have to develop strategies with a view to improving the air quality and meeting the national strategy's objectives.

Both water quality and air quality management have been greatly influenced by EU policy, whereby quality standards have been set in a range of directives. For example, the 1980 drinking water directive set numeric quality standards according to 44 parameters and offered guidance on another 22. The Drinking Water Inspectorate within the DoE, established in 1990, covers compliance with this directive. It also monitors the concentration of pesticides in drinking water, currently controlled by the Food and Environmental Protection Act 1985. Other EU directives cover other aspects of water quality, including bathing waters, shellfish waters, fish-life, treatment of urban waste water and dangerous substances. At times Britain has been reluctant to comply with the spirit as well as the letter of these directives. The initial designation of bathing waters under Directive 76/160 resulted in only 39 beaches being identified; this rose to a further 362 after the threat of legal proceedings. Whereas in 1986 only 44 per cent of coastal sea waters conformed to the bathing waters directive, by 1993 80 per cent did so (Hassan, 1995, p. 50).

The British system of air quality standards also now fits quite closely with the EU standards. The EU framework directive on Ambient Air Quality Assessment and Management No. 96/62 identifies a range of pollutants for which mandatory limits should exist, sets alert thresholds for levels where short-term exposure may pose a health risk and requires member states to undertake action to attain the mandatory limits within a specified time-scale. A series of individual directives is to set targets for some thirteen individual pollutants. While the original standards set in the National Air Quality Strategy did not fit this EU framework exactly, they have been revised so that the two approaches now complement each other.

In relation to noise pollution the local authorities have the power to set up noise abatement zones of mixed residential/industrial or commercial areas in which they can control noise levels. Local authorities also have powers to control noise from construction sites. They have a general duty, under the 1974 Control of Pollution Act, to inspect their areas from time to time to detect noise nuisance against which action can be taken. This would take the form of noise abatement notices. The maximum fine for non-compliance with such a notice is £20 000 for commercial and industrial sources. In England and Wales 7820 such notices were issued during 1993/4, 127 in Scotland in 1992/3. About 600 proceed to prosecution. Between a quarter and a half of all complaints are dealt with informally. The 1996 Noise Act creates the new offence of night-time noise. Advice on planning decisions in relation to noise is contained in PPG24 and WO Circular 16/73. Noise pollution control is a fairly technical matter depending heavily on methods of measuring noise levels. Central government provides a Code of Practice regarding noise measurement procedures. The introduction of a new British Standard BS4142/1990 is likely to introduce more stringent noise control, as it adopts a tighter standard for situations of varying noise. The EU has also considered noise pollution and recently issued a strategy document.

☐ Scotland

As in England and Wales, local authorities have responsibility for smoke and local nuisances, together with minor air pollution control. IPC is the responsibility of the Scottish Environmental Protection Agency created from HM Industrial Pollution Inspectorate for Scotland, the Hazardous Waste Inspectorate and the river purification boards, together with the waste regulation functions of district and island councils. The river purification boards had already adopted a Common Enforcement Policy since 1993 which has assisted the transition to the SEPA. The Scottish system has also been quality standard-led since 1985 when the Scottish Office introduced the Scottish Levels of Service initiative whereby the performance of the river purification boards was assessed in relation to 26 objectives including environmental quality objectives related to environmental quality standards.

☐ *Northern Ireland*

In Northern Ireland the role of pollution inspectorate is taken by the Alkali and Radiochemical Inspectorate and consultation over emissions to water is with the Environmental Protection Division of the DoE NI. The timetable for implementing IPC new processes in Northern Ireland runs one year behind that in mainland Britain.

■ Waste management

Disposing of waste is a major public and private sector activity (see Summary Box 11.6). Industry generates some 400 million tonnes per annum and households another 20 million tonnes per annum Over half of this waste is designated controlled waste. Waste disposal facilities – landfill sites, incineration plants, nuclear waste storage facilities – are usually LULUs (locally unwanted land uses) and pose difficult problems for land use planning. The more recent emphasis within waste management has, therefore, been on encouraging reuse and recycling of waste materials, as well as avoiding the creation of waste in the first place through minimisation strategies. The government's waste strategy *Making Waste Work*, Cm 3040 (DoE, 1995c) sets out a framework for waste management which encompasses all these elements. Some policies, such as reducing packaging waste through the 'producer responsibility' strategy, are part of moves towards 'greening' business, others are changes to the existing planning and pollution control regimes. Some rely mainly on exhortation and advice, others on regulation and enforcement.

Summary Box 11.6 *Waste management*

Organisation:	Environment Agency, local authorities, SEPA
Focus:	Waste stream
Aim:	Environmentally acceptable disposal, waste minimisation, recycling
Timing:	Prior licensing, continuous monitoring, ad hoc initiatives
Scope:	Disposal sites and decisions
Planning tool:	Regulation and inspection, education

The key principles of the strategy are: the proximity principle, which requires that waste should be disposed of close to its point of arising; and the self-sufficiency principle, which operates at a regional scale and aspires to each region being self-sufficient in waste disposal and treatment facilities. This is reinforced by the work on the EC Waste Framework Directive 75/442 as amended by Directive 91/156, which enshrines the 'polluter pays principle' as it relates to waste. The goal of EU waste policy is that an integrated and adequate network of disposal installations should be provided on the BATNEEC basis and following the proximity principle. While there has been a shift in emphasis towards measures which avoid the need for ultimate waste disposal, the control of waste disposal remains at the centre of waste management for the foreseeable future.

The 1990 Environmental Protection Act instituted a new regime for waste disposal. Currently some 90 per cent of waste and 70 per cent of controlled waste is disposed of in some 3500 controlled landfill sites. As previously, sites for the disposal of waste must by licensed and controlled waste can be disposed of only at a licensed site. This is known as a waste management licence and it is an additional requirement to a valid planning consent. The relevant licensing bodies or waste regulating authorities (WRAs) were: county councils in non-metropolitan England; the London Waste Regulating Authority; the Greater Manchester WRA; the Merseyside WRA; district councils in metropolitan areas outside the WRAs; district councils in Wales and Northern Ireland. As of April 1996, all local authority waste regulation functions have been taken over by the Environment Agency (or SEPA in Scotland). Licences for sites may be refused on grounds of environmental pollution, harm to human health or serious detriment to local amenities. In addition, the authorities must be satisfied that the applicant is a 'fit and proper person' before issuing a licence. Details of licences are held on a public register (subject to commercial confidentiality and national security). As with pollution control, conditions may be attached and there are powers to vary, revoke and suspend licences with appeals to the Secretary of State. The Environment Agency can charge site operators for licences and subsequent monitoring and they hold enforcement powers. They also have a duty to inspect old sites, undertake any necessary remedial work and charge owners for costs incurred. If the site poses an environmental hazard, remedial action is a mandatory requirement. Some £33 million was available in 1990/1 for such work. Central government provides technical guidance in the form of waste management papers and will in due course set standards for disposal techniques.

The remaining 10 per cent of waste used to be disposed of by dumping at sea and incineration. However sea disposal is no longer acceptable and there has, therefore, been a necessary shift towards incineration. There are

35 municipal incinerators and four specialised high-temperature incinerators; these are controlled under IPC. Incineration is likely to become more significant as landfill sites are exhausted, opposition to new sites continues and the regulatory regime for landfill tightens. For example, the EU directive on landfill will significantly affect current British practice. The first draft of this directive was initially rejected by the European Parliament in 1991 as not being sufficiently strict. The 1997 revised draft prohibits co-disposal of hazardous and non-hazardous waste as well as the landfill of certain wastes such as tyres, liquid wastes and infectious hospital waste. There will, therefore, be a need to consider alternative disposal and management strategies for these types of waste. Similarly the Royal Commission on Environmental Pollution looked at waste and concluded that incineration with energy recovery was the environmentally preferable policy direction (1993).

Under the Environmental Protection Act 1990, waste regulation had to be kept separate from waste disposal. Waste disposal authorities (WDAs) are: county councils, metropolitan WDAs, metropolitan district councils where there is no metropolitan WDA, and elsewhere district or unitary councils. Any authority that was both a WRA and a WDA had to separate these functions administratively and notify these arrangements to the Secretary of State, who had the power to direct revised arrangements. The aim was to encourage the formation of arm's-length waste disposal companies, which would work alongside private sector disposal contractors and compete with them for contracts. These arrangements remain in place even though the Environment Agency has taken over WRA responsibilities.

All parties – producers, regulators, and disposers – have a duty of care imposed on them under Section 34 of the legislation which also created greater opportunities for enforcement action. Applicants for waste management licences have to demonstrate financial and technical resources to manage sites competently. Nor can incompetent managers walk away from sites which breach their licence. They remain responsible for pollution already caused. There is a duty of after-care for sites where tipping has ceased to ensure no continuing risk of pollution. The penalty for an offence can be two years in prison and/or up to a £20 000 fine. For special wastes the prison term rises to five years. Carriers of waste have to register with the Environment Agency under 1991 Regulations implementing the 1989 Control of Pollution (Amendment) Act.

Under the 1974 Control of Pollution Act and 1992 Regulations, waste regulation authorities had to draw up waste disposal plans, now termed waste management plans, which forecast future waste generation, considered the adequacy of existing disposal facilities and set out proposals for the development of new facilities; these plans have now been taken over by the Environment Agency. Following the Waste White Paper, the Environment Agency will be updating these plans to produce a statutory waste plan. This is also a requirement under EU legislation. Under the 1991 Planning and Compensation Act, county councils and national park authorities must also prepare a waste local plan. In metropolitan areas, waste policies will be contained in the unitary development plan, and in Wales within the general local plan. These waste local plans or policies address the land use implications of authorities' waste management policies. They set out the considerations to apply in identifying sites for new treatment and disposal facilities and deciding planning applications. The waste management and waste local plans should be complementary and not conflict with each other. There will be a PPG on waste disposal facilities to advise local authorities on the preparation of such plans. Among other matters, these are likely to propose restrictions on development in the vicinity of landfill sites due to dangers from methane gas explosions.

Following the desire to have a broader waste management, rather than just a waste disposal strategy, attempts are being made to increase recycling by a system of 'recycling credits'. Under the 1991 Environmental Protection Act WDAs have a duty to pass the savings in landfill costs due to recycling on to waste collection organisations and voluntary organisations promoting recycling. This should make recycling more profitable. Local authorities are also required to draw up and publicise recycling plans and to take the provision of recycling facilities into account when granting planning permission for large shopping developments. The WDA may make agreements with waste disposal contractors to encourage recycling.

The most significant move, though, has been the introduction of a new (and possibly the only) environmental tax, that is the landfill tax. This tax has been operative since October 1996 under the Landfill Tax Regulations 1996. Under this system, the landfill operator collects £2 per tonne for inactive waste and £7 per tonne (increased to £10 in the 1998 budget) for other waste through the fees charged for landfill. Waste removed from contaminated sites or used for the restoration of sites is exempt to ensure that reclamation of derelict land is not discouraged. The receipts, which amounted to £4000 million in the first year, are then remitted to the Treasury. However, up to 20 per cent of the operator's total landfill tax liability can be passed on to an environmental body, with the operator claiming up to 90 per cent of the contribution against the tax liability. The environmental body must be registered with Entrust to ensure that they are non-profit-making and genuinely engaged in environmental protection and improvement activities. It seems likely, though, that the first impact of the landfill tax will be to promote incineration rather than more recycling, reuse and waste minimisation, although that may come in the longer term depending on the effectiveness of other policies.

Two types of waste have special additional systems of control: marine disposal and radioactive waste. Any discharge from land to sea requires the consent of the Environment Agency. Dumping or incinerating waste at sea in the past further required a licence from central government agricultural departments, that is, MAFF in England and Wales. Operational discharges from ships are the responsibility of the DoTr while discharges from off-shore installations, such as oil rigs, are under the DTI's remit. The use of the seas for waste disposal has been the subject of much international concern and bilateral or multilateral agreements. Of particular concern to Britain have been the agreements reached at the North Sea conferences. The second North Sea Conference was convened in November 1987 and agreed a ban on dumping all harmful industrial waste by 1990, a ban on incineration at sea by 1995 and a 50 per cent reduction in outputs of dangerous substances (the Red List) by 1996. An international task force was to be established to research and monitor the environmental quality of the North Sea. The third North Sea Conference was held in the spring of 1990. This further agreed that all use of polychlorinated biphenyls (PCBs) would be phased out by the end of 1999 and other pollutants discharged to sea further reduced. Dumping liquid industrial waste and fly-ash from power stations would end by 1993 and dumping sewage sludge by 1998. The timetable for ending incineration at sea was brought forward to the end of 1990; this accounted for only 2000 tonnes in 1985. However, 30 per cent of UK sewage sludge was disposed of by marine dumping, amounting to 5 million tonnes in 1985. In summer 1997 the Labour government announced that it was to stop all forms of disposal of waste at sea. The implication again is that more incineration facilities will have to be built.

Radioactive waste remains a special category. All users of such materials have to be registered, currently amounting to 7000 users. Commercial nuclear installations are inspected by the Nuclear Installations Inspectorate, part of the Health and Safety Inspectorate, which is responsible for monitoring normal working operations. Such operators have to work to a level of nuclear safety known as ALARP – as low as reasonably practicable. Transport of radioactive material is subject to DoTr regulations based on standards set by the International Atomic Energy Agency. Specific authorisation for discharge of radioactive materials is needed from the Environment Agency in England, the Welsh Office in Wales, the SEPA in Scotland and the Alkali and Radioactive Inspectorate in Northern Ireland. One thousand premises currently discharge wastes, all of which are inspected. Continuous environmental monitoring is carried out at the larger sites. Discharges from the major nuclear sites in England

---

Exhibit 11.2   *The environmental big public inquiry*

In some areas of planning policy, notably transport and energy infrastructure, the main strategic decisions are taken at central government level in a highly non-participatory manner. The only opportunities for the public and environmental groups to influence decisions is when the policy is implemented through site-specific development. In most cases major development projects, even if they receive approval through avenues other than development control, are considered at a public local inquiry (PLI). At this forum, the views of various interested parties can be put forward, first to the inspector or panel in charge of the inquiry and then, via a report, to the relevant Secretary of State. This is a participatory process which, depending on your viewpoint, allows all information to be considered before a rational planning decision is reached or allows all interests to be heard and involved in debate before a mediated conclusion is reached. But the experience of PLI procedure, particularly where major projects with environmental consequences are involved, emphasises the constraints on decision-making mediation. This was clearly apparent in a series of 'nuclear' public inquiries into: a nuclear reprocessing plant at Windscale (now Sellafield), Cumbria in 1977 (Outer Circle Policy Unit, 1979); a pressurised water reactor at Sizewell B, Suffolk in 1983–5 (Armstrong, 1985; O'Riordan *et al.*, 1988); and a fast breeder reactor/reprocessing plant at Dounreay, Scotland in 1986. These constraints take a number of forms.

The resources of environmental groups are a major constraint on their ability to participate on an equal footing with the local authority, let alone the major developer. In the case of the Windscale Inquiry, BNFL spent £750000. By the time of the Sizewell B Inquiry, the CEGB had put £20 million into the preparation for and appearance at the inquiry. The high costs and low perceived benefits were such that the Town and Country Planning Association felt it could not afford to take part in the Dounreay Inquiry. It is not just the length of the inquiry – the Sizewell B Inquiry took 340 working days – and the paperwork that are expensive. The complexity of the issues discussed means that research and expert witnesses are needed to make a case and challenge the other side. This has generated calls for third party funding to allow environmental groups to make their case.

The procedures of a PLI are another constraint. They are highly formalistic, based on a quasi-judicial model. This is reinforced by the use of solicitors and barristers to present the cases of the various parties, using techniques of cross-examination and often obscure legal language. This is a barrier to many

---

in addition require authorisation from MAFF, which monitors the levels of radioactivity in foodstuffs and other materials.

Advice on waste disposal is provided by the Radioactive Waste Management Advisory Committee but there is a commercial body, UK NIREX Ltd, whose role is to undertake such disposal. This public company is owned by BNF plc (the fuel reprocessing company), CEGB, UKAEA and the South of Scotland Electricity Board, with the Secretary of State for Energy holding a golden share. Jointly all these organisations

community groups presenting their views as they feel overawed, patronised and marginalised. The procedures also influence the debate with an emphasis on two-way claim and counterclaim, on the logical unravelling of single points and on legalistic precision in the use of words. This may not always be the best means by which to reach conclusions over environmental issues. There is often no logical order in the discussion of points either, the material presented depending on the availability of witnesses and the issues raised in cross-examination.

One major problem with development projects which implement a national policy is the division between challenging the project and challenging the policy. In the past inspectors have held that government policy could not be questioned in a PLI; the emphasis had to be on the details of the specific project, assuming that the basic need for the project had already been established. At the Windscale Inquiry only nuclear reprocessing itself could be debated, not its relation to the rest of the nuclear industry. Clearly environmental groups were unhappy with this example of 'salami politics'. Even where, as at the Sizewell B Inquiry, the issue of need for the project could be discussed, environmental groups were unhappy about the extent to which national policy could really be challenged. The inspector sought to open up a full and fair discussion on the reactor proposal but the significance of this was questioned when statements by the Secretary of State, made during the inquiry, argued that the case for nuclear power was unassailable and when the DoEn authorised CEGB contracts placing advance orders for the reactor.

For many within the environmental movement these inquiries represent a legitimation tool, used to dispel public concern and support the nuclear industry. The actions of environmental groups are a challenge to a state acting on behalf of an industrial sector. They go beyond the simple NIMBYism consistent with consumerism: deflecting a nuclear power plant to another area protects local property values and the quality of local living conditions. Challenging the nuclear power programme, and hence the location of such a plant anywhere, suggests a public commitment to a broader range of values. Similarly the groupings that arise cannot be classified in terms of class, gender or ethnicity. Rather the nuclear proposal itself generates a new basis around which a community may form and enter into negotiation, however constrained, within the planning system.

devise the strategy for radioactive waste disposal. Currently the location of long-term disposal sites is the key planning issue. Following the difficulties in finding alternative sites outlined in Chapter 3, low-level waste (gloves, overalls, laboratory equipment) is mainly disposed of at a controlled landfill site at Drigg in Cumbria; intermediate and high-level waste (totalling about 6 per cent) is currently stored at nuclear establishments. Exhibit 11.2 discusses the problems of the public local inquiry process in relation to nuclear installations.

☐ *Scotland*

In Scotland the tasks of the district and island councils as waste regulating authorities and of the river purification authorities as water authorities have been taken over by the Scottish Environmental Protection Agency. Local councils remain the WDAs but here the requirement to form arm's-length waste disposal companies does not apply. The WDAs also directly undertake recycling of waste.

■ Further reading

Again the reader is referred to the primary sources: legislation and other policy documents. The Environment Agency (and equivalent) produces annual reports and has an accessible website; much useful data, including policy details, is included in the annual *Digest of Environmental Protection and Water Statistics*. The annual White Paper on the Environment is another source of up-to-date policy information. The DETR is also producing a range of publications on environmental issues from guidance on policy and procedures (DoE 1991a, 1991b, 1991c, 1993a, 1993b, 1995a, 1995b) to research reports (Owens and Cope, 1992; Ecotec, 1993). On environmental assessment and strategic environmental assessment, there are a range of good procedural texts: Fortlage (1990), Therivel *et al.* (1992) and Glasson *et al.* (1994) for example. For the other policy areas discussed, suitable texts include: Rees (1990) on water management, Weale (1992) on pollution control, Elsom (1996) on air quality management, Gandy (1994) on waste management and Blowers (1995) on nuclear waste.

■ *Chapter 12* ■

Countryside Policy

Planning policies for the countryside attempt to balance the goals of preserving the natural features of the landscape, providing for public access and enjoyment and supporting the economic activities that occur in rural areas. The former two goals, in the view of the 1945 Sandford Committee, are not in fundamental conflict, as they both seek the conservation of the countryside although short-term and specific trade-offs may be necessary. More recent government planning policy guidance has recognised that situations of conflict may be more common than previously assumed. Certainly in the case of economic activities, principally agriculture and minerals extraction, the threats to nature and landscape conservation and public access can be severe. This conflict is now being reconsidered in the light of the goal of sustainable development and the implications of this concept for the planning of rural areas. This chapter considers countryside planning under four headings: general policies and specific designations for countryside protection together with the provision for public access; measures aimed at nature conservation; planning for rural economies, particularly agricultural activities, forestry and rural housing; and minerals planning.

■ Countryside protection and access

The general principle of countryside planning (see Summary Box 12.1), that development should benefit the rural economy *and* maintain or enhance the environment, assumes that 'the countryside can accommodate many forms of development without detriment' (PPG7, para. 1.10). Development planning and development control in the countryside should take a positive attitude in particular to rural business, tourism, sport and recreation and sensitively manage the location and detail of any new development. Outside special designations (see below) PPG7 advises that proposals for new development should take account of: the need to encourage rural enterprise; the need to protect landscape, wildlife habitats and historic features; the quality and versatility of land for use in agriculture, forestry and other rural enterprises; and the need to protect other non-renewable resources. Reuse and adaptation of rural buildings is

---

Summary Box 12.1   *Countryside protection*

Organisation:	National park authorities, local authorities, Countryside Commission, Countryside Council for Wales, Scottish Natural Heritage
Focus:	Areas of natural beauty
Aim:	Leisure and visual amenity
Timing:	Continuous
Scope:	Large and small areas
Planning tool:	Regulation and estate management

---

encouraged to prevent dereliction and avoid new build. There is, therefore, no general presumption against development in rural areas.

Development control has always sought to protect agricultural land of the best quality by resisting development on Grade 1, 2 and 3a land in England and Wales: about one-third of agricultural land in England and Wales falls into these grades. Proposals which conflict with the development plan and involve the loss of more than 20 hectares of such land require consultation with the MAFF. However, agricultural development itself used to be exempt from development control. The use of land and existing buildings for agricultural purposes, as defined in the 1990 Town and Country Planning Act, does not require planning permission since it does not constitute development. New construction, alterations or extensions to farm buildings or excavations and engineering operations do constitute development but, if reasonably necessary for the purposes of agriculture, much is permitted development under the GDO. More extensive rights are available to agricultural units of at least five hectares; more limited rights to units of 0.4–5 hectares. Details are given in PPG7.

Since 1992, however, a system of prior notification for such development operates which allows local authorities to regulate certain aspects. This is a significant innovation, affecting over 12 million hectares of agricultural and forestry land in England and Wales. Under this system the farmer or developer must give the local authority 28 days to decide whether prior approval will be necessary for the details of development: that is, siting, design and appearance. The principle of development is not open to debate. The purpose of prior approval is to safeguard the visual amenity of the landscape and promote natural and heritage conservation. Approval may be conditional and there is no right of appeal.

Such sensitive management of all development in the countryside runs alongside a range of more restrictive rural policies. The policy tools discussed here focus on special designations for small and large areas. The

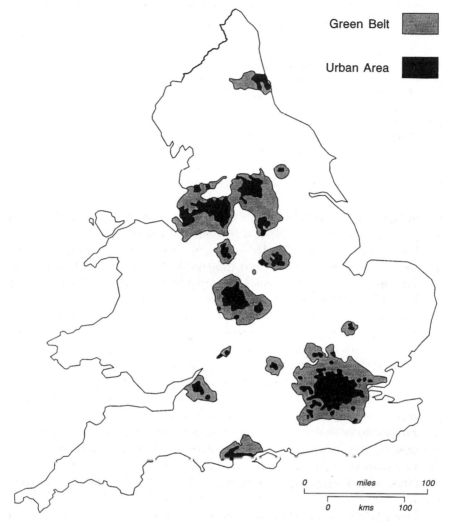

Green Belt

Urban Area

Map 12.1 *Green belts (1993)*

designations covered below are: green belts, national parks, AONBs, heritage coasts and public rights of way.

Green belts are probably the planning tool of greatest longevity and popular support. They apply to fifteen separate areas covering 15 557 km^2 or 12 per cent of England (see Map 12.1). There are no green belts in Wales; there are five in Scotland covering 1550 km^2 or 2 per cent of the country. Designation is undertaken by local authorities through the development plan process with detailed boundaries established in local plans and old-style (pre-1968) development plans. The purpose of green belts, as set out in PPG2, is fivefold:

- to check the unrestricted sprawl of large built-up areas
- to assist in safeguarding the countryside from encroachment
- to prevent neighbouring towns from merging into one another
- to preserve the setting and special character of historic towns
- to assist in urban regeneration by encouraging the recycling of derelict and other urban land

They are essentially tools for resisting and diverting urban development and largely negative in nature. The 1995 version of PPG2 on green belts stresses their positive role in providing public access to the countryside, together with space for sports and leisure, retaining and enhancing landscapes, improving damaged and derelict land, securing nature conservation and retaining land in rural uses; specific objectives for green belt policy are set out. However, green belts in themselves imply no special land management practices to this end though the new PPG commends the management activities of bodies such as the Countryside Commission. Neither is the quality of the landscape relevant to designation or a part of green belt policy implementation.

'The essential characteristic of green belts is their permanence. Their protection must be maintained as far as can be seen ahead' (PPG2, para. 2.1). This means that alteration of green belt areas and boundaries is rarely sanctioned and green belt policies in development plans will follow a longer time-scale than for other aspects. Green belts are not intended as a reservoir of development land for beyond the current plan period; other land between the urban area and green belt should be safeguarded for this purpose; this is known as 'white land'. Within green belts there is a general presumption against inappropriate development. Prior to 1995, a definition of appropriate development was given but now exceptions to inappropriate development are specified: buildings for agricultural or forestry purposes; essential facilities for outdoor sport and recreation; cemeteries and other uses of land which preserve the openness of the green belt and which do not conflict with the purposes of green belt policy. Mineral extractions may be permitted due to their locationally fixed nature. No other development is to be allowed even 'in exceptional circumstances'.

The reuse and conversion of buildings already within the green belt, arising from surplus farm buildings, is generally accepted as it can 'secure the continuing stewardship of land'. Safeguards are provided through ensuring careful development control to prevent extensions to building mass, maintain design in keeping with the surroundings and avoid a materially greater impact than the present use. The spirit of contemporary green belt policy is, however, in keeping with the promotion of economic restructuring away from a dependence on high levels of agricultural production in rural economies (see below). Redevelopment of redundant hospitals and similar institutions was a particular concern but provided it does not extend the height or mass of the building and the proposal conforms to green belt policy objectives, it is considered acceptable. Green belts are thus the exemplar of a restrictive planning policy designed to limit change in rural areas bordering on to urban concentrations. Many local authorities operate other restrictive policies for stretches of non-green-belt countryside but none carry the statutory force of green belts. Exhibit 12.1 outlines the conflicts involved in designating green belts in development plans.

Turning to more positive planning tools for the countryside, the principal major designation is the creation of ten national parks, seven in England and three in Wales, under the 1949 National Parks and Access to the Countryside Act (see Map 12.2). These are designated by the Countryside Commission in England and Countryside Council in Wales, subject to confirmation by the relevant Secretary of State. They cover 13 730 km^2 or 9 per cent of the area of England and Wales. The statutory purposes of national parks were the conservation of the natural beauty of the countryside and promotion of its public enjoyment. The 1995 Environment Act restates this purpose as relating to 'quiet enjoyment' and the understanding and conservation of wildlife and cultural heritage, thus clarifying that in cases of conflict conservation overrides public access and enjoyment. However, parks also have a duty to take full account of local communities' economic and social needs, under the Countryside Act 1968. There is a proposal to impose a statutory duty on all ministers and public agencies to take these aims of national parks into account in any development they are concerned with.

Planning for the parks used to be the responsibility of a planning board in the Lake District and Peak District, while elsewhere national park committees within county councils took on this role supported by joint advisory committees where more than one county council is affected by a national park. In January 1992, in its response to the report prepared by the ad hoc National Parks Review Panel, the government announced that it would be moving towards an independent planning authority for all national parks, thus placing them all on the same footing as the Lake District and Peak District. Following the 1995 Environment Act, this occurred with effect from April 1996 in Wales and April 1997 in England. Each new authority is the sole planning authority for the area of the park, with the responsibility to maintain a structure plan and local plan for the area (unless the Secretary of State directs that a UDP is more appropriate). However, the national park authorities are encouraged to make voluntary

---

Exhibit 12.1   *Conflict over green belts*

While green belt policy has enjoyed a high degree of consensus and support, specific green belt designations have been a focus of conflict. Central government and both tiers of local government have sought to express their own views about development allocations through representations on the appropriate boundaries of belts. This was particularly the case during the late 1970s and 1980s when green belt boundaries were being changed. The designations of postwar development plans were proving out of date. In some places, development had occurred rendering green belt notation irrelevant, but in most cases attempts were being made at the local level to extend the width of green belts to protect land from heightened development pressures. The first round of structure plans were used as the vehicle for redefining green belt areas. While this suggests that county councils were the prime movers in green belt designation, conflicts with both upper and lower tiers were equally important. The DoE sought to contain the spread of green belts, pruning back extensions, removing 'interim' status from large areas and refusing to approve some new belts. The power of the Secretary of State to approve structure plans was a strong control over county councils' actions.

The motives for this stance by central government are open to interpretation. Marxists would see this as evidence of the capture of the DoE by speculative housebuilders keen to obtain development land generally and planning permission on their land-banks in particular. On the other hand, the New Right would see this as a move against overly restrictive, anti-development policies of NIMBYist (Not In My Back Yard) local councils. The interpretation of professional planners would be that overruling local councils' policy could be justified, on the grounds of the need to mesh together county council policies on a regional scale and meet regional demographic forecasts: that is, the strategic planning needs at a higher level.

But county councils also had to deal with pressure from below, from district and parish councils. The nature of this pressure varied from locality to locality: some districts pressed for green belts; other wished to provide for more development land. In general, though, the district councils wished to retain control over detailed land allocations to meet their specific circumstances: local housing needs; the balance of inmigration the council wished to plan for; the demands of local development interests. This meant that district councils often opposed the detailed designation of green belt boundaries in county council subject plans, preferring to implement broad-brush structure plan policies through their own district plans. In many cases central government, seeing an anti-restraint alliance between the DoE and the districts, would step in and override such subject plans. This brief account of past green belt conflicts, therefore, tells of a policy being used to handle the conflicts between tiers of government, conflicts which themselves represent the balance of interests pressing their demands on the DoE or local council. The policy is shaped in detail by the adjustments that the mediation process requires and, indeed, the longevity of green belt policy can be analysed in terms of its usefulness as a mediating tool (Elson, 1986).

arrangements with neighbouring local planning authorities to prepare a joint structure plan. In 1989 the Norfolk and Suffolk Broads were given status comparable to a national park and a planning board was created to take responsibility for the area. It is likely that the Broads will formally become a national park. And in the New Forest area, a Heritage Area has been designated. The same planning principles apply to this area as to a national park although all development plan and development control matters are dealt with by the relevant local authority.

Planning responsibilities for a national park authority include, under the 1991 Planning and Compensation Act, the preparation of a single park-wide local plan and separate minerals and (in England) waste local plans. Authorities are also responsible for development control within their areas including minerals and waste applications, although in the Broads applications are first submitted to the relevant district council before being passed to the Broads Authority. Enhanced development criteria operate within the parks, ensuring a more critical approach to planning applications. Agricultural development in national parks has long been subject to a partial form of development control – the notification system that, since 1992, has been extended to all agricultural development. Certain development that carries permitted development rights outside the national park requires consent within the boundaries: some larger extensions to dwellings, industrial buildings and warehouses; roof extensions; stone cladding; satellite dishes in certain locations; microwave antennae; excavations and engineering operations. Government advice proposes a single test for considering applications for major development in parks: that such development should be demonstrated to be in the public interest before being allowed to proceed.

But national park planning implies positive management also. Each park authority prepares a national park plan which is a management plan for the area, and Exchequer funds are made available to implement this. Seventy-five per cent of national park funds are provided by central government. In 1990/1 the average net expenditure for a national park was £1.89 million with average staffing of 99 full-time staff (Crabtree, 1991). Some management functions are carried out jointly by the park committee or board and a district council – principally trees, derelict land and country parks – and district councils can act on an agency basis for the county or board. Park authorities also have powers to enter into agreements with landowners to achieve management of the land in line with park objectives. £500 000 was paid during 1989/90 under such agreements.

The 1949 National Parks and Access to the Countryside Act also provides for the designation of areas of outstanding natural beauty. There are 40 such AONBs, covering 21 220 km^2 or 15 per cent of England and Wales. AONBs may also be designated by the DoE in Northern Ireland,

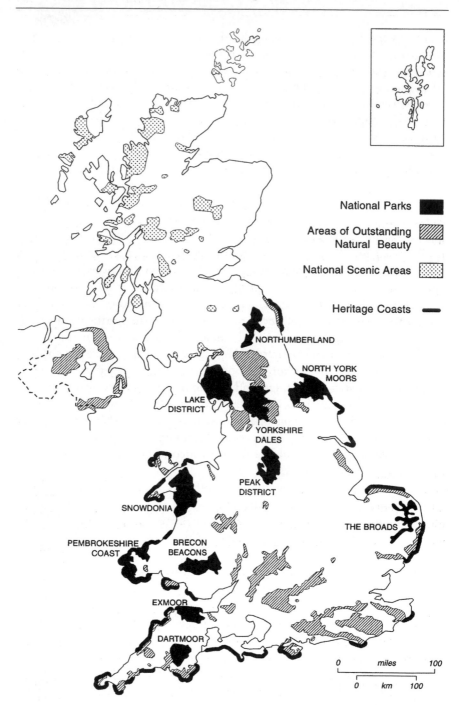

National Parks

Areas of Outstanding Natural Beauty

National Scenic Areas

Heritage Coasts

NORTHUMBERLAND

NORTH YORK MOORS

LAKE DISTRICT

YORKSHIRE DALES

PEAK DISTRICT

SNOWDONIA

THE BROADS

PEMBROKESHIRE COAST

BRECON BEACONS

EXMOOR

DARTMOOR

Map 12.2   *Countryside protection policies, 1997*

where there are nine such areas covering 20 per cent of the land area. The purpose of AONBs is to conserve the natural beauty of the landscape, rather than to provide means for public access and enjoyment. Permitted development rights are withdrawn on the same basis as in national parks, and development plans and development control are required to have regard to conservation aims. There are no special organisational provisions for AONBs and local planning authorities remain responsible for them. The Countryside Commission has recently proposed a statutory duty on local authorities to promote the management and conservation of AONBs, and formal conservation boards along the lines of the innovative Sussex Downs Conservation Board. There are Exchequer grants available for the maintenance and enhancement of AONBs, activities which are also undertaken by the local planning authority under specific powers. Grant decisions reflect the fundamental landscape conservation purpose of the designation. In 1996 £6.8 million was spent on the English AONBs, £2 million of which came through the Countryside Commission.

Certain other areas are also designated for landscape and leisure purposes. In coastal areas the local authority, in consultation with the Countryside Commission (or Countryside Council in Wales) designates heritage coasts to protect the landscape and also provide for managed recreation. Forty-four such heritage coasts cover one-third of the coastline in England and Wales or 1500 km. This is not a statutory designation and there is no withdrawal of permitted development rights but 37 of the 44 heritage coasts are in national parks or AONBs where there is enhanced protection. The designation is intended to provide a flexible management tool. In addition recent government advice on coastal planning proposes a presumption against building on all undeveloped stretches of the English coastline. Even in built-up areas, permission should be restricted to those developments which require a coastal location, such as tourism, recreation, minerals extraction, and marinas/harbours and so on. Currently some 75 per cent of the English coastline is undeveloped.

In cases of conflict between public access for recreation and nature conservation, the government advice in PPG17 on 'Sport and Recreation' makes it clear that priority should be given to conservation and the enhancement of natural beauty in national parks and heritage coasts, and conservation of natural beauty and the needs of agriculture and diversity in AONBs. Public access for leisure purposes is more specifically provided for in country parks and the provision of local authority picnic sites. Here local authorities have powers to provide special facilities for leisure activities in the countryside. The aim is not just to provide for public enjoyment but also, by doing so in selected spots, to take the pressure off other more vulnerable parts of the countryside. There has been pressure on the new Labour government to introduce a 'right to roam' as exists in

Scandinavian countries but opposition from rural landowners has prevented this.

The provision of public rights of way is the main means of ensuring continued access to the countryside. There are currently 140 000 miles of public rights of way. Under the 1949 legislation, they are set out in definitive maps, to which there have been rights of appeal and representation both to county councils, who prepared them, and the law courts of the Quarter Sessions. These definitive maps were largely completed by 1960. The 1981 Wildlife and Countryside Act provides for the continuous review of these definitive maps to give up-to-date information on public rights of access. This 1981 Act is now the reference point for such definitive maps. Local authority finance is available for footpath maintenance and signposting and the 1981 Act sets out a variety of other powers and duties concerning the enhancement of footpaths and bridleways: for example, appointment of wardens and reinstatement after ploughing. Obstructing a footpath is an offence and landowners must maintain stiles, claiming the expense from the county council. A public path can be closed or diverted only after a formal procedure, including publicity, a hearing or objections and confirmation by the Secretary of State.

Long-distance footpaths provide further sources of public enjoyment. These are initiated by county councils, in discussion with other local planning authorities, and presented to the Secretary of State for the Environment. They are eligible for Exchequer grants for maintenance, this being the responsibility of district councils. A recent footpath initiative is the Countryside Commission's parish paths partnership, a £1 million package announced as part of its 1992 'Action for the Countryside' programme. The aim is to involve local people in managing local rights of way. This is part of the Countryside Commission's general approach that bringing together voluntary and statutory groups with farming interests in the countryside is the best way of achieving the protection of rural areas, environmentally, socially and economically (see below for the application of this approach to agricultural activities in rural areas).

☐ Scotland

The general policy for development planning and development control in rural areas follows similar principles in Scotland although there is separate legislation and guidance reference points. The equivalent planning bodies in Scotland are: the Department of Agriculture, Environment and Fisheries in the Scottish Office rather than MAFF and DETR; and Scottish Natural Heritage, formed from the Countryside Commission for Scotland and the

Nature Conservancy Council in Scotland, instead of the Countryside Commission. In addition to these administrative differences, there are a number of substantive policy differences.

A major difference in countryside policy has been that there are no national parks, although the 1945 Sandford Committee clearly intended that five Scottish parks should be created alongside the English ones. National park direction orders were issued by the Secretary of State under the 1947 Town and Country Planning Act, so that all planning applications in specified areas are submitted to the Scottish Office for consideration, but no further steps were taken at that time. However a 1991 report by the Countryside Commission for Scotland (now part of Scottish Natural Heritage) entitled *Mountain Areas of Scotland* proposed four national parks in: the Cairngorms; Loch Lomond and the Trossachs; Glen Loch; Ben Nevis and Black Mount; and over parts of Wester Ross. While this did not succeed in achieving such designations at the time, it is likely that the new Scottish Parliament will consider designating national parks in Loch Lomond and the Trossachs and the Cairngorms. Neither are there any AONBs since national parks and AONBs are based on the same enabling legislation.

Instead 40 national scenic areas, covering 13 per cent of Scotland's ground area, have been identified to date. In these areas all planning applications are considered by Scottish Natural Heritage but there are no funds attached to the designation. The 1991 Natural Heritage (Scotland) Act also introduced the designation of national heritage areas. These areas are proposed by the Scottish Natural Heritage and formally designated by the Secretary of State. In these areas integrated management is to form the basis of countryside planning, focusing on positive rather than restrictive planning. In particular the negotiation of management agreements between Scottish Natural Heritage and landowners is encouraged to promote public access into the large areas of private rural land in Scotland. Existing national scenic areas may continue or, over time, be converted to national heritage areas. Coastal areas have additional protection through the means of coastal conservation zones. These are intended as areas where applications for development permission should be subject to wider consultation and stricter control. Policies for such zones are contained in local plans and a new NPPG13 on coastal planning was issued in 1997. Seventy-four per cent of the mainland and island coastlines are so designated, some 7546 km.

There is a partly implemented park system in Scotland. Country parks are established and maintained by local authorities, who may also designate areas of scenic heritage for protection under their normal planning policies. Under the 1981 Countryside (Scotland) Act provision is now made for regional parks in which the local planning authority and landowners can enter into management agreements. They are designated by the regional councils and confirmed by the Secretary of State for Scotland. There are four regional parks covering 718 km^2. The status of footpaths is also different in Scotland. There is no duty to map paths and the paths themselves are not rights of way but carry permissive powers of access. Formal rights of access are only granted following a procedure which involves the local courts. Continuous use by the public and a formal assertion by the local authority is required. Long-distance footpaths are initiated by regional councils and confirmed by the Scottish Office.

☐ *Northern Ireland*

As with most planning powers in Northern Ireland, control is largely vested in the DoE for Northern Ireland under a heavily centralised system. In addition to the occasional points made in the text, it is worth noting that the Environment Service of the DoE (NI) runs six country parks, one peatland park and two additional countryside centres, as well as coordinating a regional park. An advisory committee, the Council for Nature Conservation and the Countryside, has been established to assist the DoE (NI) in its work; this has no established staff or resources (Yearley, 1995).

■ Nature conservation

So far the emphasis has been mainly on public access and landscape conservation. However, nature conservation is an integral element of these countryside policies (see Summary Box 12.2). The main bodies responsible for ensuring that the needs of nature conservation are taken into account are the three national successors to the Nature Conservancy Council (NCC), whose duties include the provision of scientific advice, establishing and maintaining national nature reserves and developing relevant research.

Summary Box 12.2   *Nature conservation*

Organisation:	English Nature, Countryside Council for Wales, Scottish Natural Heritage, local authorities, voluntary organisations
Focus:	Habitats and species
Aim:	Wildlife conservation
Timing:	Continuous
Scope:	Local ecosystems
Planning tool:	Management

The NCC was reorganised into three national agencies under general powers contained in the 1981 Wildlife and Countryside Act, the 1990 Environmental Protection Act and the 1991 Natural Heritage (Scotland) Act. There is a NCC for England known as English Nature which works with the Countryside Commission for England; the NCC in Scotland combined with the existing Countryside Commission for Scotland to form Scottish Natural Heritage; and in Wales a new body called the Countryside Council took on the work of the NCC and Countryside Commission in Wales. There is a joint committee for international liaison and representation between the organisations, called the Joint Nature Conservation Committee. However, the 1968 Countryside Act places a duty on every local authority, government department and public body to have regard to nature conservation alongside the enhancement and maintenance of natural beauty of the countryside. Advice on nature conservation for local planning authorities is contained in PPG9. The wildlife of inland water-based areas is further protected by the specific duty imposed on the Environment Agency (see Chapter 11), water and sewerage undertakers and internal drainage boards to conserve and enhance natural beauty, and to conserve flora and fauna. Advice in DoE Circular 17/91 requires water companies to take special care in putting forward water and sewerage treatment plant proposals in areas designated for landscape and wildlife importance.

These nature conservation duties are now set within a national and international policy framework concerned with biodiversity loss at global, national and local levels. Following the convention on biodiversity agreed at the Rio Summit in 1992, the British government published its Biodiversity Strategy in 1994 (Cm 2428) and a working party was set up to investigate how the strategy should be implemented. This devised a national biodiversity action plan which identified a list of 37 key habitat types and 116 priority species that required action to ensure their continued health and existence. A programme of devising management plans for these habitats and species was set in train, identifying targets, lead actors and the resource implications. They also set out the need for local biodiversity action plans to be prepared by local authorities on a similar basis. Central government have accepted their recommendations and the result will be a comprehensive set of plans across the country aimed at maintaining biodiversity through specific local habitat and species management strategies.

Area-based provision is made for nature conservation in the form of nature reserves and SSSIs. There are 333 national nature reserves in the UK covering 1990 km^2 designated by the relevant nature conservation agency. Nature reserves are protected under management agreements between English Nature (or equivalent) and landowners. These are the responsibility of English Nature (or equivalent) though, by agreement, they may be managed by district councils. Local authorities can enter into similar agreements and create local nature reserves. There are some 487 local reserves in the UK, 250 km^2 in all. Other private and public bodies may designate non-statutory nature reserves and local authorities can identify sites of importance for nature conservation (or some equivalent name) to guide local planning. There are also marine nature reserves, designated under the Wildlife and Countryside Act 1981 and managed by English Nature (or equivalent). Seven potential sites have been identified and two designated, Lundy in 1986 and Skomer in 1990. Most recently, the habitats afforded by traditional hedgerows have been given specific protection under the 1997 Hedgerows Regulations. Under these landowners must inform the local planning authority if they propose to remove more than twenty meters of hedgerows and the authority may issue a Hedgerow Retention Order if the hedges conform to criteria relating to their conservation value. A expert group is currently considering how this protection may be strengthened.

Special additional reserves were created under the Ramsar Convention on Wetlands of International Importance especially as Waterfowl Habitat 1971 for protecting wetlands, that is, marshes, estuaries and so on. Some 88 areas in Britain have been designated by the Secretary of State under the Convention. One hundred and four special protection areas for birds have also been designated by the Secretary of State under the EC Birds Directive on Conservation of Wild Birds No. 79/409. Within Ramsar sites and special protection areas for birds, nature conservation considerations should normally outweigh the need for development projects by the water industry and local authorities are required to take special action to avoid significant deterioration of habitats. The EU has further expanded its wildlife protection work with the Habitats Directive on the Conservation of Natural Habitats and Wild Fauna and Flora No. 92/43, which sets up a European network of special conservation areas (SCAs), known as the Natura 2000 sites. Both European directives are implemented by the Conservation (Natural Habitats, etc.) Regulation 1994. In the UK the SCA sites likely to be included are bogs, heathland, dunes and key forests; the British government has put forward 255 land sites for potential designation as at November 1996. SCA designation must be taken into account in development planning and development control and work detrimental to its nature conservation value can be halted by an order. Sites can be made subject to management agreements or a special nature conservation order made by the Secretary of State. One implication of the Habitats Directive is that a valid planning permission is no longer a reasonable excuse for operations that damage a designated site.

There are also nearly 6178 sites of special scientific interest (SSSIs) in Great Britain covering 20410 km^2. They are designated by the relevant nature conservation body under Section 28 of the 1981 Wildlife and Countryside Act, which replaces the 1949 National Parks and Access to the Countryside Act in this respect. The 1981 Act requires the designation of all SSSIs to be reviewed with a view to removing the designation from damaged areas and extending boundaries where appropriate. Designation is based on scientific criteria and the sole purpose is nature conservation. Planning decisions concerning any SSSI automatically involve consultation with English Nature (or equivalent). However, the government view is that there is no presumption against development in or near SSSIs. Further protection is given under the 1981 Wildlife and Countryside Act, as amended in 1985. Under a system of reciprocal notification English Nature (or equivalent) has to inform landowners and other relevant bodies of the intent to designate an SSSI and landowners have to inform English Nature (or equivalent) of any intended operations within such a site, giving four months' notice. This does not apply to development with planning permission. The fines for not complying with these requirements are, however, relatively light. If English Nature (or equivalent) objects to proposed operations they have a limited period of time (currently four months) within which to negotiate a management agreement for the land, with compensation being payable for operations foregone by the landowner. This contrasts with other areas of planning control where there is no compensation for loss of development rights. At the end of the negotiation period English Nature (or equivalent) can apply to the Secretary of State for a Section 29 extension order. However, at the end of this extended period (of up to twelve months) the only remedy available to English Nature (or equivalent) is compulsory purchase.

Added protection is available for SSSIs of national importance, which are designated by the Secretary of State and require written approval from English Nature (or equivalent) for operations. The designation of such sites invokes compensation if the value of the land is reduced. There is a proposal for establishing consultation areas around SSSIs of major importance identified by English Nature or the Countryside Council for Wales. Sixteen areas have been proposed, ensuring wider consultation for any schemes of development or operations in or near the SSSIs. The 1981 Wildlife and Countryside Act also provides for the protection of an SSSI to be taken into account by the Minister of Agriculture in giving farm capital grants. These essentially negative measures are being supplemented by English Nature's Wildlife Enhancement Scheme which aims to promote positive management of SSSIs. Under this scheme, launched in 1991, payments will be available for wildlife protection works. These will cover the one-off costs of preparing management plans and agreements, and also annual payments for works.

In addition to these area-based policies there is a list of protected species which encourages protection of their habitats and constrains development in the vicinity, as well as preventing capture, killing and/or export in specified cases. For example the 1991 Badgers Act protects badgers' setts, requiring any disturbance to be authorised by a licence from English Nature (or equivalent). The schedules of the 1981 Wildlife and Countryside Act also detail the protection afforded various plants, animals and birds. The DETR has a Wildlife Inspectorate which seeks the implementation of the register on protected species.

☐ Scotland

As the main text has indicated, many of the provisions for nature conservation listed above are relevant in a Scottish context. There are two points of variation which are worth mentioning. First, in relation to SSSIs, an Advisory Scientific Committee has been set up to review objections to current SSSI designations and to any new designations or amendments under the current redesignation procedures. This has provoked considerable controversy as it allows landowners to appeal over the head of Scottish Natural Heritage. Second, there is a Marine Consultation Area Scheme in Scotland, under which areas identified by Scottish Natural Heritage have the protection of extended consultation arrangements over any works affecting them. This scheme was the model for proposals to establish consultation areas around SSSIs of national importance.

☐ Northern Ireland

In Northern Ireland many of the functions of English Nature are performed by the Countryside and Wildlife Branch of the DoE (NI) assisted by an advisory body, the Council for Nature Conservation and the Countryside, set up in 1989. The equivalent designation to the SSSIs is the area of special scientific interest. There are 72 such areas of special scientific interest, covering 750 km^2. These areas replace the designation of areas of scientific interest previously used.

■ Planning for rural economies

The above discussion has emphasised the protective designation of the countryside for amenity, access or nature conservation reasons. Debates

> **Summary Box 12.3**   *Rural economic development*
>
> Organisation: MAFF, the Scottish Office, local authorities,
>   Countryside Commission, Scottish Natural Heritage,
>   Countryside Council for Wales, Rural Development
>   Commission (Regional Development Agencies)
> Focus: Mainly agricultural production
> Aim: Balance economic and environmental concerns
> Timing: Continuous support
> Scope: Agricultural areas
> Planning tool: Regulation and subsidy

about countryside policy have often been cast in terms of a dispute between agricultural practices and such protection. On the one hand, protecting countryside areas requires active, economically sustained rural communities, and in practice this has meant supporting agricultural production. On the other hand, the economic activities that sustain such communities may threaten established natural habitats and landscape features (see Summary Box 12.3). For a long time it was held that supporting agricultural activity was sufficient safeguard of the countryside in itself but, more recently, the fundamental nature of the underlying conflict has been recognised. The 1986 Agriculture Act now states that a reasonable balance must be maintained between the agricultural industry, the economic and social structure of rural communities, conservation and public access.

The 1995 White Paper *Rural England: A Nation Committed to a Living Countryside* (Cm 3016) expounds on this by using the concept of sustainable development to suggest a rural policy which can ensure both rural prosperity and the protection and enhancement of the countryside. It proposes six principles:

- the pursuit of sustainable development;
- shared responsibility for the countryside as a national asset;
- dialogue to help reconcile competing priorities;
- distinctiveness, suggesting a flexible and responsive policy approach;
- economic and social diversity; and
- sound information.

This section looks at the subsidy and grant schemes for agriculture and forestry and how they have been altered to give a better balance between increased production and environmental protection. It then goes on to consider the other means of supporting rural communities, including planning for residential development in the countryside.

The main form of support to agriculture has been through the subsidies of the EU Common Agricultural Policy. The UK currently receives 341 million ECUs, amounting to 20 ECU per hectare and spread over 58 specific programmes. However, reform of the CAP through the 'agri-environment' Regulation 2078/92, in response to rising costs and overproduction, has forced a change in policy for agricultural areas. The emphasis is now on restructuring production to maintain employment opportunities for rural communities while at the same time adopting more environmentally friendly practices. Thus many subsidy schemes have been changed to reduce production, take land out of agricultural use and achieve more acceptable patterns of farming. For example, under the Extensification Scheme for Beef and Sheep, farmers received payments in return for reducing output by at least 20 per cent and doing so in an environmentally acceptable way, such as maintaining hedges, ponds, meadows, moorland and heaths. Revisions have also been made to the hill livestock compensatory allowances given to farmers in designated less favoured areas to prevent overgrazing; some 80 per cent of Wales falls in this category and 90 per cent of Scotland. Under the 1981 Wildlife and Countryside Act, applications for capital grants now trigger a series of representations and notifications, creating the potential for such applications to be refused on 'countryside' grounds. Farmers may, however, be compensated in cases of refusal. The 1981 Act also makes provision for maps of areas of moor or heath within national parks to try and protect them from ploughing and these maps are intended to inform grant decisions. In 1989 farm and conservation grants were introduced to replace grants aimed at increasing capital investment. These are targeted instead at environmental improvements such as the handling of farm waste, regeneration of woodlands and moorland and repairs to traditional buildings, hedges and walls.

In addition to restructuring the subsidy and grant schemes for agricultural production, there have been a range of initiatives aimed at developing alternative management regimes for the countryside. The most significant policy initiative is probably the Set-Aside Scheme, an EU initiative which provides for payments to the farmer where at least 20 per cent of arable land is taken out of production for five years and put to fallow, woodland or non-agricultural use. Conditions attached to these payments structure the management of the land: for example, providing for wildlife corridors, bird cover, restoring grassland and/or growing non-food crops. The reforms to the CAP in May 1992 generalise the proposal for set-aside to all farms so that reductions in guaranteed prices goes with a required set-aside of 15 per cent acreage plus compensation payments. The Countryside Premium Scheme further provides for additional payments to farmers in selected areas for managing set-aside land to the benefit of wildlife, landscape and countryside communities: for example, as feeding areas for winter geese.

In the case of forestry, schemes were introduced in 1985 (the Broadleaved Woodland Grant Scheme) and in 1988 (the Woodland Grant Scheme) to encourage high environmental standards in woodland management and provide higher rates of grant for planting native pinewoods and broadleaves. Since then grants have also been introduced for the environmental management of all woodlands, with higher rates operating for woods of special environmental value. The Pilot Farm Woodland Scheme provided supplementary grants for planting on agriculturally improved land but this has been replaced by a revision to the main Woodland Grant Scheme which now generally encourages farmers to convert farmland into woodland. This is seen as an environmentally acceptable way of taking land out of agricultural production. The grants are front-loaded to cover the costs of planting, and subject to environmental and silvicultural checks by the Forestry Authority (see below) and its consultees. Higher ratios of broadleaves within the tree mix attract more grant. Farm woodland grants are not available for ESAs (see below) and there are limits on planting in less favoured areas.

Some measures are more purely environmental in focus, not trying to marry reduced agricultural production with environmental aims. Another initiative promoted by an EC directive (No. 797/85) concerns environmentally sensitive areas (ESAs) designated by the appropriate agricultural department under the 1986 Agriculture Act (see Map 12.3). ESAs are areas of special landscape, wildlife or historic interest, considered vulnerable to agricultural intensification. Incentive payments are made to encourage farmers to maintain traditional, more ecologically sensitive farming practices. There are currently 38 such areas covering 31 080 km². Each ESA has quite distinct management agreements reflecting the special ecology of the area; the agreements last for five years in the first instance. They have no significance in relation to planning policies. Concern with the water pollution arising from farming activities has led to the designation of nitrate-sensitive areas to control nitrate leaching from soil due to fertiliser use. Monitored by the Environment Agency they encourage agreements to restrict the use of nitrate-based fertilisers in designated areas (see Chapter 11). And within the Habitat Scheme for Water Fringe Areas, farmers are encouraged to take waterside land out of production and manage it extensively to benefit wildlife. ESAs, NSAs and set-aside are all voluntary schemes run by MAFF and do not affect development planning or development control.

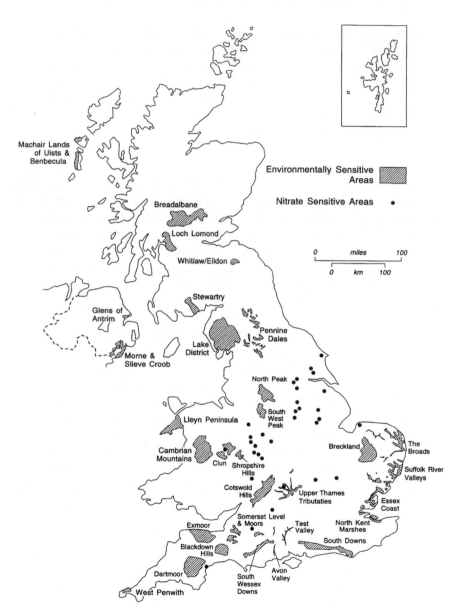

Map 12.3 *Environmental policies for farmland, 1997*

Generally the emphasis has been on a voluntary approach in encouraging the farming community to take a more responsible attitude towards nature and landscape conservation issues. The 1981 Wildlife and Countryside Act allowed for agreements for managing agricultural land. Local planning authorities can use Section 39 of the Act to enter into such agreements with farmers. The North Yorkshire Moors National Park Authority has used this means to negotiate five-year agreements with farmers by which payments are made for specified farm practices, both in the form of annual income and improvement-related grants. This voluntary approach has been supported by a wave of incentives from the DETR, mainly via the Countryside Commission (or equivalent in Scotland and Wales) and, more recently, from MAFF (and its equivalents). The Countryside Commission's 1992 Action for the Countryside programme included a number of measures aimed at agriculture, including an extended Countryside Stewardship Scheme for England. This scheme was initially run on a pilot basis by Countryside Commission for 1991–5 with consultation from English Heritage and English Nature but has now been taken over by MAFF. The aim was to bring a range of initiatives and grants under one integrated scheme. It identifies specific categories of landscape, which are seen to be under threat; currently these are chalk and limestone grassland, lowland heath, coastal land, waterside landscapes, uplands, historic landscapes, and pasture and meadow land. In these areas £13 million was originally available over three years for annual per hectare payments to farmers and landowners in the private or public sector, who enter into ten-year agreements to recreate landscapes, restore wildlife habitats and allow public access. Specified sums are set down for different types of land and works carried out, including some one-off capital payments. In its first year, 900 agreements were made. An expansion of the scheme was announced in 1995 with an additional £5 million over each of the following two years. An equivalent scheme – Tir Cymen – was set up in Wales in 1991. Another Countryside Commission initiative is the hedgerow protection scheme under which £3 million is available to complement MAFF's own hedgerow grants. As mentioned above, hedgerows now have protection under the Hedgerow Regulations.

Economic development within rural communities remains of continuing importance within countryside policy, as emphasised in the advice contained in PPG7 on the countryside. Given the somewhat reduced emphasis on agricultural production, this has involved attempts to promote forestry and other economic activities in rural areas. The Rural Development Commission (RDC) is currently charged with specific responsibility for rural economic development, though this task will be taken over by the new Regional Development Agencies (see Chapter 13). The RDC grant-aids development in 27 rural development areas designated on the basis of persistent high unemployment, narrow industrial and employment structure, lack of social services and disadvantaged as a result of their locality; these currently cover a third of England and 5 per cent of its population (see Map 12.4). The RDC encourages cooperation between local organisations to enable community-led development. The organisations include local authorities, RDC Business Services (formerly COSIRA), rural community councils and English Estates. Together they prepare rural development programmes for the next five to ten years. Local authorities are required to support such changes in the rural economy in their planning policies.

The government has published a good practice guide on *Planning for Diversification* (MAFF, 1995) to guide all bodies involved in rural planning. As well as providing a strategic planning framework, there are a number of grant schemes aimed at restructuring rural economies. The Farm Diversification Grants Scheme provides funds to enable farmers to develop farm trails, holidays, livery and similar activities to maintain their livelihood in an appropriate rural way. And the RDC runs an annual Rural Challenge (akin to the Challenge schemes within urban and regional policy – see Chapter 13). Under this £5 million was allocated to six rural development areas in 1997. But much more significant than national diversification funds have been the funds available under the EU Structural Funds, which aim to promote economic restructuring within the Union. In 1994 eleven regions of the UK were given Objective 5b status, thereby qualifying for £680 million over six years for rural development projects. (See Chapter 6 for more details on the EU Structural Funds.)

Forestry has also been pursued as an employment-generating activity and the organisation of forestry planning has reflected this. For most of this century all forestry activities have been covered by the Forestry Commission which has sought to expand tree-planting and currently owns 2 million acres worth over £2.2 billion. The Forestry Commission has been reorganised and split into two parts: the Forestry Authority which regulates all forestry, administers research and manages the grant schemes; and Forestry Enterprise which is the commercial arm, managing plantations on a self-financing basis. There is a regional structure with seven regional advisory committees. Recent changes mean that the number of environmental interests on these committees now balances the commercial forestry interests. This recognises the effect of the 1985 amendment to the Wildlife and Countryside Act which placed a duty on the Forestry Commission to balance its economic interests with conservation, countryside and wildlife concerns. British forestry policy is now placed within the framework set at the 1992 Rio Earth Summit where a Statement of Forestry Principles was agreed. In 1994 the British government issued its own strategy for *Sustainable Forestry* (Cm 2429).

Rural Development Areas

Map 12.4 *Rural development areas, 1995*

In 1991 the Countryside Commission launched a forest programme with a new National Forest in the Midlands and up to nine community forests. The National Forestry Strategy was published in 1994 with the aim of planting 30 million trees on 200 square miles over 20 years at a cost of £1 million of public money; 500 hectares would be on derelict land. The chosen site is in Leicestershire/Staffordshire. £2.2 million was also put into a National Forest Tender Scheme which would consider bids for turning both arable farmland and derelict land into forestry. Under a community woodlands supplement to the Woodland Grant Scheme, funds for planting will be provided with the aim of both increasing tree-planting and providing an appropriate location near urban areas for recreation and appropriate development.

In addition to supporting agriculture and forestry and ailing small rural businesses, it is now recognised that some residential development in the countryside is necessary to support rural communities and their economies. To this end rural housing has become a focus of planning policy in the countryside. Isolated dwellings have always been restricted to those needed by agricultural and forestry workers. Government advice has recommended functional and financial tests of whether such need is genuine and sufficient to warrant residential development and the Agricultural Development Advisory Service (ADAS) can provide an appraisal if required. Any such development is usually subject to an occupancy condition. More substantial residential development in the countryside is generally resisted. Proposals for complete new settlements were frequently put forward during the 1980s but advice in PPG3 suggests that they are appropriate only in limited circumstances. Any such development is likely to attract households from urban areas and is not intended primarily to meet rural housing needs. However, it is accepted that 'a community's need for affordable housing is a material planning consideration which may properly be taken into account in formulating development plan policies' (PPG3, para. 38). In urban locations the provision of affordable housing is encouraged using negotiation, planning obligations and conditions and controls over density. But such mechanisms work best in areas of high demand and on larger sites and may not be appropriate in rural areas. Therefore, special arrangements can be made under the rural exceptions scheme. This operates in two ways. First, local plans may include policies stating that small sites will be released for housebuilding, even in areas where housing would not normally be permitted, if they provide low-cost housing for local people. Second, in order to ensure that this housing is available for local needs, both initially and on subsequent change of occupant, housing associations are involved to prevent house price rises in open market exchanges.

☐ *Scotland*

The geography of Scotland has meant that some of the reforms of the CAP, with their focus on arable farming, have been less important than in lowland England. However, the merging of environmental and agricultural policy has had an impact here too. One issue of particular concern has been fish farming and the pollution generated in coastal locations which can severely affect local ecosystems. Fish farms are now subject to development control throughout Britain and discharges have been brought within pollution control and, therefore, subject to control by SEPA (see Chapter 11). The Scottish Office has issued draft supplementary guidelines in 1991 to the Crown Estate which is responsible for managing coastal resources as the legal owner of the seabed. This proposed identifying 44 very sensitive areas where there should be severe constraint on fish farming, with location policies identifying preferred sites for such activities elsewhere. Even outside very sensitive areas there is a presumption against very large farms. Thresholds are given for triggering environmental assessment (see Chapter 11) and separation distances specified to prevent a proliferation of such farms.

Economic development in rural Scotland remains a matter of great concern. The Agriculture Development Programme for Scottish Islands provides grants with an environmental emphasis to maintain the local economy of the islands and the Rural Enterprise Programme for the Highlands and Islands has been launched. This fits within the general work of Highlands Enterprise, formerly the Highlands and Islands Development Board.

■ Minerals planning

Minerals extraction is often regarded as an immediate and substantial threat to the countryside (see Summary Box 12.4). It disrupts surface landscapes, destroys habitats and generates considerable noise, dust and transport movements. With effective restoration, the land may in due course be returned to agricultural or alternative leisure use but no one would deny that the interim effects are not environmentally degrading. However, it has been held that the national interest (as opposed to that of local rural communities) is served by minerals extraction. The DETR produces forecasts of the demand for aggregates, using external consultants, and with the assistance of regional aggregates working parties. These provide the basis for local minerals planning and development control decisions on minerals applications. It is assumed

---

Summary Box 12.4   *Minerals planning*

Organisation:	DETR, national park authorities, local authorities
Focus:	Minerals production
Aim:	Balance national and local interests
Timing:	*Ad hoc* response, continuous monitoring
Scope:	Minerals deposits
Planning tool:	Regulation and indicative planning

---

that sites should be made available to meet forecast demand. This view is currently being challenged on the basis of principles of sustainable development (Owens and Cowell, 1996). The use of a fixed resource, such as minerals, is clearly unsustainable in the long term, but the conservation of the resource can be enhanced by encouraging recycling and substitution: that is, by demand management rather than a demand-led approach. This should also minimise the number of people adversely affected by minerals extraction in any time period. However the adoption of an approach which restricts the grant of planning permissions for minerals sites is not widely accepted, and certainly not by central government. In the specific area of opencast mining alone has expanded activity been viewed less favourably since the 1994 MPG3 *Coal Mining and Colliery Spoil Disposal*; a review announced in August 1997 is likely to reduce opencasting even further.

The main approach adopted by local authorities currently is to use development control policies to manage the release of minerals land and to influence the extraction process within a largely demand-led framework. For example, for cement quarries a plan must be drawn up by the operator for each site and discussed with the minerals planning authority to agree current operating and restoration practice. Land banks of permitted reserves are also established at each site to safeguard future cement supplies. More generally, under the 1991 Planning and Compensation Act, all county councils and national park authorities must prepare one area-wide minerals local plan. These indicate where minerals working may occur, where minerals wastes should be disposed of and where minerals resources should be safeguarded for the future. The plans also include policies for development control, restoration and after-care. National policy guidance is provided by a series of minerals planning guidance notes. Other relevant policy advice includes the PPG16 on 'Archaeology and Planning', which recommends the CBI's Code of Practice for Minerals Operators for dealing with archaeological remains on sites of excavations.

Over the past decade or so, the development control powers relating to minerals development have been greatly strengthened. The principal statutory provisions are the 1981 Town and Country Planning (Minerals) Act, incorporated in the Town and Country Planning Act 1990, and the 1995 Environment Act; aspects of the 1991 Planning and Compensation Act also apply. The most significant feature is that contained in the 1995 Act, whereby local planning authorities responsible for minerals are required to review all sites with planning permissions for minerals development (that is, the mining and working of minerals or the depositing of minerals waste) every fifteen years, imposing new conditions if necessary. Compensation is payable where the new conditions affect working rights, but not for new after-care or restoration conditions. Minerals planning authorities – generally county councils, national park authorities or metropolitan district councils – are given extensive development control powers, and a duty is placed on all minerals planning authorities to review every mining operation in their area with a view to using the full range of development control powers. Restoration and after-care conditions are particularly important to ensure proper replacement of soils and management of the site to a required standard for agricultural, forestry or recreational after-use. Approval of after-care schemes by the minerals planning authority may also be required. All planning permissions since February 1982 are subject to an implied 60-year time limit.

Most importantly, minerals planning authorities have a range of orders at their disposal. If they consider it expedient, minerals planning authorities may issue orders revoking or modifying planning permissions in relation to development that has not yet begun or uncompleted parts of the development. They can also issue a discontinuance order to stop the use of the minerals site, impose new conditions or require the alteration/removal of buildings, works or plant and machinery. Restoration and after-care conditions can also be imposed and this allows for improvements in techniques to be reflected in current minerals practice. Such discontinuance orders relate to the use of land rather than the planning permission itself and, therefore, can be used even on old (pre-1947) minerals working where there is no explicit permission. As befits such extensive powers, the order requires confirmation by the Secretary of State. On sites where work has ceased but there is an outstanding planning permission, special orders can be made. Suspension orders can be applied, to hold minerals not worked for at least twelve months for future working. This provides for temporary restoration and environmental protection. Prohibition orders can be introduced to prevent resumption of works, where no operations have been carried out for at least two years and no further working is desirable. They provide the due process for extinguishing planning permissions where development has permanently ended. The 1997 Town and Country Planning (Compensation for Restrictions on

Minerals Working and Mineral Waste Depositing) Regulations set out the compensation payable on all these orders.

Special provisions apply for permissions granted in the 1940s and for updating permissions from the 1950s, 1960s and 1970s. Some minerals operations have permissions granted as interim development orders in the mid-1940s. Prior to the 1991 Planning and Compensation Act these were valid planning consents. Under this legislation a register of interim development orders granted during 1943–8 is set up. Registered consents may be made subject to conditions meeting current-day standards for after-use and restoration. Notice is also given for the cessation of the use within 50 years' time. Where there is an interim development order on a site which has not been worked between July 1948 and April 1989, then permission is deemed to have lapsed since 1979. This means that the site comes under the Town and Country Planning Act 1990 and the minerals planning authority can decide on a new form of consent. Where there is no substantial working between April 1989 and May 1991, no working can begin until a scheme of operation and restoration conditions are determined by the planning authority.

Minerals extraction may also have implications for other areas of planning. For example, PPG14 on 'Development on Unstable Land' points out that various forms of underground mining cause subsidence and ground instability. This then becomes a factor to be taken into account in preparing development plans and determining planning applications in affected areas.

☐ *Scotland*

A broadly similar pattern of planning and control operates in Scotland since the Town and Country Planning (Minerals) Act 1981 and certain minerals-related provisions of the 1991 Planning and Compensation Act are applicable.

■ **Further reading**

As recommended before, the legislation, other policy documents and annual reports of relevant organisations, particularly English Nature and the Countryside Commission (or equivalents) should be consulted. The 1995 Rural White Paper (Cm 3016) and its updates (1996, Cm 3444) include much useful material, as does the 1994 UK *Action Plan on Biodiversity* (Cm 2428) and the documents produced by the subsequent steering group (1995). A relevant journal to consult is *Progress in Rural Policy and Planning*; this summarises rural policy developments each year.

■ *Chapter 13* ■

Regeneration and Conservation

This chapter completes the overview of the planning system by considering two different types of policy for two different categories of the built environment: the pursuit of regeneration through urban and regional policy for areas where development and change are considered essential; and the conservation of heritage areas deemed worthy of protection. Urban and regional policy has traditionally been conceived in terms of public investment and subsidy. The period of Thatcher government in the 1980s confirmed a shift towards a more market oriented approach which persists today, at the end of the 1990s, though recast in terms of partnership. In many ways urban and regional policy exemplifies the new politics of governance (see Chapters 5 and 6). The relevant policies are considered under headings of: grants for physical improvement; land transfers; and promoting regeneration through partnership. Conservation of the heritage of our built environment, by contrast, has been pursued through an enhanced form of regulation, particularly development control. This final section, therefore, returns to the land use planning system considered at the start of Part 3 in Chapter 10.

■ Regeneration: grants for physical improvement

Grants for the improvement of physical infrastructure focus on the housing sector, together with derelict and contaminated land.

Subsidies to encourage home improvement have long been available as part of the shift from a slum clearance policy to one of rehabilitation. Such subsidies have, on occasion, underpinned social change as well as physical improvement. Local authorities still have a duty to inspect housing in their area and take steps to repair, close or demolish unfit housing. Clearance areas in which extensive compulsory purchase and demolition are proposed can still be declared, but the emphasis is on improvement through grants.

The 1989 Local Government and Housing Act set out a new system of improvement grants replacing that formerly available under the 1985

Summary Box 13.1   *Grants for physical improvement*

Organisation:	Local authorities, English Partnerships (RDAs)
Focus:	Physical fabric of buildings and land
Aim:	Improvement and reclamation
Timing:	Responsive
Scope:	Urban built environment
Planning tool:	Subsidy

Housing Act. The largely consolidating Act, the 1996 Housing Grants, Construction and Regeneration Act, provides the current legislative reference point for this area. Four types of grant are available: renovation grants for improvement, repair or conversion; common parts grants for improving or repairing the common parts of buildings; disabled facilities grants for the provision of facilities for disabled persons in dwellings or the common parts of buildings; and houses in multiple occupation grants to improve or repair houses in multiple occupation or create such houses by conversion.

Grants are available to private owner-occupiers, current or intended, of dwellings and to tenants in the case of renovation or disabled facilities grants. Tenants must be responsible for carrying out the relevant works under the terms of their lease. In each case a certificate of ownership must accompany the application. Dwellings must be at least ten years old and there are no exclusions based on rateable value. Instead the amount of the grant payable is subject to means-testing based on the housing benefit system. Renovation grants must bring the dwelling up to a specified 'fitness standard'; grants beyond this standard are discretionary, not mandatory. The 1996 Act also introduced a new test of resources in relation to grant approvals. Grants may be subject to conditions regarding the nature of the works and the availability of the dwelling for letting. Grants may have to be repaid, at least in part, in the case of sale, within five years if it was intended to let the dwelling or within three years if it is owner-occupied. Minor works may also be assisted by local authority grants, for example for thermal insulation. Seventy-five per cent of eligible local authority expenditure under these provisions is met by central government grant. Higher rates of subsidy are available in renewal areas (see below).

Under the 1989 Local Government and Housing Act local housing authorities may designate renewal areas, consisting primarily of living accommodation, where living conditions are unsatisfactory. They are not intended for areas of publicly owned housing or HATs (see below). Such renewal areas replace general improvement areas and housing action areas.

A report accompanies the designation detailing the existing conditions, the powers and proposals for improvement, their costs and the resources available for implementation. Draft proposals must be publicised and account taken of representations and Secretary of State guidance. The latter currently indicates that a renewal area should be at least 75 per cent privately owned, consist of at least 300 dwellings, have at least 75 per cent of dwellings in poor physical condition and that at least 30 per cent of households should be significantly dependent on specified state benefits. Renewal areas are temporary measures intended normally to last for ten years. Within a renewal area the local authority can compulsorily purchase properties, provide housing accommodation, carry out works and assist others to carry out works. Fifty per cent of eligible expenditure will be provided by central government up to a total average expenditure of £1000 per dwelling. Local authorities are under a duty to inform residents of actions they are undertaking concerning such areas.

A further improvement subsidy provided under the 1989 Local Government and Housing Act concerns group repair schemes, otherwise known as enveloping. This refers to a programme of public sector repairs to the external fabric of a group of houses, say a row of terraced housing, which will then encourage further individual actions. Under the Act local authorities can enter into agreements to undertake enveloping of privately owned homes and recover costs as agreed between the parties. Sale of enveloped dwellings allows the local authority to recover further costs from the sale proceeds. As part of the current drive towards energy efficiency £60 million of funds were made available under the DoE's Greenhouse Programme to improve the energy efficiency of selected council estates. There are 140 or so schemes acting as demonstration projects, encouraging other local authorities to follow their example using local funds. Another estate-based programme is the Estate Action Programme, formerly the Priority Estate Project, under which funds are available for physical works and establishing new management structures. Within these schemes, the participation of tenants is seen as essential to estate renovation. Local management trusts and community refurbishment schemes are encouraged.

Grants are also available to deal with derelict land. Derelict land grant (DLG) is available for actions necessary to overcome dereliction and contamination of abandoned sites. Local authorities and English Partnerships receive funding at 100 per cent of costs in assisted areas and designated derelict land clearance areas; other bodies receive 80 per cent of costs in these areas. Outside these designated areas, 50 per cent of the net loss incurred during reclamation work is payable. Under small clearance schemes up to £30 000 may be made available to voluntary bodies as well. Derelict land is defined for the purposes of giving grants as 'land so damaged by industrial or other development that it is incapable of beneficial use without treatment'. The powers relating to DLG are held by local authorities, UDCs (see below) and English Partnerships; they are only permissive powers but are relatively unrestricted in their scope, drawing as they do on a variety of planning and other legislation. In 1985/6 the budget for approved grants was £75 million, a ninefold increase from 1974/5. Demand outstrips this allocation, with applications in 1984/5 totalling £165 million. About two-thirds of all reclamation is for hard land uses, stressing the economic rather than environmental role that much derelict land policy plays (Kivell, 1987). Local authorities are required to undertake period surveys of derelict land in their areas, and under the 1991 Derelict Land Grant Advice Note, this should occur every 4–6 years. Proposals have been discussed to give local authorities more powers in relation to derelict land with the greater use of restoration conditions and, as a last-resort measure, the provision for local authorities to reclaim sites and recover the costs from owners. Other possibilities include bonding, bank guarantee and sinking fund schemes to protect against dereliction. There are specific powers for the acquisition and restoration of derelict land within national parks under the National Parks and Access to the Countryside Act 1949.

The promotion of *ad hoc* development projects, where central government provided a substantial input of funds, is another approach that has been adopted to channel subsidies towards derelict sites. Garden festivals were promoted during the 1980s. Five festivals have been funded since 1984: Liverpool, Stoke-on-Trent, Glasgow, Gateshead and South Wales. Each cost about £50 million to turn an area of dereliction into a landscaped tourist attraction with the aim of securing longer-term investment and environmental improvement when the festival was over. About 23 per cent of the total monies went on land reclamation, with the remainder used to stage the temporary tourist event. The Millennium Dome project in Greenwich, London, is a much more grandiose scheme but with a similar approach to derelict land declamation.

Over half of all derelict sites may also be contaminated land and district councils have a duty under Section 143 of the 1990 Environmental Protection Act to compile a register of land that is also potentially contaminated, where additional aid is needed and developers will wish to be aware of the risks. The use of the term 'potentially' contaminated means that large numbers of sites are eligible for registration. The registers would identify sites, prioritise them and classify them in terms of use and need for long-term monitoring. These were due to be made public by April 1993, but concern over the effects of the register on land markets and opposition from landowners, including local authorities, led to the registers being abandoned in 1994. Under the 1995 Environmental Protection Act, the 'polluter pays principles' now applies to contaminated land, so that the responsibility for the contamination rests with the original polluter. It has been estimated that this could amount to up to £20 billion of clean-up costs (Walton, 1997). Section 61 of the 1990 Act originally required local authorities to inspect all contaminated land and take steps for its clean-up. This has now been suspended and the 1995 Act instead requires local authorities and the Environment Agency to identify and designate contaminated land and serve remediation notices on the owner or the polluter. This remediation notice is then entered on a register. The level at which a remediation notice must be served has been limited to that causing 'significant harm' to human health or the local environment. In addition local authorities have to have regard to any hardship that might result from serving the notice. There was a proposal to allow local people to sue a local authority that avoided this statutory duty, but this was dropped from the final version.

In 1993 a new urban regeneration agency, English Partnerships, was created to oversee policy for reclaiming and developing some 396 km^2 of derelict land in England. It is a policy-making executive agency with responsibility for a large slice of the DETR's budget, namely £250 million per annum for City Grant (see below) and derelict land grants, together with the work of the public sector industrial developer, English Estates. The agency has compulsory purchase powers and, in designated areas, can handle development control functions. When the new Regional Development ment Agencies are operative, English Partnerships will be restructured (see below). It should be noted that efforts are being made to shift away from a simple reliance on subsidies to solve derelict and contaminated land problems. The Groundwork Trust has long enabled local community-based projects to restore and reuse derelict land. They are to launch a national agency to support the restoration of derelict land through local community schemes. In a similar initiative, the Millennium Greens scheme was launched in October 1996 to establish small areas of open space of 10–15 hectares. While this is a Countryside Commission scheme, it is expected that 60 per cent of the 250 or so greens will be in urban locations on derelict land. It expected that the RDAs will continue this emphasis.

■ Regeneration: land transfers

A key theme throughout the 1980s was privatisation: of nationalised industries, of public utilities, and of public land (see Summary Box 13.2). The transfer of land from public to private ownership was presented as a key factor, in itself, in generating development, wealth and economic activity. The idea was that such a transfer of land would facilitate property

---

	Summary Box 13.2 *Land transfers*
Organisation:	Public corporations
Focus:	Ownership of land
Aim:	Property development
Timing:	*Ad hoc* disposal
Scope:	Public land
Planning tool:	Leverage

---

development and, thereby, property-led urban regeneration. A number of examples of this approach can be found.

Urban development corporations (UDCs) were set up by the 1980 Local Government Planning and Land Act (see Map 13.1). While emblematic of the Thatcher government approach to planning, the policy tool may continue to find new applications in the future. UDCs involved the transfer of large areas of land, usually from other public bodies such as statutory undertakers to independent corporations, often by way of a vesting instrument which short-cuts complicated and lengthy procedures for the sale of statutory undertakers' land. UDCs are designated by statutory instrument and require Parliamentary approval. Public objections to designation are possible only via a petition to the Select Committee considering the designation. The UDCs have wide-ranging powers including that of purchasing land in the designated area. A UDC can apply to the Secretary of State for a vesting order to transfer public land to the corporation's ownership. They also have powers of land assembly, reclamation, servicing land and development or disposal to developers. Substantial Treasury funds were available to package the land for sale on to the private sector as development sites. UDCs usually hold all development control powers for their areas including conservation powers over conservation areas, listed buildings and preserved trees. In some cases local authorities carry out development control functions on an agency basis for the UDC and, in the case of Cardiff UDC, a partnership arrangement was made between the UDC and the city council. Although UDCs do not have formal development planning powers, their development schemes are effectively *de facto* local plans. Such schemes are, however, corporate planning documents and not open to public consultation and scrutiny in the same way as a development plan. The UDC submits proposals directly to the Secretary of State for development of land in its area. After consultation with the local authorities the Secretary of State can then approve the proposals with or without modifications. Planning permission for all development is granted via a special development order for any conforming development.

The essence of UDCs is the discretion they have to promote the development of their areas. Altogether thirteen UDCs have been designated: Merseyside and London Docklands in 1981; Trafford Park, Cardiff Bay, the Black Country, Teesside and Tyne and Wear in 1987; Central Manchester, Leeds and Sheffield in 1988; Bristol in 1989; Birmingham Heartlands in 1992; and finally Plymouth in 1993. Later UDCs have been much reduced in scale compared to earlier ones. Those designated in 1988/9 received only £15 million each over five years compared to £443 million over 1981–8 for the London Docklands Development Corporation and approximately £150 million each over six years for those designated in between. Each UDC is a limited-life organisation and arrangements are in place for winding them up. Bristol and Leeds were wound up in 1995, Manchester in 1996 and Sheffield in 1997. As of April 1998 the Commission for New Towns will take over the remaining English UDCs, together with the six Housing Action Trusts (see below). On final winding up, the assets and liabilities should be transferred to a long-term owner, usually the local authorities and English Partnerships (or RDAs presumably). There is further discussion of UDCs in Exhibit 13.1.

It was hoped that a similar approach could be made to work for housing estates. The most well-known example of privatisation is probably the sale of individual council houses to tenants. Although the numbers sold under this initiative are now well down on the peak years, the provisions for sale still exist and a rent-to-mortgage scheme has been introduced. Tenants can purchase their home at a discount to market value and with the aid of a public sector mortgage. The 1988 Housing Act made provision for the privatisation of whole estates of council houses under the 'pick-a-landlord' scheme. The new owner could be either a developer, housing association or tenants' cooperative. But the housing privatisation initiative most closely akin to the UDC is the creation of housing action trusts (HATs) under the 1988 Housing Act. These are designated by the Secretary of State and are eligible for public funds to aid estate improvement. The designation process involves consultation with affected local authorities, a ballot of all tenants (a majority of whom must vote in favour) and debate in Parliament. However, the Secretary of State has wide discretion in making the designation. The resulting HAT is run by a small board of five to eleven people with all the housing powers of the local authority, as well as planning powers and certain public health powers. These HATs are intended to be temporary institutions with an expected life of five years. The original aim was that the housing would be disposed of before the end of the five years. On such disposal tenants become assured tenants, unless they are transferred back to a local authority. Any disposal must be to an 'approved landlord' and local authorities do have first refusal. It was

---

Exhibit 13.1   *Urban development corporations*

UDCs were the flagship of the Thatcher administration's urban policy. They arose from a classic New Right analysis of urban district councils as obstructive of the wealth-creating processes within the city. Land was being left derelict, the argument ran, because local authorities spent too much time discussing rather than facilitating, and were hostile to the very development processes that could regenerate urban areas. The UDCs thus took areas out of local authority control and placed them in the hands of well-resourced quangos with substantial discretionary powers. The quango could operate in a largely autonomous manner and, in London at least, used its powers to underpin a speculative property boom.

While successful in these terms, the LDDC also provides the ammunition for left-wing critique of UDCs (Brownill, 1990). The quango, having arisen from a dissatisfaction with elected local authorities, was explicitly divorced from local communities. It responded neither to pressure from the London boroughs nor the local groups which arose from within the Docklands communities. The New Left could readily present this as central government intervening to benefit private profit-making at the expense of local working-class people. The heavy involvement of individual property developers within the LDDC, the close relations they formed with developers working in the Dockland area and the high-handed attitude to local people all confirmed this view. The role of the LDDC in acting as the property developers' organisation meant that the degree of planning, understood as purposive, rational decision-making, was limited. Neither did the rather one-sided consultation that the LDDC engaged in lend itself to any analysis of mediation as in the institutionalist approach.

However the LDDC of the early 1980s proved to be the exception rather than the rule (Stoker, 1989b). Towards the end of the decade, the LDDC was

---

intended that the bulk of the monies would come from the private sector. The return on this private investment would be in terms of profits on sales forward or increased rents, improvement by a HAT resulting in a shift from fair rents to 'reasonable' rents, that is, an increase in rents. However, designation was dependent on local consultation and such arrangements proved unattractive to tenants and, indeed, to developers. Recent revisions to HATs maintain fair rents and allow for later transfer back to the public sector and the most common conclusion will be for the housing to be transferred back to the local authority with no change in tenants' standing.

These privatisation measures are all exemplars of the Conservative government's approach to urban regeneration. These formed part of a policy package which also included Part X registers of surplus public land and more general advice to dispose of publicly held land where possible. While the measures described above remain 'on the books' and therefore available to policy-makers and while certain examples of the implementa-

developing relations both with local councils, who decided to enter planning gain agreements with the Corporation and try thereby to salvage some benefits from the UDC designation, and with local communities through the LDDC's social programme (Brindley *et al.*, 1996). The New Left continued to see these adjustments in the Corporation's attitude as marginal and as representing a climbdown by the local community and boroughs in their struggle over the land resources of Docklands. But the experience of other UDCs suggests that a shift towards an accommodation between the local community and the corporation is the general model. In Merseyside, the lack of private sector involvement meant that, from early on, the corporation and local authorities worked together in consultation. Later UDCs were based on negotiation between quango and local government from the start. In some cases the district council operated development control and other functions for the UDC on an agency basis. In such situations the UDCs operate neither as an aloof, autonomous, professional-dominated quango nor as a representative of private capital in conflict with the local community. Rather negotiation, liaison and consultation between quango and local government, as well as infrastructure agencies and community groups, over the planning of development in an urban area becomes the norm.

This does not mean that a cosy consensus emerges. Conflicts and tensions over jurisdiction remain. Furthermore this more cooperative approach is heavily dependent on the attitudes of both local authorities and UDCs. The second-round UDCs were in areas where the local authority had already adopted a leverage style of planning due to the nature of the local property market and the other constraints they faced on their own investment activities. The UDCs also were generally more conciliatory in tone, unwilling to emulate the conflict-ridden history of the LDDC.

tion of policy remain, it is unclear how significant such land transfers will be under the new Labour government. It may be that the emphasis on land transfers as an approach to regeneration may be seen as a phenomenon of the 1980s and early 1990s, to be replaced by a more partnership-oriented approach in which the public and private sectors work together. Examples of this approach are covered in the next section.

☐ Wales

Of the agencies involved in urban regeneration in Wales, two are specifically focused on transferring land to the private sector. The Cardiff UDC is charged with transforming the Cardiff Bay area. And the Land Authority for Wales retains a role from the 1970s Community Land Scheme in buying land for resale to developers.

□   *Scotland*

UDCs, one of the main initiatives discussed above, do not apply in Scotland. Similarly the privatisation of council houses has had much less effect, with 5 per cent of the public stock sold in Scotland compared to 15 per cent in England and Wales (Midwinter *et al.*, 1991, p. 174). Direct land privatisation measures have, perhaps, been less emphasised in Scotland. But there has been considerable scope for the transfer of assets to the private sector arising from institutional change. The replacement of the SDA by Scottish Enterprise, with its change in policy emphasis, created the potential for selling the former SDA's assets, and the formation of Scottish Homes from an amalgamation of the Scottish Special Housing Association and the Housing Corporation in Scotland gives rise to similar possibilities, given that Scottish Homes was given a remit to act in a strategic planning capacity, rather than as a direct housing agency.

■   Regeneration: promoting partnership

The concept of attracting private investment into an area by grants and subsidies is not new. Regional planning was based, from the earliest days, on a combination of carrot and stick, with grants, subsidies and tax allowances offsetting the costs of investments in depressed regions – mainly in the north – while planning restrictions sought to inhibit development in the more congested, prosperous regions – mainly in the south east. In the 1980s this form of regional policy was restructured. All regional development grants were scrapped, leaving only regional selective assistance. Project-specific, these funds are available for proposals which can be demonstrated to be viable but require government assistance to go ahead. Revised boundaries for the assisted areas – development and intermediate areas – where these grants may apply, were announced in June 1992 (see Map 13.1). This limited the areas, focused them more

---

Summary Box 13.3	*Promoting regeneration by partnership*
Organisation:	DETR, local authorities, Welsh Development Agency, Scottish Enterprise (RDAs)
Focus:	Private development with social benefits
Aim:	Urban regeneration
Timing:	*Ad hoc*, opportunity-led
Scope:	Areas of marginal development interest
Planning tool:	Leverage

clearly on urban areas, and included areas in all regions of mainland Britain. The overall budget of regional aid was then cut in autumn 1992.

For most of the 1980s there was little distinction between British regional and urban policy and, while the creation of Regional Development Agencies (see below) gives an explicit regional dimension to the policy, there is still essentially a unified approach. This encompasses a concern with levering private funds into areas of depressed demand, focusing on specific projects and encouraging partnership between the private and public sectors in pursuit of these goals (see Summary Box 13.3). 'Leverage' embodies the idea that a small initial sum of public investment can attract a larger sum of private investment, with a multiplier effect ensuring the continued attraction of private funds in ever larger amounts. In the 1990s, and increasingly under the new Labour government, the concern with leverage has continued but the relationship appears more even-handed, a partnership in more than just name. This is seen in the various City Pride initiatives where the various stakeholders within a city were 'invited' by central government to prepare a Pride Prospectus for their urban area, a document which combined the functions of manifesto, advertising brochure and non-statutory plan. More significant than the document was the pattern of joint working that the Pride experiment fostered. This is likely to be the hallmark of regeneration policy for the next few years at least.

However, some of the Conservative government's policies still remain 'on the books'. Powers are still available under the 1980 Local Government, Planning and Land Act for designating enterprise zones (EZs). These are areas identified by central government, with or without local authority support, in which a range of incentives to development and business activity apply. These incentives include: exemptions from business rates; tax allowances for capital expenditure; exemption from industrial training levies; reduced requirements to provide statistical information; a simplified planning regime using an EZ scheme and rapid development control; priority handling in all regulatory regimes. In the past exemptions from IDCs and development land tax were also relevant. Such zones are designated for a period of ten years only. As a result, the first of the EZs identified in the first round in 1981 have already been wound up. A second round of twelve EZs was put forward in 1983 but central government than announced that there would be no further designation rounds. The legislation is still in force and it is possible that the scheme may be implemented again on a more substantial scale in the future, for example in response to the coal-pit closures.

In the interim period, while the Labour government rethinks its regeneration strategy, the budgetary framework for regeneration set up under the Conservatives also remains in place. The urban grant regime had

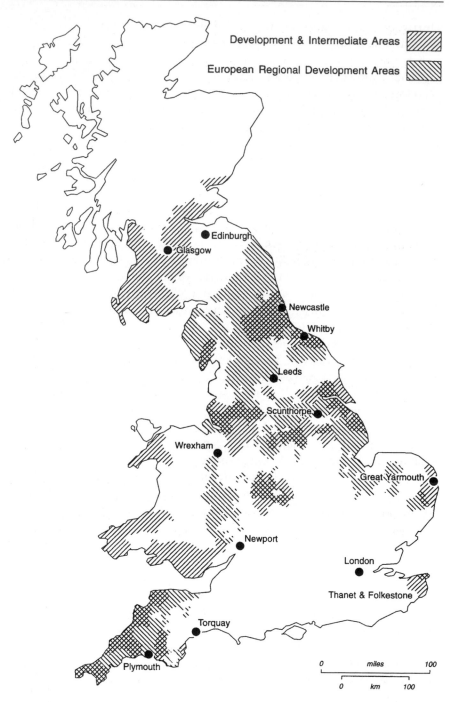

Map 13.1 *Development areas, 1995*

developed incrementally over many decades and was increasingly difficult to negotiate. Therefore, in November 1993, the Single Regeneration Budget (SRB) was announced. This incorporated no less than twenty urban policy-related spending programmes into one flexible budget trying to achieve a package of objectives: improving education and training; ensuring competitive local economies; improving poor quality housing; serving ethnic minorities; reducing crime; improving quality of life for targeted groups; and improving the environment. In 1994/5 this amounted to £1.4 billion and some 373 SRB projects were approved in the first two years. However, over the period 1994/5 to 1998/9, the SRB is projected to fall by 29 per cent in real terms (Nevin *et al.*, 1997). The budget is currently administered by the Government Offices for the Regions. There are only two main categories within the SRB: committed central government expenditure on preexisting regeneration programmes such as City Grant, UDCs, HATs and Estate Action; and a Challenge Fund in which 10 per cent of the total funds or about £122 million in 1995/6 is made available through a competitive bidding process. Particularly significant has been the competition for the five-year limited-term grants called City Challenge. £37.5 million of funding was provided in addition to the usual SRB budget for this initiative. City Challenge bids were required to show evidence of partnership between local government, the business sector and voluntary organisations and special companies were established to implement the schemes. Thirty-one schemes have been funded, eleven have completed and the remaining twenty will wind up in April 1998.

The emphasis on competitive bidding was innovative but is now accepted policy practice. All areas are eligible to bid for monies and there is no priority afforded to the urban priority areas identified under the old Urban Programme. The emphasis in making grant decisions is on output, not input; on effective use of the money, not need *per se*. To this end the demonstration of partnerships between the public and private sectors is expected, with leadership shared rather than in the hands of the local authorities. In the first and second rounds, 95 per cent and 88 per cent of successful bids respectively listed employment as a major objective of the projects bid for. The Labour government is honouring the third-round bid decisions and going ahead with the fourth round, amounting to £80 million over two years. It seems likely that the Labour government will retain an element of competition in allocating regeneration funds. It is expected, though, that the new Government will give a higher priority to schemes with a social rationale. Other suggestions include the possibility that an index of local conditions will be used to assist allocation decisions and that the concept of five–ten year agreements between central and local government and other partners will be promoted as a framework for local regeneration schemes. Regeneration policy has therefore undergone an evolutionary process from 'carrots and sticks', through project-specific grants and competitive bidding, to the current partnership approach.

The major new initiative so far in regeneration policy has come with the announcement in December 1997 of the creation of Regional Development Agencies in England, to mirror the agencies in Wales and Scotland. There will be nine RDAs operative from 1999. They have been given responsibility for social, physical and economic regeneration and coordinating inward investment, as well as site reclamation and preparation. They will have reserve planning and compulsory purchase powers but debate continues over whether they will prepare the regional planning guidance. Current indicators are that this will rest with Government Offices for the Regions and the regional planning conferences. RDAs will administer the SRB and will take over the regional regeneration work of English Partnerships and the functions of the Rural Development Commission in relation to the economic development and regeneration of rural areas. English Partnerships will retain responsibility only for national regeneration projects and the Coalfields Initiative, but will be merged with the Commission for New Towns before April 2000. The executive board of each agency will have representatives of business, local authorities, the voluntary sector and universities, and it will probably be shadowed by a regional chamber of local councillors. These agencies and chambers may also be the precursors of a more fully fledged form of regional government, but this will not occur before the next general election. It is estimated that the combined budget of the nine RDAs will amount to £750 million. This will largely come from the existing budgets of the preexisting agencies involved, together with £5 billion of loan authorisation released from the receipts of council house sales, a share of the windfall tax on the utilities and some EU funding.

A major task of the RDAs will be to attract a larger share of the increasingly important European sources of funding that many individual local authorities are already targeting. It is significant that the EU no longer links eligibility for EU funds to the national designation of eligible areas. Rather the Commission is developing a comprehensive European regional aid policy with substantial funds at its disposal. Some details of these funds are given in Exhibit 6.1 in Chapter 6. These funds have long had a regional dimension, and the reform of the CAP has led to rural restructuring and aid also becoming an important policy goal. However, more recently, there has been a concerted attempt at the European level to develop an urban policy. In May 1997 the Commission issued a communication entitled *Towards an Urban Agenda in the European Union*. This appears to have influenced the proposals for a future financial framework of the Union set out in the 1997 document *Agenda 2000: For a Stronger and Wider Europe*. Under the proposed financial arrangements, the overall budget for the Structural Funds will be frozen at 33 per cent for the period 2000–6; this represents an increase from 200 billion ECUs for 1993–9 at 1997 prices to 275 billion ECUs. However this will be targeted on 35–40 per cent of the population, rather than the 51 per cent as at present. The six objectives will be reduced to three: Objective 1 will remain unchanged and will attract two-thirds of the budget; Objective 2 will concentrate on areas undergoing industrial transformation – fragile urban areas, disadvantaged urban neighbourhoods and areas dependent on fisheries; and Objective 3 will be a new strategy for human resources. Given the changes proposed in the new Objective 2 category, this represents a significant elevation of urban areas within the European grants scheme. It follows through on the EU's Urban Initiative launched in 1994.

The promotion of regeneration in urban and regional areas has not been immune from the general 'greening' of planning (Gibbs, 1994 and 1996). There are, of course, the various measures aimed at environmental protection outlined in the previous chapters. But going beyond this, some local authorities have sought to promote economic development paths which are more sustainable in environmental terms, and restructure local economies away from unsustainable paths. This builds on local authorities' current relationships with local business and on their statutory responsibilities for local economic development. Despite the removal of many powers and resources from local authorities, they are still given a general responsibility for economic development within their areas under Section 33 of the 1986 Local Government and Housing Act and required to produce an annual statement on their policy and activities. This general role is circumscribed by guidance from central government as to the form of this activity and restrictions placed on local government by way of orders. Traditionally local government has had the power to raise the result of a 2p rate to fund such economic development. This has now been updated, following the changes in local government finance, to the product of the local authority's population and £2.50 for county councils or non-metropolitan districts, £5.00 for metropolitan districts.

During the 1980s this local economic development role was oriented so that local authorities were simply facilitating private sector business activity. Under the moves to green local economies, a much more proactive role for local government is proposed. In line with the ideas of ecological modernisation (Weale, 1992), a restructuring of the local economy is sought which will reduce the need for 'end-of-pipe' pollution control and waste management by integrating pollution prevention and waste minimisation within the economic processes. Firms would be steered towards clean technologies, recycling and energy efficiency. They would also be helped to target the new markets opening up with increased environmental regulation: for example, pollution control equipment, solar energy technology, new forms of packaging, green goods. This goal involves using the local authorities' resources towards new goals and also developing new lines of communication with the business sector. This is very much a new area of policy practice for local authorities, one in which they have yet to develop full expertise.

One more traditional way in which the shift towards a green local economy may be aided is through the provision of public transport infrastructure. The renewed importance of changed travel patterns within land use planning has already been emphasised. However, in pursuing this goal local authorities face the problem that the prevailing trend over the past decade has been towards reduced subsidy to public transport and greater private sector involvement in all transport schemes. New rail projects are expected to be virtually self-financing, including the various light rail schemes which are being implemented across the country and which are intended to have an impact on reducing road-based travel. The subsidy system within transport policy remains a significant bar to green local economic development, as it does to a more sustainable form of land use planning. The 1998 integrated transport White Paper may go some way towards remedying this.

☐ Wales

In Wales a number of agencies are involved in urban and economic regeneration activities: the Welsh Development Agency (WDA); the Development Board for Rural Wales; the Land Authority for Wales, a survivor from the Community Land Scheme of the 1970s; the Cardiff Bay Development Corporation, a UDC; the Welsh Tourist Board; and Housing for Wales, a housing association. Many of these agencies will be absorbed by the new Welsh Assembly. The WDA administers the grant schemes, including derelict land funds, and certain specific programmes: Landscape Wales and Urban Development Wales. There was also a Programme for the Valleys to run from January 1988 to March 1993 which coordinated agencies involved in regeneration of industrialised valley areas.

☐ Scotland

In Scotland the Scottish Development Agency (SDA) has pioneered a number of programmes in the past with an emphasis on a sectoral approach using local self-help to achieve economic development. The Glasgow Eastern Area Renewal (GEAR) project was one such project which operated through the 1970s and 1980s (Brindley *et al.*, 1996).

Under a 1988 White Paper, *New Life for Urban Scotland*, four further partnership initiatives were set up for Glasgow, Paisley, Edinburgh and Dundee. Many of these initiatives were instigated by the SDA. This role is now taken by Scottish Enterprise. The sister organisation, Highlands and Islands Enterprise, was created out of the Highlands and Islands Development Board. The emphasis on enterprise was a key theme in urban regeneration policy in the 1980s, as shown in the 1988 White Paper on *Scottish Enterprise: A New Approach to Training and Enterprise Creation* and the Scottish Office document *New Life for Urban Scotland* of the same year. Now the emphasis is more on public–private partnership as set out in the 1993 Scottish Office consultation paper *Progress in Partnership*. This informs the Scottish Office scheme under which it designates areas as Small Urban Renewal Initiatives within which the regeneration of town centres is linked to the renewal of nearby housing estates. Economic development remains high on the urban regeneration agenda as evidenced by the prominent role of Scotland's 22 local enterprise councils (LECs) but it should be noted that the requirement for local authorities to prepare economic development plans does not apply in Scotland. These are coordinated by Scottish Enterprise and Highlands and Islands Enterprise who continue to take on the responsibility for economic development and for central government training programmes (Fairley, 1992).

☐ Northern Ireland

In Northern Ireland, the Department of Economic Development is in charge of local economic regeneration. Because of the political and economic situation here, economic development has always had a high priority and economic development policy has been highly centralised. Historically there has been a high level of reliance on government grants, and also EU grants, and on a restricted range of major employment opportunities. The latest strategy was set out in the 1987 *Pathfinder* document which aimed to develop the area's independence from grants, subsidies, public sector employment and multinational investment.

■ Conservation

Conservation policy (see Summary Box 13.4) is concerned with protecting amenities particularly associated with the built environment. As Cullingworth states (1988, p. 196) '"Amenity" is one of the key concepts in British town and country planning, yet nowhere in the legislation is it defined.' In many cases, protection of amenity is seen as equivalent to maintaining

---

Summary Box 13.4 *Conservation*

Organisation: DETR, the Scottish Office, English Heritage, Welsh
                  Historic Monuments, Historic Scotland, district and
                  unitary councils
Focus: Heritage areas and buildings
Aim: Amenity protection
Timing: *Ad hoc*, both positive and responsive
Scope: Conservation areas, buildings, trees
Planning tool: Regulation, subsidy

---

existing buildings, trees and patterns of land use. Indeed Section 215 of the Town and Country Planning Act 1990 allows local authorities to enforce the proper maintenance of land where it is considered to affect adversely the amenity of a neighbourhood. The historic nature of urban landscapes is specifically seen as an indicator of high levels of amenity. The public estate, in the form of English Heritage (CADW in Wales and Historic Scotland north of the border), owns and maintains large numbers of historic buildings and sites. In addition, major historic buildings are managed by the Historic Royal Palaces Agency. The Secretary of State also has powers to purchase or accept a listed building or ancient monument (see below) for the public estate, local authorities may purchase a listed building by agreement and properties can be accepted into the public estate in lieu of tax liability. However, the main method of conservation planning takes the form of designating areas, sites and buildings for special protection rather than transferring property ownership.

Conservation areas are a measure whereby a district council (or English Heritage in Greater London) designates a geographic area for enhanced protection under development control. There are some 9000 conservation areas in the UK covering over 1.3 million buildings. Local authorities have a duty under the Planning (Listed Buildings and Conservation Areas) Act 1990 periodically to review their area for designating conservation areas, and the Secretary of State can also decide to designate such an area. The designation document for a conservation area undergoes consultation procedures and notification to the Secretary of State and English Heritage (or equivalent agency) before being adopted by the council. This document will include policies to be adopted in respect of the area for preservation and enhancement of amenities. Such policies must be submitted to a public meeting within the conservation area, and note taken of views expressed. However, the most significant elements of protection arise from the legislative effects of the designation. These ensure that all demolition within a conservation area constitutes development and thus requires conservation area consent unless it involves a church in use, a listed building or ancient monument, when separate provisions apply (see below).

The regime for dealing with conservation area consents is identical to that described below for listed buildings in relation to authorising works, taking enforcement action, undertaking urgent works to preserve unoccupied buildings and providing for purchase notices. As far as the operation of normal development control is concerned, the definition of material changes of use and physical alterations is interpreted more tightly within such an area. Development control within conservation areas also involves extended publicity arrangements. Furthermore, Article 4 directions under the GDO are often made to extend the definition of development for which planning permission is required. There are about 200 Article 4 directions relating to English conservation areas (EHTF, 1992). These provisions allow greater opportunity for the operation of development control as well as the inclusion of broader amenity-based material considerations in development control decision-making. Following a 1988 legal case concerning the London Borough of Camden, it was held that in all planning decisions concerning conservation areas 'special attention should be paid to the desirability of preserving or enhancing the character and appearance of that area'. This was interpreted as meaning that any permitted development should perform a positive role in meeting the conservation area's aims. However, another case in 1992, concerning the South Lakeland District Council, has reaffirmed the prior principle that development which has a neutral effect on the local area should also be permitted: only development detrimental to the amenities of a conservation area can be refused consent.

As with listed buildings, the costs of preservation and enhancement in conservation areas largely remain with owners and occupiers. However, there are two possibilities for grant aid. First, the Secretary of State and English Heritage, or equivalent organisations, can make grants or loans on a discretionary basis. In 1989/90, English Heritage allocated £33 million for such grants. Second, local authorities, singly or jointly, may enter into a town scheme agreement with the Secretary of State or English Heritage (or equivalents) which provides for a specified sum of money to be set aside for grant-aiding the repair of selected buildings over a fixed period of years. About 400 of the 7000 English conservation areas are eligible for such grants. English Heritage now proposes to assess grant applications against criteria which include: the area's inherent interest; the condition of its buildings and townscape; financial need; and the commitment to conservation. A recent additional source of funding for heritage conservation has come from the National Lottery. This bi-weekly gambling game is expected to generate £10 billion over the period 1994–

Exhibit 13.2   *Gentrification and conservation*

While conservation areas are primarily conceived of as a tool for preserving the built heritage, in practice they are also a tool of urban regeneration. This has had significant implications for the relationship of planning to local communities in these areas. At issue is the tendency for areas where conservation policies are successful to undergo gentrification, a process by which local working-class communities are displaced by a predominantly middle-class population. In some areas the process is developer-led. The refurbishment of 'lofts' in central New York (Zukin, 1988) and of dockside wharves in London by development companies has provided accommodation for new groups of high-income service workers. The distinctive physical character of these dwellings, explicitly marketed on the basis of their historic associations, has reinforced the distinctive social status of the new residents, both as new evolving occupational groups and as new occupants of previously working-class and industrial areas.

In other areas, the gentrification has been more piecemeal and led by the incoming households. In Islington and similar districts of London, old houses were refurbished by middle-class households, on a DIY plus subcontracting basis, or by small builders restoring the building and sometimes converting it into flats. Over a period of time the changing character of the area becomes apparent as tenure shifts from private renting to owner-occupation, as local services reflect the change in population and as new demands are made on the planning system (Smith and Williams, 1986).

In situations of gradual gentrification, the designation of an area as a conservation area is a central resource for the local middle-class population. Such a designation attracts certain local government funds for environmental improvements at street level. It can justify alterations in local traffic

---

2001 for the six designated 'good causes'. Heritage projects get 16.6 per cent of this which is distributed via the Heritage Lottery Fund. This is particularly targeted on physical construction projects which will enhance heritage areas and sites. In many cases, the interaction of the local property market with conservation area designation actually increases property values and this property market dynamic is part of the means by which conservation policies are achieved. This is explored in Exhibit 13.2.

The other area-based policy concerns the designation of areas of archaeological importance (AAIs) where enhanced provision is to be made for 'rescue archaeology' during development. There are five such AAIs designated under Part 2 of the 1979 Ancient Monuments and Archaeological Areas Act: York, Canterbury, Chester, Exeter and Hereford. Within designated areas of archaeological importance it is a criminal offence to carry out operations resulting in disturbance to archaeological remains without having served an operations notice on the local authority at least six weeks before operations including tipping,

management to reroute through traffic out of the area. It ensures high standards of aesthetic control on all development in the area. All these factors reinforce the social exclusivity of the area: a more pleasant local environment maintains local property prices; stringent design control raises the costs of refurbishment above the means of lower-income groups. Often the new residents use the historic nature of the area to form a community group which reflects, at one and the same time, the unique character of the built environment and the social organisation of the community around that historic environment. Such groups can be highly effective in placing pressure on local planners for further protection and enhancement of the locality.

The previous residents of such an area are relatively powerless in the face of creeping gentrification since the slow, piecemeal pace inhibits effective mobilisation of a community which, in any case, has limited time and resources for mobilisation. Where a developer is seeking to purchase a larger area for comprehensive refurbishment then there is more scope for community action to resist the shift in population implied by the development. However, the particular circumstances of each case determine the success of such community action. In New York an unsympathetic local authority meant that the local artists were unable to resist developers' attempts to evict them. In Docklands the use of largely derelict warehousing meant that some community resistance was bypassed. In Covent Garden, the support of the GLC resulted in a compromise which achieved significant economic revitalisation of the area, conservation of the historic market building and some degree of safeguards and even additional facilities for the local community (Christensen, 1979).

disturbance or flooding, are due to commence. Then an 'investigating authority' has the power to enter, inspect and excavate the site within the next four months. Thereafter it has the power to enter for inspection and recording only. Development can be delayed for up to a maximum of six months. Grants are available from the DETR and local authorities to aid such rescue archaeology, but there is no statutory funding under the legislation. Recent government advice in PPG16 on 'Archaeology and Planning' emphasises the importance of preserving nationally important archaeological remains, stating that in cases where development is proposed, there should be a presumption in favour of their physical preservation. Such nationally important remains are usually scheduled ancient monuments (see below). In other cases the relative importance of archaeology will have to be weighted against other factors. Whether scheduled or not, the desirability of preserving an ancient monument is a material consideration in development control and policies for archaeological conservation should be included in development plans. The resources of the county archaeological officer (or equivalent) who maintains the sites and monuments records can be important.

In many cases of proposed development, rescue archaeology will be the preferred option. Such rescue archaeology recognises that the excavation occurring during development often creates opportunities for archaeological exploration, through clearance of surface buildings and landscape. However, such development can of course threaten archaeological remains with disruption, damage and eventual burial. Rescue archaeology aims to influence the physical process and timing of development to allow time and opportunity for recording archaeological remains and to ensure their preservation in a form of reburial which would allow re-excavation. This is generally achieved through planning agreements and conditions attached to planning permissions. A code of practice exists for voluntary agreements between archaeologists and developers, issued jointly by the British Property Federation and the Standing Conference of Archaeological Unit Managers, through the British Archaeologists' and Developers' Liaison Group.

Marine archaeology has no equivalent system of protection as yet but an enhanced system of control for historic wrecks is being developed. The Advisory Committee on Historic Wreck Sites and the Archaeological Diving Unit have advised on new procedures of designating historic underwater sites and issuing licences for diving and other activities in their vicinity.

Inside and outside such designated areas, additional protection of important features of the built and natural environment is afforded by a variety of means. The Royal Commission on Historical Monuments, English Heritage (or equivalents) and several local authorities provide a record of historic buildings and monuments. This is currently being organised into a systematic database. Individual buildings of special architectural or historic significance throughout Britain can be 'listed' by central government. Indeed, the DETR under the Planning (Listed Buildings and Conservation Areas) Act 1990 and the Scottish Office have a duty to compile such a list or approve such lists prepared by the Commission or other relevant bodies. There are three grades of listed building: I (the highest quality), II* and II. Currently there are some 500 000 listed buildings in England, about 2 per cent of the building stock. Fifty-eight per cent of listed buildings are in rural areas; 42 per cent in urban areas. Just over half of all listed buildings are also in conservation areas: 77 per cent of urban listed buildings, 40 per cent of rural listed buildings. As of September 1996, there were 18 788 listed buildings in Wales.

The criteria for listing are set out in PPG15 and the 1990 Act. The older the building is, the more likely it is to be listed but it is not just the quality of the individual building that is important. Its location as part of a group may render it worthy of listing. If it appears that an important unlisted building is in danger of demolition or alteration which would alter its character, then local authorities can serve a building preservation notice on any unlisted building (but not a church or ancient monument) which will lead to a six-month stay of action pending the departmental listing procedure. Objection to listing may be made informally to the DETR resulting in a second opinion from an Inspector being sought. If the Department formally decides not to list the building, then the building preservation notice ceases to have effect and no further such notice can be issued for twelve months. Any owner who has received planning permission for work to an unlisted building may also apply to the Secretary of State for a certificate stating that the building will not be listed. This certificate prevents any listing, including temporary listing, for a period of five years. This can be useful where time elapses between the grant of outline planning permission and approval of reserved matters. In cases of alteration, destruction, misjudgement or mistake, buildings may be removed from the list.

The demolition of any listed building is subject to control, as are any works for alteration or extension in a manner likely to affect its character as a building of special architectural or historic interest. In each case, listed building consent is required. These powers are exercised by the relevant development control planning authority, usually the district council. But in London these functions are performed by the borough councils, subject to directions from English Heritage. Application for consent results in an extended consultation and notification procedure. Under directions from the Secretary of State consultees include English Heritage, CADW or Historic Scotland and, in the case of any proposed demolition, any amenity groups such as the Georgian Society or Civic Trust. In addition the local authority must inform the Secretary of State of any listed building consent it proposes to give, subject to notified exceptions. This creates the opportunity for the Secretary of State to call in an application. The final consent may be conditional and there is provision for appeals to the Secretary of State. Any consent for demolition must make allowance for the recording of the building by the relevant Royal Commission on Historical Monuments or Ancient and Historical Monuments in Wales. Subject to Secretary of State confirmation, local authorities may revoke or modify listed building consent, and there is an expedited procedure for so doing where the owner-occupier and all others affected do not object. The Secretary of State may also revoke or modify consents. Where development under the 1990 Town and Country Planning Act is also intended, then planning permission will be needed in addition to listed building consent. As with planning consents, listed building consents expire after five years.

Carrying out works without listed building consent is an offence punishable by a fine and/or imprisonment. Fines are exacted in proportion to the financial benefit the developer has gained, or is likely to gain. This differs from the situation with other planning consents where standard fines can be levied only for non-compliance with an enforcement notice. It is no defence to argue ignorance of the listing but it is possible to argue a defence on the basis that: there was a need for urgent works to ensure preservation of the building or for reasons of health and safety; that no temporary alteration was possible; that the extent of the works was minimised; and that the local authority was given written notice as soon as possible. The local authority or the Secretary of State can issue a listed building enforcement notice stating the breach of control, specifying remedial action, and giving the owner and occupier at least 28 days to object and lodge an appeal. If the remedial action is not taken within the stated compliance period, then the local authority may enter and undertake the works, recovering the costs from the owner. Injunctions preventing damage can also be sought.

There are a number of financial consequences arising from listed building control. Compensation may be payable by the local authority for loss arising from: refusal of listed building consent for works which would not themselves require planning permission; modification or renovation of the consent; and serving of a building preservation notice. There is an onus placed on the building owner to ensure adequate repair and maintenance for such building. Grants are available to assist in this but mainly for Grade I and some Grade II* buildings. English Heritage makes grants available for the repair of historic buildings and monuments and the National Heritage Memorial Fund is a further source for major sites. For the thirteen world heritage sites designated under the UNESCO World Heritage Convention (ratified by the British government in 1984), funds are available from the World Heritage Fund. Relief from capital taxes exists for owners of heritage properties which are opened to the public. But the responsibility for ensuring the continued contribution of such important buildings to the urban and rural environment rests with the owner and thus knowledge of any listing is important information for a prospective purchaser during the legal and planning searches. Where the owner neglects to maintain a listed building the local authority has the option of compulsory purchase. If the building has been deliberately left derelict then compulsory purchase can be at minimum compensation, if the Secretary of State so directs, which excludes all development value. Prior to such compulsory purchase the local authority must serve a repairs notice setting out the necessary repairs in detail. The local authority also has the power to execute any urgent works necessary for building preservation, provided that the building or parts of it are unoccupied and they give the owner notice. They can then recoup the cost.

While parks and gardens cannot be formally listed, English Heritage maintains a register of parks and gardens of special historic interest. This carries no statutory force but highway and local planning authorities are advised to take note of the register in their decisions by DoE Circular 8/87. There is a similar register of battlefield sites in England.

Ancient monuments are protected under the 1979 Ancient Monuments Act. The degree of protection afforded depends on whether a site is classified as a 'scheduled monument' or an 'ancient monument'. Scheduled monuments are of national importance in the view of the Secretary of State. An ancient monument is any monument of public interest in the view of the Secretary of State by virtue of historic architectural, traditional, artistic or archaeological importance. Some 20 100 monuments have been scheduled in Britain. PPG16 sets out the criteria for scheduling as: period or age; rarity; extent of documentation; group value, condition and surviving features; fragility or vulnerability; diversity; and potential. Development affecting a scheduled monument requires an additional consent in the form of scheduled monument consent from the DETR, English Heritage or equivalents; this covers proposals for demolition, destruction, damage, removal, repair, alteration, extension, flooding or covering up. The scope of control is more detailed and extensive than for listed buildings but there are six class consents in force which allow owners to undertake certain specified works without explicit consent. Crown land is subject to scheduled monument clearance which broadly follows the consent procedure, and refusal in certain limited cases gives rise to liability for compensation. It is a criminal offence to undertake prescribed operations without such a consent and injunctions preventing operations may be sought. Central government, local government and heritage agencies can all take action. There were proposals contained in a 1991 DoE Consultation Paper to tighten up the control of ancient monuments. The definition of 'damage' would be extended to any disturbance of the land. Removal of any finds, not just those using a metal detector, would be an offence and ignorance of the status of the site would not be an adequate defence, placing ancient monuments on an equivalent footing to listed buildings. Finally, works to an ancient monument to ensure public health and safety would be constrained to the minimum necessary.

Where works are urgently needed for the preservation of a scheduled monument, the Secretary of State may enter the site and undertake the works. There is no provision for recouping the costs incurred. Grants are available from heritage agencies mainly for repair, archaeological recording and consolidation of monuments. Occasionally they are available for purchase. Where the owner enters into a management agreement with central or local government or heritage agency, funds may also be made available. Any ancient monument, not just scheduled monuments, may be compulsorily purchased by the Secretary of State in order to preserve it or may be accepted into the public estate. Alternatively the Secretary of State may be appointed 'guardian' of the monument, providing for its preservation without a transfer of ownership. Public access is a condition of such guardianship.

Ecclesiastical buildings are exempt from certain listed building protection measures. They may be listed but building preservation notices, listed building consent, provisions for urgent works to unoccupied buildings and compulsory purchase provisions do not apply. This means that listed building consent is not necessary for churches in use or for demolition of redundant churches. This exemption applies only where denominations can demonstrate internal arrangements which meet with standards of a proposal code of practice. For Church of England churches an additional statutory system of protection already exists under the 1983 Pastoral Measure, operated by the Church. By agreement with the Secretary of State a non-statutory local inquiry may be held for the demolition of a listed church or one in a conservation area. The Redundant Churches Fund preserves Church of England churches of historic or architectural interest.

Trees are also covered by their equivalent of listing, in this case the placing of a tree preservation order (TPO) on an individual tree, a group of trees or a woodland. Such an order prevents cutting, topping, uprooting, wilful damage, destruction or coppicing without express permission from the district council and encourages preventative tree surgery and woodland maintenance. Permission for felling may require replanting. Dead, unsafe and dying trees are exempt. Non-compliance with a TPO may result in fines of up to £20 000 being imposed and the enforcement powers of local authorities in relation to areas have been strengthened by Section 23 of the 1991 Planning and Compensation Act, allowing applications for injunctions and warrants for right of entry. Replacement planting may also be required up to four years after non-compliance. Appeals on matters of TPOs can be made to the Secretary of State. Tree planting may also form an acceptable planning condition and, indeed, a local authority has a duty to consider the preservation and planting of trees in granting any planning permission.

☐ Scotland and Wales

As the above text has made clear, the equivalent bodies to the DETR are the Welsh Office and the Environment Department of the Scottish Office, and the equivalent heritage agencies to English Heritage are CADW, or Welsh Historic Monuments, in Wales and Historic Scotland north of the border. There are some 3000 listed buildings in Wales and 36 000 in Scotland, but resurvey is likely to increase these figures substantially. In Scotland listed buildings are graded A, B and C, not I, II* and II. The legislative basis for listed buildings and conservation area control is the 1972 Town and Country Planning (Scotland) Act and the reference point for TPOs in Scotland is Section 54 of the 1991 Planning and Compensation Act.

■ Further reading

Atkinson and Moon (1994) gives a useful overview of urban policy while Bailey *et al.* (1995) sets out case studies of the partnership approach. The reader is also referred to the references in Chapter 7 on local government and the business community, which, in considering concepts such as urban regimes and growth coalitions, also cover urban policy material. A comprehensive guide to conservation law and policy is provided by Suddards and Hargreaves (1996).

■ PART 4 ■

ASSESSING PLANNING

Part 4 ends the book with an assessment of the British planning system. Chapter 14 makes use of published research and statistics to assess the effects that the planning system has had in practice. This draws on the understanding of the operation of the planning system provided by the discussions of actors and institutions in Part 2. The different elements of the planning system are assessed under the headings used in Part 3: land use planning; environmental regulation; countryside policy; regeneration and conservation. The conclusion in Chapter 15 then reassesses the important contemporary argument for collaborative planning, suggesting a critique and proposing a more modest role for planning, perhaps more in line with the evidence on the problems that planning has had in achieving its more ambitious goals.

■ *Chapter 14* ■

The Impact of Planning

The earlier discussion of the political and economic dynamics underlying the planning system emphasised a number of themes. First, the extent and quality of the interactions between actors engaged in the networks of 'governance' are significant factors in determining policy outcomes. Second, the relevant actors, from a planning perspective, must include not only central and local government but also agencies or quangos, business interests, other pressure groups and actors at the European level. Third, there are pressures towards favouring economic interests within the planning system, both arising from the existence of urban regimes or growth coalition and the way in which professionals develop close relations with sectional interests. This is accentuated by the collective action problems which disproportionately disadvantage environmental groups compared to business groups. Fourth, the ability of professionals to influence outcomes through the exercise of discretion and the pursuit of their own interests should not be underestimated. And fifth, the economic dynamics surrounding the use of the built and natural environment result in a variety of different interests and hence a variety of pressures on the planning system. These dynamics also significantly affect the implementation of planning policy since it is only by the combined interaction of the public and private sectors that policy goals can be achieved.

In this section the extent to which policy goals have been achieved is addressed. All four areas of the planning system covered in Part 3 are discussed in terms of the impact of planning. But two different ways of assessing the policy process are used. First, the effectiveness of planning as a set of procedures is considered. Or rather, the potential weaknesses in planning as a process are outlined. Second, the outcomes of planning in terms of environmental change and protection are examined, using the available data and statistics. Much of this analysis highlights the inadequacies in the planning process in various parts of the system and the extent to which outcomes fall short of ambitions in many cases.

■ Assessing the process

□ *Implementing land use planning*

The goal of land use planning as a form of decision-making or administration is the effective management of environmental change and

319

the control of urban development. The rhetoric stresses the strengths of planning, its power to control and manage. However, research, which begins from this standpoint, has consistently found land use planning to be a weak administrative system. For example, most analyses of the development plan system emphasise its weaknesses as a strategic planning tool. Considering the planning of the south-east region, Breheny and Congdon (1989) point to the absence of regional plans, the abolition of metropolitan government, the lack of any satisfactory planning replacement and the resulting inability to deal with a succession of major strategic issues: European integration, the Channel Tunnel, London airport development. The main weak link within strategic planning has often been pinpointed as the structure plan. Originally conceived in ambitious terms as a comprehensive and integrating planning tool, structure plans were intended to take on board the range of available resources and associated constraints, and devise strategies for using them to meet sets of politically identified goals. They were to be socioeconomic in focus, operating on the spatial scale. This ideal proved to be unobtainable. Whether or not structure planning in these terms was a philosophically flawed idea, it certainly proved to be beyond the administrative and political realities of the existing system. Jowell and Noble (1981, p. 480) point to the way in which central government, through case law and DoE powers, reduced the scope of structure plans.

But, although central government may have ended the dream of integrated socioeconomic structure planning leading resource allocation, the dream was already turning sour in many local authorities. Structure planning turned out to be very costly and time-consuming. In the absence of available public sector resources it was ultimately powerless. And the integration of the various social and economic dimensions to an area's problems had to deal with the realities of a local authority divided into departments where professionals guarded their power and there were conflicts between local authorities and budget-holding public sector organisations beyond the local authority. These conclusions on structure plans have meant that the search for effective planning has focused more and more on detailed local planning and the link to development control.

Bruton and Nicholson's research on local plans (1987) found that local plans were a flexible planning instrument which could reflect local planning issues and operating environments. However, like the structure plan, local plans had weaknesses. Despite repeated procedural streamlining, they often take considerable time to prepare and full coverage has still to be achieved. The 'basic weakness of the local plan as a land use policy vehicle' (1987, p. 178) is analysed as: its inability to deal directly with local socioeconomic policies, having to deal indirectly with the land use implications of such policies; its lack of effective control over the local activities of public agencies; the lack of control over the resources necessary to implement the development proposals of local plans which are based outside the planning department or outside the local authority altogether; the difficulty of integrating local plans with other area-based policies and plans; and the problems in implementing local plans through development control.

In particular, integration of policy documents from different public sector organisations has always been a problem. The creation of a two-tier local government system in 1974 undercut the principles of structure and local plans embodied in the 1968 legislation, and as a result conflicts arose between county and district councils over development planning. Over time some local authorities have learned to establish more of a partnership over development planning. Such a joint approach is now a formal necessity in many areas as a result of local government reorganisation. However, the problem of different authorities pursuing their own interests through the development plan system continues to create at least the potential for tensions within the plan-making process. The collaborative planning approach seeks to make a virtue out of necessity by emphasising the potential for constructive discussion between parties and eventual consensus-building (Healey, 1997); this is discussed further in the next chapter. Another possible direction is to learn from the UDP process where an individual local authority has to bring together strategic and detailed development planning within one document. This is in keeping with the principles of the 1968 Act; it has also resulted in a rather more streamlined strategic planning process. This is part of a move towards rethinking the nature of the plan, which is also discussed in Chapter 15.

In addition to this tension between structure and detailed local planning, there has often been a divorce between development plans and expenditure-based plans, such as HIPs and TPPs, which the corporate planning idea of the late 1960s and 1970s never resolved and which continues to this day (Carter *et al.*, 1991). There are now also pressures for resolving interdepartmental conflicts and tensions arising from the LA21 process, which seeks to develop a holistic, integrated sustainable development strategy for the locality. Here the new policy goal is supposed both to guide decision-making within each department and policy area (housing, transport, planning and so on) and also to mesh these different elements together. It is early days for assessing such an ambitious task, but it is clear that there will be difficulties in overcoming departmental priorities in the name of this new policy objective.

Problems with development planning have led to more attention (and hope) being focused on development control. After all, the one real resource that land use planning controlled was the power to grant or deny planning permission. But the debate about development control also echoes the familiar theme of the weakness of land use planning (Kirk, 1980). Development control is a negative, reactive policy tool, responding to development pressures emanating from elsewhere in the private and public sectors. It is limited in terms of the development proposals that come before the development control planner, limited in terms of the factors it can take into account in making planning decisions, limited in terms of the conditions and agreements that can be attached to a permission. Changes such as the recent revision of the Use Classes Order serve only to weaken development control further. As Oatley points out (1991), the creation of the B1 class, intended to facilitate high-tech development, has actually allowed the conversion of high tech space into offices.

As a response to the inadequacies of development control as a policy tool, local authorities have increasingly taken advantage of the opportunities offered by planning agreements to achieve planning obligations. As Healey *et al.* (1995, p. 223) found:

> negotiating development obligations . . . had become routine across most local authorities in England by the 1990s. Although the numbers of actual agreements negotiated remain small in relation to the total number of planning decisions made, agreements are frequently used for larger and more complex applications with diverse impacts. Local authorities increasingly recognize their importance in their development plan policies. Even more significant has been the extension in the scope of agreements and the scale of obligations negotiated. There seems little sign of this tendency abating.

However they also found 'confusion, inconsistency and erratic management practices' (ibid., p. 226) in the practice of negotiating planning agreements. This is an ad hoc element of the planning system which has yet to achieve the status as development planning or other aspects of development control. As Bramley *et al.* also argue (1995, p. 235):

> the use of planning agreements to facilitate the provision of infrastructure and community facilities, and to overcome or compensate for the negative impacts of development, is a positive, permanent development to be welcomed, encouraged, but perhaps systematized.

Their hope is that 'the planning agreement approach is much more likely to promote development with local support' (ibid.).

Planning agreements may, therefore, help fill the gap that research has repeatedly found between development plans and development control. Research undertaken in 1979 by Pountney and Kingsbury (1983) in seven local plan areas found that a relatively large proportion of planning applications (24–65 per cent) were not covered by any specific reference in a local plan map or text. In a DoE study undertaken during 1982, Davies *et al.* (1986) used a checklist of planning considerations to assess policy documents and planning applications in twelve districts and six planning agencies. They concluded that 'taking all the planning considerations together, the degree of overlap between policy and control is small' (p. 207). In their analysis of a random 10 per cent sample of appeal decision letters for 1982 in England and Wales, Davies et al. (1986) found that in almost a third of all appeals there was no reference in the decision letter of any policy, national or local. Central government policy was mentioned in 35 per cent of cases. A Polytechnic of East London study (Rydin et al., 1990) of 942 appeal decisions in 24 districts in 1988 found that about two-thirds of the cases involved some discussion of local policy and central government policy was discussed in about 40 per cent of cases, DoE circulars being the most common source (27 per cent of cases).

Generally the conclusion is that many development control decisions are not necessarily based on development plans. A common finding across the research studies is that where local policy is discussed in development control it is given more emphasis if plans are statutory, up-to-date and adopted (Davies et al., 1986; Bruton and Nicholson, 1987; Rydin et al., 1990). But much of the minor and householder development which dominates the average development control officer's workload of 156 planning applications a year (Audit Commission, 1992) lies largely outside the concerns of development plans. A large proportion of development control deals with issues of importance mainly to neighbours. Admittedly the aggregate effect of many minor changes can be significant, but the planning system finds this kind of incremental change very difficult to handle in terms of its strategic impact. To summarise, Davies et al. (1986) pinpointed the problems of low overlap between plans and development control as resulting from: the partial nature of local plan coverage across districts; policies which are not geared to development control situations; policies in plans which require interpretations; and a difficulty in identifying which individual planning applications are significant from the point of view of plan policies. These problems are likely to be overcome only slowly as plan coverage spreads and policies are revised to take note of problems encountered in appeals. Furthermore, there is no systematic monitoring in most local authorities to inform the plan review process of how previous policies have fared during development control.

This lack of overlap between development planning and control does not necessarily mean that planning decisions actually conflict with development plans; the conflict between development control and developments was variously estimated at 7 per cent (Pountney and Kingsbury, 1983); 10 per cent (Kendrick, 1987), and 19 per cent (Rydin et al., 1990). Rather policy and control concern a different set of issues: for example, the impact of a development on the immediate surroundings of the site are not always spelt out in detail in plans. As Whitehand (1989, p. 412) points out, local planning authorities have rarely considered in detail what the development of a particular site should be like before the planning application is received.

Turning to the intersection of environmental regulation and land use planning, environment assessment (EA) potentially provides a significant opportunity for considering and then revising projects with a view to reducing their impact on the environment. However carrying out the procedures of EA does not necessarily imply that those procedures have been carried out well; there is no system of appeal against an inadequate EA process nor any form of quality assurance. Certainly, there was concern originally over the quality of early environmental statements (Jones *et al.*, 1991; Wood and Jones, 1991), though this situation seems to be improving. The lack of experience of many local authorities in EA is being eroded over time or county councils are stepping in to provide bridging expertise. Undoubtedly EA has introduced land use planners to a range of technical material they were not familiar with.

However, even if the EA process is undertaken properly, it can only alter the actual impact on the environment if the conclusions and recommendations are put into practice. In Britain, the main way in which the EA is taken account of is as an input into the development control process. The environmental statement becomes a material consideration. But it is only one consideration among many; there is no guarantee within the planning system that the environmental considerations revealed by the EA will not be outweighed by economic or social considerations. Neither will the negotiative mechanisms of the land use planning system necessarily be sufficient to ensure the implementation of mitigating measures recommended during the EA. The lack of a monitoring dimension to development control is also relevant here; once the permission is granted, it can be enforced but conditions and so on cannot be changed if it is found that environmental impacts in fact turn out to be too severe.

Furthermore, it may be the case that the form of the development – which is the focus of land use planning – may not be the prime issue in generating environmental impacts. Clearly where a valuable habitat or landscape is at risk from development, then the decision whether to develop or not is central to the impact. Again, where negotiation seeks to encourage passive solar energy design or protect trees on the site, say, then the environmental impact can be directly affected by the planning decision. But where it is the activities of the users of the development that is the prime cause of the environmental impact, then it can be very difficult to influence that through planning conditions, agreement and negotiation. Building design may allow for recycling facilities but this will not necessarily increase recycling rates; developments may be clustered about public transport nodes but other features of the public transport also need to be taken into account to encourage its use. Similarly green spaces can be protected from development but their value as natural habitats, leisure sites and/or visual amenities will depend on how these spaces are managed. Other measures may be needed to influence behaviour and management practices for which the control afforded by land use planning will provide only the context.

The relationship between land use planning and other environmental regulatory regimes is, therefore, relevant. Recent research by Oxford Polytechnic and ERL (1992) has indicated the extent to which pollution control and waste management concerns are already integrated into development planning and development control. Indeed there is a suggestion that the greater openness of local authorities to public pressure when compared to environmental quangos has encouraged pollution control, in particular, to become a material consideration in local land use planning. Development control has also been used to deal with perceived inadequacies in environmental policy such as protection of groundwater, post-closure pollution control for waste disposal sites and protection of the aquatic environment upon development (that is, flood prevention, land drainage and nature conservation). The research emphasised that the key problems implicit in the current situation are the lack of confidence of the public in the process and problems in consultation between environmental agencies and local authorities. The prospect that green land use planning offers is the incorporation of environmental concerns in an arena potentially open to public participation and democratic control. This contrasts with the way in which environmental quangos have operated in the past (see Chapter 6). However, as the discussion of land use planning has already indicated, there are substantial weaknesses and inequities in that system which suggest that achieving environmental protection through this route may also be problematic. There is, therefore, likely to remain a reliance on traditional modes of environmental regulation to achieve environmental policy goals.

☐ *Achieving environmental regulation*

The key problem with traditional environmental regulation has been and continues to be the political and professional will to operate stringent regulatory practices. That it has taken EU directives to prompt the necessary investment in water treatment to raise quality standards, for example, is a testimony to the weak regulatory framework that existed in Britain for many years. The 1951 Rivers (Prevention of Pollution) Act hardly scratched the surface as it dealt only with new discharges. The 1961 Rivers (Prevention of Pollution) Act extended control to existing effluent but the rush of applications meant that many were never dealt with, to potentially become deemed consents under the 1974 Control of Pollution

Act (COPA) (Beck, 1989). COPA itself was considered sufficient in theory to deal with routine direct discharges but could not control diffuse discharge such as nitrate leaching; in practice its operation was compromised by the influence of those it sought to control (Hallett *et al.*, 1991). For example Section 31 (2)(c) of COPA allowed farmers to use 'good agricultural practice' as a sufficient defence against polluting activities on the farm. The important section on water quality (Part II of COPA) was implemented in a reduced form only after sixteen years and the public disclosure requirements took ten years to be enacted!

The introduction of integrated pollution control (IPC) was supposed to remedy the weaknesses of COPA. But while long advocated from an environmental policy perspective, IPC raises considerable problems of implementation. Owens (1989) points to a number of limitations in the proposed IPC system: its focus on industrial pollution; the control over pesticides remaining within MAFF; the separate control over radioactive waste; the treatment of non-scheduled processes on a single media basis; the control over Red List substances being based on quality of receiving water rather than on best attainable abatement technology to prevent emission at source; and the location-specific nature of much BPEO assessment. A pilot BPEO audit showed that it is possible to achieve, but it is expensive in terms of time and staff (Weale *et al.*, 1991). There are clearly conceptual and administrative problems in integrating cross-media expertise and, further, reconciling integration across media with geographical integration.

These considerations lead Weale *et al.* to question whether IPC, as conceived in terms of BPEO, will ever operate (1991, p. 94): 'Conditions for the successful integration of policy are daunting in their demands, and . . . there are powerful intellectual, organisational and political reasons why the move towards IPC might fail', and, again (p. 158): 'BPEO may never be more than an imaginative statement of pollution control philosophy'. Instead Weale *et al.* see IPC being largely based on BATNEEC. This is in line with continental pollution control practice which is being imported in EU directives. A technology-led approach to regulation is more readily defined and enforced, and lends itself to an administratively accountable form of regulation (Weale *et al.*, 1991, p. 160). However, they emphasise that sector-by-sector BATNEEC, while an improvement on the discretionary, flexible and ineffective British system of the postwar years, will not bring the environmental benefits of BPEO.

Whatever the regulatory system, adequate enforcement is essential to environmental protection. There have been considerable doubts about this from the point of view of both financial resources and administrative or political will. HMIP began its life seriously understaffed; indeed, there was a strong rationalisation and efficiency-saving motive for setting up HMIP

Table 14.1   *Her Majesty's Inspectorate of Pollution staff complement*

	Professional	Administrative	Total
1988	120 (66%)	63	183
1991	134 (54%)	114	248
1992	176 (56%)	137	313

Source: Digest of Environmental Protection and Water Statistics.

(Weale *et al.*, 1991). New salaries and an increase in staff complement meant that the situation improved during the 1990s. It should be noted, though, that the increase in professional staff is much less than the total figures indicated (see Table 14.1). There has also been some concern that the HMIP contingent would be less significant within an Environment Agency in which the former NRA staff dominated numerically. Staffing clearly constrains inspections and the demands of restructuring pollution control for IPC have been acknowledged to have this effect (HMIP, 1991). In 1990/1 HMIP undertook 3876 visits covering 2092 scheduled works (or 3079 processes). In practice most sites were visited just once a year with more frequent visits to larger works. Shove (1995) suggests that there are about 50 staff responsible for enforcement and that the frequency of site visits was one-third less than in 1981.

In addition there is concern over the will to enforce. It has been argued that the ethos of HMIP (and its predecessors, see Chapter 8) acted against vigorous enforcement (Spooner *et al.*, 1992, p. 110). This attitude has, at times, been reinforced by central government attitudes, particularly in the case of pollution from sewage works. In 1986, 23 per cent of sewage treatment works tested in England and Wales were found to be in breach of approved standards. The government legalised much of this pollution by granting several water authorities 'relaxations' so that the new water companies would not be liable for prosecution for breaches after privatisation. Certainly, the number of prosecutions remains very low: prosecutions for water pollution incidents in England and Wales were 282 in 1990, 237 in 1994; this is against the background of 28 143 reported incidents in 1990, rising to 35 301 in 1994. There is the suggestion that the creation of the Environment Agency has coincided with a less conciliatory approach to pollution control but the published statistics do not yet corroborate this (see Table 14.2).

Similar concerns over the laxity of past legislation, principally COPA, and the lack of adequate enforcement have been voiced over waste management practice. Reports by HMIP and, before that by the Hazardous Waste Inspectorate, point to considerable variability in waste

Table 14.2   *Enforcement of water pollution control*

	1990		1995	
	% major incidents	% prosecutions	% major incidents	% prosecutions
Agriculture	36	44	16	38
Industry	17	27	31	40
Oil	13	7	–	–
Sewage	20	10	24	5
Other	14	12	29	16

Source: Digest of Environmental Protection and Water Statistics, Digest of Environmental Statistics.

disposal practices, with unacceptable standards at the lower end. Site licences did not prove effective in ensuring environmental protection and the ability, removed by the 1990 EPA, to surrender a licence and walk away from a site led to contaminated and contaminating sites being left as problems without anyone responsible for the solution. Leakages from landfill sites and methane generation at domestic landfill sites are two particular problems arising from poor past waste management. And the British strategy of codisposal of industrial and domestic waste has created further problems, as it is difficult to know the precise contents of sites. The Hazardous Waste Inspectorate's findings (1988, pp. 50–83), that the strength of that regulation had been subordinated to a market-led industry, could apply to the whole waste management area: 'The Inspectorate believes that the market will not sustain more realistic prices until uniformly high standards are insisted upon and achieved; until then, price cutting will deter the necessary investment in site improvements.' The new EU Landfill Directive will have a considerable impact on British practices and may improve standards here.

One area where there has been a clear and complete failure to establish a credible policy is in the case of nuclear waste management (Blowers *et al.*, 1991). Blowers and his co-researchers tell of how apparently easy options were found, one by one, to be politically or technically not feasible leading to a situation where adequate provision has clearly not been made for the varieties of waste that are arising and will increasingly arise in the future (for example, upon decommissioning a nuclear power plant). In 1976 the RCEP said that it found insufficient appreciation of the long-term requirements either by government departments or other organisations involved. In 1991 Blowers *et al.* repeat this finding. They also argue that public support for a coherent strategy has been frustrated by institutional centralisation, obsessive secrecy and a lack of openness.

The impetus for improved performance might seem to lie in pressures for more stringent regulation. Top-down pressures and traditional command-and-control policy tools seem to be the key to environmental standards and, where current performance in relation to those standards is still judged unsatisfactory, then more regulation is called for, with commensurate demands for tighter enforcement. However, despite concerns about corporatist decision-making, in many cases the participation of those being regulated is essential in order to develop workable systems of regulation. The desire to reduce enforcement costs, by having a system of regulation which parties actually prefer to comply with, also encourages close working between the regulatory agency and others. Further, while environmental groups might favour ever increasing standards for regulation to aim at, in practice the precise level of the standard and how it is interpreted need to be decided on, a task which various parties will wish to be involved in. It is also necessary to remember that environmental regulation does not only carry benefits but also costs, opportunity costs in terms of the loss of economic activity, and administrative costs, which can be measured in terms of the opportunity cost of public sector resources. Environmental regulation can demonstrate declining economies of scale, as it becomes increasingly expensive to go on reducing pollution and other impacts beyond a certain point. It may be that there is a trade-off between increased levels of regulation and some other public policy goal which deserves discussion. For all these reasons, the problem of ineffective environmental regulation may not be so easily remedied.

☐ *Agricultural interests and countryside policy*

In other areas of policy, notably countryside and urban policy, it is not the operation of procedures that is at issue, but rather the way in which the balance between different interests is achieved. In countryside policy, the chief obstacle to achieving many of the access, amenity and nature conservation goals of policy has been the overriding weight given to agricultural production interests. For most of the modern postwar period of countryside policy, security of primary production has dominated the policy's operation. Ensuring supplies of food, timber and minerals for the country's needs has driven countryside planning. This has been clear in the system of agricultural financial support, the corporate mission of the Forestry Commission, the basic assumptions of minerals planning and the access that primary producers have had to central government policy-makers. Other goals have existed alongside the production goal but rarely been accorded equal status. Even in selected areas, such as National Parks, AONBs or SSSIs, the underlying thrust of production support has often overshadowed these other concerns. Analysts are broadly agreed that the result is a series of environmental problems in rural areas.

The relative success of increasingly stringent conditions on mining operations and improved after-care can be seen in the fact that dereliction from mining is roughly static (Kivell, 1987) despite continuing growth in output; recent changes in minerals planning are likely to continue improvements in this area. However, the environmental effects of agriculture seem more intractable. This is because they affect a much larger area of the country, technological change has been rapid and environmentally harmful, and the effects become apparent only when considered over time and on a broader spatial scale. Bowers (1990, p. 2) provides a comprehensive account of the adverse environmental effects of postwar agricultural practice that have been confirmed since the publication of Rachel Carson's *Silent Spring* in 1962:

> The list of environmental 'bads' of modern agriculture is extensive: destruction and damage of natural and semi-natural habitats with attendant losses of plant and animal species; landscape damage; pesticide residues in food-chains and foodstuffs, nitrate pollution of water courses and water supplies . . . serious problems with the use and disposal of wastes from intensive livestock systems; soil degradation and erosion, health risks from crop spraying and use of agricultural chemicals.

The causes of this lie in the intensive nature of postwar agriculture and forestry, the application of more capital per hectare, the associated mechanisation and specialisation within units, all at the same time as expanding output and more rapid turnover of agricultural production (Andrews, 1990; Lowe *et al.*, 1986, p. 64). In addition to these technological causes, Andrews points to the current tendency for farmers to equate tidiness with good husbandry (1990, p. 63). Carr and Tait (1990) have shown that farmers equate stewardship of the rural environment with just the kind of tidy land management which many environmentalists see as causing ecological harm.

Buckwell (1990) has argued that although the system of agricultural support has contributed to such environmental damage, its reduction or even removal would not halt or rectify the damage. Indeed, a rapid fall in farm subsidies may lead to more environmentally damaging agricultural practices (Lowe *et al.*, 1986, p. 4). In fact the 1995 Rural White Paper admits that despite the introduction of quotas and CAP reforms, UK agricultural production has increased by about a fifth since 1973. Buckwell argues that environmental protection in rural areas needs an environmental policy. The recent policy innovations of the EU agri-environment regulation have the potential to encourage environmental protection, but their detailed operation is the key. First, the level of compensation payments relative to farm profits will determine the take-up of the schemes and the nature of the land on which take-up occurs. The current decline in farm incomes will not automatically encourage a shift towards conservation as compensation payments will fall also, although the general uncertainty in farming may mean that management agreements are seen as a way of reducing risk (Bowers, 1990, p. 32). Second, the detail of the management agreement will determine the actual environmental benefits to arise from the policy. FoE (1992) found that ESA designation had slowed the decline in environmental quality but had yet to result in positive enhancement. The policy has changed farmers' attitudes within ESAs so that they accept the need to undertake environmental care and management, but achieving that remains dependent on the structure of financial compensation, and its relation to the financial incentives for agricultural 'business as usual'.

Environmental protection will depend on the balance between compensation and profits (Lowe *et al.*, 1986, p. 3), and the negotiation of more environmentally-aware management practices between farmers and conservationists, rather than the system of regulation. Availability of resources will be a central issue in how far compensation and negotiation can work. Although the grant to the NCC/English Nature doubled in real terms from 1980/1 to 1990/1 (Pennington, 1997, p. 129), this is dwarfed by the £4 billion still spent supporting agricultural production. It has been estimated that the cost of implementing management agreements on all SSSIs alone would substantially exceed the NCC's total budget (Lowe *et al.*, 1986, p. 162).

However, it is clear that the dominance of production interests has now been challenged by the recognition of current agricultural support mechanisms as 'wasteful, inefficient, regressive and regionally biased' (Buckwell, 1990, p. 18) and it seems that environmental concerns are tentatively gaining a new ascendancy (Lowe *et al.*, 1986, p. 2). As Mowle and Evans (1990, p. 129) conclude:

> The various current initiatives are showing a greater sensitivity to conservation lobby pressures, but in an uncoordinated and ad-hoc way. It seems likely that this will continue until agriculture establishes a new set of objectives and a new consensus in the place of agriculture within which rural development emerges. Until then, progress for conservation interests is likely to be fitful and uncertain. However, it is at least possible that out of the present confusion of diverse interests a balance between conservation and development can be struck.

Following this trend, the Rural White Paper has called for dialogue and a recognition of diversity in pursuit of the accepted goal of sustainable development.

Another voice to be included in this dialogue is the leisure use of the countryside. Public access to the countryside remains limited by the adherence to a system of selected exemptions to the power of private landowners to exclude people from their land. Even in cases of public landownership, such as the estates of the Forestry Commission or Ministry of Defence, public access can be severely curtailed in the interests of the public agency's operating activities. Supporters of greater public freedom to wander in the countryside contrast this with systems, such as that in Sweden, where the right to walk across land dominates provided no harm is done to crops and animals. Again British national parks involve no transfer of landownership rights so that public access is not automatically extended upon designation, as is the case with North American national parks. Rather, there is a heavy reliance on groups such as the National Trust to buy land and either make it available for public use or, in the case of tenanted farmland, encourage the farmer to tolerate public traverse of the land. It could be argued that these restrictions on general public access to the countryside are counterproductive since they channel people towards honeypot areas where they detract from the 'quiet enjoyment' of the countryside and can generate environmental damage due to sheer numbers. The Lake District has to handle 12 million visitor days per annum, the Peak District 20 million (Crabtree, 1991).

Marion Shoard has been a rigorous critic of the British limitations on public access. She points to the problems that exist with the current network of footpaths, with frequent cases of obstruction and poor maintenance of paths, stiles, gates and signposts (1987, p. 342). She places the source of these problems with the continuation of the tradition whereby footpath maintenance is given to local interests. This may have been appropriate in the days when local people were the main users of the footpaths, but not so today when the use of the network by urban residents is resented by the local farmers and landowners who often dominate rural district and parish councils (Shoard, 1987, p. 352). After all, 74 per cent of the population walk in the countryside at least once a year, 54 per cent at least once a month (Lowe *et al.*, 1986, p. 60).

☐ *Business interests and urban regeneration*

In urban policy the apparent mismatch between the scale of the need for regeneration resources and the available public sector budget has also led to a reliance on economic production interests, particularly urban development interests, to achieve policy goals. This is a reliance which – under the banner of partnership – appears to be increasing, rather than being challenged. During the 1980s this took the form of local enterprise agencies (LEAs). There were 300 LEAs in the UK with funding of 34 million in 1988 of which 41 per cent came from the private sector, 35 per cent from central government and 24 per cent from local authorities

(Smallbone, 1991). In the early 1980s local authorities took the lead, creating arm's-length LEAs to generate local employment, focus assistance to ethnic minorities and, more ambitiously, to restructure local economies. In practice local authority-led LEAs never lived up to this goal of restructuring from below that some left-wing labour urban authorities espoused. Commenting on London, Buck *et al.* (1986, p. 188) points to a lack of capability within local authorities: 'the boroughs have sometimes seemed out of their depth when it comes to both industrial assistance and tackling employment disadvantage.' Cooke (1989, p. 299) argues that LEAs have not been effective because they have largely sought to rescue ailing companies. He contrasts them with the SDA (now Scottish Enterprise) and the WDA who have probably 'been generating between 2000 and 3000 jobs per annum since 1976' (p. 299) or 50 000 jobs in all. But these major regional agencies have 'succeeded' on this rather modest scale by strategically identifying growth sectors which locally-based LEAs are not able to do with the possible exception of LENTA in London. Furthermore the funding going into the SDA and the WDA dwarfs that available to LEAs: £60 million per annum to the WDA and £100 million per annum to the SDA by the mid-1980s (Cooke, 1989, p. 300). Each LEA is a small-budget organisation with an average budget of £108 000 in 1988 and only three full-time staff (see also Bovaird, 1992). The creation of regional development agencies may redress this imbalance.

However, much regeneration remains essentially property-led, dependent on property development to attract economic development. Past experience with property-led regeneration policies has been mixed. Enterprise Zones (EZs) were intended to comprise a package of incentives: a less-regulated form of land use control; other reductions in bureaucracy; and the financial incentives, principally capital allowances and the ten years' holiday from paying local business rates. However, all assessors have agreed that it is the financial incentives that have proved the attraction to developers moving into EZs, rather than the supposedly more relaxed planning system. As Wood and Hooper (1988) point out, a significant degree of land use control was exercised in EZs albeit through different channels than the development control system. Indeed the mixture of landlord powers, planning agreements and prior negotiation in the context of an EZ could prove more effective than the 'normal' planning system. Furthermore the later rounds of EZs seemed to demonstrate more intervention of this nature by local authorities than the first round (Barnes and Preston, 1985). Indeed Lloyd and Botham (1985) argue that local authorities were positively using EZs as an element within existing local interventionist economic strategies.

EZs were essentially a form of development subsidy presented as less restrictive planning; UDCs were an attempt to justify a development subsidy in terms of leverage, the amount of private sector money brought in per unit by public sector investment. In essentially social programmes, a low leverage ratio is acceptable: the task forces were reporting ratios of 0.5:1 in their inner city areas. However the ratio of 1:1 or 2:1 found by the National Audit Office for EZs was considered inappropriate given their rationale and, indeed, name. In practice the leverage ratios for UDCs have varied widely (from less than 0.5:1 for Merseyside to over 11:1 for the LDDC: Stoker, 1989b, p. 160). It is clear that it is the state of the local property market that determines the leverage ratio. As emphasised in Brindley *et al.* (1996), leverage policies follow market rationality and basically magnify existing disparities between areas. Thus when a recession in the property market occurs, as in 1991/2, UDCs cannot generate development and the cost of their support may seem excessive. Declines in land values in their areas also undermine their financing and rationale during a property market downturn, a point reinforced by the collection of studies in Imrie and Thomas (1993). Other relevant factors in determining a UDC's impact are the character of the relationship between the corporation and the pre-existing local authorities and the approach taken by key board members and corporation officials (Stoker, 1989b); this influences the character of the development that occurs and its relation to local community needs and established local authority policy.

Many regeneration grants comprise a project-specific form of leverage which seeks to generate net addition private investment while addressing some special social need. What UDG and LEGUP did is classic leverage: it is 'a market oriented scheme designed to cater for private sector needs with a pay-off to the public sector in terms of inner city revival' (Jacobs, 1985, p. 199). That revival is measured in physical development, not the socioeconomic benefits which are often spuriously claimed in grant applications (Matson and Whitney, 1985). It is difficult to prove 'additionality', that projects are being funded which would not otherwise have occurred, but Jacobs argues (1988, p. 198) that: 'Indications are that the nature and size of the projects coming forward would simply not have come about through the mechanism of the normal Urban Programme had it not been for the introduction of UDG', but it is a marginal effect (1988, p. 199): 'Experience shows that things have worked best when UDG has been asked to do things that the private sector actually wants to do, rather than to revive large comprehensive development plans initiated by the public sector.' This does not mean that the public sector is not involved; on the contrary, Matson and Whitney (1985) found that 67 per cent of the UDGs in their survey were public sector-led, but the public sector is edging the private sector to conform to a policy framework which is largely in line with market trends. In this way, regeneration policies remain tied to the interests of the private sector.

The only counter to this is that, as Urban Programme expenditure declined, community-based organisations have maintained their budgets so that by 1986/7 voluntary sector projects took 35 per cent of such expenditure, compared to 15 per cent in 1978/9 (Bailey, 1991). They have also had a 10 per cent share of the admittedly small Task Force budgets and been involved in City Challenge bids, which come from the local authority but require evidence of networking with the local voluntary sector. This means that community groups are now significant actors in urban policy. The National Council for Voluntary Organisation estimated that in 1988 the annual turnover of voluntary organisations in the 57 inner area programme authorities was £400 million, part grant and part trading income. As much again could be being earned in fees and payment for contract work. Bailey (1991) locates the causes of this growth in importance of community groups in the decline in local authority spending, the shift in policy towards *ad hoc* initiatives and the effects of community mobilisation over the past three decades. The move may hold benefits in terms of the empowerment of local communities and the generation of social facilities but such activity cannot, nor is it intended to, counter the underlying economic forces affecting urban areas. Such community-based policies can, in the current context, only mitigate the worst impacts of economic change and an urban policy which gives a low priority to poverty compared to economic goals (Lawless, 1991, p. 21).

■ Assessing the outputs

□ *Land use planning and urban development*

If development plans and development control are weak planning tools and there is a lack of overlap between development plans and development control, how does the planning system impact in terms of physical development? Healey, Davis, Wood and Elson (1982) emphasise the mutual interaction between planning and development processes. Development plans are not simply a framework for guiding development control. They perform two distinct functions depending on the scale of developer involved. For the smaller developers, plans act as a framework for organising their activities; for larger developers, they are a baseline for negotiation with planners. This means that development control is a much more interactive process into which development plans are just one input. As a result, the larger and more sophisticated development interests have a considerable role in influencing patterns of development. The circumstances in which planning policies are able to exert the dominant influence are identified as follows (Healey, Davis, Wood and Elson, 1982, para. 1.17):

> The policies investigated here have been effectively implemented because they relate to the central planning power of controlling the release of land in areas of high market demand, and because there has been considerable policy stability over time and consistency between levels of government about policy directions.

Thus in case studies of High Wycombe, Wokingham and Banbury, studied over 1974–80, Healey *et al.* (1982) found that local planning authorities had been successful in directing a fairly buoyant development sector to build housing and commercial property in certain locations but had found difficulties with controlling the level of employment afforded by development in particular sites, ensuring new housing was made available for local needs, phasing development in accordance with a timetable, and matching development with infrastructure provision.

In the face of such development pressure it is clear that local planning marginally adjusts market pressures, containing them and limiting the local impact. In commenting on Peter Hall and his teams' finding that planning had contained urban England (Hall *et al.*, 1973), Healey (1983, p. 41) says: 'We might conclude that the planning system has organised the process of suburbanisation but has not resisted it.' The difficulty in assessing such a statement is that the base-line against which the policy impact is being measured is not clear. What would be an indicator of the 'resistance' of the planning system: zero suburbanisation; 20 per cent of development occurring on rural land; 60 per cent; or what figure? In addition, the resistance of the planning system has always to be measured in relation to the pressure placed on it by a variable development market. In fact, government statistics show that between 1985 and 1990, an average of 68.3 km^2 of countryside was lost to urban development each year. And as at 1994, 16 per cent of England, 6 per cent of Wales, 10 per cent of Scotland and 12 per cent of Northern Ireland were categorised as urban land. The percentage of urban development occurring on previously rural land is falling from 49 per cent in 1985 to 44 per cent in 1991; comparable figures for residential development were 52 per cent in 1985, down to 39 per cent in 1993. It remains, though, a matter of normative judgement as to whether this level of 'resistance' is sufficient or not. And the contribution of the planning system to these figures is difficult to disaggregate from the dynamics of the development process.

It remains true that, in areas where more positive planning is required, where constraining private sector development is not enough, it is more difficult to identify the distinctive contribution of planning. For example, in inner city areas outside the central business core, land use planning is very dependent on the availability of public sector monies (Healey *et al.*,

1988, pp. 16–17). Again, in open land beyond the urban areas, the lack of land assembly and land management powers severely restricts the ability of local planners to influence change in the environment (Healey *et al.*, 1988, pp. 150–1). For this reason the *removal* of planning constraints within SPZs proved an inappropriate method of urban renewal in all but the most buoyant of local development markets. Research suggests that it was the financial incentives that attracted development to their predecessors, EZs, and the absence of such incentives seriously undermines SPZs as a planning tool. Recognition of these limitations of the formal land use planning system to promote development has thrown the emphasis more on developing partnerships and coalitions to identify the barriers to development as well as the means of overcoming them, and making more effective bids for financial resources from central government or the EU. However, beyond identifying individual cases where a specific project appears to have been promoted by such means, it is difficult to gauge the overall effectiveness of this form of partnership planning; in addition, it is likely that the rhetoric of partnership will overemphasise the contribution that such planning actually makes to the outcomes (Rydin, 1998a).

Who then benefits and who loses out as a result of this type of planning system? Hall *et al.*'s 1973 study argued strongly that planning was benefiting those with property interests in rural areas protected by restrictive planning, young, mobile skilled workers who would enter owner-occupation in the new suburban estates, and firms seeking large well-serviced sites. This has been at the expense of public sector tenants and those in the private rented sector who have faced less choice in housing and become increasingly trapped in inner city locations with poor amenities and limited employment opportunities. Healey and her co-researchers argue that developers have also been served by the planning system (Healey *et al.* (eds), 1982 and Healey *et al.*, 1988). Land assembly and infrastructure have been facilitated and restrictive planning waived in return for limited planning gain to encourage urban renewal and city centre redevelopment. Ambrose (1986, p. 258) notes that planning collates information with a commercial value and can prevent the oversupply of new development space that would arise from unfettered competition. He adds that the planning system can also act as a handy support for the development industry, since the planning authority's (overambitious) claim to be guiding urban change also brings with it responsibility for adverse outcomes. In addition larger landowning interests have found planning beneficial. It is these interests who are most likely to desire that new development is coordinated, concentrated and reasonably predictable in location (Healey, 1983, p. 208).

Furthermore, it seems that planning has sustained certain land values, benefiting existing landowners. One of the major conclusions of Bramley *et al.*'s study of housebuilding and planning (1995, p. 235) is that 'planning does affect the housing market, raising house prices and densities and reducing supply responsiveness', though they go on to point out that 'a very liberal planning policy on housing land release, would not eliminate these problems, or even dramatically reduce them'. While Simmie (1993, p. 173) actually favours the abolition of green belts, his review of available research echoes this conclusion. His earlier work also showed that landowners were more likely to receive planning permission unlocking the development value of their assets (Simmie, 1981).

In such a planning system, focused on negotiating with developers and landowners, certain interests can be forgotten. Recent feminist work on planning has shown how the needs of women are ignored by a patriarchal form of planning (Foulsham, 1987; Little, 1994; Greed, 1991). Much of this work has focused on the problems that women as carers face in the built environment and the physical threat posed to women by urban areas where safety has not been 'planned in' (Valentine, 1992; Trench, 1991; Oc, 1991). The specific needs of ethnic minorities have also been left out of planning policy and decision-making, an issue which the Royal Town Planning Institute is now trying to address (see also Thomas, 1994; Thomas and Krishnarayan, 1994a and 1994b).

The overall conclusion on land use planning seems to be that it is weak in relation to its aspirations and regressive in many of the impacts it does have. Marginal improvements to private sector development proposals can be achieved and local pressure groups are sometimes successful in obtaining desired changes in the built environment. But as the discussion in Part 2 has shown, pressure group politics is itself inequitable and many planning procedures are ill-suited to public participation on an open and equitable basis. The new planning theory of collaborative planning seeks to address many of these criticisms and this will be taken up in Chapter 15.

☐ *Environmental regulation and environmental protection*

The impact of such environmental regulation can often be judged in technical terms through the collection of scientific data. Furthermore, unlike in many other areas of planning, there is no shortage of scientifically-based material to draw on making an assessment. All media show some evidence of pollution or contamination: air, water and land. For air quality, government statistics show declines in many measured air pollutants, particularly as measured per unit of GDP (see Table 14.3). But this cannot be read simply as a success story for pollution control. Much of the reduction in emissions is accounted for by restructuring of British industry towards high-tech and service sectors and the introduction of new technology. Many emissions are not represented in these statistics and new industrial processes are continually producing new compounds with unknown polluting consequences. (This is also a major problem for water pollution control.) In addition, reductions in emissions are not a success if the absolute level remains too high and average levels may conceal 'hot spots' of pollution. Environmental pressure groups repeatedly point to instances of breaches of international recommended limits on particular pollutants. The debate about the thresholds for global environmental change, such as global warming, provide other criteria against which emissions may be judged too high.

In the case of water pollution, the main source on the quality of rivers, canals and estuaries is the quinquennial survey undertaken since 1970, by DoE, the NRA and now by the Environment Agency. These surveys classify stretches of water into four classes. Interpretation of these surveys has been complicated by the poor methodological base, with a variety of methods used in the former water authority areas (NRA, 1991b, p. 68). Other problems were that the surveys assessed the length of rivers of different quality regardless of width, that lengths of river were added between surveys and weather conditions greatly influenced the outcomes, as did other conditions at the point of sampling. Thus there was a 20–30 per cent chance of a stretch of water being declared to have changed from one quality class to another when there had been no real change in water quality. The Environment Agency has now introduced a new methodology, the General Quality Assessment. This is based on three determinants of quality: dissolved oxygen, biochemical oxygen demand and ammoniacal nitrogen. As a result of the new basis for assessment, figures before and after 1990 are not comparable, except for estuaries where the old National Water Council classification is still used.

Table 14.3 *Emissions to air (UK) (tonnes/GDP)*

	1970	1980	1990	1995
SO_2	18.4	11.6	6.8	4.0
Smoke	3.1	1.4	0.9	0.6
NOx	6.8	5.7	5.3	3.9
VOC	6.5	5.7	4.9	4.0
CO	18.6	16.3	13.4	9.4
CO_2	n.a.	510.0	383.0	n.a.
Methane	n.a.	14.0	10.5	n.a.

Source: Digest of Environmental Protection and Water Statistics; Digest of Environmental Statistics.

Table 14.4   *Classification of water quality in freshwater river and canals (England and Wales)*

	% water length	
	*1990**	*1995**
Good (A + B)	48	59
Fair (C + D)	37	31
Poor (E)	13	8
Bad (F)	2	1

*based on the new General Quality Assessment methodology
Source: DoE and NRA, *Water Quality Surveys*; *Digest of Environmental Statistics.*

Existing surveys indicate an increase in water quality up to 1980, with the percentage of unpolluted non-tidal rivers and canals rising from 72 per cent in 1958 to 75 per cent in 1980, and for tidal rivers from 41 per cent to 50 per cent. Thereafter it is clear that, whatever the methodological problems, there was a net downgrading of water quality in each survey up to 1990 (NRA, 1991a, p. 45). As at 1990, 48 per cent of freshwater rivers and canals were classified as good and 66 per cent of estuaries (see Table 14.4). The new classification suggests that there has since been an improvement in water quality for rivers and canals, although the data for estuaries suggests a slight decline (Table 14.5).

Any improvements in water quality are the result of investment by the water authorities in the past, and now the water companies and other industry. Deterioration, principally due to pollution from sewage works and agricultural sources, has for a long time run ahead of such investment

Table 14.5   *Classification of water quality in estuaries (England and Wales)*

	% water length		
	1980	*1990*	*1995*
Good	68	66	65
Fair	23	24	27
Poor	5	7	4
Bad	4	3	4

Source: DoE and NRA, *Water Quality Surveys*; *Digest of Environmental Statistics.*

which has only in recent years begun to make an appreciable impact. The 1990 survey (NRA, 1991a, p. 46) argued that progress was needed in relation to farm waste production and storage, leakage from contaminated land and the control of permitted discharges into water 'in order to reverse the deterioration of some of the country's best rivers and to accelerate the necessary improvement of those rivers which have long been abused'. The pressure from EU directives resulted in a substantial increase in the levels of new investment, particularly in treatment works.

As argued in Chapters 4 and 6, further impacts from environmental regulation are likely to be traced back to the growing influence of the EU in directing pollution control measures (Blowers, 1987). For example, the EC directive on large combustion plants (No. 88/609) has already had a considerable effect, bringing emissions of SO2 from power plants down to 82 per cent of their 1980 levels by 1990, only just above the 1993 target set in the directive. The directive is also responsible for some reduction in emission of nitrogen oxides from power plants. Again, following action by the EU there has been some improvement in the quality of bathing waters. Whereas in 1988 only 66 per cent of identified bathing water complied with the EC directive (and there was some controversy over the beaches which had been so identified – Blackpool was excluded), in 1995 89 per cent of UK bathing waters complied. Similarly the percentage of determinations on drinking water quality which exceed the prescribed concentration or value set down in the EC directive (or as granted in a relaxation) fell from 1.6 per cent in 1991 to 0.9 per cent in 1994. A similar effect is likely to arise from the implementation of the Urban Waste Water Treatment Plants directive; currently there are substantial numbers of cases where EU standards are not achieved.

☐ *Agricultural production and rural quality of life*

Assessing the outcomes of policy depends on the objectives of that policy and countryside policy has had a fairly clear set of objectives to date, though it now appears to be in the process of slowly shifting priorities. In terms of the overriding objective of increasing agricultural production, countryside planning can be said to have been successful. Agricultural production has risen to such an extent that indigenous needs are satisfied, foodstuffs are exported and surpluses have mounted in EU stores. For example, the European Commission's 1985 estimates were for cereal production to rise by 5.1 million tonnes over 1984/5–1990/1, an annual surplus over consumption of 43.5 million tonnes (Bowers, 1990, p. 24). The Forestry Commission achieved its own 1943 target of a three-year supply of timber in siege conditions or five million acres of afforested land in 1984 (Mather, 1991) and a Treasury study in 1972 concluded that no further afforestation was justified on the basis of the economics of timber production. Meanwhile there have been adequate supplies of minerals for energy production and construction needs. As detailed above, this over-success in promoting agricultural production prompted the recent reforms in the CAP and the introduction of set-aside policy; the result of this policy in Britain has been 748 000 hectares of set-aside in 1994 and a reduction in agricultural land of 1.6 per cent.

But concern remains at the extent of loss of habitats of nature conservation value. The historic process of the destruction of semi-natural habitats has reached a critical stage in ecological terms as many become very restricted or fragmented. For example, 22 per cent of the hedgerows existing in 1947 had been lost by 1985. Ninty-five per cent of flower-rich meadows, 40 per cent of lowland heaths, 80 per cent of chalk grasslands and 30–50 per cent of ancient woodlands have been destroyed. Half of the lowland marshes have been drained (Blowers, 1987; Lowe *et al.*, 1986, pp. 63–72). More recent figures confirm the continuation of this trend. The total length of hedgerows continues to fall from 563 000 km in 1984 to 377 500 km in 1993. Mean species numbers declined between 1978 and 1990 for all categories of arable and pastoral land other than plots of woodland or improved grassland. And in moorland and upland areas, woodlands plots saw a dramatic loss of mean species numbers of over 30 per cent during this period, though these areas showed a modest gain taken as a whole. Government statistics list some 4500 species, 15 per cent of all native species, as either at risk or already extinct.

In forestry new grant schemes have begun to have an effect. In 1983/4, 91 per cent of planting and restocking in the private estate and 98 per cent in the public estate consisted of conifers. By 1990/1 the figures had fallen to 54 per cent in the private sector but remained high at 93 per cent in the public sector. Much of this shift in planting has occurred in England, not the vast afforested areas of Scotland, and the schemes are also weakened by the fact that there is no ongoing involvement in the management of estates (Lowe *et al.*, 1986, p. 49). In any case the total expenditure on supporting broadleaved planting was less than 10 per cent of all grant aid in 1986/7 (Crabtree, 1991) and operated in a context in which broadleaved forestry had declined by a quarter since 1947 (Blowers, 1987). Any significant effect on the overall stock will take decades to become fully apparent but changes are beginning to be seen. The total stock of woodland in Britain increased from 25 200 km^2 in 1984 to 25 960 km^2 in 1990, and new planting in 1993/4 and 1994/5 reversed the trend of decades with more broadleaved planting than coniferous. However, restocking is still in favour of conifers and the proportion of the stock comprising broadleaves, mixed woodland or other non-coniferous woodland was about 50 per cent in 1984 and actually fell slightly to 49 per cent in 1990.

There is some evidence that damage to designated areas such as SSSIs may be on the decline (see Shoard, 1987, p. 440, for the past situation of unchecked damage). Recent government statistics show that of the 2022 SSSIs designated in 1996, only 287 were subject to management agreements; however, English Nature's 1996/7 survey of SSSIs found that 90 per cent are managed in a way that maintains or improves their conservation value. In 1995/6 damage affecting 231 SSSIs was reported; agricultural activities were listed as the main cause, far outstripping any other cause. However, while the number of cases of damage has remained in the range of 150–250 per annum, the area affected has fallen dramatically to 4932 hectares in 1995/6. Given the significance of these sites, this may still be considered disappointing.

But if there has been some slow improvement in environmental protection of rural areas, there remain serious socioeconomic problems in such areas. The underlying substitution of capital for labour has meant a decline in agricultural employment and in agriculture's role in the rural economy (Bowers, 1990, p. 2). Between 1960 and 1979 the number of agricultural workers halved; and between 1985 and 1995 agricultural employment fell by a quarter. Similarly technological change, although offset by the maturing of forestry estates into more labour-intensive stages, means that forestry remains a poor source of rural employment (Whitby, 1990). The system of agricultural support has failed to maintain the incomes of smaller and poorer farmers or even to maintain the gap between average industrial and agricultural incomes. Tenanted farmers have found that the financial benefits of agricultural support have almost entirely seeped through into rental increases, fuelling a shift from the rented to owner-occupied tenure in farming (Bowers, 1990, p. 29). Farming has polarised into the capitalist sector employing agricultural labour and the smaller family farm relying largely on self-labour (Symes, 1990, p. 105).

The decline in agricultural employment in rural areas has been aggravated by the decline in local rural services but has been partially offset by the shift in manufacturing jobs into the countryside. The 1995 Rural White Paper points to an increase in employee jobs in rural districts of 9.2 per cent over 1984–91 compared to an average for England of 3 per cent (though this is obviously on a small base), and an unemployment rate of 5.1 per cent in rural areas compared to 7 per cent for England as a whole. Over 1960–87 there was an increase in manufacturing jobs in rural areas of 19.7 per cent (again from a low base) compared to an overall decline in Britain of 37.5 per cent. However, Symes argues (1990, p. 111): 'rural areas are gaining an increasing share of jobs in a declining manufacturing sector! They are getting hardly any share of the expanding non-local service sector.' Certainly the Rural White Paper shows that the proportion of employees in financial and business services in rural areas is

6.2 per cent for more remote areas and 9.3 per cent for more accessible ones, compared to 15.6 per cent for metropolitan areas and 12.3 per cent for urban areas.

The result of this is a profound change in social structure in rural areas. The rural working class is becoming more attenuated. Symes identifies a process of 'accumulative causation of rural deprivation' (1990, pp. 112–13). This is made worse by central government policies on public transport and primary education in rural areas. As a result it is estimated that 25 per cent of rural households exist close to or within the margins of poverty, including many elderly people. At the same time there has been a shift in population. Depopulation of remoter rural areas continues, unstemmed by agricultural support mechanisms (Bowers, 1990, p. 2) and more accessible rural communities have acquired new populations: commuters, ex-urbanites and second-home owners. The immigration of these groups has put considerable pressure on rural housing markets, pressure which land use planning policies have been unable to deal with to ensure affordable housing for local needs (Shucksmith, 1990). Furthermore, Symes argues (1990, p. 113) that the immigrating groups have entered into political alliance with landowning farmers and other landowners to stifle debate on rural employment and low-income housing. Neither are these vital planning issues promoted by local authority officers who have tended to listen to environmental pressure groups in developing policy which benefits the 'amenity fraternity' but disadvantages the rural working class.

☐ *The cost of regeneration*

Regeneration policy faces one of the greatest challenges in urban and environmental planning, for it seeks to alter entrenched processes of economic restructuring. The evidence appears to be that taking on this challenge is very costly and, to date, has not been pursued very effectively. It has been assessed that the gap between deprived areas and the rest of the country remains as wide as it was fifteen years ago (Willmott and Hutchinson, 1992).

Evidence is available on the outcomes of a number of regeneration initiatives. Government figures on the impact of the Task Forces claim total funding of £193.5 million over 1986–91, of which 43 per cent is public funding (30 per cent spent, 13 per cent committed). As at 1991, this has generated 12 593 jobs with another 11 546 forecast: a public sector cost per job of 6600. A similar appraisal has been undertaken for a more substantial policy initiative, the EZs. Figures, from *Enterprise Zone Information* annual bulletins, suggested that substantial development had occurred in the zones: 27 per cent of land was developed at designation, 70 per cent by 1987/8. But then the second-round EZs were selected on the basis of developability (Bruton and Nicholson, 1987, p. 206). In addition to the costs of capital allowances and lost rate revenue, there had been substantial public sector investment in many of the zones, mainly on infrastructure with the rest on land acquisition. The final evaluation of EZs found that they had created 58 000 jobs at an average cost of £17–21 000 per job (Roger Tyms, 1995). However the National Audit Office's report on EZs, which effectively ended the experiment, argued that the full cost of EZs was not known, and that their effectiveness as a policy tool could not be known with any certainty (NAO, 1986). In addition it seemed that many of the jobs counted as arising from the EZ policy had probably been directed from elsewhere and the increase in land values in EZs was often at the expense of surrounding land. It is also clear that the most successful zones were those where other public sector programmes had invested resources. As Bruton and Nicholson conclude (1987, p. 209):

> Paradoxically despite the free market ideology of the EZ measure, active public sector involvement appears to be a key factor in the successful development of the zones, although this activity may bear little relation to EZ concessions and will probably use resources diverted from elsewhere.

Precisely because EZs were not an exemplar of free-market non-planning, but an unfocused, costly and interventionist policy tool, the quality of development has not proved sub-standard compared to other sites. This is because of a number of factors: the fairly effective control of new development noted above; some development in EZs had already gone through normal planning procedure; building regulations continued to apply; standardised designs, materials and construction methods were being used by developers; and owners wished their properties to maintain their investment value (Thornley, 1993, p. 197).

The other flagship regeneration policy of the 1980s, the UDCs, have similarly been criticised for their cost, their limited impact and, particularly, their social divisiveness. The LDDC is the prime example of a corporation at conflict with local authorities for most of its life and led by officers highly attuned to the requirements of the development industry. The scale of development has been substantial and developers have benefited from land sold on highly favourable terms and the extensive investment in infrastructure and site servicing that occurred before and after designation (Brownill, 1990, p. 44). By March 1989 the LDDC had received £547 million in grants with an additional £909 million planned for 1989–93; and over 1981–9 was spending 84 per cent of all income on pump-priming development; the DoTr had committed £600 million on transport; the EZ concessions were worth £130 million to 1987; and the utilities and Dockland Joint Committee (of local authorities) had invested in the area in the past. In addition by 1988/9 the LDDC was receiving 50 per cent of its income in the form of enhanced land values upon sale (Brownill, 1990, pp. 45–6).

In London's property market during the 1980s such investment was bound to generate development. However critics have consistently argued that the development did little for the employment, housing and community facilities needs of the local population. Many of Brownill's conclusions on the LDDC (1990, p. 173) hold true for all UDCs:

> The most immediate tension is how the operation of market forces and inner city policy geared to promoting the physical rebuilding of areas leads to unequal distribution of benefits, leading to the spatial exclusion of those groups who cannot afford to pay, in particular the low-paid, the working class, black people and women.

Brownill finds that landowners, property developers and some owner-occupiers were the principal beneficiaries of UDC policy. Stoker (1989b) states that UDCs produce 'a pattern of urban renewal which is broadly beneficial to the top three quarters of the income distribution' (p. 165). This is an urban policy which offers little to the urban poor.

The impacts of UDG and the Scottish equivalent LEGUP, an early form of this type of grant, have also been assessed and provide further evidence of regeneration policy over the last decade or so. Over September 1982–April 1984, 446 UDG bids were submitted, 32 per cent approved and 81 per cent of these were taken up resulting in 116 projects (Jacobs, 1985). To December 1983 some £54 million was expended on grants resulting in £221 million of private investment, a leverage ratio of 4:1. Forty per cent of grants are supporting industrial development, 35 per cent commercial and 23 per cent housing. An HRF study (1986) estimated that UDG projects were generating 129 dwellings per £1m grant or £7750 per dwelling, with higher costs where special social needs were being addressed. In Scotland, up to October 1984, £11 million of LEG-UP had levered in £46 million of private monies, a ratio of 4:1 also (Zeiger, 1985). The Scottish analysis suggests that, allowing for other relevant public monies, LEGUP created 1717 permanent jobs at £6600 per job and housing at £4700 per dwelling over September 1982–October 1984. However, various innovative funding schemes in use in Scotland means that much of the grant will be repaid to the SDA, reducing the cost per job and dwelling substantially.

So if these policies can only marginally alter the social and economic impact of urban change, have they at least accelerated physical development processes to reduce urban dereliction if not urban deprivation? In 1987 Kivell argued that: 'After 20 years of reclamation, the problem of derelict land remains as large and intractable as ever' (p. 269). He argues that relying on public sector monies to pump-prime the private sector has resulted in an overemphasis on reclaiming for hard uses (65 per cent approved reclamation up to 1984/5), insufficient funds being put into the problem and a short-term approach which stores up maintenance problems for the future. His figures show that from 1974 to 1982 derelict land increased from 43300 to 45700 hectares despite major programmes which reclaimed 17000 hectares. At reclamation rates of £44000 per hectare, current expenditure will take 26 years to clear the existing stock, ignoring any additions. An assessment from within central government (DoE, 1992) was more optimistic. It pointed to an increase in derelict land grant (DLG) expenditure to £106 million in 1992. Between 1988 and 1992 1500 hectares were reclaimed each year. But this had to be matched against the 1988 survey figure of 40 500 hectares of derelict land and a cost of £50000 per annum for recent DLG schemes.

More recent figures show that the stock of derelict land has declined from 40 500 hectares to 39 600 hectares in 1993; although 9500 hectares were reclaimed over this period, additions to the stock mean that the net reduction was only 2 per cent over the 5 year period. Expenditure under the DLG programme amounted to £118.4 m in 1993/4 when 1540 hectares were reclaimed; in 1994/5 under the English Partnerships' Land Reclamation Programme, which subsumed DLG though not in its entirety, £114 m was spent and 1700 hectares were reclaimed, including 1185 hectares of derelict land. In 1988 Lawless (1988, p. 540) stated:

> Yet any overall assessment of the policy must remain critical. In many respects it has simply not made that much difference to the inner cities and those living in them . . . the programme as a whole cannot be seen as a comprehensive strategy to address the problems of urban decline. It remains as it always has been a pragmatic *ad hoc* response to a complex series of constraints operating on the cities.

Lawless argued that any change in policy was likely to require substantial additional resources, requiring both economic growth and a change in government (1991, p. 28). While a change of government has been achieved and economic growth during the mid-1990s has been quite robust, additional resources may still prove the stumbling block. As the above figures indicate the resources devoted to this goal are not large and the impact on the stock of derelict land remains marginal.

If the improvement of the most derelict areas has not been a success, what of the conservation of the most valued features of our built environment? There is some evidence of amenity and historic heritage being preserved but, again, at a social cost. Preservation of urban and rural areas of heritage has interacted with local property markets to benefit middle- and upper class owners of property. Indeed conservation policy, as so many other types of planning policy discussed above, is directly dependent to a large extent on these property market effects to achieve its goals. English Heritage's 1992 study based on a survey of 43000 listed buildings argued that 7.3 per cent of listed buildings in England were 'at risk' and 14.6 per cent were 'vulnerable' (a less serious category of decay). But they also found that the condition of buildings was related to the existence of an appropriate and profitable use: affluence protects buildings (1992, p. 4). Ten per cent of surveyed buildings in less affluent areas were at risk, compared to 4 per cent in affluent areas. Pressure group politics reinforced these tendencies (see Chapter 7 above). Threats to amenity, such as through traffic, have been diverted to 'less valued' areas, often working-class residential areas. The vociferous pressure groups of conservation areas have reinforced the heritage protection policies of local authorities to render conservation policies one of the success stories of postwar planning in terms of the objectives of preserving the built environment (Bruton and Nicholson, 1987, p. 376; Ambrose, 1986, pp. 257–8). But it is a success which illustrates the dependence of land use planning on market processes and the potential for regressive impacts reinforced by pressure group politics.

This overriding issue of the regressive past impact of planning and its future potential for a more progressive impact is taken up in the final chapter, where the promise of collaborative planning is assessed and the preference for a more limited and modest form of planning, clearly open to challenge and redress, is outlined.

■ Further reading

This is surprising little material which attempts a systematic and comprehensive assessment of the planning system. Simmie (1993) seeks to do this for land use planning. But readers are best referred to current journals, particularly *Planning Practice and Research*, government statistics such as *Digest of Environmental Statistics* and occasional research reports undertaken for DETR or by the National Audit Office and Audit Commission.

■ *Chapter 15* ■

Conclusion: Planning for the Future

The discussion in Chapter 14 has highlighted the impacts of planning, in its various forms, as revealed through published research and data. It provides a mixed account of the success of planning in achieving its objectives. There are two broad reasons for the criticisms. First, there is the inadequacy of the policy tools that have been available to planners. Some of the tools, such as development control, are reactive in nature. In some cases, the application of protective designations is not the most appropriate approach as changes in land management practice are needed. Many types of regulation are weak, due to scope of application or problems of implementation and enforcement. Resources are not always properly distributed to achieve the policy goals; this is clearly the case with agricultural support. In some areas, as with urban regeneration, the level of resources is insufficient to deal with the scale of the problem and the pressure of market forces. And there are difficulties in raising the public support needed to implement measures which would achieve the policy goals, as with raising fuel prices sufficiently to alter travel patterns. The second reason lies in the unsatisfactory outcome of the 'politics of planning', the operation of negotiation and bargaining during the planning policy process. Charges of corporatism and inadequate public participation have been levelled at some aspects, such as pollution control; elsewhere the balance of involvement by interests has resulted in certain groups being poorly treated by the distributive impacts of planning. The distribution of costs and benefits has been emphasised in the accounts of land use planning, countryside policy and heritage conservation. The patterns of access of different groups to the planning process has not resulted in equitable outcomes. Given these difficulties, what are the arguments for planning? And what form should contemporary planning take to avoid these problems? This chapter addresses these questions and, in doing so, considers the current influential planning theory of collaborative planning, outlined in Chapter 4. While developed particularly to explain and direct land use planning, collaborative planning is a general theory of planning. As Chapter 14 showed, each area of planning covered in this book involves negotiation and conflicts of interest; since these are the central issues handled by collaborative planning, the discussion below should be of relevance to all aspects of planning.

■ The rationale for planning

Without adopting a tightly functionalist approach, it can be argued that planning is a necessary state activity. Economic and social circumstances prompt a degree of state action in managing our physical environment and trying to influence our use of that environment. There are several senses in which this is the case.

First, planning, in its most general sense, is a means of avoiding anarchy and disorder. There are strong tendencies towards such disorder in our economic system. The interaction of competitive forces in the market-place does not automatically lead along a smooth path to the public interest. Instead competition can generate the anarchy of the market, with periodic oversupply of goods, mismatch of needs and supply (or even demand and supply), underutilisation of some resources (such as labour) and over-exploitation of others (such as environmental goods and services). The cycles of boom and slump, of crisis and temporary recovery, have shaped our economy and society during the twentieth century, and will continue to do so in the foreseeable future.

These outcomes of a market system have particular consequences in the case of the natural and built environment, as change often has long-term consequences. In urban areas, the cycles of property development can leave cities scarred for many years, whether by the disruption of large-scale development activity, the dereliction of abandoned sites or the apparent irrationality of empty new buildings. The London Docklands area has seen all these stages over the past two decades: docks left to decay for years as the Port of London Authority pulled out to newer, more profitable locations; the decade of massive redevelopment and disruption for local communities under the UDC in the 1980s; and the partially empty tower of Canary Wharf standing as testimony to the collapse of yet another property boom. In the case of the natural environment, the effects of market decision-making are similarly long-term and unstable. Mining activity can change the face of a rural area completely for decades. Cessation of that activity only creates new problems of dereliction, equally persistent. Pollution flows may alter over the short term with levels of industrial output and technological change, but the impact on ecosystems can be long-term. They take time to adjust, assimilate and recover, or, more pessimistically, to adjust, alter and change irreversibly for the worse.

Planning has a role in reacting to and, more important, trying to prevent the worst excesses of this inherent instability (Hobbs, 1992). The use of knowledge about economic, social and physical environmental systems, combined with a future-oriented approach, could at least suggest scenarios for the future and propose some mechanisms for movement towards a more acceptable pattern of use of our built and natural environment. Even if it is accepted that these mechanisms for controlling the anarchy of the market are weak, the existence of the planning system represents a strong statement that the worst excesses of a market system need not be tolerated. And, in between the extremes of planning as effectively controlling instability and planning as a statement of hope, there is the prospect of a planning system limiting some of the effects without necessarily ensuring a smooth path in environmental change in urban or rural areas, or in economic, social or ecological systems.

Another role for the planning system in relation to economic and social change is in terms of accommodating long-terms shifts in structure. There has been much debate on the transition from a Fordist to post-Fordist system of production in Britain and other developed countries, and within the global economic system as a whole (Harvey, 1989; Lash and Urry, 1987; Graham, 1992). For some this is associated with a shift from modernity to postmodernity, as a distinct era in social and cultural organisation. Harvey describes the new pattern of economic activity in the late twentieth century as follows (1989, p. 147):

> It rests on flexibility with respect to labour processes, labour markets, products and patterns of consumption. It is characterized by the emergence of entirely new sectors of production, new ways of providing financial services, new markets, and above all, greatly intensified rates of commercial, technological, and organizational innovation. It has entrained rapid shifts in the patterning of uneven development, both between sectors and between geographical regions, giving rise, for example, to a vast surge in so-called 'service-sector' employment as well as to entirely new industrial ensembles in hitherto underdeveloped regions.

These broader, longer-term changes raise the question of whether the planning system is implicated in smoothing the transition to post-Fordism and postmodernism and, in the process, is reshaping itself in a post-Fordist and postmodern form. If post-Fordism involves a greater emphasis on flexible patterns of production and service delivery, with more specialised, non-standard products, then existing regimes of state influence over product and service delivery also need to adopt the flexible specialisation approach. Current changes in the management of the planning system can be seen in this light (Stoker, 1989a; Gyford, 1991, p. 122): the creation of arm's-length organisations for a variety of tasks from hearing planning appeals to disposing of waste; the emphasis on responsiveness and flexibility in all planning decisions; the attack on planning as an activity under professional control operating within a state bureaucracy.

Some already discern a postmodern form of planning developing (Harvey, 1989; Goodchild, 1990). Modernist planning was concerned with comprehensive management of the environment, conceived as a totality, and with developing master plans for planning action. Postmodern planning perceives economic processes as chaotic and uncontrollable, with change as endemic and indeed attractive. Talking specifically about urban design, Harvey (1989, p. 66) says:

> I take postmodernism broadly to signify a break with the modernist idea that planning and development should focus on large-scale, metropolitan-wide, technologically rational and efficient urban plans, backed by absolutely no-frills architecture (the austere 'functionalist' surfaces of 'international style' modernism). Postmodernism cultivates, instead, a conception of the urban fabric as necessarily fragmented, a 'palimpsest' of past forms superimposed upon each other, and a 'collage' of current uses, many of which may be ephemeral. Since the metropolis is impossible to command except in bits and pieces, urban design (and note that postmodernists design rather than plan) simply aims to be sensitive to vernacular traditions, local histories, particular wants, needs, and fancies, thus generating specialized, even highly customized architectural forms that may range from intimate, personalized spaces, through traditional monumentality, to the gaiety of spectacle.

In this way, planning can ease society on to the path towards a new pattern of organisation. It can also play a part in dealing with the inevitable side-effects of the transition process, making the process less disruptive and painful. If this seems an overly functional view of planning and its relation to economic and social change, it must be remembered that such change will generate political pressures from a broad spectrum within society looking to the state to deal with the unpleasant consequences of restructuring. It is not just in the interests of post-Fordist entrepreneurs to plan the transition, including its environmental dimension. Structural change hurts many in society, both because of the uncertainty generated and the reallocation of resources involved (but see below for further discussion of planning and distributional impacts).

Beyond these rationales for planning, in dealing with, first, periods of instability in economic activity and, second, transition during periods of restructuring, there is a third reason why planning is necessary. In relation to both the built and natural environment there is a system maintenance function for planning. This means that planning can play a part in ensuring that economic, social and ecological systems do not irreparably break down. The anarchy of market competition can threaten to undermine the basic dynamics of economic processes. The social consequences of unfettered competition can undermine the legitimacy of existing patterns of political organisation. And the unrestrained use of environmental goods and services can cause irreversible ecological damage, including damage to the life support systems of our planet. Planning is necessary to prevent such damage to the broad structures within which we live, work and exist. At different times, different aspects of the system maintenance function of planning are apparent. In periods of profound slump, the state puts its efforts into local and national economic development to promote growth, recently in a quasi-entrepreneurial style. When social movements challenge existing political structures, then the state has to put resources into meeting, or appearing to meet, demand for change (O'Connor, 1973): more extensive public consultation and participation procedures over nuclear power developments in the face of campaigns by the Campaign for Nuclear Disarmament and environmental groups; creating community programmes and encouraging business to be involved in local training and social programmes in the wake of inner city riots. Currently the growing evidence on global environmental change, particularly an enhanced greenhouse effect, is pushing governments into stepping up their environmental programmes.

Success in any of these three tasks for planning is not assured. Planning, of the environment or more directly of the economy, has not been able to sustain a steady path of growth. The process of restructuring is not frictionless, problems of adjustment occur and some sections of society lose out in the change that does occur. While Britain and other western developed countries have managed to avoid economic and social collapse, we do not yet know if ecological crisis has been averted or whether our current changes in behaviour will result in a level of climatic change to which we can adjust. But planning for the built and natural environment has an important role to play at each level of periodic, structural and systemic change.

While these processes of change provide a strong rationale for planning, there is a further, progressive argument for planning. All the processes discussed so far – the ups and downs of market-led patterns of investment, the change in mode of production, and the potential for irreparable damage to economic, social and ecological systems – have distributional consequences. The existence of these consequences can result in a broad-based support within society for planning. But planning also has the potential for dealing with the distributional impacts of change in a more equitable and democratic manner. Many of the distributional consequences take the form of spatial and environmental externalities, and planning is particularly well-suited to dealing with such externalities, regulating to prevent negative externalities, and coordinating activities to maximise positive externalities. Dealing with externalities and other distributional consequences of market activity is a primary way in which planning can encourage redistribution in society. Preventing the full impact of urban redevelopment being felt by local communities, controlling pollution which is affecting local residents in an industrial area, supporting employment opportunities for rural residents in a situation of agricultural decline, are all examples of the way in which the planning system can manage change in the pursuit of a fairer distribution of resources. But planning can play a more positive role than just reacting to the adverse consequences of market outcomes. It can actively try to redistribute resources through patterns of land use, provision of urban and transport facilities, ensuring access to leisure and beauty spots, and promoting the quality of local environments.

Of course, the message of the research reviewed in Chapter 14 is that planning has not in the past fulfilled this potential. One of the chief claims of collaborative planning is that it proposes a mode of planning practice which will be effective in achieving specific goals and fulfilling its rationale in terms of maintaining stability and adjusting to structural change, while at the same time opening up the planning system to the full range of concerned interests. Indeed it argues that planning will be more effective if it is more open – that is, a consensus for the policy approach can be built through a more open, collaborative approach – and that the resulting policy will, in its detail, be more focused on the problem, more able to generate resources and more likely to actually yield results. This is clearly a very attractive message; the next section will consider some of the emerging concerns with this approach.

■ The potential of collaborative planning

Healey's collaborative planning is widely acknowledged as the contemporary face of planning theory and rightly lauded for its attempt to develop a new normative approach to planning activity following the multi-faceted critiques of planning in the 1970s and 1980s, from the Right and the Left. It represents a serious attempt to develop a model for planning practice appropriate to a period in which the claims of modernism and modernist planning, exemplified by the procedural planning theory approach, can no longer be supported. However, any serious theoretical approach deserves a critical engagement and this is now emerging in relation to collaborative planning; this section represents part of that engagement. There are four points of engagement.

First, there is the view of language integral to the approach. Collaborative planning is based on an appreciation that language makes a difference; the way in which communication occurs affects outcomes. In particular, the language used can create barriers between actors, as in the case of gender-blind or colour-blind language. Therefore attention to the detail of communication can ensure that specific groups are not 'talked out' of planning debate. This is not just a matter of translation or political correctness. Rather it is a matter of considering whether the concerns, concepts and ways of thinking of specific groups are reflected in planning deliberations. Conversely, language can help forge alliances by building or borrowing a shared means of communication – planners using the language of business have found it easier to work with business interests or gain grants from a pro-business government (Newman, 1996; Hastings, 1996; Rydin, 1998a). The format of arenas will also be important in reinforcing the exclusive or inclusive nature of the planning system (Bryson and Crosby 1993). However, other work on language and social action suggests that much more is involved in manipulating the language of planning than this view implies. There are a variety of different types of such work.

At the most structuralist end, there is Foucault's work, which is becoming influential within planning theory as a counter to collaborative planning. Foucault explicitly examined the power of discourse, the hypothesis that 'in every society the production of discourse is at once controlled, selected, organized and redistributed by a certain number of procedures whose role is to ward off its powers and dangers, to gain mastery over its chance events, to evade its ponderous, formidable materiality' (1984, p. 109). Just as discourse is prevalent throughout society, so power is a diffused phenomenon, in one sense oppressing us all, though not equally. This analysis was, of course, developed through immense studies of the history of sexuality, madness and the disciplinary basis of the academy. In these, the controlling influence of prohibitions on forbidden speech, of the defining line of madness and of the Enlightenment project of the 'will to truth' are all explored. Particular emphasis has been put on the role of the state, at least in recent centuries, as a disciplinary state, enforcing compliance through discursive means. The metaphor of the Panoptican – the ideal model of a prison where a centrally located warder can observe prisoners, without prisoners in separate wings seeing each other – is used to encapsulate this. So planning language is only allowed into the Panoptican if it has been safely disciplined. The central problem this kind of analysis throws up is how then is any change to be achieved.

Hajer has drawn on Foucault's ideas, and moved on from them to present an analysis of environmental politics which looks at the way that storylines run through political debate, focusing particularly on acid rain politics (1995). These storylines are promulgated through a variety of discursive means and are significant because of the way in which they mesh together different actors involved in a particular policy process. These connections are not found in physical proximity or interpersonal communication – attendance at meetings, correspondence, debate within formal arenas – as with collaborative planning, but through common adoption of the assumptions, concepts and lines of analysis of the storylines. Such discourse coalitions will include members of political coalitions but also those who never meet or are even aware of each other. Yet the widespread adoption of a storyline can add credence to the claims of specific groups and render those of other groups less credible. It also means that certain interests do not need to continually push for their position since the prevailing storyline implies that some of their claims have already been accepted. And this very longevity and independent existence of storylines means that historic coalitions will continue to influence policy development in the present. From this perspective, promoting a new storyline will be a difficult task, involving dismantling previous storylines and confronting the interests who were able to achieve prominence for their claims and viewpoint. Hajer's analysis emphasises the difficulties of achieving change in pursuit of goals which challenge dominant economic and political interests. Thus the conclusion is drawn that concepts such as sustainable development and ecological modernisation only achieve a place on the policy agenda if they do not challenge these interests fundamentally. 'We are all Greens now' (1995, p. 14), but nothing has really changed.

A less structuralist approach to the interaction of power and language is provided by the range of work which draws on focus groups to investigate the ways in which 'lay' and 'expert' groups actively construct meanings around environmental issues and the relative influence of these meanings within the policy process. Following a social constructionist line, this work argues that the ways in which we define issues, understand problems and delimit possible solutions are all active processes that actors engage in, contingent upon the social situation in which they are located (Harrison and Burgess 1994). This actor-centred approach emphasises the interplay of these different understandings within the policy process, the differential 'voice' given to different actors, the implications of labelling certain understandings as 'lay' or 'expert' and the difficulties of constructing a consensus out of the different voices (a point returned to later).

Closely related work on the sociology of scientific knowledge (Irwin, 1995; Wynne, 1996), which often considers environmental issues, has stressed the relationship between lay and expert understandings, so that lay perceptions are determined in part by the prevailing constitution of expert knowledge but also by the extent of trust or scepticism conferred on expertise. It becomes difficult to achieve policy goals when a substantive gap in viewpoints exists between expert and lay constituencies and trust is absent, in part due to the prior exercise of power by the expert groups. Policy recommendations arising from such work usually involve greater acknowledgement of the meaningful knowledge held by lay groups and improved two-way (not one-way) communication between groups to achieve goals. Such a message also comes from the risk communication literature (Muir and Veenendall, 1996). However it is difficult to envisage how communication will effectively close the gap of itself and dispel memories of past inequities.

The second basis of engagement concerns the potential for creating consensus out of conflict, an issue which Allmendinger and Tewdwr-Jones have also examined (1998). Reference has already been made to the work on lay and expert representations which identifies the existence of differently constructed meanings. It may prove difficult to meld these differences into a common commitment to a policy goal. There may not even be agreement between parties as to when a consensus has been reached! Paying attention to communication may be a necessary but certainly not sufficient condition to setting out, let alone achieving agreement on, planning goals. The Habermasian position is that consensus is inherent in the communicative act, although everyday conditions prevent this being realised. However if one drops this assumption – for which there seems to be no supporting evidence – then the issue of conflicts of interest becomes a much more pressing problem. We may have to accept that dissent is inevitable. As Mouffe baldly states, 'all forms of consensus are based on acts of exclusion' (1993, p. 81); and she further argues that we 'need to abandon the illusions of direct democracy and perfect consensus in a completely transparent society' (p. 77). There may even be situations in which dissensus is desirable and performs useful functions; Ingham (1996) provides a case study from Montana, USA, in which the discourse of conflict between actors helped forge the identity of the local community, which had previously been somewhat amorphous and latent.

The problem of the treatment of conflict, particularly within conditions of postmodernity, is one that has been preoccupying much contemporary social political theory. Commentators have found themselves torn in trying to characterise postmodernity politically. On the one hand, some acclaim the benefits of many groups newly finding a voice and identifying the empowerment potential of polyphony, literally 'many voices'. On the other hand, many fear a collapse of solidarity for collective action into a morass of cultural relativism, in which no case can be made for one view above another (and that includes arguments for sustainability), and in which all concepts such as 'justice' or 'truth' are seen as discourse-dependent. As Squires points out, this is ironic since most of those who engage in deconstructing the narrative of modernity do so in the name of marginalised or oppressed groups (or the environment) and, after the event, become concerned 'at the extent to which questions of meaning and interpretation have superseded questions of judgement and value' (Squires, 1993, p. 5).

The discussion around these questions has suggested that much more careful attention needs to be paid to the way in which democracy, in all its forums, deals with difference, in order to find a path between treating everyone identically in the name of universalism and facing a fragmented collection of groups and individuals. Rather, to 'resolve differences in a democratic fashion, a more fluid explicitly relational concept of difference is needed in order to recognize heterogeneity and interspersion of groups' (Squires, 1993, p. 7). As Harvey points out, much of the postmodern fragmentation is the result of the play of power within capitalism, and a free polyphony is unlikely to challenge that (1993).The search is for the possibility of 'togetherness in difference', recognising the existence of injustice and oppression and ensuring that the advocacy of these fundamental values (or any others) is not inconsistent with an allowance for difference. As Squires acknowledges though, postmodernism offers little in the way of concrete guidance on how to achieve this.

There are three possibilities worth exploring to render 'togetherness in difference' more real. First, it has been suggested that reinterpreting difference in terms of community may be helpful. A community is characterised by a common internal identity, which distinguishes members from others and supports claims from the community, but also by the notion of responsibilities which community members owe both to each other and the broader society; duty to the society modifies the notion of community rights. This can be used to embrace the environmental obligations of communities, both internally, globally and over time. Second, considering difference in linguistic terms also encourages the recognition of interconnectedness as well as opposition. Each group may adopt its own discourse in order to enable and reinforce both internal communication and to distinguish that group from others. But that does not preclude communication with others via translation and learning and/ or interactive debate. Communication may not imply consensus but it does imply inter-relation. And third, there is the political programme mapped out by Giddens (1994) for resolving the dilemma of solidarity and difference. This comprises:

- a concern to repair damaged solidarities, recognising reciprocity and interdependence;
- promoting 'active trust' and renewing personal and social responsibility for others;
- focusing on life politics, the politics of lifestyle, not life changes; developing generative politics which allows individuals and groups to make things happen, not just comment;
- creating dialogic democracy in which voices can engage in dialogue and thereby generate not consensus but mutual tolerance and active trust;

- democratising democracy through mobilising social movements and encouraging diversity; and
- rethinking the postwar welfare state.

He should perhaps have added the need to develop recognised means of resolving conflicts which achieve legitimacy, an issue of the design of political institutions and public trust of the state. Similarly while Giddens recognises the importance of 'necessary silence' so that individuals and groups can get on with their lives without continual renegotiation of the conditions for doing so, he does not spell out the enduring necessity of formal safeguards in preserving this necessary silence. This requires that previous negotiations are enshrined in formal rules and institutions which individuals and groups can call on when needed.

The third criticism to be explored concerns the nature of collective action. So far the discussion has stressed the need to include rather than exclude whenever possible, and the problems of managing to achieve an inclusive policy process. However an additional requirement, not acknowledged by collaborative planning, is identified through the focus of public choice theory on collective action problems (Olson, 1978). While Giddens mentions that some people do and indeed should be able to ignore politics if they wish, he never considers the existence of this collective action problem. This argues that the balance of benefits to be gained from engaging in politics as against the costs of such political engagement means that it may not be worthwhile for some individuals or groups to become politically active, either through direct lobbying or collective action. Incorporating collective action problems in the analysis reinforces the need for procedural safeguards for those who do not choose to be empowered for whatever reason. It also suggests an additional strategy, namely the design of institutions which alter the choice situation facing those potentially involved in collective action. Such a strategy has been proposed by Ostrom (1990), whose work on the management of common pool resources has highlighted how institutions can be designed to create and maintain social capital (including the active trust identified by Giddens). This social capital comprises a variety of practices, attitudes and knowledge which enables cooperation to manage the resource in question. In the context of such institutions, the balance of costs and benefits from collaboration that individuals and groups face can be altered so that it is worthwhile engaging in joint management rather than passively being excluded by the collective action problem. Institutions which overcome this problem are various in kind but include common property regimes where property rights are (re)distributed to emphasise interrelationships between actors, the mutual network of rights and responsibilities within a defined group; in effect such a property regime creates and sustains a community as already defined. Property regimes can be a mechanism for creating the communitarian ideal of social relations.

The fourth criticism relates to the role of professions in the policy process, which again is a point that Allmendinger and Tewdwr-Jones (1988) highlight. The justification of professional involvement in the collaborative planning of Healey is twofold. The professional may bring advice and expertise to the policy process, enabling other groups to engage in dialogue on more equal terms. The expertise of the professional becomes a means of empowerment. The second justification arises precisely because the collaborative process may not yield a consensus or it may yield a consensus which does not accord with what was considered the desirable policy direction. Consider the situation where an empowering dialogue within a local community has been sensitively facilitated by professionals attuned to the language of different subcommunities and offering up their specialist knowledge and expertise. What if the community decide on a path which the professional deems unsustainable? It can be argued that the professional can be the guiding light for public interest policy goals such as sustainability, talking others into the desired values and outcomes.

This raises several questions about such professionals. What of the interests of professionals as a group, which may constrain any programme for reform, particularly where genuine empowerment for other groups is involved? Why should professionals give up their control or at least influence over decision-making? The public choice approach has pointed out how state bureaucrats, which many of these professionals are, may skew public policy in pursuit of their interests, as measured by budgets and status (Dunleavy, 1991). Perhaps value systems can overcome such simple self-interest. But what are the values that professionals bring to the policy process? Do they incorporate a commitment to empowerment? How do professionals accommodate these to other values they may hold, such as equity, redistribution, aesthetic quality or economic regeneration? And finally, there is the matter of the expertise which some professional groups may bring to the process. The expertise claims of generalists within the policy process may be suspect for their lack of grounding in specific specialisms. Professionals may be called on to mediate but where are their skills in this task? And isn't this a job for the political system? All these issues of sectional interests, values and claims to expertise are compounded by the formal processes of professionalisation which many policy actors go through (Evans and Rydin, 1997).

A particularly pertinent point in the 1990s and beyond is the question of how the view of the planner within collaborative planning, with its emphasis on the use of discretion, active negotiation and broking of deals, fits with the post-Nolan view of public sector employees. The Nolan

Committee reports on public life have emphasised the need for accountability and reinforced the audit culture within the public sector, whereby paper evidence for policy actions must be available. It is not clear how the collaborative planner could operate within these conditions; there appear to be tensions between the need for flexibility and the need for accountability. As Innes has shown (1996), the outcomes of collaborative processes are often reached by a circuitous route in which it is not always apparent who is responsible for which decision and during which individual actors may take on many different roles. The outcome is collective and it can be justified *post hoc*, but the process may not be as transparent as Nolan envisages.

Therefore, however attractive collaborative planning may appear, particularly to planners, there are question marks over it theoretically and practically. The critique should, hopefully, take the discussion of planning forwards rather than backwards though. Collaborative planning emphasises the need to consider the range of interests within planning and how they are involved. But the interests of planners themselves also need to be considered. The question of safeguards within the planning system needs to be set alongside the consideration of arenas and procedures for democratic decision-making, which recognise and allow for: difference; the current exercise of power by sectional interests including through the use of language; the limited capacity of professionals; and the collective action problem. This suggests the need for specific institutions to support communities and overcome the collective action problem, perhaps even with common property regimes. It also suggests requirements for formal public safeguards within the policy process on: access to information and decision-making arenas; recognition of status within the policy process; and rights of redress, safeguards which also allow action against professionals within the policy process. The emphasis here is on providing a 'safe' institutional context within which new norms, values and ways of talking can develop.

■ The role of the plan

The discussion so far has focused on the process of planning. What of the plan? Is there still a place for strategy in planning and if so what form should that strategy take? This final section looks at the role of the plan and the associated issue of incrementalism.

It can be argued that one of the failures of planning has been its pursuit of rather grandiose visions of the future, visions which it was in any case incapable of implementing. The pursuit of a comprehensive goal resulted in many interests being ignored during the process of attempted implementation and the mistakes that resulted were on a similarly grandiose scale. The critique of procedural planning theory in the 1970s emphasised the dangers of this approach. Therefore, a relevant question for contemporary planning is the form that the plan should take. In effect this involves giving meaning to the type of order that planning is seeking to achieve, bearing in mind the rationale for planning given at the start of this chapter.

A plan or strategy can take many different forms. At one end of the spectrum is the view of a strategy as a mission statement or vision which sets objectives but little in the way of detail concerning how those objectives are to be achieved. Such a strategy indicates that policy should be goal-driven and it is generally recognised that to be effective the strategy should be the manifestation of a consensus among key policy actors. The need to build consensus emphasises the view of relationships between key actors in terms of communication, identification of common interests and the broking of mutually acceptable policy solutions, that is, the basic view of collaborative planning. Networking and partnerships are common ways of describing such relationships. The danger, in this view, is that the strategy is defined only in terms of the currently achievable consensus and the needs of the contemporary partnership, with the longer term being sacrificed. Could such an approach establish a consensus on and a real commitment to protecting the environment for future generations? Another factor is that implementation, in this model, may be devolved to various partners. Their involvement in the partnership should ensure that all parties 'own' the strategy and that implementation should follow from the development of the strategy, but problems of achieving objectives can still arise.

At the opposite end of the spectrum, there is the view of a strategy as a detailed plan which not only sets out objectives but also details the mechanisms by which the objectives are to be realised. The result may be a master plan or blueprint in the sense of a thorough picture of the future state of an area or some particular aspect of planning in that area. This version of a strategy raises issues of whether the powers exist to implement this detailed picture and can suggest, in turn, a view of the relationships between key actors which is hierarchical. Past experience, particularly in land use planning, suggests that hierarchical relationships have the potential for conflict between parties. The development of any strategy at the level of a higher tier requires attention to the ways in which that strategy may be implemented. There is a potential tension here, between implementing a broader view and maintaining good relations between the tiers of governance.

Between these extremes there is the possibility to identify a strategy which builds on short-term alliances and agreements and yet develops a longer-term view with some broader policy goals. It could combine the local partnership with some goals originating from the centre. One good model for this approach is that developed as part of the work on the Biodiversity Action Plan, arising from the Biodiversity Convention agreed at the Rio Summit. This model suggests that strategies should be limited to identifying:

- clear goals and specific targets for the policy area;
- potential mechanisms for achieving these targets;
- the lead agencies charged with implementing the strategy to achieve the targets and developing detailed plans; and
- any resource implications of the strategy.

Such a strategy would be developed by a partnership specific to the issue involved, so that all relevant parties would 'own' the strategy. The result should be a consistent and coordinated document which has consensual support and builds on any existing strategies and alliances between groups. However, the emphasis on targets against which policy can be monitored provides a stricter framework than the looser-vision documents of many existing partnerships.

There might be some concern that such an approach is unable to deliver substantial change in policy direction that could result either from a strong plan backed by top-down powers or an emphasis on the immediately achievable results identified by a limited coalition. A distinction, therefore, needs to be drawn between the types of policy that are seeking to alter the context for decisions and those where the emphasis is on decisions on a more specific project, site, case or initiative. The context for any detailed form of planning usually needs to be set at the central level through policy which structures economic decision-making: setting taxes and subsidies; allocating property rights; establishing the basis on which markets operate. Chapter 14 has repeatedly shown this to be the case. Changing this context will be the most effective way of achieving substantial and rapid change. But within this overall context, more detailed planning can help achieve specific objectives. They can do so more effectively where a phased approach is adopted, with interim targets being set and policy achievements monitored against them. This is, in effect, a form of planned incrementalism (Rydin, 1998b).

■ So to conclude . . .

What is not needed is a plan-making process which is time-consuming and expensive, which emphasises the 'big policy issues' but which cannot effectively address them. There is little point in strategies which cannot be implemented due to lack of appropriate policy tools and which cannot be assessed for lack of data on urban, regional and environmental change. Neither should the emphasis within the planning process suggest open, democratic debate and the pursuit of consensus when the activities of a short-term goal-oriented coalition are actually involved. Above all, planning should not contribute to a form of diversionary politics, where attention is focused away from the most serious issues facing us. Rather planning should aim for strategies which set out specific goals that are based on a consensus among key actors but not thereby limited to the lowest common denominator of planning politics. There needs to be flexibility in thinking on how to achieve those goals and the encouragement of innovation to suggest new paths towards them. Planning tools which have proved effective in the past should be emphasised and throughout there should be more monitoring of outcomes against specific criteria, targets or indicators derived from the goals. This requires data and monitoring systems.

Within this framework, the ideas of collaborative planning can prove fruitful. These include: the emphasis on developing organisations for collaboration and looking at the modes of communication, but always remembering that this may not be sufficient; the pursuit of consensus but not at the expense of either long-term and broader goals or the protection of weaker voices within the planning debate; the encouragement of voice within planning but not forgetting the collective action problem, that the most powerful often shout the loudest and that too many voices can be problematic as well. Planning can provide a space for debate on important policy issues. But in practice, it rarely leads to consensus. Neither does planning readily achieve a shift of resources towards the least well-off. Planning activities will always be constrained by the prevailing distribution of resources and the use of those resources to exercise power. The effective path to altering this lies in action at the central level to redistribute resources through a variety of means, principally fiscal measures and allocating property rights. What planning can do is give more of a voice to those who routinely bear the costs of environmental change. This may help protect those groups in the face of economic and social change and mitigate the inequitable results of planning decisions.

Since participation carries burdens and those with the most to gain financially and politically have already, by and large, ensured their place in the participatory processes of planning, the least the planning system should offer in these cases is the right to challenge the state when decisions are judged unequitable and undesirable by the community affected. For not every group can be included within a participatory schema and the right of an excluded group (even if excluded by their own choice for passivity) to challenge planning decisions remains an important principle of open planning. Allowing challenges to planning from outside, rather than just changing planning practice from within, may prove the most effective means of shaping a planning system for the twenty first century. For planning has not to date been able to overcome the barriers towards achieving its progressive potential. As Healey (1992a, p. 43) says: 'the weakness of the system lies in the limited powers available to citizens, and all those economic, environmental and social interests which do not have a property interest in a specific site, to challenge political and administrative decisions'. Yet planners continue to make statements which emphasise both their ability to manage many aspects of built and natural environmental change and the intention to do so in the name of the public interest, balancing interests and protecting the least powerful groups. Thus many current activities within the planning system are diversionary, appearing to promote social change but making only limited moves in practice. The language of apparent commitment is at least as important to the analyst of planning as the substantive outcomes on social groups. Indeed the diversionary nature of much planning activity is a contributory factor in preventing further movement towards redistribution and openness.

There are good reasons why planning should contain elements which are essentially diversionary. The planning system has characteristics of a bureaucracy and bureaucrats do seek to extend their arenas of influence. Given the weaknesses of many planning tools and hence the problems in achieving stated planning goals, there are incentives to extend planning activity in other directions. Vested interests will usually exist who benefit from an area of planning activity and will lend support to its maintenance and even extension. This means that a critique of planning and planners is an essential part of a move towards a planning system which fulfils its progressive potential. Complacency is perhaps the most dangerous feature of a planning system in this respect. It is not the ambition or scope of the planning system which necessarily needs to be questioned. Rather, the operation of planning in all its facets needs to be criticised from outside and inside. Indeed robust internal criticism is likely to render the planning system more able to stand up to external criticism, a problem it has faced in the past. Self-criticism will raise questions of performance in the various sectors of the planning system and, more important, of priorities. The essential and diversionary elements of the planning system can then be disentangled. Such self-criticism is being institutionalised in the form of audits and assessments of planning activity. While such activities can themselves be criticised for the time and resources they consume, they may offer the scope to an internal reassessment of planning which identifies the diversionary elements and prepares the way for a change of emphasis within planning. This assumes, of course, that the goal against which planning is audited and assessed includes redistributive and democratic aims.

For such an assessment not to degenerate into another futile, bureaucratic procedure, it needs to operate in the context of debate. Such debate may occur in many different arenas: community, professional, political, and academic. Implicit in all such debate, as this book has tried to argue, are one or more theoretical views on planning, the role of the state, professionals and the public, and the relation between planning and the market. Even if not explicitly stated, there is a theoretical stance behind statements and views. This is, I believe, to be welcomed, not deprecated. Theories help us organise our ideas and relate them one to another. They link general issues about our society to specific issues of concern within a particular planning situation. Most important, theories exist in opposition to each other and holding one theoretical viewpoint inevitably involves conflict with others. Debate is intrinsic to theoretical discussion and theoretical debate should underpin the ongoing assessment of planning. In this hope, the interaction of theory, policy, procedure and data in this book is offered to the reader, with a view to stimulating debate and argument about the British planning system.

■ Further reading

Readers may care to look at Blowers and Evans (1997) which contains a number of views of how planning should develop towards the twenty-first century.

Bibliography

Academic texts and selected HMSO publications only are included in this bibliography. The numerous specific policy documents and various documents of largely historic interest are detailed in the text itself. The place of publication is London unless otherwise stated.

Adam Smith Institute (1983) *Omega Report on Local Government Policy* (ASI).

Adams, D. (1994) *Urban Planning and the Development Process* (UCL Press).

Allmendinger, P. and Tewdwr-Jones, M. (1998) 'Deconstructing communicative rationality: a critique of Habermasian collaborative planning', *Environment and Planning A*.

Ambrose, P. (1986) *Whatever Happened to Planning?* (Methuen).

Ambrose, P. and Colenutt, B. (1975) *The Property Machine* (Penguin).

Amin, A. and Thrift, N. (eds) (1995) *Globalisation, Institutions and Regional Development in Europe* (Oxford: OUP).

Andrews, J. (1990) 'The relationship between agriculture and wildlife', in J. Bowers (ed.), *Agriculture and Rural Land Use: Into the 1990s* (Swindon: ESRC) pp. 58–69.

Armstrong, J. (1985) *The Sizewell Report: A New Approach for Major Public Inquiries* (TCPA).

Arnstein, S. (1969) 'A ladder of citizen participation', *Journal of American Institute of Planners*, 35 (4) pp. 216–24.

Ashworth, W. (1954) *The Genesis of Modern British Town Planning* (Routledge & Kegan Paul).

Atkinson, R. and Moon, G. (1994) *Urban Policy in Britain* (Macmillan).

Audit Commission (1992) *Building in Quality: A Study of Development Control* (HMSO).

Bailey, N. (1991) 'Community Development Trusts: an essential component of urban regeneration strategies', paper presented to AESOP Congress, Oxford Polytechnic, June.

Bailey, N. with Barker, A. and MacDonald, K. (1995) *Partnership Agencies in British Urban Policy* (UCL Press).

Baker, S., Kousis, M., Richardson, D. and Young, S. (1997) *The Politics of Sustainable Development: Theory, Policy and Practice within the European Union* (Routledge).

Balchin, P. and Bull, G. (1987) *Regional and Urban Economics* (Harper & Row).

Ball, M. (1984) *Housing Policy and Economic Power* (Methuen).

—— (1988) *Rebuilding Construction* (Routledge).

Barnes, I. And Preston, J. (1985) 'The Scunthorpe Enterprise Zone: an example of muddled interventionism', *Public Administration*, 63, pp. 171—81.

Barrett, S. and Fudge, C. (eds) (1981) *Policy and Action* (Methuen).

Baumol, W. and Oates, W. (1975) *The Theory of Environmental Policy* (Englewood Clifs, NJ: Prentice-Hall).

Beck, L. (1989) 'Farm waste pollution', in Institute of Water Engineers and Managers, *Agriculture and the Environment*, Technical Papers of Annual Symposium, University of York (IWEM) pp. 5.1–5.24.

Bennie, L. and Maloney, W. (1996) 'Representing the Green identity: a party and pressure group compared', paper to Political Studies Association Annual Conference, University of Glasgow, April.

Biodiversity Steering Group (1995) *Biodiversity: The UK Steering Group Report*, Vols 1 and 2 (HMSO).

Blowers, A. (1987) 'Transition or transformation? Environmental policy under Thatcher', *Public Administration*, 65, pp. 277–94.

—— (1995) 'Nuclear waste disposal: a technical problem in search of a political solution', in T. Gray (ed.), *UK Environmental Policy in the 1990s* (Macmillan) pp. 210—36.

Blowers, A. and Evans, B. (eds) (1997) *Town Planning into the 21st Century* (Routledge).

Blowers, A., Lowry, D. and Solomon, B. D. (1991) *The International Politics of Nuclear Waste* (Macmillan).

Blunkett, D. and Jackson, K. (1987) *Democracy in Crisis: The Town Halls Respond* (Hogarth Press).

Boddy, M. and Fudge, C. (eds) (1984) *Local Socialism? Labour Councils and New Left Alternatives* (Macmillan).

Bomberg, E. (1996) 'Greens in the European Parliament', *Environmental Politics*, 5 (2) pp. 324–31.

Bovaird, T. (1992) 'Local economic development and the city', *Urban Studies*, 29 (3/4) pp. 343–68.

Bowers, J. (1990) 'The consequences of declining support for agriculture', in J. Bowers (ed.), *Agriculture and Rural Land Use: Into the 1990s* (Swindon: ESRC) pp. 23–34.

Bramley, G., Bartlett, W. and Lambert, C. (1995) *Planning, the Market and Private Housebuilding* (UCL Press).

Braybrooke, D. and Lindblom, C. (1963) *A Strategy of Decision: Policy Evaluation as a Social Process* (Collier-Macmillan).

Breheny, M. (1995) 'The compact city and transport energy consumption', *Transactions of the Institute of British Geographers*, 20 (1) pp. 81–101.

Breheny, M. and Congdon, P. (eds) (1989) *Growth and Change in a Core Region* (Pion).

Breheny, M., Gordon, I. and Archer, S. (1997) 'Can planning for a more sustainable city secure sustainable levels of urban travel in the London region?', paper to ESRC London Seminar, London School of Economics, January.

Brindley, T., Rydin, Y. and Stoker, G. (1996) *Remaking Planning* (Routledge).

Broadbent, T. A. (1977) *Planning and Profit in the Urban Economy* (Methuen).

Brownill, S. (1990) *Developing London's Dockland* (Paul Chapman).

Brugman, J. (1997) 'Is there a method in our measurement? The use of indicators in local sustainable development planning', *Local Environment*, 2 (1) pp. 59–72.

Bruton, M. and Nicholson, D. (1987) *Local Planning in Practice* (Hutchinson).

Bryson, J. and Crosby, B. (1993) 'Policy planning and the design of forums, arenas and courts', *Environment and Planning B*, 20 (2), pp. 223—52.

Buck, N., Gordon, I., Young, K. with Ermish, J. and Mills, L. (1986) *The London Employment Problem* (Oxford: Oxford University Press).

Buckwell, A. (1990) 'Economic signals, farmers' response and environmental change', in J. Bowers (ed.), *Agriculture and Rural Land Use: Into the 1990s* (Swindon: ESRC) pp. 7–22.

Burke, T. (1995) 'View from the inside: UK environmental policy seen from a practitioner's perspective', in T. Gray (ed.), *UK Environmental Policy in the 1990s* (Macmillan) pp. 11–17.

Burkitt, B. (1984) *Radical Political Economy* (Brighton: Wheatsheaf).

Burns, D. (1988) 'The decentralisation of local authority planning', paper to Radical Planning Initiatives Conference, Polytechnic of Central London, January.

Burns, D., Hambleton, R. and Hoggett, P. (1994) *The Politics of Decentralisation* (Macmillan).

Butt Philip, A. and Gray, O. (eds) (1996) *Directory of Pressure Groups in the European Union*, 2nd edn (Cartermill Publishing).

Button, K. (1995) 'UK environmental policy and transport', in T. Gray (ed.), *UK Environmental Policy in the 1990s* (Macmillan) pp. 173–88.

Byrne, T. (1986) *Local Government in Britain* (Penguin).

Carr, S. and Tait, J. (1990) 'Farmers' attitude to consumption', *Built Environment*, 16 (3) pp. 218–31.

Carter, N., Brown, T. and Abbott, T. (1991) *The Relationship between Expenditure-based Plans and Development Plans*, Final Report, School of the Built Environment, Leicester Polytechnic.

Castells, M. (1977) *The Urban Question*, English edn (Edward Arnold).

—— (1978) *City, Class and Power* (Macmillan).

—— (1983) *The City and the Grass Roots: A Cross-Cultural Theory of Urban Social Movements* (Edward Arnold).

Chapman, R. A. (1984) *Leadership in the British Civil Service* (Croom Helm).

Cherry, G. (1972) *Urban Change and Planning* (Henley on Thames: Foulis).

—— (1974) *The Evolution of British Town Planning* (1914–74) (Lawrence Hill).

—— (1996) *Town Planning in Britain since 1900* (Oxford: Blackwell).

Child, J. (1977) *Organization: A Guide to Problems and Practice* (Harper & Row).

Christensen, T. (1979) *Neighbourhood Survival* (Prism).

Clark, M. and Herington, J. (1988) *The Role of EA in the Planning Process* (Mansell).

Clotworthy, J. and Harris, N. (1996) 'Planning policy implications of local government reorganisation', in M. Tewdwr-Jones (ed.), *British Planning Policy in Transition* (UCL Press) pp. 100–23.

Collins, R. (1990) 'Changing conceptions in the sociology of the professions', in R. Torstendahl and M. Burrage (eds), *The Formation of Professions: Knowledge, State and Strategy* (Sage) pp. 11–23.

Cooke, P. (1983) Theories of Planning and Spatial Development (Hutchinson)

Cooke, P. (1989) 'The local question – revival or survival?', in P. Cooke (ed.), *Localities* (Unwin Hyman) pp. 296–306.

Cox, A. (1984) *Adversary Politics and Land* (Cambridge: Cambridge University Press).

Crabtree, J. R. (1991) 'National Park designation in Scotland', *Land Use Policy*, 8 (3) pp. 241–52.

Cullingworth, J. B. (1975a) *Environmental Planning Vol. 1: Reconstruction and Land Use Planning 1939–47* (HMSO).

—— (1975b) *Environmental Planning Vol. 2: National Parks and Recreation in the Countryside* (HMSO).

—— (1979) *Environmental Planning Vol. 3: New Town Policies* (HMSO).

—— (1980) *Environmental Planning Vol. 4: Land Values, Compensation and Betterment* (HMSO).

—— (1988) *Town and Country Planning* (Unwin Hyman).

Cullingworth, J. B. and Nadin, V. (1994) *Town and Country Planning in Britain*, 11th edn (Routledge).

Daly, H. (1992) *Steady State Economics*, 2nd edn (Earthscan).

Davies, H., Edwards, D., Roberts, C., Rosborough, L. and Sales, R. (1986) *The Relationship between Development Plans and Development Control and Appeals*, Working Papers in Land Management and Development Nos 10, 11, 12, Department of Land Management, University of Reading.

Davies, J. (1972) *The Evangelistic Bureaucrat* (Tavistock).

Dearlove, J. (1973) *The Politics of Policy in Local Government* (Cambridge: Cambridge University Press).

de la Court, T. (1990) *Beyond Brundtland* (Zed).

Dennis, N. (1972) *Public Participation and Planner's Blight* (Faber).

Desai, M. (1979) *Marxian Economics* (Oxford: Basil Blackwell).

Dobson, A. (1995) *Green Political Thought* 2nd edn (Routledge).

DoE (1988) *Enterprise Zones Information 1987/8* (HMSO).

—— (1991a) *Policy Appraisal and the Environment* (HMSO).

—— (1991b) *Environmental Assessment: A Guide to the Procedures* (HMSO).

—— (1991c) *Monitoring Environmental Assessment and Planning* (HMSO).

—— (1992) *Derelict Land Grant – Developments and Achievements Report 1988–92* (DoE).

—— (1993a) *Making Markets Work for the Environment* (HMSO).

—— (1993b) *Environmental Assessment of Development Plans: A Good Practice Guide* (HMSO).

—— (1995a) *PPG13: A Good Practice Guide* (HMSO).

—— (1995b) *Preparation of Environmental Statements for Planning Projects That Require Environmental Assessment: A Good Practice Guide* (HMSO).

—— (1995c) *Making Waste Work*, Cm 3040 (HMSO).

DoE/Welsh Office (1986) *River Quality in England and Wales 1985* (HMSO).

Doran, P. (1996) 'The UN Commission on sustainable development', *Environmental Politics*, 5 (1) pp. 100–7.

Dowding, K. (1995a) 'Model or metaphor? A critical review of the policy network approach', *Political Studies*, 43 (1) pp. 136–58.

—— (1995b) *The Civil Service* (Routledge).

Dryzeck, J. (1996) *Democracy in Capitalist Times* (Oxford: OUP).

Dunleavy, P. (1980) *Urban Political Analysis* (Macmillan).

—— (1981) *The Politics of Mass Housing in Britain 1945–75* (Oxford: Clarendon Press).

—— (1991) *Democracy, Bureaucracy and Public Choice* (Hemel Hempstead: Harvester Wheatsheaf).

Dunleavy, P. and O'Leary, B. (1987) *Theories of the State: The Politics of Liberal Democracy* (Macmillan).

Ecotec Research and Consulting Ltd. with Transportation Planning Associates (1993) *Reducing Transport Emissions through Planning* (HMSO)

Eggertson, T. (1990) *Economic Behaviour and Institutions* (Cambridge: Cambridge University Press).

Elkin, S. (1974) *Politics and Land Use Planning: The London Experience* (Cambridge: Cambridge University Press).

Elkington, J. (1987) *The Green Capitalists: How Industry Can Make Money and Protect the Environment* (Gollancz).

Elsom, D. (1996) *Smog Alert* (Earthscan).

Elson, M. (1986) *Green Belts* (Heinemann).

Engels, F. (1969) *The condition of the Working Class in England* (first published in 1892) (St Albans: Panther)

English Heritage (1992) *Buildings at Risk: A Sample Survey* (English Heritage).

English Historic Towns Forum (1992) *Townscape in Trouble* (Butterworths).

Ennis, F. (1996) 'The implementation of planning obligations', *Planning Practice and Research*, 11 (4) pp. 349–64.

Evans, A. (1973) *The Economics of Residential Location* (Macmillan).

—— (1987) 'House Prices and Land Prices in the South East' – a Review', paper prepared for the House Builders' Federation, HD87.308 (HBF).

Evans, B. and Rydin, Y. (1997) 'Planning, professionalism and sustainability' in A. Blowers and B. Evans (eds), *Town Planning into the 21st Century* (Routledge) pp. 55–70.

Fairley, J. (1992) 'Scottish local authorities and local enterprise companies: a developing relationship?', *Regional Studies*, 26 (2) pp. 193–207.

Faludi, A. (1973) *Planning Theory* (Oxford: Pergamon).

Faludi, A. (ed.) (1973) *A Reader in Planning Theory* (Oxford: Pergamon).

Faulks, J. (1991) 'The changing attitude towards liability for damage to the environment under European Community law', *European Environment*, 1 (3) pp. 17–20.

Fennell, R. (1990) 'Socio-structural initiatives under the CAP', in J. Bowers (ed.), *Agriculture and Rural Land Use: Into the 1990s* (Swindon: ESRC) pp. 91–102.

Foley, D. (1960) 'British town planning: one ideology or three?', *British Journal of Sociology*, 11 (3) pp. 211–31.

Forester, J. (1989) *Planning in the Face of Power* (Berkeley: University of California Press).

Fortlage, C. (1990) *Environmental Assessment: Or Practical Guide* (Aldershot: Gower).

Foucault, M. (1984) *The Care of the Self: The History of Sexuality*, Vol. 3 (trans. R. Hurley) (Penguin).

Foulsham, J. (1987) 'Women's needs and planning practice: a critical evaluation of recent local authority practice', paper to Radical Planning Initiatives Workshop, Polytechnic of Central London, January.

Fraser, W. (1984) *Principles of Property Investment and Pricing* (Macmillan).

Freidson, E. (1984) 'Are professions necessary?' in T. Haskell (ed.), *The Authority of Experts* (Bloomington: Indiana University Press).

Friends of the Earth (1992) *Environmentally Sensitive Areas: Assessment and Recommendations* (FoE).

Galbraith, J. (1981) *The Galbraith Reader*, selected by the editors of *Gambit* (Penguin).

Game, C. (1997) 'How many, when, where and how? Taking stock of local government reorganisation', *Local Government Policy Making*, 23 (4) pp. 3–9.

Gandy, M. (1994) *Recycling and the Politics of Urban Waste* (Earthscan).

Gatenby, I. and Williams, C. (1996) 'Interpreting planning law', in M. Tewdwr-Jones (ed.), *British Planning Policy in Transition* (UCL Press) pp. 137–54.

Geddes, P. (1905) *Civics as Applied Sociology*, reprinted in H. Meller (ed.), *The Ideal City* (Leicester: Leicester University Press).

—— (1949) *Cities in Evolution* (first published 1915) (Williams & Norgate Ltd).

Gibbs, D. (1994) 'Towards the sustainable city: greening the local economy', *Town Planning Review*, 65 (1) pp. 99–109.

—— (1996) 'On course for a sustainable future? European environmental policy and local economic development', *Local Environment*, 1 (3) pp. 247–58.

Giddens, A. (1994) *Beyond Left and Right: The Future of Radical Politics* (Cambridge: Polity Press).

Gissurarson, H. (1984) 'The only truly progressive policy', in N. Barry *et al.*, *Hayek's* Serfdom *Revisited* (IEA).

Glasson, J., Therivel, R. and Chadwick, A. (1994) *Introduction to Environmental Impact Assessment* (UCL Press).

Godschalk, D. (1991) 'Negotiating intergovernmental development policy conflicts: practice-based guidelines', paper to AESOP Conference, Oxford Polytechnic, July.

Goldsmith, F. and Warren, A. (eds.) (1993) *Conservation in Progress* (Chichester: Wiley).

Golub, J. (1996) 'British sovereignty and the development of EC environmental policy', *Environmental Politics*, 5 (4) pp. 700–28.

Goodchild, B. (1990) 'Planning and the modern/postmodern debate', *Town Planning Review*, 61 (2) pp. 119–37.

Goodwin, M. and Painter, J. (1997) 'Local governance, the crisis of Fordism and the changing geographies of regulation', *Transactions of the Institute of British Geographers*, 22 (4) pp. 635–48.

Gore, T. and Nicholson, D. (1991) 'Models of the land-development process: a critical review', *Environment and Planning* A, 23, pp. 705–30.

Graham, J. (1992) 'Post-Fordism as politics: the political consequences of narratives on the left', *Environment and Planning D: Society and Space*, 10, pp. 393–410

Granovetter, M. and Swedberg, R. (1992) *The Sociology of Economic Life* (Boulder, Colorado: Westview Press).

Gray, J. (1984) 'The road to Serfdom: 40 years on', in N. Barry *et al.*, *Hayek's* Serfdom *revisited* (IEA).

Gray, T. (1995) *UK Environmental Policy in the 1990s* (Macmillan).

Greed, C. (1991) *Surveying Sisters* (Routledge).

—— (1994) *Women and Planning: Creating Gendered Realities* (Routledge).

—— (1996) *Implementing Town Planning: The Role of Town Planning in the Development Process* (Longman).

Grimley J.R. Eve in association with Thames Polytechnic and Alsop Wilkinson (1992) *The Use of Planning Agreements* (HMSO).

Gyford, J. (1985) *The Politics of Local Socialism* (Allen & Unwin).

—— (1991) *Citizens, Consumers and Councils* (Macmillan).

Hague, C. (1984) *The Development of Planning Thought: A Critical Perspective* (Hutchinson).

Hajer, M. (1995) *The Politics of Environmental Discourse* (Oxford: OUP).

Hall, P., Gracey, H., Drewett, R., and Thomas, R. (1973) *The Containment of Urban England* (Allen & Unwin).

Hall, P. and Taylor, R. (1996) 'Political science and the three new institutionalisms', *Political Studies*, XLIIV, pp. 936–57.

Hall, S. (1988) *The Hard Road to Renewal: Thatcherism and the Crisis of the Left* (Verve).

Hallett, S., Hanley, N., Moffatt, I. and Taylor-Duncan, K. (1991) 'UK water pollution control: a review of legislation and practice', *European Environment*, 1 (3) pp. 7–13.

Hambleton, R. and Hoggett, P. (eds) (1984) *The Politics of Decentralisation*, Working Paper No. 46, School for Advanced Urban Studies, University of Bristol.

Harding, A. (1990) 'Property interests and urban growth coalitions in the UK: a brief encounter', paper to Property-led Urban Regeneration Seminar, University of Newcastle, March.

—— (1994) 'Urban regimes and growth machines: towards a cross-national research agenda', *Urban Affairs Quarterly*, 29 (3) pp. 356–82.

Harrison, A. (1977) *Economics and Land Use Planning* (Newbury: Policy Journals).

Harrison, C. and Burgess, J. 1994) 'Social construction of nature: a case study of conflicts over the development of Rainham Marshes', *Transactions of Institute of British Geographers*, 19 (3) pp. 291–310.

Harvey, D. (1973) *Social Justice and the City* (Edward Arnold).

—— (1985) *The Urbanisation of Capital* (Oxford: Basil Blackwell).

—— (1989) *The Condition of Postmodernity* (Oxford: Basil Blackwell).

—— (1993) 'Class relations, social justice and the politics of difference', in J. Squires (ed.), *Principled Positions* (Lawrence & Wishart).

—— (1996) *Justice, Nature and the Geography of Difference* (Oxford: Blackwell).

Hassan, J. (1995) 'The impact of European Union environmental policy on water industry reform', *European Environment*, 5 pp. 45–51.

Hasselgren, J. (1982) 'What is living and what is dead in the work of Patrick Geddes', in *Patrick Geddes: A Symposium*, Occasional Paper in Town and Regional Planning, Duncan of Jordanstone College of Art/University of Dundee.

Hastings, A. (1996) 'Unraveling the process of "partnership" in urban regeneration policy', *Urban Studies*, 33, pp. 253–68.

Hayek, F. (1944) *The Road to Serfdom* (Routledge & Kegan Paul).

Hazardous Waste Inspectorate (1988) *Third Report* (HMSO).

Healey, P. (1983) *Local Plans in British Land Use Planning* (Oxford: Pergamon).

—— (1990) 'Policy processes in planning', *Policy and Politics*, 18 (1) pp. 91–103.

—— (1992a) 'An institutional model of the development process', *Journal of Property Research*, 9 (1) pp. 33–44.

—— (1992b) 'A planner's day: knowledge and action in communicative practice', *American Planning Association Journal*, Winter, pp. 9–20.

—— (1997) *Collaborative Planning: Shaping Places in Fragmented Societies* (Macmillan).

Healey, P. and Barrett, S. (1990) 'Structure and agency in land and property development processes: some ideas for research', *Urban Studies*, 27 (1) pp. 89–104.

Healey, P. and Gilroy, R. (1990) 'Towards a people-sensitive planning', *Planning Practice and Research*, 5 (2) pp. 21–29.

Healey, P. and Nabarro, R. (eds) (1990) *Land and Property Development in a Changing Context* (Aldershot: Gower).

Healey, P., McDougall, G. and Thomas, M. (eds) (1982) *Planning Theory: Prospects for the 1980s* (Oxford: Pergamon).

Healey, P., Davis, J., Wood, M. and Elson, M. (1982) *The Implementation of Development Plans*, report of an exploratory study for DoE (Oxford Polytechnic, Department of Town Planning).

Healey, P., McNamara, P., Elson, M. and Doak, A. (1988) *Land Use Planning and the Mediation of Urban Change* (Cambridge: Cambridge University Press).

Healey, P., Purdue, M. and Ennis, F. (1995) *Negotiating Planning Gain* (E & FN Spon).

Hebbert, M. (1982) 'Retrospective on the Outlook Tower', in *Patrick Geddes: A Symposium*, Occasional Paper in Town and Regional Planning, Duncan of Jordanstone College of Art/University of Dundee.

Heilbronner, R. (1983) *The Worldly Philosophers* (Penguin).

Heiman, M. K. (1996) 'Race, waste and class: new perspectives on environmental justice', *Antipode*, 28 (2) pp. 111–21.

Herington, J. (1984) *The Outer City* (Harper & Row).

HMIP (Her Majesty's Inspectorate of Pollution) (1991) *Fourth Annual Report (1990–91)* (HMSO).

Hobbs, P. (1992) 'The economic determinants of post-war British town planning', *Progress in Planning*, 38 (3) pp. 180–300.

Hodgson, G. (1988) *Economics and Institutions* (Cambridge: Polity Press).

Holder, J. (ed.) (1997) *The Impact of EC Environmental Law in the UK* (Chichester: Wiley).

HRF (Housing Research Foundation) (1986) *Impact of UDG/DLG on Urban Dwelling and Greenfield Development*, report by Coopers & Lybrand Association (HRF).

Howard, E. (1902) *Garden Cities of Tomorrow* (Swan Sonnenschein & Co.).

Howells, P. and Rydin, Y. (1990) 'The case for property investment and the implications of a unitized property market', *Land Development Studies* 7 pp. 15–30.

Imrie, R. and Thomas, H. (eds) (1993) *British Urban Policy and the Urban Development Corporations* (Paul Chapman Publishing).

Ingham, Z. (1996) 'Landscape, drama and dissensus: the rhetorical education of Red Lodge, Montana', in C. Herndl and S. Brown (eds), *Green Culture* (Madison: University of Wisconsin Press).

Innes, J. (1996) 'Consensus building as role-playing and bricolage: toward a theory of Collaborative planning', paper for ACSP/AESOP Congress, Toronto, Canada, July.

Investment Property Databank (1997) *Annual Report* (IPD).

Irwin, A. (1995) *Citizen Science: A Study of People, Expertise and Sustainable Development* (Routledge).

Jacobs, J. (1985) 'The Urban Development Grant', *Policy and Politics*, 13 (2) pp. 191–9.

Jacobs, M. (1994) 'The limits to neoclassicism: towards an institutional environmental economics', in M. Redclift and T. Benton (eds), *Social Theory and the Global Environment* (Routledge).

—— (1997) *Making Sense of Environmental Capacity* (CPRE).

Jessop, B. (1990) *State Theory: Putting the Capitalist State in its Place* (Cambridge: Polity Press).

Johnson, S. (1973) *The Politics of the Environment* (Tom Stacey).

Johnson, T. (1972) *Professions and Power* (Macmillan).

—— (1993) 'Expertise and the state', in M. Gare and T. Johnson (eds), *Foucault's New Domains* (Routledge) pp. 139–52.

Johnston, R. (1989) *Environmental Problems: Nature, Economy and State* (Belhaven).

Johnston, R. and Pattic, C. (1996) 'Intra-local conflict, public opinion and local government restructuring in England, 1993–5', *Geoforum*, 27 (1) pp. 97–114.

Jones, C., Lee, N. and Wood, C. (1991) *UK Environmental Statements 1988–1900*, Occasional Paper 29, Department of Planning and Landscape, University of Manchester.

Jones, R. (1982) *Town and Country Chaos* (ASI).

Jowell, J. and Noble, D. (1981) 'Structure plans as instruments of social and economic policy', *Journal of Planning and Environmental Law* (July) pp. 466–80.

Kendrick, M. (1987), 'Planning appeals in Northamptonshire 1979–86', paper prepared in the Planning Department, Northampton County Council.

Kimber, R. and Richardson, J. (1974) *Pressure Groups in Britain: A Reader* (Dent).

Kirk, G. (1980) *Urban Planning in a Capitalist Society* (Croom Helm).

Kitchen, T. (1997) *People, Politics, Policies and Plans* (Paul Chapman Publishing).

Kivell, P. (1987) 'Derelict land in England: policy responses to a continuing problem', *Regional Studies*, 21 (3) pp. 265–9.

Kuper, R. (1997) 'Deliberating waste: the Hertfordshire Citizens Jury', *Local Environment*, 2 (2) pp. 139–54.

Labour Party (1994) *In Trust for Tomorrow* (Labour Party).

—— (1997) *The First 100 Achievements* (Labour Party).

Laffin, M. and Young, K. (1990) *Professionalism in Local Government: Change and Challenge* (Longman).

Larson, M. S. (1984) 'The production of expertise and the constitution of expert power', in T. Haskell (ed.), *The Authority of Expertise* (Bloomington: Indiana University Press) pp. 28–80.

—— (1990) 'In the matter of experts and professionals, or how impossible it is to leave anything unsaid', in R. Torstendahl and M. Burrage (eds), *The Formation of Professions* (Stockholm: Swedish Collegium for Advanced Study) pp. 1–10.

Lash, S. and Urry, J. (1987) *The End of Organised Capitalism* (Cambridge: Polity).

Laumann, E. and Knoke, D. (1987) *The Organisational State* (Madison: University of Wisconsin Press).

Lawless, P. (1988) 'British inner urban policy: a review', *Regional Studies*, 22 (6) pp. 531–40.

—— (1991) 'Urban policy in the Thatcher decade: English inner city policy 1979–90', *Environment and Planning*, 9, pp. 15–30.

Leach, S. (1989) 'Strengthening local democracy? The government's response to Widdicombe', in J. Stewart and G. Stoker (eds), *The Future of Local Government* (Macmillan) pp. 101–22.

Leach, S. and Stoker, G. (1997) 'Understanding the local government review: a restrospective analysis', *Public Administration*, 75 (Spring) pp. 1–20.

Lehmbruch, G. and Schmitter, P. (eds) (1982) *Patterns of Corporatist Policy Making* (Sage).

Leyland, D. (1986) 'Town planning and business strategy', in K. G. Willis (ed.), *Contemporary Issues in Town Planning* (Aldershot: Gower) pp. 31–43.

Leyshon, A. and Thrift, N. (1997) *Money/Space: Geographies of Monetary Transformation* (Routledge).

Lindblom, C. (1977) *Politics and Markets* (New York: Basic Books).

Little, J. (1994) *Gender, Planning and the Policy Process* (Oxford: Pergamon).

Livingstone, K. (1987) *If Voting Changed Anything They'd Abolish It* (William Collins).

Llewelyn Davies (1997) *Exploring Urban Potential for Housing*, report to the North West Association and Government Office for the North West.

Lloyd, M. and Botham, R. (1985) 'The ideology and implementation of Enterprise Zones in Britain', *Urban Law and Policy*, 7 (1) pp. 33–55.

Logan, J. and Molotch, H. (1987) *Urban Fortunes: The Political Economy of Place* (Berkeley: University of California Press).

Loveless, J. (1987) *Why Wasteland? Towards an Urban Renaissance* (ASI).

Lowe, P. (1986) *Urban Social Movements: The City After Castells* (Macmillan).

Lowe, P. and Goyder, J. (1983) *Environmental Groups in Politics* (George Allen & Unwin).

Lowe, P., Cox, G., MacEwan, M., Winter, T. and Winter, M. (1986) *Countryside Conflicts: The Politics of Farming, Forestry and Conservation* (Temple Smith/Gower).

Lowe, P. and Ward, S. (eds) (1998) *British Environmental Policy and Europe* (Routledge).

McCormick, J. (1991) *British Politics and the Environment* (Earthscan).

MacEwan, A. and MacEwan, M. (1987) Greenprints for the countryside? *The Story of Britain's National Parks* (Allen & Unwin).

MAFF (1995) *Planning for Diversification* (HMSO).

Maitland, R. and Newman, P. (1989) 'Meet the new management of planning', *Planning*, 846, pp. 32–3.

Mandelbaum, S., Mazza, L. and Burchell, R. (eds) (1996) *Explorations in Planning Theory* (New Brunswick, New Jersey: Rutgers).

March, J. and Olsen, J. (1989) *Rediscovering Institutions: The Organisational Basis of Politics* (New York: Free Press).

Marriott, O. (1969) *The Property Boom* (Pan).

Martinez-Allier, J. (1987) *Ecological Economics* (Oxford: Blackwell).

Massey, D. and Catalano, A. (1978) *Capital and Land* (Edward Arnold).

Mather, A. S. (1991) 'Pressures on British forest policy: prologue to the post-industrial forest?', *Area*, 23 (3) pp. 245–53.

Matson, M. and Whitney, D. (1985) 'Urban Development Grants: evaluation of practice in Yorkshire and Humberside', paper to Conference on Research in Local Land Use Planning, Oxford Polytechnic, 31 May/1 June.

Midwinter, A., Keating, M. and Mitchell, J. (1991) *Politics and Public Policy in Scotland* (Macmillan).

Montgomery, J. and Thornley, A. (1990) *Radical Planning Initiatives* (Aldershot: Gower).

Morphet, J. (1992a) 'Continental doors open to mobile professionals', *Planning*, 900 pp. 26–7.

—— (1992b) 'A question of control over professional entry routes', *Planning 955* p. 17.

Mouffe, C. (1993) 'Liberal socialism and pluralism: which citizenship?', in J. Squires (ed.), *Principled Positions* (Lawrence & Wishart) pp. 69–84.

Mowle, A. and Evans, S. (1990) 'Conserving the rural environment – reconciling farmer and nature in the less favoured areas', in J. Bowers (ed.), *Agriculture and Rural Land Use: Into the 1990s* (Swindon: ESRC) pp. 118–31.

Muir, S. and Veenendall, T. (1996) *Earthtalk: Community Empowerment for Environmental Action* (Westport, Connecticut: Praeger).

Murphy, S. (1988) *Social Closure* (Oxford: Clarendon Press).

Myerson, G. and Rydin, Y. (1991) 'Language and argument in people-sensitive planning', *Planning Practice and Research*, 6 (1) pp. 31–3.

Myrdal, G. (1957) *Economic Theory and Under-developed Regions* (Duckworth).

National Audit Office (1986) *Enterprise Zones* (HMSO).

NRA (National Rivers Authority) (1991a) *The Quality of Rivers, Canals and Estuaries in England and Wales* (NRA).

Nevin, B., Loftman, P. and Beazley, M. (1997) 'Cities in crisis: is growth the answer? An analysis of the 1st and 2nd rounds of the "Single Regeneration Budget Challenge Fund"' *Town Planning Review*, 68 (2) pp. 145–64.

Newell, M. (1977) *An Introduction to the Economics of Urban Land Use* (Estates Gazette).

Newman, I. (1996) 'Discourse and the public sector', *Local Government Policy Making*, 23, pp. 52–9.

Newman, P. (1991) 'Quality, democracy and directions for local government', *Planning Practice and Research,* 6, pp. 29–30.

—— (1994) 'Urban regime theory and comparative urban politics', paper to IFRESI Conference on Cities, Enterprises and Society at the Eve of the 21st Century, Lille, March.

Nolan Committee (Committee on Standards in Public Life) (1997) *Third Report – Standards of Conduct in Local Government in England, Scotland, and Wales,* Vol. 1, Cm 3702-1 (HMSO).

Nownes, A., and Neeley, G. (1996) 'Public interest group entrepreneurship and theories of group mobilisation', *Political Research Quarterly*, 49 (1) pp. 119–46.

—— (1991b) *Statutory Water Quality Objectives Scheme* (NRA).

Oatley, N. (1991) 'Streamlining the system: implications of the B1 business class for planning policy', *Planning Practice and Research*, 6 (1) pp. 19–28.

O'Brien, M. and Penna, S. (1997) 'European policy and the politics of environmental governance', *Policy and Politics*, 25 (2) pp. 185–200.

Oc, T. (1991) 'Planning natural surveillance back into city centres', *Town and Country Planning* (September) pp. 237–9.

O'Connor, J. (1973) *The Fiscal Crisis of the State* (New York: St Martin's Press).

O'Connor, M. (ed.) (1994) *Is Capitalism Sustainable? Political Economy and the Politics of Ecology* (New York: Guildford Press).

Office of Water Services (1991) *Paying for Water: A Time for Decisions* (Ofwat).

Olson, M. (1978) *The Logic of Collective Action* (Cambridge, Mass.: Harvard University Press).

O'Riordan, T., Kemp, R. and Purdue, M. (1988) *Sizewell B: An Anatomy of the Inquiry* (Macmillan).

O'Riordan, T., and Turner, K. (eds) (1983) *An Annotated Reader in Environmental Planning and Management* (Oxford: Pergamon).

O'Riordan, T. and Jordan, A. (1995) 'British environmental politics in the 1990s', *Environmental Politics*, 4 (4) pp. 237–46.

Ostrom, E. (1990) *Governing the Commons* (Cambridge: CUP).

Outer Circle Policy Unit, with Justice and Council for Science and Society (1979) *The Big Public Inquiry* (Outer Circle Policy Unit).

Owen, G. (1996) 'Continuity and change: sub-national government in Great Britain', *Public Policy and Administration*, 11 (3) pp. 67–82.

Owens, S. (1989) 'Integrated pollution control in the United Kingdom: prospects and problems', *Environment and Planning C: Government and Policy*, 3, pp. 81–91.

—— (1994) 'Land, limits and sustainability: a conceptual framework and some dilemmas for the planning system', *Transactions of the Institute of British Geographers*, 19 (4) pp. 439–56.

Owens, S. and Cope, D. (1992) *Land Use Planning and Climate Change*, DoE Research Report (HMSO).

Owens, S. and Cowell, R. (1996) *Rocks and Hard Places: Minerals Resource Planning and Sustainability* (CPRE).

Oxford Polytechnic and ERL Consultants (1992) *Planning, Pollution and Waste Management*, DoE Research Report (HMSO).

Pahl, R. (1975) *Whose City?* (Penguin).

Pearce, D., Markandya, A. and Barbier, E. (1989) *Blueprint for a Green Economy* (Penguin).

Pearce, D. and Turner, R.K. (1990) *Economics of Natural Resources and the Environment* (Hemel Hempstead: Harvester Wheatsheaf).

Pennington, M. (1997) 'Property rights, public choice and urban containment', PhD thesis, University of London.

Pepper, D. (1984) *The Roots of Modern Environmentalism* (Croom Helm).

Pickvance, C. (ed.) (1976) *Urban Sociology: Critical Essays* (Tavistock).

Pollit, C., Lewis, L., Negro, J. and Patten, J. (eds) (1979) *Public Policy in Theory and Practice* (Hodder & Stoughton).

Pountney, M. and Kingsbury, P. (1983) 'Aspects of development control', *Town Planning Review*, 54 (2) pp. 138–54 and (3) pp. 285–303.

Ranson, S., Jones, G. and Walsh K. (eds) (1985) *Between Centre and Locality* (Allen & Unwin).

Ratcliffe, J. and Stubbs, M. (1996) *Urban Planning and Real Estate Development* (UCL Press).

RCEP (Royal Commission on Environmental Pollution) (1993) *The Incineration of Waste*, Cm 2181 (HMSO).

—— (1995) *Transport and the Environment* (first published in 1994) (Oxford: OUP).

Reade, E. (1987) *British Town and Country Planning* (Milton Keynes: Open University Press).

Redclift, M. (1987) *Sustainable Development* (Methuen).

Rees, J. (1990) *Natural Resources* (Methuen).

Rhodes, R. (1981) *Control and Power in Central–Local Relations* (Aldershot: Gower).

Richardson, J. (ed.) (1993) *Pressure Groups* (Oxford: OUP).

Roberts, J., Elliott, D. and Houghton, T. (1991) *Privatising Electricity: The Politics of Power* (Belhaven).

Robinson, M. (1992) *The Greening of British Party Politics* (Manchester: Manchester University Press).

Roger Tyms and Ptnrs (1995) *Enterprise Zones Monitoring* (Roger Tyms & ptnrs).

Rowbotham, S., Segal, L. and Wainwright, H. (1980) *Beyond the Fragments: Feminism and the Making of Socialism* (Merlin).

Rydin, Y. (1986) *Housing Land Policy* (Aldershot: Gower).

—— (1988) 'Joint Housing Studies: housebuilders, planners and the availability of land', *Local Government Studies*, 14 (2) pp. 69–80.

—— (1998a) 'The local enabling state: rhetoric, resources and planning in East London', *Urban Studies*, 35 (2) pp. 175–191.

—— (1998b) 'The context of incremental planning', *Planning Theory*.

Rydin, Y. and Myerson, G. (1990) 'Explaining and interpreting ideological effects: a rhetorical approach to "green belts"', *Environment and Planning D: Society and Space*, 7, pp. 463–79.

Rydin, Y., Home, R. and Taylor, K. (1990) *The Policy Implications of the Planning Appeals System*, report to Association of District Councils, Department of Land Management, Polytechnic of East London.

Saunders, P. (1979) *Urban Politics: A Sociological Interpretation* (Hutchinson).

—— (1981) *Social Theory and the Urban Question* (Hutchinson).

—— (1985) 'The forgotten dimension of central–local relations: theorising the "regional state"', *Environment and Planning C: Government and Policy*, 3, pp. 149–62.

Self, P. and Storing, H. (1962) *The State and the Farmer* (Allen & Unwin).

Selman, P. (ed.) (1988) *Countryside Planning in Practice: The Scottish Experience* (Stirling: Stirling University Press).

—— (1996) *Local Sustainability* (Paul Chapman Publishing).

Selman, P. and Parker, J. (1997) 'Citizenship, civicness and social capital in Local Agenda 21', *Local Environment*, 2 (2) pp. 171–84.

Shaw, K. (1990) 'The lost world of local politics revisited: in search of the non-elected local state', *Regional Studies*, 24 (2) pp. 180–4.

Sheail, J. (1981) *Rural Conservation in Inter-war Britain* (Oxford: Clarendon).

Shoard, M. (1987) *This Land is Our Land* (Paladin).

Short, J. (1984) *The Urban Arena: Capital, State and Community in Contemporary Britain* (Macmillan).

Short, J., Fleming, S. and Witt, S. (1986) *Housebuilding, Planning and Community Action* (Routledge & Kegan Paul).

Shove, E. (1995) 'Constructing regulations and regulating construction: the practicalities of environmental policy', in T. Gray (ed.), *UK Environmental Policy in the 1990s* (Macmillan).

Shucksmith, M. (1990) *Housebuilding in Britain's Countryside* (Routledge).

Simmie, J. (1981) *Power, Property and Corporatism* (Macmillan).

—— (1993) *Planning at the Crossroads* (UCL Press).

Smallbone, D. (1991) 'Enterprise agencies in local economic development: some policy issues', paper to AESOP Congress, Oxford Polytechnic, June.

Smith, N. and Williams, P. (1986) *Gentrification of the City* (Allen & Unwin).

Spencer, K. (1989) 'Local government and the housing reforms', in J. Stewart and G. Stoker (eds), *The Future of Local Government* (Macmillan) pp. 78–100.

Spooner, D., Arnett, R. and Justice, M. (1992) 'Building a geographical base for integrated pollution control: some problems', *Area*, 24 (2) pp. 105–12.

Squires, J. (ed.) (1993) *Principled Positions* (Lawrence & Wishart).

Stewart, J. (1995) 'A future for local authorities as community government', in J. Stewart and G. Stoker (eds), *Local Government in the 1990s* (Macmillan) pp. 249–68.

Stewart, J. and Stoker, G. (eds) (1989) *The Future of Local Government* (Macmillan).

Stewart, J. and Stoker, G. (eds) (1995) *Local Government in the 1990s* (Macmillan).

Stoker, G. (1989a) 'Creating a local government for a post-Fordist society: the Thatcherite project?', in G. Stoker and J. Stewart (eds), *The Future of Local Government* (Macmillan) pp. 141–70.

—— (1989b) 'Urban Development Corporations: a review', *Regional Studies*, 23 (2) pp. 159–67.

—— (1991) *The Politics of Local Government*, 2nd edn (Macmillan).

—— (1996) 'Governance as Theory: Five Propositions' Paper to Enjeux Des Debates Sur la Governance, Université de Lausanne, November.

Stoker, G. and Mossberger, K. (1994) 'Urban regime theory in comparative perspective', *Government and Policy*, 12 195–212.

Stoker, G. and Wilson, D. (1991) 'The lost world of British local pressure groups', *Public Policy and Administration*, 6 (2) pp. 20–34.

Stone, C. (1989) *Regime Politics: Governing Atlanta 1946–88* (Lawrence: University Press of Kansas).

Suddards, R. and Hargreaves, J. (1996) *Listed Buildings: The Law and Practice of Historic Buildings, Ancient Monuments and Conservation Areas* (Sweet & Maxwell).

Sutcliffe, A. (1981) *British Town Planning: The Formative Years* (Leicester: Leicester University Press).

Swenarton, M. (1981) *Homes Fit for Heroes* (Heinemann).

Symes, D. (1990) 'The rural community in lowland Britain: counting the garden gnomes', in J. Bowers (ed.), *Agriculture and Rural Land Use: Into the 1990s* (Swindon: ESRC) pp. 103–17.

Tewdwr-Jones, M. (ed.) (1996) *British Planning Policy in Transition* (UCL Press).

Therivel, R., Wilson, E., Thompson, S., Heaney, D. and Pritchard, D. (1992) *Strategic Environmental Assessment* (Earthscan).

Thomas, H. (1994) 'The New Right: "race" and planning in Britain in the 1980s and 1990s', *Planning Practice and Research*, 9 (4) pp. 353–66.

—— (1996) 'Public participation in planning', in M. Tewdwr-Jones (ed.) *British Planning Policy in Transition* (UCL Press) pp. 168–88.

Thomas, H. and Krishnarayan, V. (1994a) '"Race", disadvantage and policy processes in British planning', *Environment and Planning A*, 26, pp. 1891–1910.

—— (1994b) 'Race and planning in London', *Cities*, 11 (4) pp. 264–70.

Thomas, K. (1997) *Development Control: Principles and Practice* (UCL Press).

Thornley, A. (1993) *Urban Planning under Thatcherism: The Challenge of the Market*, 2nd edn (Routledge).

Torstendahl, R. (1990) 'Introduction: promotion and strategies of knowledge-based groups', in R. Torstendahl and M. Burrage (eds), *The Formation of Professions* (Stockholm: Swedish Collegium for Advanced Study) pp. 1–10.

Trench, S. (1991) 'Reclaiming the night', *Town and Country Planning* (September) pp. 235–7.

Udehn, L. (1996) *The Limits of Public Choice* (Routledge).

Underwood, J. (1980) *Town Planners in Search of a Role*, Occasional Paper No. 6, School for Advanced Urban Studies, University of Bristol.

UK Round Table on Sustainable Development (1997) *Housing and Urban Capacity* (UK Round Table on SD).

Valentine, G. (1992) 'Images of danger: women's sources of information about the spatial distribution of male violence', *Area*, 24 (1) pp. 22–9.

Veblen, T. (1976) *The Portable Veblen*, edited and with an introduction by M. Lerner (Penguin).

Wainwright, H. (1987) *Labour: A Tale of Two Cities* (Hogarth Press).

Walker, J. (1991) *Mobilizing Interest Groups in American: Patrons, Professions and Social Movements* (Ann Arbor: University of Michigan Press).

Walton, W. (1997) 'Bad land and bad law: the role of local authorities in the formulation of new legislation and guidance for contaminated land in the UK', *Government and Policy*, 15 (2) pp. 229–43.

Ward, S. (1996) *Planning and Urban Change* (Paul Chapman Publishing).

Wates, N. (1976) *The Battle for Tolmers Square* (Routledge & Kegan Paul).

Weale, A. (1992) *The New Politics of Pollution* (Manchester: Manchester University Press).

Weale, A., O'Riordan, T. and Kramme, L. (1991) *Controlling Pollution in the Round* (Anglo-German Foundation).

Whitby, M. (1990) 'Ex-post and ex-ante view of forest employment: to the future with the wisdom of hindsight?', in J. Bowers (ed.), *Agriculture and Rural Land Use; Into the 1990s* (Swindon: ESRC) pp. 50–7.

Whitehand, J. (1989) 'Development pressure, development control and suburban townscape change', *Town Planning Review*, 60 (4) pp. 403–20.

Wilder, C. L. and Plant, G. (1992) 'What environmental institutions does the UK need?', background paper, Second Round Table Conference, London School of Economics, Centre for Environmental Law and Policy, July.

Williams, R. H. (ed.) (1996) *European Union Spatial Policy and Planning* (Paul Chapman Publishing).

Willmott, P. and Hutchinson, R. (eds), (1992) *Urban Trends* I (Policy Studies Institute).

Wood, C. and Hooper, P. (1988) 'The effects of the relaxation of planning controls in enterprise zones on industrial pollution', paper to Planning Practice and Research Conference, Polytechnic of Central London, January.

Wood, C. and Jones, C. (1991) *Monitoring Environmental Assessment and Planning*, report of Department of the Environment Research Project (HMSO).

WCED (World Commission on Environment and Development) (1987) *Our Common Future* (Oxford: Oxford University Press).

Wynne, B. (1996) 'May the sheep safely graze? A reflexive view of the expert–lay knowledge divide', in S. Lash, B. Szerszynski and B. Wynne (eds), *Risk, Environment and Modernity* (Sage) pp. 44–83.

Yearley, S. (1995) 'UK Environmental policy and the politics of the environment in Northern Ireland in the 1990s' in T. Gray (ed.) *UK Environmental Policy in the 1990s* (Macmillan), pp. 35–100.

Yearley, S. and Milton, K. (1990) 'Environmentalism and direct rule', *Built Environment*, 16 (3) pp. 192–202.

Young, S. (1997) 'Participation strategies in the context of Local Agenda 21', paper for ESRC Local Governance Programme Conference, University of Glasgow, April.

Zeiger, H. (1985) 'LEG-UP: Local Enterprise Grants for Urban Projects', *Policy and Politics*, 13 (2) pp. 199–210.

Zukin, S. (1988) *Loft Living* (Radius).

Index

Note: Page numbers in **bold** type refer to illustrative figures or tables.